CIVIL ISLAM

PRINCETON STUDIES IN MUSLIM POLITICS

Dale F. Eickelman and James Piscatori, Editors

CIVIL ISLAM

MUSLIMS AND DEMOCRATIZATION IN INDONESIA

ROBERT W. HEFNER

PRINCETON UNIVERSITY PRESS

PRINCETON AND OXFORD

Library of Congress Cataloging-in-Publication Data

Hefner, Robert W., 1952–

Civil Islam : Muslims and democratization in Indonesia / Robert W. Hefner.

p. cm. — (Princeton studies in Muslim politics)

Includes bibliographical references and index.

ISBN 0-691-05046-5 (cloth : alk. paper) — ISBN 0-691-05047-3 (pbk. : alk. paper)

1. Islam and state—Indonesia. 2. Islam and politics—Indonesia. 3. Democracy—Religious
aspects—Islam. 4. N.U. (Organization) 5. Indonesia—Politics and government—1966–1988.
6. Indonesia—Politics and government—1998– I. Title. II. Series.

BP63.I5 H44 2000

322'.1'09598—dc21   00-020486

This book has been composed in Berkeley Book

www.pup.princeton.edu

Printed in the United States of America

10 9 8 7 6 5 4 3 2 1

10 9 8 7 6 5 4 3 2 1

(pbk)

CONTENTS

FOREWORD

FEW SUBJECTS in the Muslim world in the late 1990s commanded the attention of analysts and policy makers as much as Islam's compatibility with democracy, and few countries aroused more interest than Indonesia. Revolutionary developments engulfed the world's largest "Muslim" state, from the popular unrest that led to the overthrow of President Soeharto after thirty-two years in power to the holding of the first relatively free, multiparty elections since the 1950s to the bloody events in East Timor that brought an unprecedented foreign military intervention to an independent Indonesia. These startling events, along with the unexpected regional economic malaise, excited concern that Indonesia had become the sick man of Asia and even prompted some to wonder whether this archipelago of thousands of islands could survive as an integrated state. Robert Hefner's singular contribution is to put this roiling tableau into perspective and to explain the long-term trend, barely visible at times to the international public, of an evolving Muslim politics of pluralism.

The received wisdom that Muslim societies are democracy-resistant owes much, of course, to a revival of nineteenth-century formulations that civilizations and cultures are all-encompassing and determining. Islamic civilization, it is often argued, does not value intermediary institutions between the government and the people, thus precluding the emergence of civil society, and is based on a legal culture of rigidity, thus placing a premium on obedience and social conformity rather than on critical inquiry and individual initiative. Social scientists have added to this pessimistic view by emphasizing the adverse effects of social and economic stratification and especially the weaknesses of the middle classes. While sensitive to the myriad social trends at work, Hefner places the search for democratization in its shifting cultural contexts and stresses that the "rhythm" of democratic development varies according to specific milieu. More than elections, wealth, and constitutional arrangements, democracy depends, in his view, on "a virtuous circle of values and associations that varies in its cultural expressions." Debates over the meaning of Islamic traditions and contestation over Islamic symbols are fully covered in the discussion that follows, but Hefner does not assume that Indonesians inevitably live according to a fixed normative code or that Islamic influences are invariable.

Highlighting the role of Islamic groups like the Nahdlatul Ulama (NU), Masjumi, and the Association of Indonesian Muslim Intellectuals (ICMI), this work argues that current Muslim demands for greater political participation must be seen against a historical background of cultural and social pluralism as well as state violence. Soeharto's New Order regime came into existence in 1965–66 on a wave of civil unrest and killings of an unprecedented scale, and went out in 1998 in a deliberately contrived atmosphere of sectarian and ethnic conflict. In addition to the important economic forces that were at work, a sea of change of growing Muslim self-assertiveness had been occurring. The government, which could not afford, in the long run, to ignore this revivalist sentiment and which sought alternately to harness and divide it, was ultimately undermined by Muslims of varying views and institutional affiliations who joined together in a democratic opposition.

Hefner's study puts Indonesia alongside post-Franco Spain or postcommunist Eastern Europe as a key case study of democratic transition. It persuasively concludes that although democracies are not everywhere uniform and their development is incremental, the linkages forged between state and civil society are decisive for the success of democratizaton. Where there are well-established roots of pluralism in Indonesia and a "depth of civil-democratic conviction," the existence of a civil society is not sufficient for a viable democracy to develop; the state, too, must become civil or, to use the author's word, *civilized*. Contrary to what some have suggested, state and society are not mutually exclusive but must work together in tandem. A strong state is not a problem itself as long as it is committed to basic rules of tolerance and adheres to fundamental limitations. Institutions are doubtless significant in this process, but the social imaginary, in Charles Taylor's phrase, is vital. Simply put, the political and moral imperative of democracy depends on how one thinks about the state or, broadly, its cultural underpinnings.

As Professor Hefner shows, the Indonesian public sphere has inescapably been shaped by forces that have also been present in other Muslim societies. Abetted, in significant part, by a literacy rate of nearly 90 percent and the expansion of the public educational sector since 1965, Indonesians have acquired the means to develop and articulate alternative political—and Islamic—visions. This process of formalization, or what we call "objectification," of Islam is a contributor to the fragmentation of authority at the same time as it is a marker of intellectual creativity. Although the government labored to coerce all mass organizations to accept the official, nonsectarian ideology of *Pancasila* and adopted the twin policies of repression and co-optation toward that end, multiple individual and collective voices have been heard and diverse Islamic and political interpretations have emerged.

Hefner's assumption that a "social logic" of transformation is under way is minutely demonstrated. The discussion on ICMI indeed documents its various components and uses this fragmentation to explain both the association's ability to push the pluralist agenda forward and the government's capacity in the past to manipulate the group in the hope of sustaining a conformist Islam. This work also provides a fuller picture than has otherwise prevailed of the role of the Islamic media, the changes in organization, ideology, and tactics of major groups, and the social and political contributions of such intellectuals as the independent Nurcholish Madjid and the NU's Abdurrahman Wahid. In the increasing inability of the government—especially a secular-minded military elite—to impose a uniform reading of Islam lies both the uncertainty of Muslim politics and the possibility of pluralism. The imprint of multiple ideas of Islam on public debates and the de facto registration of competing groups in the public order point to portentous openings.

Robert Hefner's analysis is thus both empirically rich and theoretically suggestive: It rescues Islam from the peripheral status to which it has customarily been relegated in Indonesian studies; it also provides a corrective to those who would assert that the Muslim majority world, by inclination, is antithetical to democracy. Indeed, by providing a "social anthropology of democratization," Professor Hefner not only challenges such assumptions, he masterfully places Indonesia at the forefront of our understanding of transitions from authoritarianism.

James Piscatori
Dale F. Eickelman

PREFACE

WHEN I BEGAN research on Islam and democratization in Indonesia a decade ago, friends expressed surprise at my interest. Although I had published on Indonesian religion, political economy, and nation making since the late 1970s, most of my research had been of a familiar anthropological sort, focused on the life-worlds and history of ordinary Indonesians, especially on the island of Java. Indonesian friends were curious about what an anthropologist might have to say about so unparochial a topic as Islam and democracy. The project differed from the anthropology to which they were accustomed. Indonesian anthropologists had long projected an image of themselves as specialists of peasants, small-scale communities, and otherwise peripheral peoples. The topics of Islam and democracy were left to political scientists, sociologists, and others concerned with the central rhythms of the modern era rather than its discordant margins.

For different reasons, some of my colleagues in American anthropology were also skeptical of the idea of an anthropology of democracy. Some questioned outright whether notions like democracy and civil society can ever be anything more than culture-bound constructs of the modern West. Inasmuch as there was an anthropological consensus on these matters in the 1980s, it leaned in this relativist direction. The incommensurability of cultures, it was widely believed, made efforts to apply political ideals across cultural divides an act of hermeneutic naiveté at best, or cultural imperialism at worst.

In 1992 I was reminded of the strength of this opinion among some of my colleagues after presenting some preliminary reflections on Islam and democratization in a West Coast Department of Anthropology. As I finished my remarks a friend raised his hand to challenge me. Doesn't the work of Michel Foucault demonstrate, he said, that concepts like democracy and democratization are ethnocentric constructs that even in a Western setting occlude the processes of domination and subordination intrinsic to "democratic" political systems? And don't these Enlightenment-derived ideals only perpetuate a cultural hegemony that has violated the very values to which this world-conquering discourse lays claim?

In my pre-anthropological days in the early 1970s I had been an occasional writer on French philosophy and social criticism. So I was familiar with the demand that concepts drawn from Western political theory be subject to critical deconstruction. In the mid-1970s I had left French critical theory to enter a discipline I hoped might provide a more encompassing perspective on the problems of our age. As a social anthropologist years later, then, I was sensitive to the claim that questions of cross-cultural translation cannot simply be waved aside. Indeed, debates in the early 1990s only underscored the still vexing nature of these issues. With the rivalry between communism and liberal democracy apparently finished, some Western observers began to give voice to a naively triumphalist Occidentalism (chapter 1). One of its premises was that with communism out of the way the world had achieved a finished consensus on liberal democracy. As Bhikku Parekh observed at the time, this triumphalism aroused anxiety in parts of the non-Western world, "especially those which were until recently at the receiving end of the western civilizing mission."[1]

As the euphoria died down, however, skepticism as to the generalizability of democratic values was again voiced, this time from influential policy circles. In the early 1990s no less a figure than Samuel Huntington—senior professor of government at Harvard University (and, in 1997–98, chairman of a seminar in which I participated on cultural globalization at the Harvard Center for International Affairs)—published several provocative essays in which he suggested that democracy may not be viable beyond Western shores. With the polarizing tensions of the Cold War done, it seemed, cultural relativism was attracting mixed ideological company indeed.

Rather than the fitful fashions of Western academia, however, it was the practical interests of my Indonesian colleagues, particularly Muslim intellectuals, that pushed me to a more nuanced understanding of these questions. One incident early on in my research had a particularly lasting impact on me. It was June 1991, during the first of what were to become annual summer visits to Indonesia during the 1990s to talk with Muslim intellectuals, business people, and activists about democracy, markets, and social justice. Shortly after my arrival in Jakarta I was invited to the national headquarters of Nahdlatul Ulama (NU). With more than thirty million supporters, NU is the largest of Indonesia's Muslim organizations, typically (if simplistically) identified as "traditionalist" in its theology. The invitation to speak came from NU's youth wing, a group well known for its willingness to take on serious political issues. Although I was familiar with the youth group's reputation, I nonetheless felt uneasy about the invitation. The young man who came to my hotel room to invite me to speak explained that his friends hoped I would talk about the role of Muslims in the mass killings of Communists during 1965–66.

Before the killings, Indonesia had had the largest communist party in the noncommunist world. Consuming 500,000 lives in just five months, the destruction of the Communist Party marked a turning point in modern Indonesian history (chapter 4). The military-backed regime that came to power in the aftermath of the violence reversed the country's leftward course. Under the guidance of Western-trained economists, it stabilized the currency and halted the inflation ravaging the economy. Over the next few years it launched programs that boosted rice production, expanded the nation's decrepit transport infrastructure, lifted literacy rates from 40 to 90 percent of the population, and implemented one of the developing world's most successful family planning programs. Despite corruption of titanic proportions, the economy grew over most of the next thirty years at a rate of 6–7 percent annually. In the 1990s, however, the crony capitalism of the presidential family became so pervasive that it contributed to an awful economic collapse (chapter 7).

The economic crisis of the late 1990s also demonstrated that Indonesia's growth had come at a high political price. Its down payment had been the killings of 1965–66. Despite repeated promises of liberalization, in the aftermath of the 1965 violence the government imposed strict limits on the press, subjected the country's political parties to draconian controls, and muzzled critics. These two peculiar developmental processes—state-managed growth and political authoritarianism—are the backdrop to the Muslim reformation I discuss in this book.

This historical background was also partly why I was uneasy about speaking at the NU headquarters. During 1965–66 Nahdlatul Ulama had been a willing and, especially in East Java, powerful partner in the military-civilian alliance that carried out mass killings. In the countryside where I had conducted research in the late 1970s and again in 1985 the memories of the violence were still raw. Earlier, in the 1960s, the majority of people in these villages had been either "Javanist" Muslims, casual about the performance of devotional duties, or Hindus and Christians. As was typical in eastern Java at this time, villages of non- or nominally Islamic persuasion tended to support the Indonesian Nationalist Party (PNI), in part because the party opposed calls for the establishment of an Islamic state. A smaller number of people in these villages were affiliated with the Communist Party, which also opposed creation of an Islamic state. Only a few residents in my villages identified themselves as supporters of the Nahdlatul Ulama. Although a minority in my villages, NU comprised the majority in communities just a few kilometers away. Indeed, the regency of Pasuruan where I lived had long had a reputation as the most powerful stronghold of Nahdlatul Ulama on the island of Java.

During the awful chaos that swept Java from October 1965 to January 1966 militants associated with the Nahdlatul Ulama, armed and backed up by military advisers, came from the countryside just below my villages to arrest, interrogate, and execute suspected Communists. Even non-Communist nationalists were terrorized by the bloodletting. Their fears were fueled by reports that those targeted for execution included people better known for their opposition to Islamic orthodoxy than for left-wing views.

In 1990 I had published a book on my research in those villages, *The Political Economy of Mountain Java: An Interpretive History*.[2] In it, I had among other things attempted to present a social anthropological account of the killings. Before the book's publication I had shown the manuscript to Muslim-Indonesian friends, asking if they found my presentation fair. Several read the manuscript and commented that although they felt it important for Muslim scholars to reflect on the violence, the lessons of the period might yet be difficult for conservatives to accept. "Yes, we were used by outside forces in those years," one scholar told me during a visit to the United States in 1989. "But the real tragedy is that to this day some of our colleagues have no regrets that they were exploited for antidemocratic ends. Our failure to learn from that experience has impeded Indonesia's democratization."

As I traveled to the NU national headquarters that afternoon in June 1991 I was nervous that some in the audience might have read my book and considered my comments on NU unfair. Although unaware of my concerns, the young man who had invited me to speak had seemed to sense my anxiety about the proposed topic of discussion. He reassured me by explaining that the group wanted me to speak on the violence because a team of young NU scholars had been commissioned to visit East Java and investigate the 1965–66 violence. "We have to learn from the past, and we have heard that you might have something to tell us." Although intended to reassure me, at the time this comment only increased my anxiety. How had they learned that I had written on the killings? How might they react to my descriptions of the way NU landlords and religious leaders joined in the violence?

As I prepared for my talk I reminded myself that since the early 1980s Nahdlatul Ulama had come under the leadership of a charismatic and ecumenical leader, Abdurrahman Wahid. Reversing many of the organization's earlier policies, Wahid had become an outspoken opponent of Islamic "fundamentalism" and the idea of an Islamic state. He had also distinguished himself as an ardent spokesperson for religious minorities and pluralist democracy. But I also knew that Wahid had many enemies and that the Jakartan intellectual scene was rife with tensions, not least of all in Muslim circles. I worried that my comments might inadvertently compromise my relationship with some in this community.

Despite these reservations, I had agreed to speak. NU was simply too important on the national scene for me to forego an opportunity to meet with its activists. Besides, one of the issues with which my new project was concerned was Muslim reflection on 1965–66. So on the way to the NU headquarters the day of my presentation I used my free time in a traffic jam to reflect on how I might present the violence without offending people. I resolved to present a short history of the conflict and then offer a few comments on tolerance and civility. No need to get specific, I thought, and, above all, no need to point my finger.

When I got to the meeting room my confidence drained. The small hall was packed with young activists. My name and title were scrawled on the blackboard in back of the lectern, along with the announced topic of my presentation, "The Violence in Java: Its Meaning for NU and Democracy." I started at what struck me as a provocative title. Should I turn around and leave? No, I thought, I will go on. I gathered my courage and moved to the front of the hall, determined to speak in as safe and generalized a way as I could.

In the end, my presentation that June afternoon was politely received. I spoke largely as I had planned, providing a none-too-detailed summary of what we know about 1965–66, adding a few blandly uplifting remarks on tolerance in political life. Anxious not to step over that invisible line of allowable speech in Soeharto's Indonesia, I opted at the last minute to omit any details on the violence in my villages of research in East Java.

When I had finished my presentation, the audience sat quietly for a moment, as if they were expecting me to say more. Finally a fresh-faced, intense young man stood to pose a question. He introduced himself by saying that he was a participant in the NU-sponsored project on the killings in East Java. He paused, and then looked me straight in the eye, extending his hand forcefully in my direction in what, in my still anxious state, seemed like an accusatory gesture: "Professor Hefner," he said, "is it not true that you conducted research and have written on the violence in certain portions of East Java?" My mind raced, and I thought, "Uh-oh. Where is he going with this question?" I feared the worst.

"Yes, I have," I responded, "just as I explained in my talk." He continued: "But you said very little about your own work and what you have written about Nahdlatul Ulama." I braced myself. "Have you not written that landlords associated with the Nahdlatul Ulama were directly involved in the violence and that some of the violence had nothing to do with Islam but with wealthy landlords using religious symbols to mobilize sentiment against peasant supporters of land reform?"

My face flushed at the question, as I sensed I was about to hear an indictment. I was utterly unprepared for what the young man then said: "Professor Hefner," he began, his voice now trembling, as he turned back to face the audience in a manner that told me his prosecutorial tone was directed not at me but at his comrades and NU. "Professor Hefner, I believe your findings are correct. We, too, have found that wealthy farmers and religious leaders participated in the massacres, not out of religious conviction but because they had been told that they would lose their land to Communists. Our research also has shown that people who were good Muslims allowed themselves to be used by those who would inflame us to strike at their enemies for reasons having nothing to do with Islam. Those involved in the killings acted contrary to Islamic law and social justice."

I could scarcely believe what I was hearing. His voice shaking with conviction, the young man turned back to me. "And you, Professor Hefner. Does the horror of this violence not make you wonder whether Indonesian Muslims can be democratic? Can you tell us whether you think Islam can be a force for democracy or are we doomed to repeat the errors of the past? We need to know what Western social science can teach us about achieving democracy. Can Muslims create a civil society? This is what we hope to learn from you today. Can you please give us an answer?"

I have only a dim recollection of what followed during the remaining ten minutes until we adjourned. I stammered awkwardly, saying something about Indonesia having a long and proud democratic tradition and about Muslims being a part of that. But my response lacked spirit. I felt inadequate to answer the young man's question, embarrassed at my inability to be helpful. I even felt somewhat ashamed at my initial anxieties to address comparative questions on Islam and democracy in the face of this remarkable group of Muslim youths who found these issues urgent. I with all my fine scruples about cross-cultural difference, was unable to provide an answer.

The anthropology of the 1980s had taught me to value "reflexive" interaction with the people and society where one works—recognizing that the "other" with whom one interacts in a field setting is a full and dignified human being, with his or her own voice and initiative. But nothing in my anthropological training had prepared me for questions from an "other" that reflected a greater level of concern with the central political issues of our age than I myself commanded. Although its drama was special, the exchange that June afternoon was not an isolated occurrence. Over the years that followed, in conversations with students, writers, intellectuals, and ordinary people, I was asked again and again what Western history and political theory can teach Muslims about the conditions required for democracy and civility. Although all were not so self-critical as this young man from NU, Muslim friends regularly asked me what the Western experience could teach them about the prospects for "civil society" (*masyarakat sipil, masyarakat madani*) in the Muslim world. Their questions emerged from an Indonesian and Muslim context. But rather than reflecting an incommensurable "otherness," these men and women expressed an abiding conviction that we moderns share a common humanity and common political dilemmas.

At the beginning of my research in 1991 I shared my discipline's concerns that questions like these on civility and democracy may be misplaced or inappropriate because enunciated in a language that, formally at least, had originated in the West. But my conversations over the next eight years convinced me that, properly contextualized, these issues are not culture-bound constructs relevant only in a Western context. Certainly, as their questions on Western history indicated, most of my Indonesian colleagues understood that the terms of democratic theory had been colored by their early genealogy in the West. All were also familiar with their government's position on these matters. Citing the uniqueness of "Asian values," the New Order (1966–98) regime was a virulent proponent of the idea that "liberal" notions, like democracy and human rights, were incompatible with Indonesian culture. The force of this message, however, eventually rang hollow. Many of my friends had come to believe that the passage of democratic ideals out of the West had not compromised their truth but rather enlarged it.

In time I came to believe that these Muslim thinkers had it right, and that a dialogical and transcultural perspective is a better point of entry to modern democracy's meanings than is a narrowly philological approach that freezes the notions in a mythic Western past. I resolved to go beyond the confines of my own academic training and come to terms with how one might think about democracy and religious reformation in a non-Western tradition.

To my great relief, intellectual developments in anthropology and the human sciences helped in my redirection. The anthropology of the early 1990s was itself caught in the throes of a great transformation. The passing away of the small-scale societies with which anthropology had long been concerned and the movement of anthropologists into the study of complex societies provoked deep soul-searching in the field. Growing numbers of anthropologists grew impatient with the discipline's earlier habit of neglecting history and emphasizing the seamless integrity of local worlds. The change was also related to the end of the Cold War and attempts to apply programs of economic liberalization and democratic reform to different societies. In the face of these and other "globalizations," anthropologists and researchers in related disciplines threw themselves into the study of translocal processes, as seen in everything from nationalism, religious conversion, and the culture of capitalism to diasporas and democratic movements. Modernity was now seen not as seamless or unitary but hybridic and multiple.[3]

In Indonesian studies this shift to global forces and the heterogeneity of culture seemed especially welcome. In the early 1990s pathbreaking studies by the historians Denys Lombard and Anthony Reid had demonstrated that this archipelagic world had long been, in Lombard's famous phrase, a "crossroads" (*carrefour*) of civilizations, characterized more by its peculiar genius at integrating disparate influences than a stable cultural core.[4] Since the beginning of the common era, island Southeast Asia had assimilated Hinduism, Buddhism, Chinese commercial technologies, Islamic mysticism and political philosophy, and a host of other influences. In the modern era the region was further transformed by colonial capitalism, state bureaucracies, print culture, intra-Asian diasporas, Islamic reform, and national liberation movements. If any region of the world seemed well suited for the new issues of hybridity and globality, it was Southeast Asia.

This book, then, is the product of my engagement with these events and an exploration of their relevance for an understanding of Islam and democracy. Its immediate concern is to explain the emergence of a democratic, religiously ecumenical, and boldly reformist movement in Indonesian Islam in the 1980s and 1990s. From a comparative perspective, this movement ranks as one of the remarkable if little discussed events in the contemporary Muslim world. As the title of this book indicates, a key feature of this movement was the repudiation of, as Aswab Mahasin (a Muslim NGO, [nongovernmental organization] activist and human rights writer), once put it, "the mythology of the

Islamic state," that is, a state based on a totalizing understanding of Islamic "law" (*shariah*) and a monopolistic fusion of religious and political authority. The movement also promoted women's rights, inter-religious dialogue, and the struggle to create a democratic and pluralist polity.

The account I provide in this book seeks first to explain the cultural and historical background to this *civil* Islam. My analysis is not meant to suggest that democratic Islam will necessarily prevail in Indonesia. There are other, more conservative streams in Indonesian society, and, although I am personally optimistic, the long-term outcome of today's democratic achievements are still unclear. For reasons I explain in the chapters that follow, the fate of the democratic movement will ultimately depend not only on the struggle for a civil society but on efforts to reform the state.

Soeharto, having courted moderate Islam in the late-1980s, switched gears in the mid-1990s and began to cultivate allies among ultraconservative Islamists. The regime did so in reaction to growing opposition from the middle class and because Muslim democrats were joining forces with non-Muslim reformers. The counterattack had a devastating impact on Muslim democrats and the prodemocracy movement. Whereas in the early 1990s many Indonesians had hoped that a resurgent Islam might carry the democratic banner, by the late 1990s many feared the regime might succeed in using ethnoreligious divides to block political reform. The subsequent failure of Soeharto's efforts, and the role of democratic Muslims in the overthrow of Soeharto, stand as remarkable democratic achievements in their own right.

Rather than a simple celebration of civil Islam, however, this book attempts to provide a social anthropology of democratization in a majority Muslim society seen through its achievements *and* setbacks. Analysis of these issues begins with the paradox of how, out of the maelstrom of the mid-1960s, a movement of Muslim democratic renewal emerged. Certainly when the New Order was founded in 1966, few would have forecast such an eventuality. Just how and why it occurred is a story that sheds light on the conditions facilitating democratic reformation not only in Indonesia but in the Muslim world as a whole.

Let me conclude these prefatory remarks with two qualifications about this book's organization. First, the approach I adopt on Indonesian politics is biased toward the Muslim perspective. My reasons for this are twofold. First, in most accounts of Islam in today's world, Indonesia is conspicuous for its absence, despite the fact that with some 88 percent of its 210 million citizens officially professing Islam it is the largest majority-Muslim society in the world. In the past this marginalization has been justified on the grounds that Indonesia is far from the historical heartland of Muslim and, especially, Arab civilization. Inasmuch as the study of Islam in the West initially developed through research on Muslim law and classical Islamic commentaries, there were perhaps grounds for this exclusion. In an age when more Muslims live in Asia than on any other continent and when all face similar political challenges, however, this exclusion can no longer be justified.

A second reason for my Muslim angle on Indonesian politics and culture is that in Indonesian studies Islam has often not been given its due. Although the Dutch scholars who pioneered Indonesian studies in the early twentieth century were concerned with Islam, specialists of Indonesia in the United States often assumed that Islam was a minority or superficial element in Indonesian culture. Although the anthropologist Clifford Geertz has sometimes been blamed for this bias, his *Religion of Java*[5] shows a considerable understanding of Javanese Islam. In his summary remarks in later works, however, Geertz was at times too casual. Among other things, as Marshall Hodgson has observed,[6] he applied so narrow and "modernist" a perspective on Islam that he ended up identifying many of the practices and beliefs of Indonesian Muslims as "Hindu-Buddhist" rather than as subaltern streams in Southeast Asian Islam. What was in Geertz a minor theme became a central emphasis among less careful American Indonesianists. We were treated to repeated sightings of "Hindu-Buddhist" wildlife in the Indonesian forest, even when much of what was being discussed was explicitly identified by its believers as part of *their* profession of Islam.

In adopting a Muslim perspective on Indonesian democratization, then, I seek to correct for the earlier marginalization of Islam in Indonesian studies. I should emphasize, however, that I am interested in the politics and culture of the *full* Muslim community, not merely self-professed Islamists or supporters of an Islamic state. In this book, then, "Muslim politics" refers to any and all kinds of political actions based on a person's conviction as a Muslim, whether or not the resulting behavior embraces the idea of an "Islamic" state.

The second qualification I should make about this book's presentation is that it is intended as a work in the tradition of *both* historical sociology and social anthropology. Although collaboration between these two disciplines is lamentably rare, there seem few grounds anymore for not bringing the two disciplines into dialogue. Having moved to study complex societies, it would be an unfortunate conceit if anthropologists were not to recognize that they have much to learn from the historical sociologists who have long labored there. Conversely, as sociologists become more cross-cultural in their concerns, it behooves them to attend to the remarkable archive of non-Western cultures that anthropologists have stored.

In emphasizing that this is a work of social anthropology and historical sociology, I also mean to indicate that the methodology I have utilized is not that of the classical historian, with its careful amassing of chronological detail. My presentation involves a selective sampling of key moments and events. From these I seek to draw general conclusions on how Muslim politics works and how it relates to the process of democratization. From a historian's perspective, this approach may appear woefully selective. For analytic purposes, however, this method of presentation allows me to reach general conclusions, some of which, it is hoped, are relevant for understanding democratization in other parts of the world, including the West.

A Note on References

Throughout the book I cite endnotes that provide publication details on a reference the first time it is given. The index provides a full list of authors cited, and readers interested in a particular author or work can locate full bibliographic information by referring to the endnotes.

ACKNOWLEDGMENTS

A LONG PROJECT like the one that made this book possible incurs great debts. My research trips to Indonesia during 1991–98 were supported by several foundations. I must thank, first of all, Karen Colvard of the Harry Frank Guggenheim Foundation for funding during 1993–95 to carry out a first wave of interviews and analysis on Muslim discussions of violence and democracy. Without the foundation's inspired commitment to the comparative study of the causes of and cures for social violence, this project would have never been possible.

Under the direction of Mary Zurbuchen, the Ford Foundation, Jakarta, financed visits for the last phases of this study (1997–98), as well as a later study (1999) on Javanese traditions of pluralism and tolerance that will form the focus of a separate book. I am honored to have worked with the foundation and deeply grateful for its support.

Between the Guggenheim and Ford funding, I received generous support for annual visits to Indonesia from the German Bertelsmann Wissenschafts Stiftung, as part of a twelve-country study of pluralism and tolerance directed by my colleague at the Institute for the Study of Economic Culture (ISEC) at Boston University, Peter L. Berger. I extend special thanks to Volker Than at Bertelsmann for his generosity during my visits to Stiftung events in London and Berlin. I thank Peter for his kind support of the Indonesia project, my work as director of the ISEC project on civil society (1993–98), and, more generally, for ten years of warm collegiality. Final write up of the research was made possible by a generous grant to ISEC by an anonymous donor, for which I am also grateful. Also at ISEC, finally, I thank Adam Seligman and Robert Weller for years of shared reflection on democracy across cultures.

In Indonesia I thank the Indonesian Council of Sciences (LIPI) for acting as local sponsor of several research projects over the years and the Department of Religion for supporting my trip to Indonesia to help organize a conference on Islam and modernity in 1995. I also want to express my deep gratitude to Enceng Shobirin and my friends at LP3ES, a Jakarta nongovernmental organization. Each summer during the 1990s Shobirin and his colleagues used their considerable knowledge of the Jakartan scene to arrange interviews, making my study both feasible and enjoyable. My debt to the more than four hundred people I interviewed in Indonesia, many of whom became dear friends, is too great to detail. However, I must single out four people for special mention: Nurcholish Madjid, Mochtar Pabotinggi, Abdurrahman Wahid, and Adnan Buyung Nasution. The actions of these great democrats provided me with the inspiration needed to write this book.

At Princeton University Press I thank Mary Murrell for shepherding this book through publication and the Muslim Politics series editors, Dale F. Eickelman and James Piscatori. The work done by Dale and James on Muslim politics has had a profound influence on my own.

Finally, I thank my wife, Nancy Smith-Hefner, who tolerated my long absences during summers over eight long years even though she had her own teaching and research commitments. Without our long walks and shared lives, what would any of this be worth? My thanks and love also go to our two children, Claire-Marie and William Francisco, who also put up with their dad's absences, although not without lament. Me, too!

ABBREVIATIONS

ABRI	The Indonesian Armed Forces
BAIS	Indonesian Military Intelligence
BKAM	Coordinating Body for Muslim Good Works
BPPT	Agency for the Assessment and Application of Technology
CIDES	Center for Information and Development Studies
CPDS	Center for Policy and Development Studies
CSIS	Center for Strategic and International Studies
DDII	Dewan Dakwah Islamiyah Indonesia (Indonesian Council for Islamic Predication)
DPR	Indonesian Parliament
Gemsos	Socialist Student Movement
GMKI	The Movement of Protestant Indonesian Students
HMI	Association of Islamic Students
IAIN	State Islamic Institute Colleges
ICMI	Association of Indonesian Muslim Intellectuals
IPKI	Association of Supporters of Independence
IPS	Institute for Policy Studies
IPTN	Nusantara Aircraft Industry
ISMI	Association of Muslim Indonesian Scholars
KAMI	Indonesian Student Action Group
KAPPI	(high school counterpart of KAMI)
KISDI	Indonesian Committee for Solidarity with the Islamic World
Komnas HAM	National Human Rights Commission
KOPASSUS	military special forces
KOSTRAD	Army Strategic Reserve Command
LBH	Lembaga Bantuan Hukum (Indonesian's first legal aid society)
LP3ES	Institute for Socioeconomic Research, Education, and Application, a leading Jakarta NGO
LSAF	Institute for Religious and Philosophical Studies
MI	*Mahasiswa Indonesia* [Indonesian student]
MPR	People's Consultative Assembly
MUI	government-sponsored Council of Indonesian Ulama
MPRS	Provisional People's Consultative Assembly
NASAKOM	Soekarno's government of national unity (from the first letters of the Indonesian terms for *nationalism, religion,* and *communism*)
NGO	Nongovernmental Organization

NU	Nahdlatual Ulama
PAN	Partai Amanat Nasional (Party of Amien Rais)
PMII	Student Organization linked to the Nahdlatul Ulama
PMKRI	Association of Catholic Students
PDI	Indonesian Democratic Party
PDI-P	Indonesian Democratic Party–struggle (founded by Megawati.)
PI or PII	Indonesian Muslim Pupils
PKB	Party of National Renaissance, NU-linked
PKI	Indonesian Communist Party
PNI	Indonesian Nationalist Party
PPMI	Federation of Indonesian Students
PPP	Unity and Development Party
PRD	The People's Democratic Party
PRRI	Revolutionary Government of the Republic of Indonesia
PSI	Indonesian Socialist Party
RPKAD	Army Paracommando Regiment
RMI	Rabithah Ma'ahid Islamiyah (organization of *pesantren* affiliated with Nahdlatul Ulama)
SIUPP	Surat Izin Usaha Penerbitan Pers (General publication license)
SOBSI	Sentral Organisasi Buruh Seluruh Indonesia (PKI-dominated labor federation), Central Organization of All-Indonesia Workers
SOKSI	Central Organization of Indonesian Workers
SOPSI	Government-controlled national labor federation
SOSPOL	armed forces' Bureau for Social and Political Affairs

CIVIL ISLAM

Chapter One

DEMOCRATIZATION IN AN AGE OF

RELIGIOUS REVITALIZATION

G LOBAL POLITICS at the turn of the millennium has been marked by two far-reaching events. The first has been the diffusion of democratic ideas to disparate peoples and cultures around the world. A skeptic might point out that politics varies greatly among societies and movements waving the democratic banner, and political civility is not guaranteed by good words alone. Nonetheless, as with the earlier notion of nationalism (equally varied in its ideals and practice), there can be little doubt that the cross-cultural diffusion of democratic ideas is one of the defining globalizations of our age.

The second event marking world politics at the turn of the millennium has been the forceful reappearance of ethnic and religious issues in public affairs. Whether with Hindu nationalism in India, Islam and citizenship in France, the culture wars in the United States, or Islamist movements in the Muslim world, the end of the twentieth century demonstrated convincingly that high modernist reports of the demise of religion and ethnicity were, to say the least, premature.[1] The scale of the ethnoreligious resurgence also reminded us that the cultural globalization so rampant in our age does not bring bland homogenization. Rather than making everything the same, globalization brings with it vibrant contestation and localization. The growing demand for ethnic and religious "authenticity" is a notable example of this trend.[2] Whether the resulting upsurge of ethnic and religious identities is compatible with democracy and civil peace is a question central to this book.

Of these two developments, the diffusion of the idea of democracy at first caused the least surprise. After all, for decades it has been a truism of Western political thought that with industrialization, education, and the development of a middle class, pressures for popular political participation increase, unleashing democratic struggles like those that transformed the modern West. In the euphoria following the collapse of communism in 1989–90, policy makers' faith in this modernist credo was, if anything, only strengthened. The Eastern European revolutions, we heard, proved that the world had arrived at "the end point of mankind's ideological evolution and the universalization of Western liberal democracy as the final form of human government."[3] Having sailed through the troubled seas of middle modernity, it seemed, the world was about to pass into a pacific ocean of market economies and liberal democracy.

Just a few years after the fall of the Berlin Wall, however, these titanic visions of an ideology-annihilating "end to history" hit an iceberg. Political realignments in Eastern Europe were followed by an upsurge in ethnic and regional conflict.[4] In India, Bosnia, Burma, Ruanda, and several Western countries, ethnoreligious issues asserted themselves with a force not felt since the Second World War.[5] Where before there was talk of an end to history, now there were warnings of its resumption "on traditional lines, but on a yet vaster scale—an epoch of Malthusian wars and religious convulsions, of ecological catastrophes and mass deaths of a magnitude far greater even than those of our century."[6]

Not all observers of international events were moved to such grimly apocalyptic conclusions. But the surge in ethnoreligious violence gave rise to a new pessimism concerning democracy's possibility. One of the more startling changes of heart was that of Harvard political scientist and U.S. State Department adviser Samuel Huntington. An upbeat spokesperson for democracy's "third wave" a few years earlier,[7] in 1993 Huntington presented a deeply relativistic reassessment of democracy's future. We are mistaken to assume that all societies can develop democratic institutions, Huntington argued, because the principles of democracy are incompatible with the cultures of many. The list of alleged incompatibilities underscored the enormity of the problem. "Western ideas of individualism, liberalism, constitutionalism, human rights, equality, liberty, the rule of law, democracy, free markets, and the separation of church and state have little resonance in Islamic, Confucian, Japanese, Hindu, Buddhist, or Orthodox culture." Although Huntington conceded that a few civilizations might yet be won to the democratic cause, most, he implied, would not. The new world order was not to be that of democracy triumphant, it seems, but of primordialism resurgent.

Professor Huntington went on to argue that some among these undemocratic nations will develop interests deeply contrary to those of the West. "The fault lines between civilizations," he warned, may soon replace "the political and ideological boundaries of the Cold War as the flash points for crisis and bloodshed."[8] Among the most likely trouble spots on the horizon, Huntington advised, was the Muslim world. "Conflict along the fault line between Western and Islamic civilizations has been going on for 1,300 years," he observed, and in the future this "*military interaction* between the West and Islam is unlikely to decline" (emphasis added).[9] Other commentators sounded equally dire warnings, hinting of a new Cold War in which a resurgent Islam might play the role earlier assumed by Leninism.

In these and other examples, analysts assessed the relationship between democratization and ethnoreligious revival, and some concluded that the two processes are often antithetical. For these commentators, there was no better example of this negative relationship than the religious resurgence shaking the Muslim world. In the face of the slaughter in Algeria or Taliban brutalization in Afghanistan, it seemed reasonable to these observers to conclude that there was a general incompatibility between democracy and Islam.[10] The silence of some Western leaders in the face of the dismemberment of democratic Bosnia suggested that these views of the Muslim question were, sadly, no longer merely academic.

In the face of this ferment, the attitude of Western policy makers toward democracy's future went from breezy confidence to edgy uncertainty. Eastern Europe's cruel communist winter was not everywhere followed by a democratic spring. Capitalist growth in East and Southeast Asia did not automatically bring democratic decency. And the Muslim world seemed awash in violence. Examples like these lent credence to a newly minted cultural relativism which asserted that democracy is, in the end, incompatible with many non-Western cultures.[11]

Some suggested, however, that there is another way of viewing these deviations from the democratic plan. Rather than proving it is only possible in Western settings, these setbacks show that democracy's achievement depends heavily on local cultural resources. For proponents of this view, democracy requires more than elections and constitutions. It depends on traditions and organizations that teach ordinary citizens habits of the democratic heart. Embedded as democracy is in local life worlds, its culture and organization will vary across societies, too. Buoyed by this confidence, students of comparative politics in the 1990s moved beyond formal institutions to understand the informal conditions that, to borrow Robert Putnam's now famous phrase, "make democracy work."[12]

This new wave of research stood in striking contrast to earlier discussions of democracy in Western political theory. During the 1970s and early 1980s that theory had been dominated by arid philosophical debates over democracy's first principles. "This American liberal doctrine understood political philosophy to be a branch of legal theory."[13] Rather than focusing on legalistic principles, research in the 1990s took a sociological or anthropological turn. There was a heightened awareness of the multicultural nature of the contemporary world and the need to attend to this pluralism when considering democracy's possibility.[14] Now even "the West" was understood to be diverse in its cultural genealogies. With this recognition, there was a parallel expansion of interest in the variety of cultures within which democracy can work. What conditions encourage tolerance and democratic participation? Can human rights take hold in cultures whose concepts of personhood differ from those of liberal individualism? Can democracy tolerate or even benefit from the energies of public religion?[15] Questions like these showed that, for students of comparative politics, the conditions of democracy's cross-cultural possibility had become the order of the day.

ISLAMIZATION AND DEMOCRATIZATION

In this book I examine the relationship of Islam to democratization in the majority-Muslim nation of Indonesia. For many Western observers, of course, Indonesia is not what first comes to mind when one thinks of the Muslim world. The average Westerner is perhaps more familiar with its ancient Hindu-Buddhist temples and graceful Balinese arts than with the fact that Indonesia—the fourth most populous nation in the world—is also the world's largest majority-Muslim country. Some 88 percent of this nation's 210 million people officially profess Islam. On these grounds alone, what Indonesian Muslims think and do should be a matter of general interest. An investigation of Muslim politics in this tropical milieu, however, has another benefit. It allows us to distinguish features of Muslim politics that owe more to Middle Eastern circumstances than Islamic civilization as a whole. Marginalized in treatments of classical Islam, Indonesia must be central to any effort to come to terms with the diversity of modern Muslim politics.

Islam and politics in Indonesia are also of interest because, after years of sustained economic growth, this nation ranks as one of Asia's political and economic giants. With its huge domestic market and manufacturing industry, Indonesia in the early 1990s seemed poised to join the ranks of the world's largest economies early in the twenty-first century. By the end of 1998, however, this achievement was in doubt. The financial crisis that erupted in East Asian markets in August 1997 had an especially destructive impact on Indonesia. After growing at a brisk annual rate of 6–7 percent for almost thirty years,[16] Indonesia's gross domestic product shrank almost 14 percent in 1998. A poverty rate that had declined to just 13.7 percent of the population in early 1997 had [the figures have been revised down recently] shot back up to 40 percent eighteen months later. Equally alarming, a country long praised for its multicultural tolerance found itself caught in a downward spiral of ethnoreligious violence. Better off than most of the public, Chinese Indonesians (3 percent of the population) became the target of angry Muslim crowds. In a cycle of anti-Christian violence never before seen in Indonesian history, some four-hundred churches, many owned by Chinese-Indonesian congregations, were damaged or destroyed between 1997 and 1998. Indonesia's rare flower seemed to be wilting.

The political and economic crises of 1997–99 dampened the optimism of those who had hoped that Indonesia might serve as a beacon for democracy to the larger Muslim world. For other observers, the crisis only confirmed the dim prospects for democratization in any Muslim nation. Both of these conclusions, however, miss the larger point. Indonesia *does* have rich civic precedents, as well as the world's largest movement for a democratic and pluralist Islam. At the same time, however, the regime that ruled Indonesia from 1966 until the fall of President Soeharto in May 1998 was also one of the world's most shrewdly authoritarian. The crisis of 1997–99 did not prove the earlier claims of democratic Islam a fraud, then, but underscored the scale of the challenge faced by Indonesian democrats of all faiths. This fact only makes more urgent the task of understanding Muslim politics in Indonesia and the circumstances that lead some Muslims to embrace democratic ideals.

The Pluralism of Muslim Politics

To come to terms with questions like these requires that we rethink some of our basic assumptions on Islam and democratization. The first step in such an effort is to recognize that Muslim politics is not monolithic but, like politics in all civilizations, plural. Several recent studies have reminded us that this was always the case.[17] Even in the Umayyad and Abbasid empires of Islam's first centuries there was a lively pattern of extra-state religious organizations, centered around the twin institutions of learned Muslim scholars (the *ulama*) and religious law; neither was totally controlled by the state.[18] From a sociological perspective, the differentiation of religious and political authorities was inevitable as the Muslim community developed from a small, relatively homogeneous movement into a vast, multiethnic empire. From a religious perspective, too, the separation was necessary if the transcendent truth of Islam was not to be subordinated to the whims of all-too-human rulers.

More than Western Europe during the same period, medieval Muslim society was religiously plural, with Muslims living alongside Christians, Jews, Hindus, and others. There were several notable attempts to develop a practice of toleration, although, as in every other premodern tradition, no systematic theology on the matter was ever devised.[19] Contrary to the claims of conservative Islamists today, the medieval Muslim world also knew an extensive separation of religious authority from state authority. In most Muslim countries, religious scholars developed the healthy habit of holding themselves at a distance from government.[20] So, too, did many of the great mystical brotherhoods that served as vehicles for popular religious participation.[21] During the long Muslim middle ages, concepts of sacred kingship coexisted in uneasy tension with contractual notions of governance, with the result that religious leaders sometimes challenged rulers' authority.[22] For reasons that will become clearer in the Indonesian case, Muslim scholars in this era were reluctant to amplify these latter precedents into an explicit theory of political checks and balances. The full reformation of Muslim politics awaited the great upheavals of the modern era.

In the early modern era, reform-minded rulers in the Muslim world initiated modernizations intended to respond to the political challenge of the West. The enormity of Western colonization also prompted Muslim reformists outside the state to demand that the door of religious interpretation (*ijtihad*) be reopened. Over the course of its long history, the Muslim world had seen a series of religious reformations, most of which called for a return to scripture and the recorded example of the Prophet Muhammad. But the reformers of the late nineteenth and early twentieth century gave this scripturalist imperative a new twist. For them, the message of Islam required that Muslims avail themselves of science, education, and modern forms of association. *This* reformation was intended to give Muslims not just the purity of the Word but the means for achieving cultural modernity.[23]

By the middle of the twentieth century, however, Islamic modernism seemed to have settled into a staid orthodoxy. Certainly, in several Middle Eastern countries, Muslim brotherhoods continued to call for the establishment of an Islamic state.[24] But these movements did not play a determinant role in the politics of their homelands nor did they critically engage the terms of Muslim politics. In the postwar period the dominant political discourse in most Muslim countries was socialist and secular nationalist, not Islamist. Politics was visualized through the shapes and colors of the nation-state, and the nation to which the state was supposed to conform had, if any, an only vaguely Islamic hue.[25]

However secure the idea of the nation might have appeared, the world of ordinary Muslims was anything but stable. In the early twentieth century most Muslims still lived in predominantly agrarian societies.[26] In the aftermath of the Second World War and independence, however, the circumstances of ordinary Muslims changed forever. Nationalist regimes launched ambitious programs of mass education. They also developed roads, markets, mass media, and intrusive state administrations. Local communities were opened wider than ever to outside ideas and powers. Mass migrations to cities and distant nations furthered this detraditionalization, forcing whole populations to develop new habits of livelihood and association. In the 1980s and 1990s this restructuring of life-worlds went further with the expansion of high-speed travel and electronic communications, both of which made Muslim societies even more permeable to new information and lifestyles. As in other parts of the world, the resulting "global ecumene"[27] heightened popular awareness of the world's pluralism and posed serious challenges to established authorities and moralities.

In this manner, social change in our age has drawn great masses of Muslims onto a teeming public stage. Having done so, it has given special urgency to the question of the political and ethical scripts by which they are to act once there. As in the nineteenth- and twentieth-century West, one response to these changes has been to call for equality, freedom, and democracy. Whatever their historical etymology, in most of the Muslim world these ideas are no longer just the stuff of Westernized academics or coffee-house intellectuals. Drawn down from the academic stratosphere into local life-worlds, democratic ideas have become one stream in the larger effort to give ethical shape to public life.[28]

Some observers have interpreted this diffusion of democratic ideas as "Westernization" pure and simple. Native conservatives agree, although they typically equate the process with spiritual pollution. What is really at play in this process, however, is a more subtle interaction between the local and the (relatively) global.[29] Viewed from the ground of everyday practice rather than the dizzying heights of official canons, the normative diversity of preindustrial societies was always greater than implied in classical Western sociology. In all societies there are values and practices that hover closer to the ground and carry latent possibilities, some of which may have egalitarian or democratic dimensions.[30] These low-lying precedents may not be heard in high-flying canons. Nonetheless they are in some sense available to those reflecting on what to become when the world takes a new turn. As Robert Weller has shown in his study of China's prodemocracy movement, local actors there seized on what at first looked like the exogenous idioms of democracy and civil society to legitimate principles of equality and participation in public life. Weller demonstrates that these principles were already "present" in indigenous Chinese kinship and folk Confucianism, although in an undeveloped and politically bracketed way. [31] The concept of democracy proved useful for Chinese activists, then, not just because it was in the global air (although this certainly helped) but because it amplified a long latent potential in Chinese society.[32]

It is for Muslim democrats as it is for Chinese. The tumult of recent decades has led many to aspire to a just and egalitarian public order. Although broadly democratic, the political discourse these Muslims are forging is not identical to Western liberalism. One reason this is so is that Muslims have looked to their religion to provide some of the terms for this new public ethic.[33]

It is now a truism of comparative studies that religion in the post-Enlightenment West was marked by widespread "privatization," which is to say, the growing tendency to see religion as a matter of personal ethics rather than public order.[34] The reasons for this development are too complex to detail here. We now realize, however, that the change had more to do with the peculiarities of European history and Western Christianity than with any universal modernizing tendency. We also know that this privatization was never as extensive as portrayed by some enthusiasts of Enlightenment secularism. After all, the post-Enlightenment West witnessed not merely attacks on public religion but new religious movements, such as Methodism in England, Pietism in Germany, and the Great Awakening in the United States.[35] It was no accident that the great French sociologist Alexis de Tocqueville concluded that congregational Christianity was a vital element in the democratic culture of early-nineteenth-century America.[36] De Tocqueville understood that the American separation of church and state took government out of the business of coercing conformity, but it did not take religion out of public life. The arrangement relocated religion not so much to the private musings of isolated individuals but to a civil sphere of voluntary association and public debate. The result was not religion's decline but an extraordinary efflorescence characterized by vigorous denominational competition and continual public argument. Renouncing the union of church and state, religion in America was pluralized and contested, but it was not reduced to the realm of the purely private.[37]

In light of our revised understanding of Western religion and modernity, it should come as no surprise to us that the privatized model of religion has not gained great ground in the contemporary Muslim world.[38] Although classical liberals might wish otherwise, most Muslims still look to their religion for principles of public order as well as personal spirituality. What they take from their tradition, however, is not immutably fixed but reflects an ongoing interpretation informed by the changing circumstances of our world.

The participatory revolution now sweeping the Muslim world has, for example, provoked fierce debates over questions of Islam's social meaning and by whose authority it is defined. In a pattern that resembles the competition between Protestant fundamentalists and liberal modernists in the United States a century ago,[39] the destabilization of hierarchies in the Muslim world has unleashed "competition and contest over both the interpretation of [religious] symbols and control of the institutions, formal and informal, that produce and sustain them."[40] Mass education and mass marketing have intensified the competition, creating vast but segmented audiences for Islamic books, newspapers, and arts.[41]

This pluralized landscape has also seen the appearance of a host of religious activists with backgrounds and interests different from those of classically educated Muslim scholars (the *ulama*). Today populist preachers, neotraditionalist Sufi masters, and secularly educated "new Muslim intellectuals" challenge the monopoly of religious power earlier enjoyed by the *ulama*.[42] Having originated in circles apart from the *ulama*, these new activists orient themselves to a broad public rather than to a few religious adepts. In place of esoteric legal debates, the spokespersons for this public Islam present their faith in quasi-ideological terms, as a source of practical knowledge "that can be differentiated from others and consciously reworked."[43] Traditional scholars find the discourse of the new Muslim activism bizarrely eclectic. It mixes passages from the Qur'an with discussions of current affairs, modern moral dilemmas, and, sometimes, Western political theory. But it is precisely this heady mix that allows the new public Islam to address a diverse mass audience.

In this manner, Islam in recent years has drifted away from its earlier elite moorings into an unsteady societal sea. In a fashion that resembles the expansion of evangelical Protestantism in contemporary Latin America,[44] one segment of the new Islamic leadership has moved down-market in its appeals, crafting its message for an audience of ordinary and, sometimes, destitute Muslims. More than is the case for Latin American evangelicals (although not unlike their North American counterparts), however, others have moved up-market into the political and philosophical debates of public intellectuals. A few others, finally, have been drawn into the netherworld of off-stage intrigue and statist violence. The long-term fate of Muslim politics everywhere depends on the balance struck between these divergent tendencies.

A Muslim Public Sphere?

In many respects, what is happening in the Muslim world resembles what the German sociologist Jurgen Habermas described some years ago as the emergence of the "public sphere" in the West.[45] Habermas's study of eighteenth-century European society emphasized that public arenas, like coffee houses, literary clubs, journals, and "moral weeklies," helped to create an open and egalitarian culture of participation. Habermas suggests that this development provided vital precedent for the next century's struggles for democratic representation.

Habermas has been criticized for overlooking the degree to which there were competing notions of public interaction in eighteenth-century Europe and other public spheres, not least of all religious. Habermas has also been rightly faulted for exaggerating the egalitarianism of the eighteenth-century public by overlooking exclusions based on wealth, gender, and religion.[46] Like Alexis de Tocqueville's observations on democracy in America, however, Habermas's analysis has the virtue of emphasizing that democratic life depends not just on government but on resources and habits in society at large. Formal democracy requires a culture and organization greater than itself.

The question this comparison raises, of course, is whether the heightened participation and pluralization so visible in the Muslim world heralds an impending acceleration of the democratization process. For some observers, the answer to this question is a resounding no. These skeptics argue that the Muslim resurgence contradicts one of the central premises of democratic and Habermasian theory, namely, that for a society to democratize, religion must retreat from the public stage to the privacy of personal belief.[47] Privatization, critics insist, is a condition of democratic peace.[48]

As noted above, our revised understanding of religion in the West now casts doubt on this unitary view of democracy and modernity. Nonetheless some specialists of Islam have lent their voices to this pessimistic view by arguing that Muslims have a unique cultural malady that makes it difficult for them to get noxious religious emissions out of the public air. Bernard Lewis, a respected historian of Turkey and the Middle East, has invoked the oft-cited phrase that Islam is *din wa dawla*, "religion and state," to observe that Muslims have an entirely different understanding of religion from that of liberal Christianity or the post-Enlightenment West:

> When we in the Western world, nurtured in the Western tradition, use the words "Islam" and "Islamic," we tend to make a natural error and assume that religion means the same for Muslims as it has meant in the Western world, even in medieval times; that is to say, a section or compartment of life reserved for certain matters. . . . That was not so in the Islamic world. It was never so in the past, and the attempt in

modern times to make it so may perhaps be seen, in the longer perspective of history, as an unnatural aberration which in Iran has ended and in some other Islamic countries may also be nearing its end.[49]

Lewis is right to emphasize that many Muslims regard their religion as a model for public order as well as personal ethics.[50] His generalization is too sweeping, however, if it implies that no good Western democrat has ever viewed religion in so comprehensive a manner. His generalization also misleads if it implies that Muslims have just one way of interpreting *din wa dawla*, and one way, therefore, of organizing Muslim politics.

Recent history has demonstrated that there is an enormous range of opinion among Muslims on precisely these matters. Some new activists *do* invoke the idea of Islam as "religion and state" to justify harshly coercive policies. They advocate a fusion of state and society into an unchecked monolith they call an "Islamic" state. They insist that the only way to enforce the high standards of Muslim morality is to dissolve the boundary between public and private and use the disciplinary powers of the state to police both spheres. The Qur'an of course knows no such concept of an "Islamic" state, least of all one with the coercive powers of a modern leviathan. The Qur'an also abhors compulsion in religion. For believers, however, the biggest problem with this arrangement is that it ends by degrading religion itself. By concentrating power in rulers' hands, statist Islam only increases the likelihood that Islam's high ideals will be subordinated to vulgar political intrigues. Time and time again we see unscrupulous despots wrap themselves in the mantle of Muslim piety. Not coincidentally, the Islam they promote is typically a neofundamentalism hostile to pluralism, justice, and civil decency.[51]

But the Islamic reformation[52] of the late-modern era is greater than the claims of hypocritical dictators. In part this is so because the Qur'an and its commentaries are rich with other, pluralistic possibilities. This is also the case, however, because the politics of the Muslim reformation depends not only on the recovery of hallowed textual truths but on a reading of the realities of the larger modern world. To quote the great Syrian Muslim democrat Mohammad Shahrour, Muslims "have been used to reading this book [the Qur'an] with borrowed eyes for hundreds of years."[53] More are reading it today with their own eyes. Like all thoughtful readers, however, they draw on what they see around them to enrich their understanding of the text. In so doing, they notice meanings previously overlooked. For many Muslims, the charge of this new reading is to recover and amplify Islam's democratic endowments so as to provide the ethical resources for Muslims in a plural, mobile, and participatory world.

Civil pluralist Islam is an emergent tradition and comes in a variety of forms.[54] Most versions begin, however, by denying the wisdom of a monolithic "Islamic" state and instead affirming democracy, voluntarism, and a balance of countervailing powers in a state and society.[55] In embracing the ideals of civil society, this democratic Islam insists that formal democracy cannot prevail unless government power is checked by strong civic associations. At the same time, it is said, civic associations and democratic culture cannot thrive unless they are protected by a state that respects society by upholding its commitment to the rule of law.

Recovering and amplifying elements of Islamic tradition, civil Islam is not merely a facsimile of a Western original. As Bhiku Parekh has noted, Atlantic liberalism (the version most popular among liberal philosophers in Great Britain and the United States) "defines the individual in austere and minimalist terms . . . as an essentially self-contained and solitary being."[56] Of course, recent debates in the United States have reminded us that contrary to philosophical portrayals, real-and-existing democracy must always find ways to accommodate social as well as individual goods.[57] As Adam Seligman and Michael Sandel have both emphasized,[58] it is nonetheless true that the language of modern liberalism, with its image of the "autonomous agentic individual," has often made the affirmation of social goods difficult.

As will become clearer in the following chapters, Muslim democrats, like those in Indonesia, tend to be more *civil* democratic or Tocquevillian than they are (Atlantic) liberal in spirit. They deny the need for an Islamic state. But they insist that society involves more than autonomous individuals, and democracy more than markets and the state. Democracy requires a noncoercive culture that encourages citizens to respect the rights of others as well as to cherish their own. This public culture depends on mediating institutions in which citizens develop habits of free speech, participation, and toleration. In all this, they say, there is nothing undemocratic about Muslim voluntary associations (as well as those of other religions) playing a role in the *public* life of civil society as well as in personal ethics.[59]

The success of civil Islam will ultimately depend on more than the ideas of a few good thinkers. In all modern traditions, religious reformation requires a delicate balance between a changing society and its orienting ideas. The ideas must be expansive enough to attract and guide the attention of a fast-moving people. But the ideas must not run so far ahead that they leave the great mass behind. It is a premise of the present book that a democratic politics is indeed developing in the Islamic world, and it is not too far ahead of those whom it would guide. In sociological terms, the reformation depends on achieving a delicate balance between structural changes in state and society, on the one hand, and public culture and ethics, on the other.

In this book, of course, I am especially interested in the trials and tribulations of civil Islam in the Southeast Asian nation of Indonesia. The Indonesian example is interesting for several reasons. It provides a striking illustration of the varied ways in which a universal religion has been adapted to local worlds. The example challenges most of our stereotypes of Muslim history and politics.

It also enlarges our sense of the plural nature of modernity and the way the modern world has presented similar challenges to believers in all the world's religions, even while allowing them different outcomes.

CIVIC SEEDLINGS

Although an earlier generation of Western scholars identified its most distinctive trait as the strength of so-called Hindu-Buddhist survivals, the more distinctive quality of Indonesian Islam has long been its remarkable cultural pluralism. The archipelago that in modern times became Indonesia and Malaysia was never conquered by invading Muslim armies, smothered under a centralized empire, or supervised by an omnipresent clergy. Certainly there was the occasional despot who aspired to religious absolutism. But the striking feature of political organization in the early modern archipelago is that it was organized around a "pluricentric" pattern of mercantile city-states, inland agrarian kingdoms, and tribal hinterlands. In comparative terms, regional organization here resembled not so much the great empires of China, India, or Byzantium as the pluralized polities of early modern Europe (chapter 2).

The variety of states and societies in the archipelago had a profound influence on the subsequent development of Muslim politics and culture. Even in an era when virtually all Javanese, Malays, or Minangkabau called themselves Muslims, neither the courts nor religious scholars (the *ulama*) exercised monopolistic control over the practice of Islam. There were always different Muslim rulers, diverse religious associations, and alternative ideas as to how to be Muslim. From the beginning, people in the region grappled with what social theorists today sometimes regard as a uniquely modern problem—cultural pluralism.

There was nothing inevitable about the outcome of this engagement. Distributed across a vast territorial expanse and three hundred ethnic groups, the Muslim community could have dissolved into a maelstrom of ethno-Islams, in which each community claimed an opposed understanding of religion's truth. At times local Muslim rulers did encourage exclusive or chauvinistic professions of the faith. From early on, however, the mainstream tradition recognized that there were different ways of being Muslim, and different balances of divine commandment and local culture (*adat*). This cultural precedent may well explain why, in the late colonial period, so many Indonesian Muslims rallied to the nationalist cause (chapter 3). In Indonesia at least, the nationalism they embraced was plural and multiethnic rather than, as in so much of Europe, premised on a single ethnic prototype.

This pattern of political and ethnoreligious pluralism was put to a test in the colonial era. The Dutch replaced the archipelago's many states with a unified empire. The colonial government placed strict limits on Muslim participation in public affairs, trying to squeeze Islam into an illiberal version of Enlightenment privatism. Rather than reinforcing a union of religion and state, then, colonialism pushed Muslims away from the corridors of power and out into villages and society. In the eighteenth and nineteenth centuries a vast network of Qur'anic schools spread across the archipelago. The leaders of these schools were suspicious of Europeans and their native allies, and they located their institutions at a safe distance from state capitals. In the early twentieth century, when the first modern Muslim organizations were established, most showed a similarly healthy skepticism toward the pretensions of rulers.

These practical precedents for civic autonomy and a balance of social powers, however, did not yet enjoy sufficient cultural authority to serve as the basis for a reformed Muslim politics. Indeed, on this point the struggle for national independence after 1910 introduced contradictory trends (chapters 3, 4). Many Muslims, including pious ones, rejected the notion that Islam requires an Islamic state. Joined by Christians, Hindus, Buddhists, and secular nationalists, these Muslims advocated a plural and democratic nation-state. Others in the Muslim community, however, insisted that the end of colonialism heralded a new age of cooperation with the state. Muslims' ascent into government, these leaders argued, was the answer to their prayers for a deeper Islamization of state and society.[60]

This dream, of course, was not merely a matter of political ambition. As in other parts of the Muslim world, Islamic reformists in the early independence era were determined to put an end to the mysticism, saint cults, and ancestral veneration widespread in native society, all of which they regarded as polytheistic deviations from Islam.[61] In some of the archipelago these campaigns for religious purification were an unqualified success. On the densely populated island of Java (and a few other areas), however, the results were mixed. Javanese Muslims were divided between those committed to a more or less normative profession of the faith, known as *santri*, and those who spiced their piety with Javanese customs, known as *abangan*.[62] The reformist campaign left a few *abangan* wondering whether they were really Muslims at all.[63] By the 1920s many were looking away from Islamic orthodoxy to socialism, secular nationalism, and Marxism to make sense of their new world (chapter 3). Although in some parts of the archipelago reformist Muslims could portray their rivals as backward heathen, then, this was not the case in Java. The *abangan* leadership was educated and organized.[64] The conflict between Javanists and reformist Muslims did not pit parochial traditionalists against cosmopolitan modernizers. It set two rival visions of religion and nation against each other. This was to become the basis for an enduring political argument.

By the time Indonesia declared its independence on August 17, 1945, then, the neat union of Islam and ethnicity among Javanese had been shattered; politics and religion had been pluralized.[65] Indonesians favoring a formal Islamization of state faced increasing opposition as the independence era advanced. By the late 1950s the anti-Islamist opposition included most of the military leadership, which had done battle with Muslim separatists; Christians, Hindus, and Buddhists, all disproportionately represented in the ranks of the middle class; secular nationalists and modernizers; the Communist Party; and most of the Javanist community.

As time went on, the debate between Islamists and nonconfessional nationalists became even more strident. Contrary to general expectations, Muslim parties failed to win a majority of the vote in the first national elections in 1955. The vote was evenly divided between nonconfessional nationalists and proponents of an Islamic state. With the impasse at the nation's center, the big political parties launched furious mass mobilizations, organizing peasant associations, labor unions, cooperatives, and religious clubs. Although 88 percent of their support was concentrated on the island of Java (where 55 percent of the population lived), the Communist Party proved the most skilled at this mobilization. Having won 18 percent of the vote in the 1955 elections, the party went on to recruit twenty million people to its affiliate organizations. By 1960 Indonesia had the largest Communist Party in the noncommunist world (chapters 3, 4).

The rapid pace of the Communist Party's growth hid a fatal organizational flaw. Although less massive than their communist rival, Muslim organizations were more evenly dispersed across the country and more deeply rooted in society. The Communists were also at a disadvantage in that they were bitterly opposed by the army high command. This struggle between the Communists, on one side, and the military and the Muslims, on the other, came to a tragic climax in the aftermath of a failed left-wing officers' coup on September 30, 1965. In the weeks that followed, Muslims joined forces with the conservative army leadership to destroy the Communist Party; as many as half a million people died. Muslim organizations sacralized the campaign, calling it a holy war or *jihad*. The Muslim heritage of civil autonomy and skepticism toward state power seemed a faded memory indeed.

In the aftermath of 1965–66, the military-dominated "New Order" government made political and economic stabilization its top priority (chapter 4). To the surprise of Muslim leaders, the regime also moved gingerly to restrict independent political parties, especially—now that the nationalist left was destroyed—Muslim ones. In the face of government repression, the Muslim community split into two camps. Some sought to defend the faith through a program of Islamic appeal (*dakwah*), intended over the long run to revive the Islamic parties and recapture the state. Another group in the Muslim community, however, criticized this reduction of Muslim interests to state-centered struggle. The obsession with party politics in the 1950s, they said, had only polarized the nation and impeded Muslim progress. What was really needed, then, was not another campaign to capture the state but a vigorous program of education and renewal in society. The ultimate goal of this program should be the creation of a Muslim civil society to counterbalance the state and promote a public culture of pluralism and participation (chapter 5).

This intra-Muslim debate might well have remained an insignificant issue had Indonesian politics remained in a steady state. Instead, however, the rivalry between these two visions of Islam and nation eventually became one of the defining features of the New Order. This had to do with changes in society. Contrary to the expectations of its rulers, in the late 1970s and early 1980s Indonesia experienced a historically unprecedented Islamic resurgence (chapters 5, 6). There was an upsurge in mosque construction, Friday worship, religious education, alms-collection (*zakat*), and pilgrimage to Mecca. In 1977 the Unity and Development Party (PPP), a government-tolerated Muslim party, astonished the nation by winning the lion's share of the vote in the capital.

Government programs had unwittingly contributed to the resurgence. Between 1965 and 1990, the percentage of young adults with basic literacy skills skyrocketed from 40 percent to 90 percent.[66] The percentage of youths completing senior high school was equally impressive, rising from 4 percent in 1970 to more than 30 percent today.[67] The educational expansion occurred after 1966, when regulations mandating religious instruction in all schools were enforced with a new vigor. Before Soeharto's rise, most schools had implemented requirements for religious education casually, if at all. But by the early 1970s all elementary school students were receiving the same religious instruction from state-certified teachers.

A second influence on the resurgence was that many Indonesians in these years were searching for a new ethical compass for their fast changing world. They were doing so, moreover, at a time when other arenas for public association and debate had been closed.[68] Islam was "seen as a safe alternative to the heavily circumscribed political structure."[69] After street battles in January 1974 the regime muzzled the news media. In 1978 it clamped down on campus politics. Between 1983 and 1985 the government required mass organizations to recognize the state ideology, or *Pancasila* ("five principles"), as their "sole foundation"; those that refused were banned. Nothing escaped the regime's reach. It launched regular sweeps against campus activists, labor organizations, and even independent business associations.[70] The regime also reduced the two official political parties, the nationalist-oriented Democratic Party (PDI) and the Muslim-oriented Unity and Development Party, to pliant ineffectuality.

The Soeharto government also regularly meddled in Muslim affairs (chapters 5–7).[71] Muslim associations were nonetheless better able to withstand the state's repressive storm. Indeed, in their campaigns against the national sports lottery, against government regulations on marriage,[72] and in support of Islamic banking, among others, Muslim organizations showed a striking ability to circumvent the state and influence public policy.

Although the Islamic resurgence displayed the pluralization of authority seen in other Muslim countries, it also showed the impact of state controls.

With its regulations recognizing only five faiths (Islam, Protestantism, Catholicism, Hinduism, and Buddhism) as legitimate options for its citizens, the New Order effectively outlawed the indigenous religions practiced in local communities across eastern Indonesia, Kalimantan, and interior Sumatra. Anthropologists working in these areas in the 1970s and 1980s provided vivid accounts of the deleterious impact of these policies on indigenous religions, and, conversely, their role in catalyzing conversion to Christianity or Islam.[73] State policies had a similar impact on *abangan* Islam. Over the past thirty years the institutions through which Javanist Islam once operated as a *public* alternative to orthodox Islam have declined, whereas institutions for Islamic education and devotion have grown (chapter 4).[74] Upset by Muslim participation in the anticommunist massacres,[75] some 3 percent of ethnic Javanese converted to Hinduism or Christianity in the first years of the New Order.[76] Others took shelter in mystical associations. Both developments pale, however, in comparison with the growing numbers of Javanists who have adopted a more pious profession of Islam.

Political observers have long suspected that the relative decline of Javanist Islam has serious political implications. In the 1950s, after all, secular and *abangan* Muslims formed the core of the Communist and Nationalist Parties. Opposition to political Islam became one of the rallying cries of the populist left. The conversion of nominal Muslims to a more mainstream Islam has been seen by many observers, then, as portending enormous changes in Indonesia's political landscape.

The consequences of the resurgence are more complex, however, than a simple shift from secular-nationalism to "conservative" Islam. As the growing public interest in Sufi mysticism has illustrated, many Indonesians prefer an independent and tolerant spirituality to the controlled Islam of the state.[77] Equally important, as Muslim students in the anti-Soeharto movement showed, many pious youth find democratic and egalitarian values in their reading of Islam. Indeed, although conservative Islamists disapprove, the remarkable feature of the resurgence was that its central streams were democratic and pluralist (chapters 6, 7).[78] In the 1990s Muslims were the single largest constituency in the prodemocracy movement against Soeharto.

But not all has been sweetness and light for Indonesian Muslims. In the last years of his rule, Soeharto changed course and, rather than suppressing Muslims, courted them. The president's rapprochement was in part intended to counterbalance his worsening relationship with powerful military commanders. But Soeharto's actions also reflected his awareness of the strength of the Islamic resurgence (chapters 6, 7). Whatever his precise motives, the president's policies had an electrifying impact on Muslim affairs. Having obstructed organized Islam for twenty years, in his last twelve Soeharto encouraged it. He supported the establishment of an Islamic bank, expansion of the authority of Muslim courts, an end to the prohibition on the wearing of the veil (*jilbab*) in schools, the founding of an Islamic newspaper, abolition of the state lottery, expanded Muslim programming on television, increased funding for Muslim schools, and the appointment of armed forces leaders sympathetic to (conservative) Islam.[79] Among conservative Muslims in the 1990s there was talk of a "honeymoon" with Soeharto.

In political terms, however, the opening to the Muslim community was always circumscribed. Muslims seen as too critical or democratic were excluded from presidential favor. Rather than a *civil* Islam, in other words, Soeharto sought to create a *regimist* Islam untroubled by his authoritarian ways. As it became clear that mainstream Muslims *were* interested in democratic reforms, the president upped his ante. From 1996 on, his strategists began to make stridently anti-Christian and anti-Chinese appeals in an effort to divide the opposition along ethnic and religious lines. Responding to these overtures, a few Muslim ultraconservatives moved out of the opposition into alliance with the regime. They collaborated in the campaigns of intimidation and terror that marked Soeharto's final years (chapters 6, 7).

Soeharto's actions betrayed the principles of *Pancasila* pluralism earlier promoted, if often hypocritically, by his regime.[80] In exploiting ethnoreligious divisions for personal power, Soeharto also made a dangerous run on the reserves of civic decency in society. Civil society, and civil Islam, were threatened by the uncivil depredations of the state.

The state itself was far from unitary, however. By the end of Soeharto's rule, there were many decent people in the military and bureaucracy who were shocked by Soeharto's desperate dealings. In the face of Soeharto's repression the state elite split into rival factions—some opposing the president, others supporting him. The state's loss, however, was not civil society's gain. As had been the case in the final years of Soekarno's rule,[81] intra-state rivalries led some among the elite only to intensify their efforts to exploit divisions in society. Fortunately many in the state, and the great majority of people in society, rejected these uncivil abuses. In the first months of 1998 Muslim and secular democrats joined forces in a prodemocracy campaign that ultimately brought Soeharto down (chapter 7).

What guided Soeharto throughout his career was not, as many once thought, his commitment to a consistent ideology, least of all the tolerant Javanism attributed to him a generation ago. Soeharto's obsession was power, and he was happy to change ideological garb to keep it. A master of divide and conquer, he played religious rivals against one another until none could stand on their own. On this point Soeharto's actions reflected less an "idea of power" unique to Javanese culture than a strategy of divisive control widely used by authoritarian rulers. The tactic threatened the most precious of Indonesia's democratic resources: the depth of tolerance and nationalist pride among citizens of all faiths.

In the end, Indonesia survived Soeharto. Its long-term prospects look hopeful, although its democratic transition is still young. More specifically, although

Soeharto stepped down in May 1998, most of his supporters did not. Despite the victory of pro-reform parties in the elections of June 1999, then, the road toward justice and reconciliation is still far from clear.

What is apparent, however, is that democratic consolidation will require not just a civil society of independent associations (although these are important too) but a public culture of equality, justice, and universal citizenship. In this majority-Muslim society, and in the aftermath of a great Islamic revival, the creation of such a public culture of democratic civility will be impossible unless it can build on the solid ground of civil Islam. While affirming the legitimacy of religion in public life, civil Islam rejects the mirage of the "Islamic" state, recognizing that this formula for fusing religious and state authority ignores the lessons of Muslim history itself. Worse yet, without checks and balances in state and society, the "Islamic" state subordinates Muslim ideals to the dark intrigues of party bosses and religious thugs.

The Indonesian example reminds us, then, that while a civil society and civic culture are required to make democracy work, by themselves they are still not enough. A healthy civil society requires a *civilized* state. In the Indonesian case, such a state would work with, rather than against, the greatness of its citizens and the humanitarianism of civil Islam. On the challenge of these achievements, the Indonesian story has much to tell.

Chapter Two

CIVIL PRECEDENCE

A KEY THEME in modern social theory has been that the traditions a society inherits from the past shape its ability to respond to the present, often in ways actors themselves do not fully understand. Dutifully engaged in business in an effort to confirm he is among God's elect, the Calvinist entrepreneur who helps create modern capitalism in Max Weber's *The Protestant Ethic and the Spirit of Capitalism*[1] provides the prototype for this sort of analysis, in which a precedent from the past is projected into the present to create something unexpectedly new. In the heyday of modernization theory in the 1950s and 1960s, social scientists set out for non-Western locales in the hope of finding precedents for modern development like these. Like Weber, most researchers were interested in cultural inheritances that might facilitate the emergence of the two institutions thought pivotal to the making of the modern world—market economies and political democracy.

From the start this kind of comparative inquiry was plagued by conceptual shortcomings. The models of democracy and capitalism used in these investigations, first of all, were often so idealized as to undermine comparison with non-Western societies. Typically, for example, the image of the West used in the analysis was a stripped-down model of the Anglo-American experience, squeezed of its political complexity so as to fit into the modernization corset. Convinced of the benefits of such simplifications, researchers often found themselves confused upon arriving in a foreign setting, uncertain of what they should look for. In identifying precedents for modern market economies, for example, should one look for a tradition of moneymaking? Or is the critical issue technology and efficient institutions for capital accumulation? Or is the key perhaps an entrepreneurial class willing and able to extract surplus value from a reluctant labor force?

The answer to these questions all depends on what one believes is essential for a modern economy and society. Rather than grappling with questions like these, however, modernization theorists tended to create simplified prototypes of the modern West and then look for their counterpart in developing societies. Inspired by an exuberant reading of Weber's *Protestant Ethic* (and ignoring the complex analyses of his *Economy and Society*),[2] field researchers interested in capitalism looked for local miniatures of Weber's Calvinist entrepreneur—as if market growth did not also depend on an array of "embedding" institutions in state and society.[3]

In the years since modernization theory's demise, social researchers have achieved a deeper understanding of the difficulties of such cross-cultural comparison. They have done so in part by recognizing that the West is not unitary but richly plural in its traditions. They have also recognized that the social and historical richness of the "non-Western" world cannot be adequately conveyed by simplistic polarities of modernity and tradition. Modernity is multiple, and the premodern world equally so.

Buoyed by this critical confidence, comparative research on politics and democratization in the 1980s and 1990s took an anthropological turn. Researchers realized that even in the West the roads to political modernity have been many, not one. The history of democratic government in England has differed significantly from that in Germany, and Germany's history differs from that of Italy or the United States. Rather than assuming that democratic government everywhere emerges from the same *specific* institutions or events, then, scholars began to look for something more general—a polymorphous social resource that, in different times and places, provides a precedent for democratic life.

Two social entities popularly identified as having these generic qualities are "social capital" and "civil society." Social capital consists of accumulative cultural endowments that facilitate the performance of certain social tasks.[4] Stated differently, and to steal a sentence from the Harvard political scientist Robert Putnam, social capital refers to "features of social organization, such as trust, norms, and networks, that can improve the efficiency of society by facilitating coordinated actions."[5] Based on an analogy with economic capital, the idea here is that the effective performance of social tasks requires not merely material goods but institutions for coordinating specifically *social* resources as well.

Expressed in so general a fashion, one could imagine social capital for all kinds of purposes: to heighten religious piety; to maintain sexual virtue; or perhaps to promote a public appetite for bird watching. In most contemporary research, however, the concept has been applied to a narrower array of issues, based on theories of what it is that has made the world modern. Like modernization theorists a generation ago, researchers have been particularly intent on identifying social capital that might enhance the prospects for modern markets and democracy.

In cross-cultural studies of capitalism, the social capital paradigm has helped to correct the view that all that is needed for economic growth is to clear the market of political obstacles, "get prices right," and let the market do its job. As was made apparent by efforts in the 1990s to introduce a market economy to Russia, however, real-and-existing markets are never self-contained or naturally self-organizing. They are affected by, among other things, the politics, work habits, and morality of their host society. Rather than being everywhere the same, then, capitalism varies across cultures. The state and law play a minor role in business in Taiwan compared to the United States and Western Europe. Multimillion dollar deals that in the United States are struck only after scrutiny by a small army of lawyers are, among overseas Chinese, settled with a handshake.[6] Every market is embedded in society in ways like these, and capitalism depends on a social capital of networks and norms not everywhere the same.[7]

Building on insights like these from economic sociology, political researchers have deployed the concept of social capital in an analogous fashion to analyze the conditions that make democracy work. Studies of this sort emphasize that democratic governance depends not just on formal elections or constitutions but on informal endowments found in society as a whole. These endowments include a political culture emphasizing citizen independence, trust in one's fellows, tolerance, and respect for the rule of law. These cultural resources are in turn best fostered, it has been argued, through a peculiar social organization known as civil society.

The concept of civil society means widely differing things in different theoretical traditions. In its most common usage in the 1990s, however, the notion refers to the clubs, religious organizations, business groups, labor unions, human rights groups, and other associations located between the household and the state and organized on the basis of voluntarism and mutuality. The idea here is that for formal democratic institutions to work, citizens have first to acquire the habit of participating in local voluntary associations. It is through such "networks of civil engagement," one hears said, that citizens learn the habits of participation and initiative later generalized to the whole of political society.

Much of the inspiration for this idea originated in Alexis de Tocqueville's famous nineteenth-century study *Democracy in America*. Drawing on ideas first developed by Montesquieu, de Tocqueville regarded intermediary associations as vital for healthy democracy. Fascinated by Americans' ability to develop democratic institutions compared to the French inability to do so, de Tocqueville argued that the key difference was that Americans had "carried to the highest perfection" the civic habit of common effort in organizations independent of the state.[8] In attempting to explain this peculiar American aptitude, de Tocqueville highlighted the role of churches and small-town government. These institutions draw Americans out from the confines of their private lives, de Tocqueville said, into public projects where they learn "habits of the heart" conducive to a democratic good.

Building on this Tocquevillian premise, contemporary enthusiasts of social capital and civil society have set out for distant shores to look for participatory precedents like these. In an influential study, for example, Robert D. Putnam has examined why patterns of government vary so greatly between northern and southern Italy. In the south, he claims, politics has long been plagued by corruption, violence, and organized crime. "The southerner . . . has sought refuge in vertical bonds of patronage and clientelism, employed for both economic and political ends."[9] By contrast, local government in the north works relatively well because, Putnam argues, people have long relied on "networks of civic engagement." The latter are evident in everything from choral groups and lay religious associations to business partnerships and political parties.

When, in good Tocquevillian fashion, Putnam turns to explain the difference between northern and southern Italy, he finds that "social patterns plainly traceable from early medieval Italy to today turn out to be decisive in explaining why, on the verge of the twenty-first century, some communities are better able than others to manage collective life and sustain effective institutions."[10] Indeed, since the great Norman kingdom of the twelfth century, Putnam argues, the south has been characterized by an autocratic political culture. The Norman kingdom that created this uncivil polity has long since passed, but, Putnam implies, its lawlessness, patron-clientage, and corruption live on.

In contrast to the south, Putnam observes, northern Italy, even in medieval times, began to create self-governing communes, "oases amidst the feudal forest." The north did so because it responded to the violence and anarchy of medieval Europe with horizontal collaboration rather than vertical hierarchy. Although the communal system was not democratic in the modern sense (because full rights of participation were restricted to patricians), civic life drew large numbers of people into horizontal associations.[11] The resulting networks of civic engagement heightened public trust, smoothed institutional performance, and provided a "culturally defined template for future collaboration."[12]

Putnam's thoughtful insights became axioms of the 1990s' literature on civil society. Especially influential was his structuralist claim that the real key to democratic culture is popular participation in laterally organized "civic" associations. Putnam gave this conviction an almost mathematical precision, saying that "the more horizontally structured an organization, the more it should foster institutional success in the broader community." Conversely, Putnam observed, "membership rates in hierarchically ordered organizations . . . should be negatively associated with good government."[13] Horizontal groupings are "democracy-good," it seems, and vertical ones "democracy-bad."

In retrospect, this appealing little formula appears too simple. As America's extremist militias remind us, "horizontalism" is no guarantee of democratic civility. Organizations like right-wing militias or the Ku Klux Klan may well display the independence from government and rank-and-file effervescence we associate with civil society. Contrary to Putnam's alluring formula, however, these exclusive associations can also breed intolerance and sectarianism. From examples like these, it is apparent that lateral association does not guarantee any specific political outcome. The political impact of civic associations depends not just on their formal structure but on the discourse and practice they help promote. In assessing whether associations "make democracy work," then, we have to look carefully at what their members actually say and do. In particular, we have to examine the way their members relate to one another *and* to outsiders, and ask whether the overall pattern contributes to a public culture of inclusion and participation or uncivil exclusivity.

This first shortcoming in the civic-associational model of democratization points to a second. If horizontalism is not all good, not all verticalism is bad. Vertical structures may not only coexist with civic organizations, but, by preserving the peace or building bridges over troubled waters, they may actually strengthen a public culture of civility and participation. This was famously the case, for example, in the eighteenth- and nineteenth-century Netherlands. There the social peace was threatened by the uncivil rivalries among the country's three major religious groupings: Roman Catholics, Orthodox Protestants, and Liberal Protestants. (In the late nineteenth century secular humanists were added to the mix.) Peace among these social groupings was maintained by vertical organizations coordinated by nonclerical representatives from each pillar. The idea behind this arrangement was that pillar leaders should negotiate an equitable share of state resources so as to ensure that their followers did not fight with people from rival pillars. In this manner, vertical coordination helped to maintain horizontal peace. As the Dutch sociologist Anton Zijderveld has observed, this arrangement was in some ways "authoritarian and elitist." But it nonetheless allowed a "remarkable social and political pacification," one that eventually facilitated modern Dutch democracy.[14]

Examples like these remind us that associational explanations of what "makes democracy work" are inherently incomplete. One has to examine not just civic organizations but their synergistic interaction with public culture and the state. This conclusion also implies that modern democratization always involves more than just projecting old associations into new social terrains. As Peter Evans has remarked in a review of the literature on social capital, there is nothing simple about " 'scaling up' micro-level social capital to generate solidary ties and social action on a scale that is politically and economically efficacious" for society as a whole.[15] Institution-building efforts like these depend not only on civic associations but on the state. Without a state to expand their democratic role, "networks of civic engagement" may get lost in the backstreets of society rather than open on to a democratic public sphere.

These simple theoretical lessons are directly relevant to the Indonesian example. Modern Indonesia has been plagued by a recurring inability to make good on the promise of its civic endowments. Indonesian society in general, and Muslim society in particular, has been blessed with an abundance of civic resources. Muslims learned long ago to live with ethnic and regional diversity.[16] They showed a healthy skepticism toward the all-controlling state. These cultural precedents might well have served as the raw material for a Muslim political reformation. But their amplification into public discourses and practices has often proved difficult. This was partly so because most of the ruling elite who dominated Indonesian society, rather than consolidating precedents for civility and pluralism, ignored or abused them. The colonial policy of divide and conquer had an especially corrosive impact on native civic traditions. The postcolonial state continued this legacy; the Soeharto regime brought it to perfection.

This failure of civic consolidation, however, has not been the state's fault alone. The movements for Islamic reform that arose in the nineteenth century decried many of the accommodations devised by local Muslims to live in a plural world. Rather than drawing on local history to deepen democratic precedents, many reformists looked away from their world, back to an idealized golden age. As specialists of Islam have emphasized (chapter 1), there are abundant resources in Muslim tradition for democratic politics. But for these raw materials to become effective democratic endowments, Muslim thinkers have to be willing to learn from their own history as well as from high doctrines. Politics in Indonesia has often made this delicate balance of religious idealism and political empiricism a difficult achievement indeed.

PROMISE BROKEN

At first sight, the archipelagan region that today makes up Indonesia seems an unlikely candidate for ever having enjoyed even a limited culture of pluralism and participation. After all, in the early modern era (sixteenth to seventeenth century), the region was inhabited by more than three hundred ethnic groups living on some six thousand inhabited islands separated by marked divisions of language and culture. Although by the early modern period the majority of coastal people in the area had come to profess Islam, many of the larger islands' hinterlands maintained locally oriented ethnic religions. Even coastal Muslim territories were cross-cut by regional and ethnic divides.

Trained in modernization theory, a Westerner reflecting on this diversity might be tempted to conclude that it was the result of traditional societies long lost in historyless slumber and about to be awakened by the detraditionalizing energies of the West. Like the polarity of "tradition" and "modernity" on which it is based, however, such a conclusion overlooks the dynamism that has long characterized this region.[17] The archipelago's diversity is not the result of traditional torpor but a decidedly unlinear encounter with forces at work in this region for the better part of a thousand years. European colonialism had a major influence on the latter stages of this history, but its role was less progressive than modernization models typically imply. In fact, the European interregnum reinforced absolutism, reified ethnicity, and undercut integrative processes already at work across ethnic and territorial divides.

By the time the Dutch began to make regular appearances in the archipelago in the early seventeenth century, the region's coastal principalities were in the second century of an economically expansive and Muslim-pioneered "age of commerce."[18] The trade that moved through this great commercial zone was multifaceted, but its most lucrative circuits involved the transport of spices, cloth, rice, and gold from eastern Indonesia to commercial centers in southern Sulawesi, Java, the Malay Peninsula, and Sumatra. From these ports goods were shipped to China, India, and southern Arabia, creating a trading zone comparable in scale to that of the eastern Mediterranean in the early modern period.

As in the Mediterranean world, the archipelagan trade had long influenced regional culture and politics. Earlier, in the first centuries of the common era, commercial exchange between the archipelago and India and China catalyzed the emergence of the area's first states. Shortly thereafter, this same trade facilitated the diffusion of Buddhism and Hinduism from India to royal courts throughout the region. Although the remote islands of eastern Indonesia and the inaccessible interiors in the west were not dramatically transformed by this movement of people, goods, and ideas, the region's major states were forever changed.

Many of the more conspicuous elements in this cultural complex showed strong Indian influences. These included the use of Sanskrit-derived alphabets; Indian legal ideas; political regalia emphasizing the divinity of the ruler; and, consistent with the cult of sacred kings, rituals identifying the court as a microcosm of the universe and a meeting point between heaven and earth. In the peculiar blend of Hinduism and Buddhism characteristic of the archipelago, some rulers were presented as incarnations of Buddhist *boddhisattvas*, Hindu gods, or both. As this example shows, high religion in the pre-Islamic era was hitched to the cart of dynastic politics.[19]

By the time Europeans finally arrived, then, the Indonesian archipelago had enjoyed more than a thousand years of civilizational efflorescence. In fact, at the time of the European arrival, the archipelago was experiencing a vast renewal of cultural and commercial energies, on a scale that invites comparison with renaissance Europe. Trading expeditions from India and, especially, southern China (after the ascent of the Ming dynasty in 1368) stimulated commercial activity. This in turn had a far-reaching impact on archipelagan society. Rather than stimulating the growth of empire, political power remained dispersed across a host of mercantile city-states and inland agrarian kingdoms. Until the Europeans imposed their rule the archipelago never knew a centralized empire like those in the Middle East or China. If anything, in fact, the region's state organization resembled the pluricentric pattern of early modern Europe. Historical sociologists like Max Weber, Ernest Gellner, and John Hall, among others, have long identified Europe's multipolar organization as one of the keys to its gradual democratization.[20] There were times when it looked as if the archipelago's pluralism held a similar democratic promise.

The civilizational dynamic at work in the early-modern archipelago was evident in many spheres. At the time of the European arrival, Malay—a language originally spoken in small settlements on the Malay Peninsula and in Borneo—was becoming the lingua franca for regional commerce and religion.[21] Malay achieved this prominence not through conquest but as the public language for a multiethnic world. Islam was also spreading across coastal portions of the archipelago at this time, in a manner that invites comparison with the expansion of Protestantism in early modern Europe. The Muslim advance came not on the heels of conquering nomads or slave armies but through commerce, urban growth, and a new cosmopolitan culture.[22]

There had long been a limited Muslim presence in the archipelago. Arab and Central Asian Muslims had played an important role in southern China's trade as early as the eighth century. No doubt a few had settled for short periods in archipelagan ports, but in this early period they appear to have been quarantined within small communities of expatriate foreigners.[23] Significant local conversion to Islam occurred only later, after the Indian branch of the Southeast Asian trade fell into Muslim hands after the great Muslim conquests of the twelfth and thirteenth centuries.[24] With the Indian and Chinese branches of the trade in Muslim hands, and with trade itself heightening social intercourse, Islam spread to trading posts around the archipelago from the thirteenth to the seventeenth century. For a while, the new religion even found a significant following in coastal Thailand and Cambodia.[25] In the Philippines, Islam's advance from the south toward Luzon in the north was halted only by the sixteenth-century arrival of the Spanish.[26]

Keeping the comparison with European Protestantism in mind, scholars have long wondered how much the Islamization of insular Southeast Asia was related to a (relatively) "democratic" transformation in political and ethical culture. For the early centuries of Islam's diffusion the answer to this question seems to be, rather little. The longer-term answer, however, requires a more complex assessment.

Clearly, in the first instance, the coming of Islam to the Indonesian region replaced a hierarchical Hindu-Buddhism with a religio-political tradition that was almost equally "raja-centric," to borrow a phrase from the historian Anthony Milner.[27] Ordinary people's identification as Muslim usually followed the ruler's conversion to the new religion. Once established, some of these now Muslim states engaged in warfare with their heathen neighbors. A most famous case occurred on the island of Java, where north-coast principalities joined forces in the sixteenth century to attack older Hindu kingdoms in the center and west of the island.[28] In most of the Indonesian region, however, one sees little evidence of the systematic destruction of Hindu temples that marked Muslim conquest in India or the vehement and often bloody iconoclasm of Reformation Europe.

All was not a matter of quietistic conversion, however, as implied in Clifford Geertz's *Islam Observed.*[29] From Theodore G. Th. Pigeaud's monumental *Java in the Fourteenth Century*, we know that pre-Islamic Java had a vast network of Hindu-Buddhist monasteries, temples, and shrines. In comparison with South Asia, where Hindu temples survived Muslim conquest, the temple tradition in Java seems to have experienced a sudden and stupendous collapse. Syncretistic compromises survived, of course. As with the *wayang* tradition of shadow puppetry in Java, however, the great majority did so by clothing themselves in what was at least superficially an Islamic garb.[30] On Java, travelers in the sixteenth and seventeenth centuries occasionally stumbled on odd mountain hermits and mystics, many of whom called themselves Muslim even though their ritual clearly owed much to the pre-Islamic tradition.[31] Even in these instances, however, the tendency was for public religion to be represented as Islamic, even though pious Muslims might question the accuracy of such characterizations. In this manner, and with the exception of Hindu kingdoms in Bali and a small pocket of Hindus in eastern Java, no Hindu clergy, communities, or temples survived in Islamized areas of the archipelago.

IMPERIAL ISLAM AND ITS OTHER

Eventually imperial Islam became the state religion in most of the archipelago's coastal kingdoms.[32] The *raja* was identified as supreme defender of the faith and, not coincidentally, religious scholars (*ulama*) were subordinated to the authority of the court. In Java, the Malay Peninsula, and southern Sulawesi this raja-centric Islam also helped to create an environment in which the concern for Islamic orthodoxy was relaxed, allowing localized or syncretic traditions to survive in court ritual and folk religion.[33] At a few times and in a few places, of course, some Muslim rulers promoted a strict application of Islamic law. We know, for example, that there was a peak of scriptural influence in the early seventeenth century, when some of the most powerful sultans acquired the trappings of absolutist rule.[34] In Aceh, Ternate, and Banten (in West Java) apostates were threatened with execution, and religious minorities were forced to convert.[35] Some of these absolutist states also enforced classical Islam's harsh criminal penalties (*hudud*), including amputation of limbs for theft. It was no coincidence that this period of strict application of the *shariah* (divine commandments or law) coincided with the archipelago's commercial boom and the efforts of local sultans to tighten their grip on society.

In most of the early modern archipelago, however, the law was applied with a gentler and more pluralistic hand. Where Muslim judges (*qadi*) operated at all, they were appointed by the ruler, often on the basis of family ties rather than a mastery of Islamic law.[36] *Shariah* was not used as the sole source of law in most regional courts. Religious scholars did consult Muslim legal digests, some of which incorporated recognized elements of the *shariah*, particularly on matters of marriage, divorce, sexuality, inheritance, slavery, and commerce. In general, however, legal codes in precolonial times drew on varied sources, and the application of *shariah* was at the discretionary judgment of the ruler. As Sir Thomas Raffles remarked of Java's legal administration in 1817, this discretionary power was "a prerogative liberally exercised."[37]

Whatever their influence in matters of law, during most of the early modern period Muslim rulers experienced serious checks on their authority. The great commercial boom of the sixteenth and seventeenth centuries, in particular, gave rise to struggles to limit royal authority. When the Dutch and English first arrived in the archipelago, they "were frustrated by the difficulty of finding monarchs who could make decisions binding on their subjects."[38] In trading centers like Melaka (to the northwest of today's Singapore), royal authority sat lightly on the local population, and the merchant class, especially, enjoyed considerable freedom. In matters of state, a pluralist balance of political power was seen in institutions like the dual monarchy in Sulawesi, where power was divided between a king and chancellor. Elsewhere in eastern Indonesia councils of wealthy merchants advised and even appointed kings.[39] In the trading city-state of Buton in eastern Indonesia, the checks on royal power went even further. In that kingdom, local governance was organized with reference to the Sufi doctrine of the Seven Grades of Being. Here, however, this well-known Sufi doctrine was deployed in a way that severely curtailed the sultan's power. The result was that sixteen of twenty-eight Butonese sultans were relieved of their positions, and one was actually executed.[40]

Such precedents for pluralism and participation in state affairs can be dismissed on the grounds that, as was indeed the case, most of them drew on indigenous political ideas as well as Islamic ones. But this overlooks the fact that Muslim politics must always be contextualized in a way that allows its general principles to operate locally. At the very least, the history of the early modern archipelago shows that there was no inherent "civilizational" obstacle to Muslims pressing for a devolution and pluralization of power. It is equally clear, however, that subsequent developments in the archipelago ensured that these efforts to restrict royal power would not be amplified into a serious alternative to *raja*-centered Islam.

The single most important reason for this turn of events is that the arrival of Europeans brought about a decisive shift in the balance of power between rulers and urban merchants. The Europeans were determined to secure a monopoly over the most lucrative sectors of the archipelago trade, especially Indonesian spices. On their arrival in the area in 1499 the Portuguese "sank or plundered every Muslim spice ship they could."[41] When treaty arrangements proved ineffectual the Europeans seized Melaka, a prosperous entrepot which Europeans called "Venice of the East." Over the next century the Portuguese and Dutch captured or sunk most of the large-tonnage junks used by native peoples, destroying one of the world's great private shipping fleets. In seventeenth-century eastern Indonesia the Dutch went further, seizing control of the spice islands and even enslaving populations who resisted Dutch demands for monopoly control of the trade.

What had once been a dynamic and multipolar civilization, then, began in the early modern era to move in an absolutist direction. The Europeans destroyed the independent trading class, and tilted the balance of regional power to centralizing despots willing to collaborate with Europeans against native merchants. It is, of course, foolish to speculate as to what Southeast Asia might have become had Europeans not colonized the region. At the very least, however, we can see from this brief history that Muslim politics in the Southeast Asian region was varied from the start. At a few times and in a few places, there were pluralist tendencies not just in politics but in literature and religious practice as well. In his epic examination of culture and society in the Malay world the historian Denys Lombard observes that during the early modern period one began to see the "emergence of the notion of the individual" in law, education, and literary creation. Javanese and Malay legal traditions emphasized individual rather than collective responsibility; the tradition of trial by ordeal was suppressed; education was opened to people from varied social backgrounds; and the *hikayat* literature of urban areas highlighted real heroes rather than idealized archetypes. One exception to these trends concerned women: they were excluded from this emerging culture of moral individualism, even though their role in pre-Islamic times had been one of complementary balance rather than subordination.[42]

However varied its possibilities, this social momentum was not sustained so as to allow an enduring reformation of Muslim politics and culture. There were uncivil forces waiting in the wings, and in the eighteenth and nineteenth centuries they triumphed. European colonialism imposed a system of racial and ethnic apartheid on native society and drained these civic energies. Having allied with royalty against the merchant class, the Europeans eventually turned on the aristocracy, subjecting them, too, to the cunning of colonial control. Ironically, however, the European usurpation of royal authority revived the fortunes of popular Islam, creating unexpected political opportunities.

When reflecting on this example of reformation manqué, it is helpful to remember how fitful was the comparable process of political democratization in Western Europe. The first limited experiments in civic republicanism in northern Italy in the early modern period were largely extinguished by the wars with Spain. Republican ideals then made their way to the Netherlands and England, where they played a role in efforts to limit royal power.[43] Even then, however, the evolution of civil society was fitful and uncertain, awaiting a modern economic change that would do away once and for all with the settled hierarchies of old. For a brief period Muslim Southeast Asia, too, showed signs of a struggle for a more pluricentric and participatory polity. Its revival would have to await the great transformations of the modern era.

FROM DYNASTIC TO PROTONATIONAL ISLAM

After its initial adventures, Dutch colonialism advanced in a piecemeal fashion across the archipelago. A few territories, such as coastal Java, were colonized as early as the seventeenth and eighteenth centuries. Others, however, such as the sultanate of Aceh on the northern tip of Sumatra, were not effectively subjugated until the early twentieth century, and even then only at a great military cost.[44] Only in the mid-nineteenth century were the Dutch able to launch a systematic colonization of native society. Their effort was stimulated by their rivalry with the British, whose swift progress in nearby Malaya encouraged the Dutch to transform their piecemeal holdings into a continuous colonial expanse.

The colonial government's attitude on Islam ranged from cautiously suspicious to openly hostile. Viewing Muslim *ulama* through much the same Calvinist lens as they did the Church of Rome, Dutch authorities in the early nineteenth century required "Mohammedan priests" to secure passports for travel around the East Indies. In 1825 colonial authorities raised the cost of passports for the Mecca pilgrimage. Several years later they issued instructions discouraging native officials from making the pilgrimage and forced returned pilgrims to take examinations before allowing them to use the honorary title, *haji*. At the end of the nineteenth century the authorities launched a program of secular education designed to, among other things, immunize the native elite against Islamic appeals. The crown jewel in the Dutch policy was set in place in 1889, with the implementation of recommendations from the renowned orientalist Snouck Hurgronje, relaxing controls on "religious" Islam while stiffening those on "political" Islam. This approach, and the secular-modernist perception of religion it implied, was to have a lasting effect on state-Muslim relations.[45]

Surveying the variety of cultures across the archipelago, some government advisers argued that Islam was no more than "thin veneer" over a largely non-Islamic culture. This idea appealed to those who wished to justify the suppression of Islam on the grounds that it was a threat to colonial rule.[46] In Java, in particular, nineteenth-century colonial administrators developed a "structure of not seeing,"[47] overlooking Islamic influences in Javanese tradition, while exaggerating and essentializing the influence of pre-Islamic ideals. In the aftermath of the brutal Java War (1825–30), colonial scholars worked to create a canon of Javanese literature that romanticized pre-Islamic literature as part of a Javanese golden age spoiled by the arrival of Islam. Dutch Orientalism overlooked the fact that the proportion of Islamic-oriented literature in modern court collections was much greater than the so-called renaissance literature (pre-Islamic classics rendered in modern Javanese verse) presented by colonial scholars as the essence of things Javanese.[48] A similar purging of Islamic influences from Javanese traditions took place in some high arts, most notably in the *wayang* tradition of shadow puppetry.[49]

Colonial legal policies effected a similar essentialization. Under the direction of Cornelis van Vollenhoven, the "*adat* law school" worked under state direction to develop what amounted to a system of legal apartheid. A classic example of the colonial "invention of tradition,"[50] European experts divided the native peoples of the Indies into nineteen separate legal communities. Islamic law was recognized in each community's legal canons only to the extent that colonial advisers ruled that local custom (*adat*) explicitly acknowledged it.[51] In this manner, colonial authorities reified the distinction between *adat* and Islam. As James Siegel's study of Aceh and Taufik Abdullah's of Minangkabau both demonstrate,[52] the Europeans' distinction between endogenous "custom" and exogenous "Islam" imposed an artificial separation on a highly unstable relationship. In the decades preceding the European conquest, legal traditions in western Indonesia had already begun to accord a greater role to Muslim textual commentaries.[53] Growing Muslim influence only stiffened the Dutch resolve to implement their Islam-restricting policy.[54]

This policy of co-opting elites while subjugating society eventually undermined the authority of the native rulers who collaborated with the Europeans. Pressed by colonial programs, the peasantry came to see their rulers as mere lackeys of the Europeans. As indigenous rulers lost their legitimacy, that of the Muslim leadership only increased. The great historian of Java, Sartono Kartodirjo, has described the consequences of this leadership crisis in the case of Java. He notes that while in the previous era some Islamic scholars (the *ulama*) had been employed in royal service, the Dutch secularized government administration, removing religious leaders from influential posts. Marginalized in government circles, Muslim leaders nonetheless "displaced that elite in exercising political authority over the peasantry."[55] As colonial programs penetrated the countryside, native society was shaken by peasant protest movements. At first these were of a localist nature, but many eventually acquired a more general face:

> The potential following of earlier social movements was . . . limited by their particularized demands and the narrowing effect of reliance on regional cultural traditions. At a time when increasing communication was broadening the horizons of the peasantry and making localized groups aware of their common sufferings, common aims, and common adversaries, the time had come to develop an intellectual or ideological definition of this wider community. Since a modern-style nationalist ideology did not exist, it was natural that Islam should fulfill this need. . . .. For an important period in the history of Java, then, Islam was seen not as marking off one segment of society from the rest, but as supplying the political definition of "national" identity and the focus of resistance toward the colonial ruler.[56]

Through these and other activities, European colonialism forever changed Muslim politics in Indonesia. The Europeans destroyed imperial Islam, undermined the authority of native rulers, and unwittingly reinvigorated popular Islam. This new, societally based Islam was different, of course, from the *raja*-centric traditions of the sixteenth and seventeenth centuries. European control of the state led Muslim leaders to develop a cautious and critical attitude toward government, and forced them to rely on their own resources to develop their institutions. Their situation contrasts with the experience of Muslims in much of the Middle East or even nearby Malaya. In Malaya, particularly in the native states subject to indirect rule (where sultans retained a significant measure of authority), the British encouraged cooperation between state authorities and Muslim leaders, not least of all by vesting sultans with the responsibility for guarding and promoting the faith.[57]

In Indonesia little such collaboration existed between colonial rulers and Muslims. The tendency instead was for Muslim institutions to distance themselves from the state by locating themselves deep in native society. In Java and other areas of the archipelago, for example, the eighteenth and nineteenth centuries saw the spread of a vigorous little institution known as the *pesantren*, a Javanese variant of the pan-Indonesian Qur'anic boarding school. As the Dutch pacified the countryside, improved roads, and introduced economic programs, Java's native population steadily grew. The population fanned out across the countryside, opening the last of the island's frontier regions to settlement. Muslim teachers took advantage of these migrations, moving out from the north coast, where they had earlier been concentrated, and establishing *pesantren* across the interior of the island, where the influence of textual Islam had been weak. These Islamic boarding schools have continued to play a central role in the religious and political life of traditionalist Islam to this day (chapter 4).[58]

Pesantren are organized around the leadership of a Muslim scholar (Arabic, *alim*; pl. *ulama*) and his retinue of students (Jav., *santri*). In earlier times the institution depended for its sustenance on gifts from the pious as well as on the economic activities (usually agricultural) of student boarders. The schools served as centers for the study of the Qur'an, *hadith* (words and deeds of the prophet as recorded in written canon tradition), and classical Islamic commentaries; their educational function was made all the more important by state hostility toward Islam. Colonial-era *pesantren* were also important because they provided a translocal network for native authority apart from the state. In Java and Sumatra many of the movements of prenationalist anticolonialism were led by graduates of these schools. In the national era (1945 on), Islamic scholars have provided the leadership for Indonesia's largest social and political organization, the *Nahdlatul Ulama*.[59]

In the late nineteenth and early twentieth centuries this same community of independent Muslims supplied the lion's share of native entrepreneurs. In contrast, Javanese political elites recruited to government service were notorious for their disdain of hard work and lack of commercial acumen. Their preferred avenue of social mobility was government office, which they used as a platform for meddling in business affairs. Although in colonial times most large enterprise was controlled by Europeans or Chinese, *pesantren* nurtured an ethic of initiative and independence.[60] The struggle for national independence would give the bearers of this tradition an opportunity to expand their social role.

CONCLUSION: SCALING UP AND SHUTTING DOWN

As these remarks on *pesantren* illustrate, there was a significant *organizational* precedent for extra-state Muslim associations in late colonial Indonesia.[61] Their vitality was all the more impressive in light of the fact that although nominally committed to a variant of European liberalism, in practice colonial authorities institutionalized a system of centralized power, state monopolies, and racial chauvinism. In comparison with the English in Malaya and India, the Dutch commitment to education and political participation was also meager.

In such an environment it is not surprising that Muslim institutions survived by keeping their distance from state power and emphasizing autonomous self-organization. Despite this civic precedent, however, Muslim leaders had difficulty using this experience as a source of new political *ideals*, for several reasons. One had to do with the nature of authority in traditionalist Islam itself. Although Muslim society as a whole was characterized by considerable economic initiative and pluricentric organization, the structure of authority in most Muslim institutions remained unambiguously hierarchical.[62] Religious leaders exercised a near-total authority within Qur'anic schools, buttressed by popular beliefs in their sacral powers. As Abdurrahman Wahid (the leader of Nahdlatul Ulama elected president of Indonesia in 1999) observed in 1977, in traditional *pesantren* the chief resident scholar (*kyai*) exercised an "absolute authority" over his students and staff. Pedagogical methods (known as *srogan*) emphasized rote memorization and silence in the presence of the *kyai*. Although a few senior students (*santri ndalem*) might be allowed to eat with the *kyai*, his living space and family were otherwise segregated from students. Even after leaving school, senior *santri* were supposed to show obedience to their teacher, visiting him at the end of the annual fasting month and sending the best among their own students to study with him. The *kyai*'s authority was based on the perception of him as not merely a teacher but an heir to knowledge and power transmitted in an unbroken line from the Prophet Muhammed. Consistent with this view, the offspring of *kyai* were (and still are today) regarded as possessing an in-born knowledge (*ilmu laduni*) giving them a special capacity for learning and leadership.[63]

Unlike the all-encompassing hierarchy of, say, caste in premodern India, this institutional authority was not linked to a uniform hierarchy in society as a whole. Java's wars, religious pluralism, and colonial conquest made a settled hierarchy of this sort impossible for any but restricted portions of the population. Nonetheless, the nature of authority in *pesantren* made it difficult for Muslim leaders to draw on the institution's critical relationship with the state as a precedent for a democratic reformation of Muslim politics.

The example again underscores that, by itself, a vigorous tradition of extra-state association does not guarantee a democratic public culture. For civil *structures* to become effective precedents for civic *ideals*, at least three additional conditions must be met. First, native intellectuals have to look into their own social experience and derive from it a model of political *culture* that affirms principles of autonomy, mutual respect, and voluntarism. Second, and equally important, influential actors and organizations must then work to generalize these democratic values and organizations beyond their original confines to a broader public sphere. Third, and last, if these principles are to endure, they must be buttressed by an array of supporting institutions, including those of the state.

In early twentieth-century Indonesia there were few incentives for traditionalist Muslims to engage in such a critical rethinking of their political tradition. Prestige hierarchies in the traditionalist community rewarded traditional religious skills, such as memorizing the Qur'an, studying law, or mastering mystical arts. There was little reason to depart from this pattern, especially if innovation might only offend other believers.

Certain considerations reinforced these structural disincentives. Early on, the Dutch authorities concluded that the most effective policy toward mass-based Islam was noninterference in religious affairs combined with forceful repression of political activism.[64] Although in nineteenth-century Java numerous rebellions took place under the banner of Islam, *pesantren* leaders soon recognized the dangers of political involvements that were too direct. A few years after its founding in 1926, for example, at a time when nationalist Indonesians were calling for changes in the colonial order, the traditionalist *Nahdlatul Ulama* issued a statement affirming the compatibility of European rule with Islam.[65]

There was little in traditionalist society in the late colonial period, then, to leverage a critical reflection on Muslim experience and abstract from it the terms for a revitalized Muslim politics. As we shall see, the potential for such a creative reformulation was not entirely lacking. However, it would be another half-century before events would bring forth a generation of leaders willing and able to view their own history as a cultural resource for political reformation. By then, however, the project of Muslim renewal would face a host of new obstacles.

Chapter Three

CONTESTS OF NATION

NO IDEA HAS HAD so profound an influence on the refiguration of Muslim politics in modern Indonesia as has nationalism. In the first decades of this century Muslim leaders shifted their sights away from earlier dreams of resurrecting a pan-Islamic polity toward the goal of a multi-ethnic nation coincident with the territorial borders of the Dutch East Indies.[1] Still today, almost a century later, the great majority of Indonesian Muslims are not only resigned to the idea of the Indonesian nation but are among its most ardent promoters. Inasmuch as nationalism has been one of the driving forces of modern politics throughout the world, this fact may not be surprising. Nonetheless it illustrates that Muslim politics is not singular and unchanging but always in dialogue with the ideas and struggles of its age.[2]

In this chapter I examine Indonesian Muslims' commitment to the idea of the nation and its implications for Muslim politics as a whole. I focus on two critical moments in this history: first, the early years leading up to independence (1945), with their great debates over the ideological foundations of the Indonesian state, and, second, the collapse of the Soekarno regime and the rise of the New Order during 1965–1966. These two periods were vital transitions in the making of modern Indonesia. The debates in each period shed light on the varieties of Muslim politics and the questions Muslims faced in deciding what precedents to take from their past to meet the challenge of the present.

ISLAM AND NATIONALISM

During the first decades of the twentieth century, the idea of nationalism was the focus of fierce political debate in the Muslim world.[3] Some Muslim intellectuals objected to the idea on the grounds that the principle of popular sovereignty violates principles of divine law and universal religious community (*ummat*). The South Asian poet and philosopher Muhammad Iqbal, for example, insisted that Islam demands a borderless community, and lamented that European colonialism had destroyed the pristine unity of the Islamic world. Like many of his contemporaries, however, Iqbal was eventually resigned to the fact that the reconstitution of a universal Muslim polity is currently impossible and that therefore each Muslim territory should struggle for its own independence.[4] To this day a few nonconformists decry a principle of state that they feel elevates human will above the divine. Nonetheless, as James Piscatori has shown, the central tendency during the twentieth century has been for Muslims to accept the legitimacy of the nation-state and orient their politics within its horizons.[5]

To say that today most Muslims accept the legitimacy of the nation-state, however, is not to say that they agree on the precise terms of its organization or ideology. Nationalism is not sewn of one cloth. However much some Western theories imply otherwise, *religious* ideals have played a key role in many twentieth-century nationalisms, including those of Western Europe.[6] Nowhere has the weave of religious ideals into the nationalist cloth been more fiercely debated, however, than in the Muslim world. For more than a century Muslims have struggled with the question of how to accommodate Muslim politics to nationhood and citizenship. In the late twentieth century the struggle between secular or "nonconfessional" nationalism[7] and Islamic nationalism has given the argument new vigor.[8]

In Indonesia the question of the role Islam should play in the idea and practice of the nation has been a point of contention for the better part of a century. The first modern mass organization for native political rights, the Sarikat Islam (Islamic Union), was established in 1912 and quickly achieved a mass following in central portions of the archipelago, especially on the island of Java.[9] The organization eventually foundered, however, on precisely this question of Islam's role in an independent state. Established to defend the interests of Muslim merchants against Chinese rivals, Sarikat Islam (SI) at first relied heavily on Islamic appeals. As it gained followers, however, the organization was torn by ideological strife between members committed to the conventional Muslim politics and those inclined toward Marxism and secular nationalism.[10] In 1921 the rivalry between the two factions came to a head with the expulsion of left-wing delegates from the organization. Over the next five years leftists (known as "red" SI) and Muslims (known as "white") vied for control of SI's local chapters. Coinciding as it did with growing state repression, the rivalry shattered the fledgling organization and left the native struggle for independence in disarray.

With Sarikat Islam's demise, leadership of the nationalist struggle passed into the hands of nonreligious nationalists, the most important of whom were affiliated with the Indonesian Nationalist Party. Established in 1927 under the leadership of a Dutch-educated engineer, Ahmad Soekarno, the PNI was based on multiethnic nationalism (*kebangsaan*), not religion or ethno-nationalism. Although raised a Muslim, Soekarno received his advanced education in the plural environment of colonial schools. He was the sort of "creole functionary" whom Benedict Anderson, in his much-read essay on nationalism, has identified as the prototypical carrier of the (secular) nationalist idea.[11] Trained at a time when the colonial state required growing numbers of native administrators, Soekarno was attracted to the ideas of European Enlightenment and socialist liberalism. Like many other native Indonesians, this experience led Soekarno to embrace a concept of nation that transcended ethnicity, region, and religion.

Soekarno's nonconfessional conviction was reinforced by his belief that "historical Islam," as he called it, had diverged from Islam's original ideals and, in so doing, only exacerbated the plight of Muslims relative to the West. Influenced by secular nationalist reformers in Turkey and the Middle East, the young Soekarno argued that the union of religion and state in traditional Muslim governance had contributed to the Muslim world's stagnation.[12] Separating Islam from state, Soekarno argued, would liberate Islam from the tutelage of corrupt rulers and unleash its progressive potentialities. In making this case, the young Soekarno took pains to point out that he was not a secularist opposed to Islamic values. On the contrary, in his view religious disestablishment would facilitate their more effective realization in society.

In the eyes of many Islamic politicians at this time, however, Soekarno's nationalist notions seemed a shallow basis on which to build a new political order. While a small segment of the native population had the privilege of Western education, many more had made a different social pilgrimage through a network of mosques and Islamic schools that reached across the archipelago all the way to Arabia. The speed with which Middle Eastern reformist ideas spread through this network in the eighteenth and nineteenth centuries demonstrates that Islamic education was not solely a localized institution, as some Western scholarship has implied.[13] A channel for Islamic reformism in the nineteenth century, in the twentieth this network of scholars and schools helped transmit ideas of Islamic nationalism.[14]

The carriers of this Muslim nationalism were convinced that Islam, not secular liberalism or socialism, was the proper ground on which to build the nation. For these thinkers, Soekarnoist nationalism was a too-Western creation. This fact was easily apparent, these Muslim thinkers felt, in the educational background of most of the secular nationalist leadership, which drew heavily from the ranks of graduates of European schools. To these Muslim writers, secular nationalism looked like a modern version of the tribal and ethnic solidarities (ʿasabiyah) which had divided the Arabs in pre-Islamic times and against which Prophet Muhammad had struggled.[15] Islam, these writers insisted, provides a more meaningful basis for fraternity than Western-derived notions of ethnicity and socialism.[16] In addition, Muslim leaders said, Islam is not merely a matter of individual piety and private belief, like modern Christianity. It is a civilization and social order, which is to say a complete and self-sufficient "system" unto itself. Its components cannot be artificially separated from one another, as Western liberalism's separation of religion and state would require. This image of Islam as an eternal and "complete" (Arabic, kaffah) social order (Arabic, al-nizam al-islami) has been a recurrent theme in modern Islamist politics, and it divides Indonesian Muslims to this day.[17]

Influenced by the writings of Middle Eastern reformists like Muhammad Abduh and Sayyid Jamal al-Din al-Afghani, reformist Muslims in Indonesia were keen to formulate a systematic response to the challenge of the West.[18] In Indonesia several reformist organizations arose in the early twentieth century to take up this charge. The most influential of these was the "Followers of Muhammad" or Muhammadiyah. Founded in 1912 in Central Java by a minor religious official in the Javanese courts, the Muhammadiyah focused its attention on education, health, and care for the poor rather than formal politics. In the last years of the colonial era, the Muhammadiyah spread to most corners of the archipelago; today it boasts some twenty-five million followers.[19] The Muhammadiyah showed none of traditionalist Islam's reserve toward Western education, technology, and science; it was unabashedly modernist.[20] Organizationally, too, the Muhammadiyah repudiated the traditionalists' emphasis on charismatic religious leadership and developed organizations with rule-governed bureaucracies and open elections.

However bold their innovations in education and association, the modernists were timid on the question of the state. Some insisted that the Qur'an and the recorded example of the Prophet Muhammad (*sunna*) provided no comprehensive blueprint for political organization, least of all one that might be regarded as an Islamic state. What Islam offers, these thinkers felt, is generalized principles of equality, mutual consultation, and social justice, values compatible with modern democracy. Others among the Muslim reformists, however, insisted that the normative precedents for an Islamic politics are more systematic than general principles alone. An Islamic politics must affirm the details and not merely the spirit of divine law (*shariah*) and seek its full implementation in state and society.

In the late colonial period Muslim political writers were aware that they could not reach a consensus on these matters. Sarikat Islam's collapse provided a painful illustration of their community's schisms. Modernist writers responded to this problem by deferring any detailed reexamination of Muslim political theory and focusing instead on general issues of native rights, education, and welfare.[21] A more definitive formulation of state principles and organization would have to await some future moment. To force consensus too quickly, it was said, would only weaken the Muslim community. However judicious this conclusion from the perspective of Muslim solidarity, this strategy meant that most Muslim intellectuals continued to look away from their own history as a source of empirical insight into just what is needed to create a modern and democratic Muslim politics.

Faced with this same challenge of political renewal, other Indonesians found themselves drawn to the ideals of a secular or nonreligious nationalism. Even many pious Muslims argued that a compromise of this sort was necessary if the independence movement was not to pit Muslims against secular nationalists and non-Muslim minorities.[22] Although in the 1930s they comprised only 7 to 8 percent of the Dutch Indies' population (as opposed to 12 percent today), most non-Muslims were concentrated in remote and relatively cohesive territories, especially in the islands of eastern Indonesia and in inland portions of Sumatra, Kalimantan, and Sulawesi. In the late colonial period the state's administrative infrastructure in these regions was still weak, and a well-organized secessionist movement might well have presented a serious challenge to the fledgling republic.

Debate over the basis of a future Indonesian state raged in the months leading up to August 17, 1945. Indonesians' declaration of independence on that day made it clear that they had yet to reach a workable agreement on the basis of the state.

PLURALISM POLITICIZED

During the first months of 1942 Japanese armies swept into the East Indies and put an end to Dutch colonialism. Although the Dutch later attempted to reimpose their rule, the Japanese occupation marked a new era for Indonesian politics and Islam. Recognizing the strong ties of Muslim leaders to the populace, the Japanese showed none of the hesitation of the Dutch about drawing Muslims into state administration. They established a Department of Religious Affairs, largely for Muslim concerns; supported the creation of a unified Muslim political federation, known as Masyumi; and, eventually, as the threat of Allied invasion loomed large, trained Muslim militias. The Japanese were also aware of the depth of religious division in the native community, however, and they balanced their courtship of Muslims with initiatives for non-Muslims and secular nationalists.[23] In most instances, in fact, the Japanese gave secular nationalists a larger role in the occupation government. They also gave them the lion's share of leadership positions in the auxiliary army established in October 1943. In the final months of the occupation, the balance of power the Japanese had maintained between Muslim and secular nationalists collapsed into open rivalry.[24]

With an allied invasion imminent, the Japanese, on March 1, 1945, allowed the native community to form an Investigative Committee for the Preparation of Indonesian Independence (*Badan Penyelidik Usaha Persiapan Kemerdekaan*). Charged with outlining the political structure of an independent Indonesia, the committee reached agreement on basic economic and constitutional issues. But it deadlocked on the thorny issue of Islam's role in the state. On June 1, 1945, Soekarno attempted to resolve the crisis by proposing the "five principles," or *Pancasila*, as the philosophical foundation for an independent Indonesia.[25] Soekarno's *Pancasila* was a unique synthesis of nationalist, Muslim,

Marxist, liberal democratic, and populist-Indonesian ideas. The Javanese leader hoped the doctrine's woolly eclecticism would satisfy both secular and Islamic nationalists.

Muslim leaders, however, regarded the *Pancasila's* pronouncements on religion as hopelessly vague at best and anti-Islamic at worst. The first principle declared that the Indonesian nation was founded on "belief in God." Unspecific as it was, this principle left wiggle room for heretical mystics, apostates, ethnic religionists, Communists, and others whom Muslims felt undeserving of recognition. There was also no mention of state support for Islam. Faced with Muslim objections, then, a committee revised and expanded the first principle from simple belief in God to "belief in God *with the obligation for adherents of Islam to carry out Islamic law [shariah]*" (my emphasis).

Now it was the turn of secularists and non-Muslims to protest. They objected that the revised formulation left vague just who was to enforce Islamic law. There was also no mention of what penalties might be imposed for Muslims who refused to abide by the terms of the law. Muslim leaders held their ground, however, insisting that the clause had to stay in the statement of national principles. Eventually known as the "Jakarta Charter," this principle of state support for Islamic law was to be a bone of contention for years to come.[26]

On August 18, just one day after the Indonesian declaration of independence, Soekarno and Mohammad Hatta (co-declarers of Indonesian independence) yielded to the appeals of Christians, Hindus, and nonreligious nationalists and dropped the Jakarta Charter from the preamble to the Indonesian Constitution. At the recommendation of Muslim leaders in Nahdlatul Ulama, however, Soekarno added a clause to the first principle of the Pancasila so that it read not just as "belief in God" but "belief in a singular God" (*ketuhanan yang Maha Esa*). The concession brought the first principle closer to the central Muslim doctrine of *tauhid*, the affirmation of God's indivisible oneness. This was to prove a significant amendment. In years to come, this revised phrasing would legitimate state efforts to proscribe animism and polytheism as acceptable religious options for citizens.[27] For those who had hoped for a formal linkage of Islam and state, however, this new phrasing was still a poor substitute for the Jakarta Charter. Coming as it did in the aftermath of weeks of negotiations, many Muslim leaders felt betrayed.[28]

During the first years of independence, this compromise formulation remained the focus of heated political controversy. The contention was exacerbated by the uncertainties surrounding the state constitution. After 1950 the state operated under a provisional constitution. Influenced by the United Nation's 1948 universal declaration of human rights, this provisional document affirmed the importance of human rights and the rule of law, and instituted a strong parliament with a weak presidency.[29] The constitution also specified that an elected Constitutional Assembly, known as the Konstituante, was eventually to draw up a new and definitive constitution. Delegates to this body were to be chosen in a second round of elections held after the first national elections, the precise date for which was to be arranged by the new National Assembly. Irritated by the earlier deletion of the Jakarta Charter and alarmed by the growing popularity of the Communist Party, the Muslim leadership was determined not to be outmaneuvered. With their extensive rural organization, Muslim leaders wanted early elections. They were confident that they would emerge the winners from the elections and, from there, go on to establish an Islamic state.

To the surprise of almost everyone, however, the 1955 elections yielded not a Muslim victory but a standoff between the two main Muslim parties and their Nationalist and Communist rivals. From an electoral field of more than thirty parties, the Nationalist Party won 22.3 percent of the vote; Masyumi (modernist Muslims), 20.9 percent; Nahdlatul Ulama (traditionalist Muslims), 18.4 percent; and the Communist Party, 16.4 percent.[30] The proportion of the vote for Muslim parties was almost exactly equal to that for Nationalist, Communist, and Christian parties. The elections had not given Muslim parties their expected victory.

The second round of voting for the Constituent Assembly in late 1955 produced much the same result, with delegates divided evenly between Muslims and nonreligious nationalists. The assembly was charged with drafting a constitution to replace the provisional one under which the country had operated since 1950. To do so, however, the assembly had to resolve, once and for all, the question of whether Indonesia was to be a nonreligious state or some kind of Islamic one.[31] Although the assembly reached agreement on most constitutional details, it deadlocked on the vexing issue of Islam and state.[32]

Meanwhile, conflicts that had simmered since the first days of the republic erupted with a new ferocity. In Sumatra in 1958 a group of regional military commanders opposed to the centralizing policies of the Jakarta leadership established a rebel Revolutionary Government of the Republic of Indonesia (PRRI). The PRRI leadership eventually joined forces with other regional rebels, especially those involved in a Muslim-led insurrection in Sulawesi. Supporters of the PRRI government insisted that they did not intend to secede from the nation but only wanted to pressure the Jakarta leadership to devolve greater power to the regions. This, they hoped, would allow a more equitable distribution of state revenues, but it would also counterbalance the growing influence of the Communist Party in Java. When word got out that the PRRI was receiving clandestine assistance from the American CIA, however, support for the rebels dropped precipitously. Soekarno appealed to Indonesian national pride and succeeded in discrediting the rebels as agents of Western imperialism.

With the collapse of the PRRI, Muslim leaders who had sided with the rebel effort found themselves further marginalized from national politics. Rather than undermining Communist influence in the government, then, the PRRI rebellion strengthened it. The rebellion and the impasse in the Constituent

Assembly also provided Soekarno with a pretext to talk, in late 1958, of the need for a new political order. Rather than a parliamentary democracy founded on "Western" liberal principles, he argued, the country needed a "Guided Democracy" based on "Indonesian" values. Although its details were vague, what was clear was that the president intended to reduce parliament's power and expand his own.

At first President Soekarno submitted his plan for Guided Democracy to the Constituent Assembly, hoping to win the body's approval. The assembly immediately rejected the proposal as undemocratic. When, in mid-1959, the assembly again failed to agree on the bases of the state, the president, with the full backing of the armed forces, saw his opportunity. He dissolved the assembly, announced a return to the executive-heavy Constitution of 1945, and declared that Indonesia would henceforth operate under the terms of Guided Democracy.

Although the Nationalist and Communist leadership, as well as the Muslim NU, eventually went along with the president's initiative, the modernist Masyumi, the largest of the Muslim parties, vehemently opposed it. Masyumi was joined in its criticisms by the Indonesian Socialist Party (PSI), which shared Masyumi's passion for constitutional proceduralism and its hostility to the presidential cult of personality. A year after the declaration of Guided Democracy, Soekarno struck back at these critics. He banned Masyumi and the PSI on the grounds that their leadership had supported the regional rebellions. Eventually, to the dismay of Muslim and Social Democrats alike, the senior leadership of these parties was imprisoned. Among those jailed were the PSI's Sutan Sjahrir and Masyumi's Mohammed Natsir. Both were heroes of the revolution, former prime ministers, and renowned for their commitment to clean government and constitutionalism.[33]

Over the next six years, Muslim influence in national politics steadily declined. Shortly after his declaration of Guided Democracy, President Soekarno announced the creation of a government of national unity, known as NASAKOM (from the first letters of the Indonesian terms for nationalism, religion, and communism). NASAKOM was Soekarno's answer to what he regarded as the hopeless factionalism of parliamentary democracy. In principle, the government of national unity was supposed to unite all progressive political groupings. In Soekarno's eyes, this meant the Nationalists, the Communists, and Muslims from the traditionalist Nahdlatul Ulama. In practice, however, the president depended most heavily on the Nationalist Party and, as time went on, the Communists. The influence of the Muslim NU was largely limited to the Department of Religion.

NASAKOM was also part of Soekarno's strategy to maintain his role as leader of the revolution in the face of the escalating rivalry between Communists and the army. Soekarno had come to regard the military—especially the army, which received extensive American equipment and training, unlike the much smaller navy and air force, which received aid from the Soviet Union—as a conservative drag on the Indonesian revolution. With the outbreak of regional rebellions in the late 1950s and the declaration of martial law in 1957, the military's role in national politics had expanded exponentially. From the military's perspective, there were strong grounds for this political involvement. During the independence war, the military had established a shadow adminis- tration that reached from the national level down to district-level government. Initially this apparatus was intended to dampen the factionalism crippling the republican effort against the Dutch. Once in place, however, this parallel ad- ministration became as important as the civilian administration itself.

Military discontent with the civilian government increased in the final years of the parliamentary era. The military blamed the political parties for having divided the country and causing the regional rebellions of the late 1950s. They also blamed the parliamentary system for having allowed the Communist Party to grow, by the late 1950s, into the largest of the nation's parties. At the same time that President Soekarno was speaking of the need for a Guided Democ- racy, then, the army chief of staff, Major General Abdul Haris Nasution, was outlining a policy whereby the military would operate as both a military and sociopolitical force. Identified by Nasution as a "middle way" between military authoritarianism and confinement to the barracks, in the New Order period this doctrine came to be known as *dwifungsi*, or the "two functions."[34] Although their interests actually diverged from the president's, the military supported his appeal for Guided Democracy and a return to the executive-heavy Constitu- tion of 1945.[35]

The military's rivalry with the Communists intensified after 1959. The army command was alarmed by what they regarded as the president's growing reli- ance on the PKI (Partai Komunis Indonesia, or Indonesian Communist Party). Unwilling to challenge Soekarno directly, the army leadership realized it could counter the Communist advance by developing a network of organizations to serve as an alternative to the political parties. In the early 1950s such an ambi- tious initiative would have been beyond the capacities of the military. But the army's ability to finance and organize initiatives in society increased after Soekarno seized Dutch properties between 1957 and 1959. Fearful that the PKI might capture these economic prizes, the army command took control of most of the new state enterprises. In the meantime, as PKI power grew, the army's involvements moved offstage, into a netherworld of patronage and se- cret alliances. Indonesia's constitutional proceduralism was giving way to a new politics of secrecy and underground alliances.

For President Soekarno, of course, NASAKOM was not a distortion of Indo- nesian democracy nor an artificial invention of tradition but rather a return to a culturally appropriate, "Indonesian" politics. He believed he could diffuse the country's growing political tensions through the fusion of the major parties into a national union.[36] No doubt, as many Western analysts have suggested, this idea was influenced by (elite) Javanese ideals of social harmony. But NASAKOM was less a return to political tradition than a strategic response to the worsening competition between Muslims, Communists, and the military. If not contained, that rivalry threatened to sweep the president himself from power. More than any traditional "idea of power," then, it was Soekarno's determination to stave off this eventuality that led him to attempt this implausible alliance of Nationalists, Communists, and traditionalist Muslims.[37]

Notably absent from the NASAKOM arrangement, of course, were the two parties best identified with democratic proceduralism: the party of Muslim modernists, Masyumi, and the Western-oriented, social democratic Indonesian Socialist Party. Although the PSI had won only 2 percent of the vote in the 1955 elections, it was popular among intellectuals, a segment of the bureaucracy, and the military leadership of the Siliwangi Division of the army (chapter 4). Based in West Java, the Siliwangi Division had long been regarded as the most professional of army divisions. Although, as the American political scientist R. William Liddle has noted, "from 1955 to 1965 PSI-type secular modernizing intellectuals were out of style in Indonesian politics,"[38] they continued to circulate among the student population, particularly in Jakarta and Bandung. PSI intellectuals also had contacts with military commanders and the anticommunist democratic opposition. Although supporters of democratic proceduralism, some among these "secular modernizing intellectuals" (as Liddle has aptly called them) were learning to play by the rules of a new game (chapter 4).

Forced from the public stage, Masyumi leaders were left with little choice but to engage in similarly clandestine activities. For them the exclusion had even more serious consequences than for the PSI. Unlike the PSI, Masyumi had been one of Indonesia's great mass parties. Outside of Java, it had been the single largest vote-getter in the 1955 elections. Its exclusion from government and its failure to achieve even modest political goals left the reformist community deeply disheartened. The consequences of this experience were not merely psychological. The crisis had a profound impact on the internal balance of power in Masyumi and, through it, the whole modernist Muslim community.

As the Australian political scientist Herbert Feith remarked many years ago,[39] Masyumi had from its inception been a "loosely knit organization, whose membership was in practice not clearly defined" and whose leadership "was openly split by factional disagreement." The party leadership included people with vastly different understandings of Muslim politics. One wing of that coalition, in the beginning a rather marginal one, had long been skeptical of constitutional government, convinced it was liberal and Western rather than Islamic. For these conservative reformists, Islam had no need of "outside" resources since it was an all-encompassing "system" in its own right. The failure of the Masyumi leadership to demonstrate that constitutional proceduralism could get results only confirmed the conservative reformists' skepticism.

Conducting research in the modernist community in the first years of the (post-1966) New Order, the American political scientist Allan A. Samson is one of the few Western observers to have grasped the significance of this crisis for Muslim modernists. Leadership in the community, he observed, was divided among "fundamentalists," "reformists," and "accommodationists." The "fundamentalists" were those who saw politics as the "implementation of the sacral" rather than, as was the case for the accommodationists, "the art of the possible." For this group the give-and-take inevitable in democratic governance only guaranteed Islam's betrayal. The accommodationists were also committed to Islamic values, but they assessed them in light of their practical impact on Muslims' socioeconomic welfare. Emphasizing the need for flexibility, the accommodationists were dealers and brokers, not dreamy idealists, and often found grounds for cooperating with secular organizations. They also accepted the legitimacy of the *Pancasila* state.

The largest and most influential of Masyumi's political factions, however, was what Samson calls the "reformists." This group was headed by Mohammed Natsir, Anwar Harjono, Lukman Harun, and Muhammad Roem—men who would go on to play important roles in the New Order period (see chapters 6, 7). Samson described the group:

> This group, the reformists, perceived Islam as a relevant religion for the modern age, consonant with science and reason, and attempted to utilize politics to inculcate broad Islamic values in society. In this sense the reformists occupied a middle ground between fundamentalists and accommodationists—willing to cooperate with secular groups if this would forward desired social and political ends, but adamant to the point of fundamentalist militancy in regard to Islamic goals.[40]

Anwar Harjono illustrated well the complexity of this middle group. Well known for his lawyerly manner, Anwar was convinced that the rule of law and constitutional governance were compatible with, indeed *required for*, effective Islamic government.[41] But Masyumi's bitter treatment left him with little to show for his high ideals, and he eventually became disillusioned with democratic proceduralism (see chapter 7).

Outlawed in 1960, the Masyumi did not disappear entirely. The organization's youthful supporters took refuge in the Association of Islamic Students, or HMI (Himpunan Mahasiswa Islam). Officially at least, HMI was fully independent of Masyumi. During the 1955 elections, for example, it had counseled its membership merely to vote for good Muslim candidates rather than directly for Masyumi. Like its high school counterpart, the PII (Indonesian Muslim Pupils; Pelajar Islam Indonesia), however, HMI was modernist in its theology and organization, and many of its members were linked by ties of friendship and family to Masyumi. The Communist leadership understood this well. Buoyed by Masyumi's abolition in 1960, the PKI targeted these student organizations on the grounds that they were counterrevolutionary fronts for Masyumi.[42]

The counterrevolutionary charge had at least one grain of truth. After 1960 youthful modernists in the HMI and PII worked furiously to check the advance of the PKI wherever they could. Driven from public politics, the Muslim activists had nowhere to go but underground. They responded by forging secret alliances with other anticommunist politicians, including people from the PSI, Christian parties, Nahdlatul Ulama, conservative nationalists, and sympathetic members of the armed forces. In East and Central Java, the collaboration between modernists and the military included young Muslims' infiltration of Communist front organizations and the gathering of intelligence, including lists of party members.[43] Public association and democratic proceduralism had given way to a netherworld politics indeed.

Modernist Muslims also responded to Masyumi's forced dissolution by intensifying their programs of religious proselytization. Many of the Masyumi rank and file were members of the Muhammadiyah, Indonesia's largest reformist organization. Soekarno did not take action against this organization, and after Masyumi's ban, the Muhammadiyah intensified its religious proselytization.[44] Lance Castles's study of Muslim politics in north-central Java provides a clear picture of this reorientation of modernist activism at this time. Castles notes that "after the defeat and eventual dissolution of the Masjumi, a new wave of reformist proselytization seems to have begun. . . . The membership of Muhammadijah has increased and subbranches (*ranting*) have appeared in villages hitherto untouched by reformism. . . . There are three times as many *muballighs* [preachers] engaged in this work as there were five years earlier."[45] The ground was being laid for the Islamic resurgence of the 1970s and 1980s (chapter 5).

Despite these efforts, Soekarno's authoritarianism and the Communist Party's advance greatly diminished Muslim political influence. Muslim modernists, in particular, were driven from the public stage. No longer benefiting from government patronage, their business supporters also declined. Unable to compete for followers, modernist Muslims watched with dismay as Communist organizations mobilized vast followings among Java's and Bali's poor.

The PKI would soon put its new organization to the test in a bold campaign of land reform. As the campaign progressed, however, the Communist Party discovered that the Muslims' retreat to the margins had not entirely extinguished their political power. The constitutional proceduralism to which the Masyumi leadership had earlier been dedicated was finished. But the awesome power of organized Islam was not.

ENDGAME

The year 1965 was one that brought Indonesia's woes to a new low. Earlier, in late 1963, President Soekarno had announced a "Crush Malaysia" campaign intended to force the former British colony into the Indonesian republic.

Alarmed by the president's radicalism, the military paid lip service to the confrontation but took steps to minimize the threat of direct violence by making secret contact with Malaysian officials.[46] The campaign ultimately exacerbated Indonesia's economic difficulties and destabilized its politics.

The Crush Malaysia campaign also strained Indonesia's relations with the West. It squeezed out what remained of foreign investment, disrupted exports, and pushed the economy further down the road to ruin. With revenues from foreign trade dwindling, the government printed more paper money to finance its operations. The resulting inflationary spiral reached 600 percent per annum in 1965. To make matters worst, Indonesia was beset with volcanic eruptions in 1963 and drought in 1964–65. In Bali, in 1964, some eighteen thousand people were starving; in Central Java the number was put at one million.[47] It was not just the poor who faced economic ruin, however. The urban middle class was in crisis, too, as job opportunities dwindled and the purchasing value of salaries plummeted. At times during 1965 the government was unable even to provide the monthly rice rations promised civil servants. By mid-1965 the economy was near collapse, and per-capita income had fallen to a postwar low.

The year 1965 was also one of great political gambles and, eventually, horrific violence. A little over a year earlier, in late 1963 and early 1964, the PKI had launched a campaign of peasant mobilization designed to force implementation of the nation's new Agrarian Law (passed in September 1960) and Share-cropping Law (approved in November 1959). Setting legal limits on landholdings and a landlord's share of the harvest in tenancy, this legislation was the fruit of collaboration between the Communist Party and populist reformers in the Nationalist Party. Although the nationalists helped craft this legislation, it was the Communist Party that pressed for its implementation. It did so through an ambitious and, in light of its previous caution, unprecedented campaign of "unilateral actions" (*aksi sepihak*) in the countryside. The party hoped to use the campaign not merely to implement agrarian reform but to expand its mass base and pressure its allies in the NASAKOM government for a greater share of power. The PKI also hoped that the campaign would provide it with "a means of creating safe places of retreat in case the army should succeed in turning the tables on the party in a showdown."[48]

Such go-it-alone mobilization was a serious break with the strategy pursued by the Communists since the end of the independence war. Under the leadership of Chairman D. N. Aidit, the PKI had pursued a cautious program of party consolidation for most of the 1950s. It had good reason for caution, in light of the strong opposition to the party in military and Muslim circles. The party's opponents harbored bitter memories of events a few years earlier, in the pre-Aidit era, when the PKI had thrown caution to the wind and pursued a path of radical adventurism.

It was in September 1948, at the height of the independence war, that an influential wing of the PKI rebelled against the republican leadership, accusing it of selling out to the Dutch. The Communist rebellion was prompted by disputes among the republic's civilian and military leadership over plans to reduce the size of its vast and poorly coordinated armed forces. The forces included several hundred thousand irregulars as well as three hundred thousand regular soldiers. In July and August 1948 local commanders, opposed to this consolidation, clashed with pro-government units in several areas of Java. In this already explosive environment, a more radical leadership came to power in the Communist Party, in the aftermath of struggles provoked by the return of the Stalinist leader Musso from a twenty-two-year exile in the Soviet Union. Having won control of the leadership, Musso set out to impose Stalinist discipline on his party and radicalize the national struggle. He brought the hodgepodge of organizations affiliated with the PKI under centralized command. Unhappy with the pace of the nationalist struggle, he then encouraged strikes and land seizures in an effort to transform the independence struggle into a social revolution. These initiatives exacerbated the PKI's relations with Muslim organizations, since the landlords targeted by the Communists tended to be disproportionately from the ranks of *santri* Muslims with ties to the Islamic party Masyumi (which at this point in its history included Nahdlatul Ulama in its ranks).[49]

By mid-September 1948 these varied conflicts had escalated into violent clashes between pro-PKI and pro-government forces around Yogyakarta and Surakarta in Central Java and around Kudus on the north coast. The government's Siliwangi army division attempted to stop the conflict by driving PKI supporters from the strategically important city of Surakarta. But this tactic merely relocated the violence rather than suppressing it, as PKI forces quickly amassed in the East Javanese city of Madiun. As they took control of the city, PKI militias began to kill anticommunist officials. Musso and the PKI leadership rushed to the city, where they announced in a radio broadcast that the republican government headed by Soekarno and Hatta had been replaced with a new government of national revolution.

As the violence intensified it took an ugly, communal turn. As pro-government forces marched on Madiun in the last week of September, Communist rebels began slaughtering officials linked to Masyumi and the Nationalist Party. In the countryside, *abangan* supporters of the Communists—alarmed by reports that their own leaders were being killed—began to kill their *santri* neighbors. When Madiun finally fell to pro-government forces, angry *santri* in nearby Surakarta took vengeance on local *abangan*, executing suspected rebel sympathizers.

Despite its limited scale, the Madiun rebellion had a lasting impact on Indonesian politics. For the military command, the Madiun affair would be remembered as a dastardly "stab in the back" at a time when the republic was reeling from Dutch assaults. The affair provided the regular army leadership with an excuse to purge its rank and file of Communist sympathizers, giving the army a greater measure of ideological cohesion. Muslim leaders would remember the Madiun rebellion in equally bitter terms, as proof of communism's incompatibility with Islam. No doubt, the bizarre cruelty of the anti-Islamic violence was aggravated by the panic that set in among the Communist rebels as they realized that their cause was lost. However, as George Kahin has observed, "members of the Masjumi appeared to be singled out for cruel treatment, sometimes this being limited to robbery, but frequently extending to torture and execution."[50] Four years later, when a team of American researchers conducted research in an area of East Java not far from Madiun, they found that villagers had vivid memories of the killings, which worsened tensions between *abangan* and *santri*.[51]

Against this historic backdrop, in the early 1950s the PKI, under Aidit, proceeded cautiously. The Communists worked hard to rehabilitate their image by positioning themselves as faithful allies of President Soekarno. Party statements emphasized the ideological affinities between its own anti-imperialism and the president's ardent nationalism; they also affirmed that at this point in Indonesian history the struggle against imperialism took precedence over domestic class struggle.[52] During most of this period the party avoided class-based conflicts and "operated within the dominant values set by the society and the regime—nationalist perspectives, consensus politics, and *aliran* forms of representation."[53] The party was also reluctant to become too directly involved in rural campaigns, fearing that a clash might invite an army crackdown. In short, although the program drawn up at the 1954 party congress identified the Indonesian revolution as "above all an agrarian revolution,"[54] the PKI's tactics were "above all" nationalist and Soekarno-focused.

The party's success at rebuilding its cadres and, especially after 1957, transforming itself into the largest of Indonesia's political parties, however, created strong pressures in the PKI for a bolder program of mass mobilization. The nation's economic infrastructure decayed from 1950 to 1965, worsening the plight of the rural poor and creating a constituency desperate for radical action, especially in Java. The more important influence on the PKI's program of rural mobilization, however, was the party's uncertain position in the Soekarno-led government. Although officially the PKI was an equal partner in NASAKOM, in practice it was opposed by Muslims, the armed forces, and conservative nationalists. Only the president and the left wing of the Nationalist Party welcomed PKI participation. These tensions only made the PKI more dependent on Soekarno and stiffened the party's resolve to find a way to force its unwilling partners to give it a greater share of power.

Rural mobilization appeared the surest way to get this leverage. In 1959 the PKI began its first rural land campaign. Modeled on a Chinese Communist program undertaken before that country's land reform in the 1950s, the PKI's "Go Down" campaign exhorted its cadres to go into the countryside, study the rural poor, and educate the populace in party policies.[55] The program was also designed to enhance the class awareness of the party rural cadres, many of whom came from middle and even wealthy peasant backgrounds.[56]

At first, the Go Down movement emphasized gradualist reform rather than open class struggle. At a PKI-sponsored peasants' conference in 1959 Chairman Aidit again stressed that anti-imperialism—meaning, in effect, the international campaigns promoted by President Soekarno—should take precedence over the "antifeudal" struggle for agrarian change. Party propaganda also limited its demand for confiscation of landholdings to land owned by foreigners and "traitor" landholders. Traitor landlords included landowners who, in places like West Java, South Sulawesi, and Sumatra, had supported the rebellions of the late 1950s. There was a hint of anti-Islamic sentiment in this demand, since people involved in those rebellions were disproportionately linked to Muslim organizations like the Masyumi.

The rural campaign intensified after 1959, in a manner that brought the PKI into growing conflict with Muslims and the military. A bill on land rents and sharecropping passed by the national assembly in late 1959 stipulated that landowners could take only 50% of harvest from tenants. The passage in September 1960 of the new Agrarian Law set strict limits on the amount of land a family could control.[57] Both laws represented a direct challenge to the *santri* Muslims disproportionately represented in the ranks of the nation's large landowners.

At first, however, the PKI leadership proceeded with caution in its new campaign. During 1960 and 1961 the party limited itself to media appeals demanding enforcement of the new regulations. After several serious incidents, however, in September 1963 the party escalated its campaign.[58] In a notable departure from the policies of the 1950s, party propaganda began to speak loudly of the class struggle in the countryside. What marked the campaign as radical was not just this language of class conflict or its attempt to redistribute land by force but its implicit repudiation of the party's cautious collaboration with others in NASAKOM. Buoyed by the spectacular growth of its membership, the PKI leaders were convinced that the time had come to escape the separate but unequal stalemate of NASAKOM.

Other developments reinforced the PKI leadership's confidence. On several occasions in 1964 the president made clear that he now regarded the PKI as the vanguard of Indonesia's revolution; he had shifted his foreign policy accordingly, tilting toward alliance with Beijing. In the same year the president signaled his impatience with the slow progress of land reform. Even in the indirect language of Indonesian politics, these comments offered a green light for a more ambitious effort. The PKI leadership also felt that it now had little to lose since, with the notable exception of the Nahdlatul Ulama,[59] none of the PKI's partners in the government of national unity had a rural organization capable of challenging a mobilized Communist force. Finally, the PKI leadership hoped that the campaign would shift national attention away from the divisive religious issues that had dogged the party's image since the Madiun affair and allow the party to highlight its commitment to class struggle.

The campaign presented serious organizational and political problems. The Agrarian Law provided few details on how to carry out land redistribution. At the very least, such an undertaking required a small army of technical cadres to identify and register holdings. Having grown so rapidly since 1957, most of the PKI cadres were ill equipped for such a daunting task. Equally serious, noncommunist villagers rejected Communist investigators as biased partisans. Moreover, as indicated by repeated criticisms in the PKI press of wealthy peasants among its members, not even all PKI officials were keen on distributing land.

Although originally government officials had predicted that the reform would make one million hectares of land available for redistribution, by 1963 the government estimated that no more than thirty-five thousand hectares had actually been reallocated.[60] The original estimates of available land in Java and Bali had been grossly exaggerated. Despite significant relative inequality in landholding, the majority of Javanese and Balinese landowners controlled farms of Lilliputian proportions, averaging a mere three-quarters of a hectare. The number of farmers who owned landholdings above the limits specified in the agrarian law was, in fact, small, though a greater number controlled amounts above the legal limit through rental and sharecropping.[61]

The most serious obstacle to the land reform, however, was not technical but political: the alliance of landowners and local officials determined to obstruct the law's enforcement. Pious Muslims were disproportionately represented in the ranks of these opponents. Their opposition was based on a complex mixture of economic and religious motives. Some attacked the legislation on the grounds that there was no precedent for it in religious law. But Muslim critics also felt that their communities were being unfairly singled out by the new regulations. At least since colonial times, *santri* Indonesians had tended to be more affluent than their less pious neighbors, both because of the predominance of *santri* in the merchant class and because in many rural areas *santri* habits of investment and consumption encouraged a spare, disciplined economic ethic. Qur'anic schools across Indonesia have always depended on gifts from wealthy landowners and on produce from lands controlled by the school owner. Endowments (*waqaf*) to religious institutions are strongly sanctioned in Islamic law, linked as they are to the reproduction of institutions at the heart of religious life. This circulation of wealth from economic to religious elites (themselves sometimes from the ranks of the former) is all part of the way differences of wealth and class are moralized in traditionalist Muslim communities. In Java this moral economy has long distinguished *santri* from *abangan* communities, providing each with distinct mechanisms of accumulation and investment, and different economic ethics.[62]

This linkage of wealth and religion ensured that the PKI's land reform campaign was seen by rural *santri* as nothing less than a challenge to their religion and way of life.[63] Not surprisingly, then, religio-communal tensions appeared from the start of the campaign. There was a clash between Muslims and Communists around the Lirboyo *pesantren* near Kediri in late 1964.[64] A more serious incident occurred south of Kediri in the village of Kanigoro on January 13, 1965, which quickly acquired near-mythological notoriety in the Muslim community.[65] On that morning a large group of PKI cadres invaded a school run by the Muslim Pupils Association, the modernist group close to the then banned Masyumi. After a short fight the Communists seized the Muslim youths, bound their hands, and marched them six kilometers to a police station where they were handed over as counterrevolutionaries. The incident provoked outrage in Muslim circles. The Muslim press highlighted the allegation that the Communists had violated the sanctity of the Kanigoro mosque by entering it without removing their shoes. The invaders were also alleged to have manhandled the school's teacher and trampled on the Qur'an.[66]

In fact, direct assaults by the PKI on Islamic institutions were uncommon during the land reform campaign. The PKI's propaganda took pains to insist that it was not Islam that was the problem but the "counterrevolutionary" Muslims of Masyumi, PII, and the HMI. As an American who worked in East Java at this time noted, "The PKI never acknowledged that it had any differences with a legal party, even the aroused NU."[67] Nonetheless, time and time again the targets of the land campaign were disproportionately Muslim. Against the memory of the Madiun affair, Soekarno's ban on Masyumi, the PKI's attacks on the HMI and PII, the collapse of *santri* businesses, and the efforts of some Javanists to repudiate Islam outright, Muslim leaders felt pushed to the limit. Many insisted they would retreat no more.

Despite several small victories, then, the larger PKI campaign misfired, provoking fierce resistance on the part of landlords and Muslims. The campaign had the unintended consequence of cementing regional anticommunist alliances. In the Javanese countryside the most important partners in the anticommunist network were Nahdlatul Ulama; members of the now-banned Masyumi and modernist youth organizations like the HMI and PII; conservative nationalists; and the armed forces. In Muslim territories outside Java, Masyumi played the main role in this informal alliance. In Hindu Bali, anticommunist cadres were recruited from the ranks of conservative nationalists and anticommunist socialists. In the capital and among the intelligentsia, finally, the Indonesian Socialist Party was also influential, although more for its ideas and elite connections than any mass following.

Although officially allied with the Communists in the NASAKOM government, the leadership of Nahdlatul Ulama took its participation in the anticommunist alliance one step further when, in remote corners of East Java, its militias began joint training exercises with the military.[68] HMI youth in Malang,

Surabaya, and other areas of East Java received similar training as civilian vigi-lantes. The movement from public and democratic politics to offstage syndical-ism was in full gear.

In retrospect, clearly the PKI had seriously misperceived its own strength and the weakness of its rivals. In the final months of 1964 the Commu-nist leadership indicated that it understood as much, acknowledging that "counterrevolutionaries" had successfully blocked the rural campaign. In De-cember President Soekarno attempted to dampen tensions by sponsoring a gathering of his NASAKOM allies. The meeting ended with a declaration of national unity that urged peasants to use consultation to resolve disputes. In joining in this declaration the PKI signaled its desire to pull back from the land campaign.[69]

The campaign's failure showed that the party did not comprehend the nature of Muslim social power, a power premised on the intersection of religious, political, and class interests. The campaign failure also cemented a heretofore unwieldy alliance of anticommunists. Not a simple matter of state against soci-ety, this alliance linked factions in the state elite to mass organizations in soci-ety. This vertical network was about to be put to a new and awful test.

Conclusion: State-Society Agonistes

In a widely cited essay on the development of the modern Indonesian state, Benedict Anderson has suggested that policy outcomes in Indonesia and many other nation-states can be understood as products of the shifting balance be-tween two competing interests: those of a "participatory" society and those of a controlling state. Anderson portrays the state in psychological terms, as a needful creature characterized by its "self-preserving and self-aggrandizing im-pulses, which at any moment are 'expressed' through its living members but which cannot be reduced to their passing personal ambitions."[70] Anderson goes on to suggest that this oscillating tension between state and society underlies the twists and turns of twentieth-century Indonesian politics. Thus, with its "emphasis on popular representation and on extra-state political organization and activity," parliamentary democracy "expressed the current preponderance of nation and society over the state." In contrast, Anderson argues, the New Order's rise to power after 1965–66 can be understood as "the resurrection of the state and its triumph vis-à-vis society and nation." [71]

The agonistic opposition Anderson has described here captures certain fea-tures of modern Indonesian politics well. For example, it correctly implies that a modern polity depends on a delicate balance between the capacities of the state and those of society. But in one very critical regard the zero-sum imagery of Anderson's model is seriously misleading. Whether in Indonesia or else-where, the interaction between state and society is *not* always an agonistic circle in which the state's gain is society's loss. Other outcomes are possible because power is not a fixed quantity, and the interaction of a state with a society is capable of engendering dynamics more complex than the simple addition and subtraction of a fixed sum of power.

Certainly this image of a never-ending tug-of-war over a fixed quantity of power is common in many popular political ideologies, including, as Anderson has argued, that which was at one point dominant in Java.[72] But modern history has shown that a strong state need not mean a weak or pliant society, and a strong society need not mean an ineffectual state. Some modern states, those we like to describe as democratic, have been able to achieve a civil decency by being strong and self-denying at the same time. Because they are strong, they are able to provide a host of services unthinkable under a weak or ineffectual state, including protections for human rights, an equitable rule of law, mass education, and procedures for subjecting political leaders to the will of the people. As Michael Mann has argued,[73] the provision of these services to large populations living in vast territories is not something traditional states either attempted or desired. Yet uniform and equitable access to state protections and services is a condition of the possibility of the egalitarian citizenship at the heart of the idea of nationalism. From the perspective of democratic theory, then, there is no inherent antagonism between state and a civil society. A strong but self-limiting state is not merely compatible with a vibrant civil society; it is one of its preconditions.[74]

Conversely, we know that broad-based participation in "society" is a precondition for a civil and democratic polity. By itself, however, this participation is no guarantee of good political health. In the Indonesian case, the political mobilization of society that had begun in the revolution (1945–49) was momentarily dampened during the early years of parliamentary democracy. But the competition revived with a fury in the run up to the national elections of 1955 and the regional elections of 1957. Shortly thereafter it assumed a more dangerous, subterranean form, as parliamentary politics gave way to clientage, offstage alliance, and violence. Anderson himself has described this process insightfully, developing a theme earlier enunciated by Clifford Geertz:

> The punctuational rhythms and legislative focus of parliamentary constitutionalism were replaced by an accelerando of mass politics penetrating ever more widely down and across Indonesian society. The major political parties of the period—the PKI, the PNI, and the conservative Muslim NU—threw themselves into expanding not merely their own memberships but those of affiliated associations of youth, women, students, farmers, workers, intellectuals, and others . . . which competed fiercely for influence in every sphere of life and on a round-the-clock basis. Hence the popular penetration of the state, which had been stemmed, and even reversed, after the declaration of martial law in 1957, resumed.[75]

This "popular" mobilization certainly diminished the effectiveness of the state, but—illustrating again the inadequacy of zero-sum portrayals of state-society dynamics—the state's loss was not society's gain. On the contrary, as the state's capacity to adjudicate social conflict declined, as it lost its ability to provide a stable fiscal environment, and as politics moved from public institutions into netherworld patronage and vigilantism, there was a desperate and inequitable scramble for resources. In such downward-spiraling free-for-alls, the prospects for subjecting power to democratic accountability *decrease* while the influence of mobilized and violent syndicates increases.

In circumstances like these, it makes little sense to speak of a uniform increase in "societal" power, as if, in good democratic fashion, the power relinquished by state institutions is automatically redistributed to the members of an undifferentiated "society." Whether in Indonesia or anywhere else, no such undifferentiated society has ever existed. In the Indonesian case, only those actors linked to mobilized political syndicates had any chance of benefiting from the deteriorating national situation, and even their gain was uncertain. The poor, the marginal, the middle peasant who just wanted to be left alone, and the intellectual unwilling to play by the rules of big-power politics—all these people were left with little room and even less power. Their choice was to submit to the rules of this cruel game or endure further suffering.

As the coordinating power of the constitutional state declined, then, what occurred was not an increase in societal power but a ferocious competition among factional syndicates who decimated democratic institutions, devastated the economy, and left most people poorer and less powerful than before. Power devolved not from a monolithic "state" into a uniform "society" but into the hands of segmental political organizations able to mobilize followers, coerce the weak, and, where necessary, bludgeon their enemies. The conflict corroded civil decencies, undermined what was good in state institutions, and left political hooligans the winner.

It was this fight to the finish into which the main players in Indonesian politics in 1964–65 had been drawn. The process of political mobilization through extralegal means diminished the likelihood that the political structures to emerge from this struggle would be more democratic. Popular sovereignty was yielding to factionalist privilege and state-sponsored gangsterism. In this kind of contest, winners were not likely to feel much allegiance to the self-limiting give-and-take of civil democracy. *This* was the essential fact of Indonesian politics in 1964–65. The outcome of this struggle would leave both "state" and "society" diminished.

Chapter Four

AMBIVALENT ALLIANCES:

RELIGION AND POLITICS IN THE EARLY NEW ORDER

ALTHOUGH SOME details remain a mystery, the course of events that began with the attempted leftist officers' coup of September 30, 1965, and culminated in the installation of Soeharto's New Order regime in mid-1966 is now more or less clear. The events of 1965–66 marked the end of one chapter in modern Indonesian history and the beginning of another. By the time the transition was complete, everything in the nation's politics had changed. The charismatic leader who had dominated most of the independence era, President Achmad Sukarno, was stripped of his power; the political parties that had raucously vied for influence on the national stage were marginalized; the once powerful Communist Left was destroyed; and a military coalition headed by a clever young general was in power. What all these changes were to mean for Muslims was still unclear. Few understood that the events they had witnessed were to change their political fortunes forever.

In this chapter I briefly review religion and politics in the transition to the New Order. My purpose is not to offer yet another overview of the traumatic beginning of the Soeharto regime, of which there are already excellent accounts,[1] but to provide a context in which to understand the changing actions and aspirations of organized Islam. The violence of 1965–66 provides insights into the challenges faced by Indonesians, both Muslim and non-Muslim, hoping to advance the cause of pluralism and democracy. The new regime's machinery of centralized power and ideological control destroyed most that remained of Indonesia's formal democratic institutions. The killings of hundreds of thousands of Communists left a legacy of vigilante violence that would haunt Indonesia for years to come. Yet out of this maelstrom of cruelty, civil voices, including Muslim ones, were soon heard.

Having been marginalized from national politics and economic life in the final years of the Soekarno regime, Muslims looked with high hopes toward the regime that came to power during 1965–66. Indeed, to many it seemed to offer the possibility of a "new order," one that would restore organized Islam to its rightful position in public life. From early on, however, there were signs that some among the regime's advisers were ambivalent about Muslim political organizations and civilian politics as a whole. Rather than suppressing Muslim activism and secularizing politics (as some of the elite recommended), the government adopted a mixed regimen that combined severe controls on political

Islam with guarded support for Islamic spirituality. Regime strategists looked to organized religion as a ground for public morality, a shield against Western liberalism, and an antidote to communism. Animated by this conviction, the New Order regime not only tolerated depoliticized forms of religion but encouraged their penetration into all corners of society.

Over the life of Soeharto's New Order (1966–98), this peculiar tactic of suppressing Muslim politics while encouraging Muslim piety offered more room for Muslims than other society-based organizations. Muslim associations became centers for frank discussions of politics and public morality. From the beginning, the discourses Muslims developed in these discussions were varied. Rather than being a weakness (as some conservative Islamists believed), however, the diversity and debate within the Muslim community provided it with the flexibility to experiment with new initiatives, some of which thrived in the altered circumstances of the New Order. Mass education and the growth of a Muslim middle class also allowed for the emergence of a new type of Muslim leader. These "new Muslim intellectuals" were public figures whose views on Muslim politics owed as much to general education, new print media, and the encounter with Western social theories as it did to Qur'anic boarding schools and classical legalism. Buoyed by these developments, the Muslim community in the 1980s experienced a social renaissance unprecedented in modern Indonesian history. By the late 1980s the renaissance gave rise to new political pressures as well, as members of the Muslim middle class pressed for greater representation in government and society.

Eventually the resurgence forced Soeharto to rethink his policies on Islam. Some among Soeharto's advisers continued to speak as if nothing had changed and urged the regime to promote "cultural" Islam while strictly suppressing Muslim politics. But the resurgence was too powerful and too tempting to turn back in so simple a manner. Facing new challenges, Soeharto eventually tried to harness conservative Islam to his own cart. He was to learn, however, that the forces he was dealing with had a political and moral integrity all their own.

OUT OF THE PAN

The attempted coup of September 30, 1965, came as no surprise to many Indonesian observers. As we have seen, 1964–65 had already witnessed extensive agrarian violence and furious ideological exchanges. Tensions in the capital reached new heights in early 1965, when rumors circulated of a plot to overthrow the president. The rumors increased in early August after President Soekarno fell ill unexpectedly, fueling (as it would turn out, unjustified) reports that he was near death. Jakarta took on a crisis atmosphere, and the major factions in Indonesia's off-stage polity worked furiously to position themselves for the tumult that was sure to follow Soekarno's passing. The Communist

Party warned of an imminent right-wing putsch. Muslim organizations feared that the president was about to grant the Communists new powers.

It was the armed forces, especially the army, however, that presented the most powerful rival to the PKI. Confident that it had the technical and organizational capacity to face down the PKI in any fire fight,[2] the military command was nonetheless worried about divisions in its own ranks. Although the army generals in Jakarta were united in their opposition to the PKI, they were uncertain about the loyalties of their regional command, particularly in the strategically important provinces of East and Central Java. There, much of the middle officer corps was known to be loyal to President Soekarno. The army command was equally concerned about the loyalties of the air force and navy, elements of which were also sympathetic to the president and the political Left.

Army concerns heightened when, early in 1965, President Soekarno, the PKI, and the left-leaning commander of the air force, Omar Dhani, all began to speak of the need for a "fifth" armed force in society. Although its precise details were never clarified, the gist of the plan was to create revolutionary militias, consisting of workers and peasants, trained by representatives of the armed forces but operationally independent of them. Proposals for such a force represented a none-too-subtle effort on the part of President Soekarno and the Communists to take Indonesia's social revolution one step further, mobilizing the masses into a state of armed readiness. All parties in the national struggle were aware that if this plan went forward the military's monopoly on armed power would be over. The militias would also provide the PKI with the armed force it had sorely lacked since the 1948 Madiun disaster.

After weeks of rumors, tensions finally came to a climax the night of September 30, 1965. Late in the night, leftist forces led by junior army officers kidnapped six generals and a lieutenant from their homes in central residential districts of the capital. Three of the generals were shot and killed in their homes as they resisted their abductors. The others were taken to the Halim air force base in eastern Jakarta, where, in the presence of Communist cadres as well as rebel officers, they were executed and their bodies (along with those of the three officers killed earlier) dumped in a well. The most senior military officer targeted by the dissidents, General Abdul Haris Nasution, evaded capture by leaping a fence in his backyard, although his daughter was mortally wounded in the rebel attack.

With these actions, the coup leaders had in just a few hours achieved one of their primary goals: neutralization of the senior, and most anticommunist, army command. It is not clear that the rebels had originally intended to execute the generals; they may have simply wanted to arrest them and hand them over to the president on charges that they had conspired against him. Convinced, in any case, that they could sway the remaining military leadership to their side, the coup leaders left less prominent senior officers untouched.

Calling themselves the "Thirtieth of September Movement," the next day the coup leaders declared they had taken action on behalf of the army in conjunction with other branches of the armed forces, under the leadership of a certain Lieutenant Colonel Untung, a battalion commander in President Soekarno's elite palace guard. The coup leaders claimed to have uncovered plans for a coup against President Soekarno by senior army officers associated with a shadowy "council of Generals" (*Dewan Jenderal*). The council, the statement explained, "is a subversive movement sponsored by the CIA," consisting of "power-mad generals and officers who have neglected the lot of their men and who above the accumulated sufferings of their men have lived in luxury, led a gay life, insulted our women and wasted government funds."[3] The council's goal, the rebels implied, was to overthrow President Soekarno and reverse the Indonesian revolution.[4] The rebels portrayed themselves, then, as loyal supporters of the president, forced into action by the treachery of the senior command.

The rebel statement also announced the establishment of a Revolutionary Council in Jakarta, charged with carrying out Soekarno's policies and neutralizing counterrevolutionary opponents; similar councils, they explained, would soon be established in the provinces. Late in the afternoon of the same day the commander of the air force, General Omar Dhani, delivered a broadcast in which he pledged his support to this and "all progressive-revolutionary movements" and referred to the Thirtieth of September Movement as "safeguarding the Revolution . . . against CIA Subversion." The killing of the generals, he added, had been a "purge within the army."[5] Dhani's statement showed that the rebels had won the support of the leadership of at least one branch of the armed forces.

If a purge of the army leadership was their primary goal,[6] the rebels had erred in assuming that they could win the remaining military command to their side. Central Java was the only province in which local commanders publicly lent their support to the rebel cause. Five of the province's seven infantry battalions went over to the rebel cause after junior officers deposed their commanders; in Yogyakarta the commander and chief of staff were abducted and killed. Although in Bandung and Surabaya there were desultory efforts by junior officers to rally support for Untung's movement, the armed forces in the other provinces remained wary of events in Jakarta.

By the end of the next day (October 1) the Jakartan wing of the rebellion had, for all intents and purposes, collapsed. The rebels had calculated that the polite commander of the Army Strategic Reserve Command (KOSTRAD), Major General Soeharto—whom several of the rebels knew personally—would be easily swayed to their side once presented with the fact of the coup.[7] This proved to be a serious mistake. Informed the morning of the coup that the most senior army general (General Yani) was missing, Soeharto consulted with other army commanders and assumed control of the army. Late that same day his emissaries convinced the rebel leaders deployed in Jakarta's Merdeka Square to give up their cause. After recapturing the capital's radio station, Soeharto addressed the nation. He condemned the Thirtieth of September Movement as counterrevolutionary and appealed to all the armed forces to join him in crushing the rebellion. The tide had already turned against the rebels.

Early the next day (October 2) elite army paracommandos under the leadership of a close Soeharto ally, Colonel Sarwo Edhie, occupied Halim air force base. It was later learned that President Soekarno himself had spent most of the previous day at the rebel base in the company of Omar Dhani (the air force commander who had declared his support for the coup) and several senior members of the PKI leadership. As General Soeharto's forces recaptured the base, Dhani, Soekarno, PKI-Chief Aidit, and the leaders of the Thirtieth of September Movement fled, fueling speculation that, somehow, all had been secretly involved in the rebellion.

Had the rebellion not involved the killing of the army leadership, and had the country not already reached economic collapse, the coup attempt might have been seen in later years as little more than a nasty bump in the already erratic course of the Soekarnoist revolution, an intramilitary spat gone awry. However, the coup effort took place in a context of radical economic decline and incendiary political contestation. In addition, by killing the senior command, the rebels violated a fundamental rule of Indonesian military rivalry. Equally provocative in anticommunist eyes was the presence of the PKI chairman, Aidit, at Halim on October 1, along with members of the Communist mass organizations Gerwani (the Communist women's organization) and Pemuda Rakyat (the organization of Communist youth). Whatever their actual complicity, which appears to have been limited at best, the mere presence of PKI leaders at the base made the leadership vulnerable to the charge that they were behind the coup. Compromising the Communist position even further was the fact that in Central Java the PKI made broadcasts and sponsored demonstrations supporting the Thirtieth of September movement; in Jakarta the PKI newspaper, *Harian Rakjat*, also praised Colonel Untung. Some observers have speculated that this activity may have actually been encouraged by anticommunist infiltrators in the PKI intent on discrediting the organization. In the unsettled context of the coup, however, the actions of the party leaders nonetheless amounted to a strategic blunder of disastrous proportions.[8]

Alarmed by the murder of the generals and convinced that other commanders would react harshly to news of the killings, President Soekarno disappointed the coup leaders by refusing to support their actions; indeed, he demanded that the rebellion end. On October 2 Soekarno took steps to reassert his own authority over the armed forces, hoping these actions would allow him to mediate between the two sides in the conflict. The president appointed Major General Pranoto Reksosamudro, a man known to be cordial with PKI officials, to serve as his representative to the armed forces.[9] Soeharto immediately rejected the appointment, however, insisting that it was inappropriate until the fate of the missing generals was resolved. This was the first clear hint that Soeharto intended to restore order on terms other than those of the Soekarnoist status quo.[10]

Soekarno's strategy for responding to the campaign against the Thirtieth of September Movement was to downplay its seriousness by portraying it as an intra-military conflict. Aware of the growing strength of his opponents, he was anxious to defend his supporters in the military and prevent the rising tide of condemnation from turning into an anticommunist bloodbath. He was well aware that the destruction of the PKI would deprive him of an important base of support. Events were already more seriously out of control, however, than the president realized. General Soeharto's camp had begun a carefully orchestrated propaganda campaign to highlight the horrors of the coup attempt and to prove the PKI's complicity in it. On October 4, with photographers and television crews in attendance, the bodies of the slain generals were removed from the well on the Halim air force base. The condition of the bodies—dispatched with gunshot, dumped into a well, and decaying in the tropical heat—seemed to lend credence to the Soeharto group's claims that the generals had been tortured by PKI units before their execution. These accounts placed blame for the killings on members of the Communist Youth and PKI's women's unit groups that indeed had been present on the base at the time of the generals' murder. Official army accounts alleged that these groups had not merely witnessed the killings but had carried them out themselves after first subjecting the generals to hideous torture. Afterward, the official story claimed, the women killers engaged in a lascivious orgy with PKI cadres. Over the months that followed the attempted coup, this fabricated allegation of Communist treachery, torture, and licentiousness was repeated endlessly in the media. Not surprisingly, this propaganda spurred horrendous acts of violence against innocent local women associated with the Gerwani.[11]

The military leadership was aware that they risked provoking a civil war if they moved too swiftly against President Soekarno—a point of which Soekarno himself reminded them. There was still strong support for Soekarno in the civilian population, as well as in some branches of the military. Soekarno even had supporters among the leadership of the party of traditionalist Islam, Nahdlatul Ulama—this despite the fact that by now NU cadres in East and Central Java had taken the lead in the killing of Communists.

Well known for his cunning in political affairs, General Soeharto devised a plan for continuing the assault on Soekarno and the PKI without plunging the country into civil war. The solution had two components. The first involved a sustained propaganda campaign against the president, so as to restrict his influence and, if need be, drive him from power. It was important that this initiative not be seen as emanating from the military but from civilian groupings unhappy with Soekarno rule. The second element in the Soeharto campaign was equally high-risk: the physical liquidation of the PKI. Soeharto and his allies recognized that this bloodshed must not be seen as a military campaign but the product of the spontaneous fury of ordinary citizens. To create this impression, the armed forces would have to mobilize hundreds of thousands of civilian vigilantes across the country. The civilians would aid in the identification, arrest, and execution of PKI cadres. Even as they reached deep into society, the killings would have to be carried out without obvious military support or extensive media coverage, so as not to provoke Soekarno.

Although the campaign to destroy the PKI was one of the twentieth century's worst mass slaughters, in the end it went largely unrecorded in Indonesia's mass media. Although violent denunciations of the PKI were regularly featured in the media, the killings themselves received almost no coverage. People in towns remote from the killing fields were often unaware of the enormity of the bloodshed or the systematic nature of its conduct.[12]

There were nonetheless indirect indications of the enormity of the violence. Perhaps most revealing were the vitriolic denunciations of what was now presented as a PKI coup and the horrific accounts of Communist lasciviousness and torture they highlighted. With these accounts came regular exhortations for all citizens—Muslims, Christians, nationalists, and even noncommunist socialists—to join in the hunt for the perpetrators of this hideous crime. By late October 1965 government and press reports portrayed the PKI's crime not merely as a coup in the capital but as part of a larger plan to seize power and execute religious and social leaders across the country. In towns and villages where the PKI had large followings, assaults on the hapless membership were preceded by the discovery of lists of local people slated for execution by the Thirtieth of September Movement.

In the months that followed, President Soekarno made a series of desperate attempts to save what remained of the disintegrating Communist Party. He rejected demands that the party be banned and, in several public settings, chastised Muslims for their role in the killings. Ironically, by resisting demands for the PKI's dissolution, Soekarno may have inadvertently exacerbated the scale of the killings. Determined to destroy the PKI by any means possible, militant anticommunists in East Java, Central Java, and Bali (provinces that accounted for the greatest proportion of the killings) took advantage of the crisis to unleash even more furious waves of death. Even if the anticommunist alliance failed to secure the PKI's official dissolution, they hoped the party's mass base would be so decimated that it would never revive.[13]

The greatest portion of the killing was completed by the end of December 1965, although scattered incidents of killing continued into mid-1966; there were also renewed executions in Central Java and East Java in 1968 and 1969.[14] By the time it was over most of the PKI's core cadres had been eliminated, and some five hundred thousand people had been killed. Before the coup, the

Communist Party had been Indonesia's largest party, with some three million members, of whom perhaps 10 percent were trained cadres. There were an additional fifteen to twenty million members in organizations affiliated with the party.[15] Having twice recovered from earlier disasters, this time the PKI was fatally wounded.

In an insightful overview of the Indonesian killings, the historian Robert Cribb has observed that the scale of the killings was largely "gratuitous." By this he means that their enormity was disproportionate relative to the modest scale of the political change they ushered in. Despite the scope of the killings, he observes (agreeing with an earlier comment by Harold Crouch), the ascent of the New Order regime was marked by as much continuity—in particular, of army influence and bureaucratic dominance—as change.

From an institutional or structural perspective, this observation is no doubt correct. The Indonesian military was deeply involved in politics and enterprise before the New Order's ascent, and even more so afterward. However, this structural continuity should not obscure the important fact that in terms of the *process* of state politics there was a rupture of fundamental proportions between the Soekarno regime and the New Order. While in the first years of independence the state administration had enjoyed a measure of social and ideological unity, by the end of the Soekarno era there was no state qua unitary agent, least of all one capable of acting in a rational and efficient manner to achieve desired ends.

Under these circumstances the image of structural continuity obscures as much as it illuminates. As Michael Langenberg has observed, at the height of the 1965 violence there was no "efficient, centralized government to issue a coherent policy of genocide or mass extermination of political enemies."[16] Rather than reducing the likelihood of gratuitous violence, this volatile fragmentation of the state apparatus only increased it. State and society were in segmental turmoil. The primary characteristic of this segmental struggle was that rival political factions created extra-constitutional alliances that linked forces in the state with those in society against rival syndicates organized in an equally segmentary manner. In circumstances like these it makes no sense to talk of a well-demarcated "state" acting in opposition to a "society," since the rival groupings incorporated elements from both.[17]

The continuity of state structures from the Guided Democracy era to the New Order, then, obscures a deep and abiding discontinuity. By 1965 the state administration had lost its ideological and organizational cohesiveness; even the armed forces were factionalized. Rival groupings then reached out into society to achieve the leverage they needed to break the deadlock with the enemy. In doing so, however, they made the political conflict in state and society even worse. The state was so split by rival alliances that the only likely outcome was that winners would take all and losers would lose horribly.

The state that emerged in the aftermath of this conflict was more powerful, more centralized, and more ideologically cohesive—"considerably more centralized and more functionally effective over the civil society at large than at any time since 1942."[18] It was also a state that had destroyed the infrastructure of civil organization in such a way as to ensure that, henceforth, the state would not hesitate to use violence in the interest of power. A key element in the military's arsenal of violence was to be civilian vigilantes, some of whom were recruited from the ranks of Indonesia's growing population of urban gangsters.[19] Although the violence of 1965–66 would subside, this habit of uncivil governance would endure.

AMBIVALENT ALLIES

In contrast to the offstage campaign against the PKI, the effort to restrict the power of President Soekarno proceeded in the manner of high drama. Although, by late 1965, the army had destroyed the president's base of support in the Communist Party, Soekarno seemed only more determined to develop a new base. The president had managed to protect some of his noncommunist supporters in the military. To the irritation of the army command, he also continued to reject calls for a formal dissolution of the Communist Party, implying that the NASAKOM formula uniting nationalists, Muslims, and Communists was still the basis of the government. NASAKOM required some kind of reconstituted Communist Party, perhaps under a new party name and party organization.

By late December 1965 the president was speaking out even more boldly in defense of the Communists, reminding the nation of the Communist contribution to the independence struggle, and implicitly challenging the army leadership. In mid-January 1966, in response to demonstrations against him, Soekarno appealed to his supporters to organize themselves into columns (*barisan*) for his defense. Caught off guard, the army leadership responded by declaring its loyalty to the president, while secretly working to bring the newly formed Soekarno columns under military control.[20] In early 1966, Soekarno traveled around the country attempting to build support among the leadership of the political parties. In his boldest move, on February 21, 1966, he reshuffled his cabinet, dismissing anti-communist ministers while retaining those sympathetic to the PKI.[21] By reshuffling military personnel in the cabinet, the president also strengthened the hand of Soekarnoist officers in the military.

Caught off guard again, the army leaders faced the dilemma of either acquiescing to the president or publicly challenging him. The latter strategy carried the risk of alienating Soekarnoists in the Central and East Javanese command. In the end, the senior leadership devised an ingenius middle strategy: to allow a group of anti-Soekarnoist officers to take covert actions against the new cabinet and Soekarno's policies. The most important of these officers were the three New Order "radicals," Brigadier General Kemal Idris, head of the Army Strategic Reserve Command (KOSTRAD); Colonel Sarwo Edhie, commander of the elite Army Paracommando Regiment (RPKAD) and a key figure in the suppression of the PKI in Central Java and Bali; and Major General Hartono Rekso Dharsono, former chief of the Siliwangi Division of the army and now working in the army headquarters.[22] All three of these officers had a long history of ties to anti-Soekarnoist forces, especially among students and intellectuals in Jakarta, Bandung, and Bogor. In the 1950s, for example, Kemal Idris was well known as a sympathizer of the social-democratic but anticommunist Indonesian Socialist Party. Before its banning by Soekarno in 1960, this Western-oriented, technocratic party had enjoyed the support of anti-Soekarnoist officers, especially in the West Javanese Siliwangi division.[23] Even after the PSI and Masyumi were banned in 1960, members of both groups were active in the opposition to Sukarno, and most had regular contacts with army officers. Youth groups such as the modernist Association of Muslim Students and the Movement of Socialist Youth (Gemsos, Gerakan Mahasiswa Sosialis) were above-ground platforms for a much larger underground network (chapter 3).

It was these networks that were mobilized during 1965 and 1966 for the purpose of creating a "civilian" opposition to Soekarno. In histories of the New Order, October 5 is the date most conventionally cited as the beginning of the student movement against the PKI and Sukarno. However, PSI and HMI activists are quick to point out that, in fact, both groups made secret contact with their military patrons on October 2 even before the outcome of the coup was clear. The HMI leadership met the night of October 1 to discuss strategies in light of the still unfolding coup. On October 2, representatives from the HMI leadership met with officers from Kostrad to begin planning the anticommunist alliance.[24] Several weeks later, in an effort to expand student-military collaboration, Minister of Higher Education and Science Major General Sjarif Tajeb invited representatives from the leading student groups to his office on October 25 to form an action group against the Communists and remnants of the Thirtieth of September Movement. This organization, the Indonesian Student Action Group (KAMI, Kesatuan Aksi Mahasiswa Indonesia) was designed to serve as a more manageable (from the military's perspective) organizational vehicle than the existing Federation of Indonesian Students (PPMI). Although in the days following the coup the federation had publicly condemned the PKI, the PPMI had many Soekarnoists in its ranks. They insisted that criticism of the PKI not extend to the president.

KAMI suffered from no such ambivalence. The eight student groups that comprised KAMI were united in opposition to the PKI and support of political reform, including changes to the presidency. Despite agreeing on these issues, KAMI's constituent bodies were divided on other matters, especially the question of Islam and state. Among its eight constituents, KAMI included Muslim-nationalist organizations like the HMI (modernist Islam) and the PMII (*Perhimpunan Mahasiswa Islam Indonesia*, linked to the Nahdlatul Ulama), as well as student organizations committed to nonreligious nationalism. Most important among the latter were the Association of Catholic Students (PMKRI), the Protestant Indonesian Students movement (GMKI), and the PSI-oriented Socialist Students movement (Gemsos).[25] In terms of membership, HMI was the largest of KAMI's subgroupings. But Catholics wielded influence disproportionate to their numbers, owing to their education, organizational discipline, and financial backing by wealthy Chinese Catholics.[26]

During the uncertain months following the Thirtieth of September coup, KAMI briefly became one of the most influential civilian forces in the struggle to ban the Communist Party and restrict President Soekarno's power. Aided by their high school counterpart KAPPI (founded on February 9, 1966), they took control of the streets away from their rivals in the "Soekarno Columns" mobilized by the president.[27] Throughout this period, of course, the anti-Soekarno action groups were thoroughly dependent on their military patrons. They were vulnerable because the military still counted many Soekarnoists in its ranks. In the face of this pro-Soekarno opposition, KAMI and KAPPI leaders maintained regular contact with General Ali Moertopo, a personal adviser to General Soeharto.[28] Through him and the Siliwangi radicals they secured tactical support for their activities. The student action groups helped military opponents of Soekarno to block the president's efforts to regain power, while making it difficult to blame the campaign on the anti-Soekarnoist military.

The students' role proved decisive in the unsettled period from January to March 1966, when Soekarno made one last attempt to push back his challengers. In early January KAMI leaders participated in a meeting on the campus of the University of Indonesia which brought together academics, bureaucrats, and military officers (including General Nasution, then Minister of Defense and Security) who called for nothing less than a total political-economic restructuring of government.[29] On January 10 the students came together with Colonel Sarwo Edhie, commander of the elite RPKAD regiment, and formulated the famous "Three Demands of the People" (*Tri Tuntutan Rakyat*, or *Tritura*): dissolution of the PKI, reorganization of the government, and the lowering of prices for basic goods and services. On January 15 students marched to the presidential palace to meet with Soekarno, violating the prior agreement that only a handful of student representatives would come to the palace. The president received the students but used the occasion to plea for an end to the killings. On January 20 the president escalated his rhetoric against the organization, accusing KAMI of being a tool of "neocolonial and imperialist forces." Clashes ensued in the capital between KAMI and the president's student supporters.

The crisis deepened in February as KAMI students launched strikes in Bandung and Jakarta. It was in this context, then, that on February 21 Soekarno reshuffled his cabinet, firing General Nasution, the minister of defense and one of KAMI's most ardent supporters, while retaining ministers opposed to the KAMI demonstrators.[30] The students responded with a new wave of protests, including, on February 24, a march on the presidential palace to prevent the inaugural meeting of the new cabinet. The next day Soekarno responded in kind, banning KAMI. At this point, the anti-Soekarnoist military intervened in a manner that openly defied the president's instructions, providing protection for the banned organization on the campus of the University of Indonesia. With this military assistance, the students went on the offensive again in early March, staging more demonstrations against the cabinet. On March 10 they sacked the Consulate General of the People's Republic of China.

This contest between Soekarno, on the one hand, and the students and anti-Soekarnoist military, on the other, reached a climax on March 11. As on February 14 the students blocked access to the presidential palace, forcing the ministers to make their way to the palace by helicopter. As the cabinet meeting got under way, the president was informed that six Siliwangi divisions were taking up positions on the outskirts of the capital and a coup was imminent. With two of his ministers, the president immediately flew by helicopter to his Bogor palace. There he received three officers sent by Major General Soeharto. Shaken by the day's events and convinced that Soeharto was among the moderate army leadership, Soekarno signed over to General Soeharto broad powers "for the reestablishment of order."

The next day Soekarno learned that the first step taken by Soeharto with the powers conveyed through the "Letter of March 11" (widely known as the "Supersemar")[31] was to ban the PKI. Six days later, fifteen of the president's left-leaning ministers were arrested. Over the next six months a purge of left-wing Soekarnoists was carried out in the government bureaucracy and military. Soekarno had been outwitted.

Although in July and August 1966 Soekarno attempted to challenge Soeharto's far-reaching interpretation of the Supersemar transfer of powers, the March incident marked a turning point in the balance of power between the president and his military rivals. In the aftermath of the Supersemar, members of the action fronts began to speak of the birth of a "New Order" that would usher in dramatic political change. Student activists continued to call for the resignation and trial of President Soekarno. The army leadership was reluctant to take such radical measures, however, fearing they could provoke violent reaction in the army's Central and East Javanese divisions. Urged on by the New Order radicals Kemal Idris, Dharsono, and Sarwo Edhie, in the last months of 1966 KAMI and KAPPI demonstrators helped to create an atmosphere in which the president's support only declined further.

In mid-March, 1967 the anti-Soekarno movement came to a startling conclusion. With some eighty thousand crack army troops ringing the city, the People's Consultative Assembly (MPR), the representative body charged with electing Indonesian presidents and formulating the broad outlines of state policy, stripped Soekarno of his presidential powers and named Soeharto acting president. Soeharto would receive the title of president a year later. Soekarno was not subjected to trial or public humiliations, but he remained under effective house arrest until his death in June 1970. The Soekarno era had ended; the New Order had been born.

Power in Search of Policy

From the easy chair of retrospective history, it is easy to dismiss KAMI and the other action groups as puppets of the army leadership, manipulated for military ends and with no integrity of their own. When, a few years after their formation, they began to challenge New Order policies, the action groups were easily suppressed and several of their leaders imprisoned.

At the time of their founding, however, KAMI and the other action groups attracted not just fanatical anticommunists but principled proponents of democratic reform. Many writers, artists, and public intellectuals, including many from the noncommunist Left, had resented the ideological controls of the late Soekarno era. These people hoped that the New Order would put the nation back on the road to freedom, democracy, and prosperity. Long after KAMI's activities were restricted, the organization's heady experience of open debate and participatory activism would serve as a reference point for those who came to be known as the "generation of '66" (*angkatan '66*). In later years some of these activists went on to become Indonesia's most prominent journalists, artists, and legal rights activists.

In what follows I sketch some of the ideological fervor of this period from the perspective of several organizations that participated in the New Order's rise. In providing this account, I want to weave a path between, on the one hand, those who believe implausibly that students and civilian groupings were the primary agents for the New Order's ascent, and, on the other, critics who insist that the New Order was a military coup pure and simple and its ideological debates no more than a superstructural charade. In recent years the former view has been the subject of animated discussion, particularly in the ranks of the generation of '66, some of whom clearly regret their role in assisting Soeharto's rise.[32]

The evidence shows that the action groups played a vital role in legitimating the change of regime and muting Soekarnoist opposition in the armed forces. On the matter of the mass killings, in addition, the participation of the action groups helped to shift responsibility for the PKI's destruction away from the military and onto the population as a whole. This shared responsibility diminished the likelihood of anti-military recrimination.

As in all struggles for state power, however, seizure of the state was just one, albeit decisive, moment in an ongoing process of regime consolidation. New Order rulers were convinced of the need to assert military control over the state and greatly restrict mass political participation. Confident in these matters, the military commanders were less certain of the policies they should adopt on fiscal management, the party system, and organized Islam. The regime was forced to look to civilian advisers and technicians. It soon became apparent, however, that these advisers did not share a common political vision.

Nowhere was this disagreement clearer than on the question of Islam. Rather than a singular opposition to Islam or a strong commitment to Javanism, as some early accounts of the New Order suggested, the ruling elite had contradictory views on organized Islam. During its first years, then, the regime stumbled through a series of inconsistent policies, often with unanticipated political consequences. To illustrate the complexity of these policies I examine, in the remainder of this chapter, the experience of three different groups involved with the government during its earliest years. The three are the "secular-modernizers,"[33] moderate social democrats who were heir to the mantle of the Indonesian Socialist Party; the loosely organized array of Javanese mystical groups known as *aliran kepercayaan* (streams of belief); and the party of Muslim traditionalists, Nahdlatul Ulama. In the next chapter I extend this same inquiry into the experience of a fourth group, modernist Muslims.

There were other actors involved in this struggle to shape New Order religious policy. Taken together, however, the experience of these four groupings illustrates the complex evolution of religious politics in the early New Order. Two issues stand out from this history. First, however much some in the regime's inner circle had strong Javanist or secularist convictions, over the long term the regime's policies were primarily shaped by political considerations of a thoroughly "nonreligious" sort. Religious interests ranked low on the hierarchy of values with which Soeharto was concerned. His basic preoccupation was to hold power, stabilize the economy, and reap the benefits of development for himself and his family. When circumstances demanded it, the president did not hesitate to play one religious group against another, in a manner that left a bitterly uncivil legacy in Indonesian society.

In the first years of the New Order, the most prominent victims of this power politics were organized Muslim groups, especially those associated with the Muslim parties of the Soekarno era. The restrictions and harassment to which these organizations were subjected convinced a generation of Western experts that Soeharto and his advisers were fervent Javanists opposed to Islam. When, in the late 1980s, power considerations dictated a change in policy, however, the Soeharto regime quickly reversed course, courting conservative Muslims and leaving its Javanist and non-Muslim friends high and dry. Soeharto's religious policies were inconsistent because they responded not to the cultural logic of Javanism but to the insistent demands of unchecked power.

The inconsistency of New Order religious policies raises a second point. However adept at neutralizing its challengers, the Soeharto regime repeatedly failed to grasp the nature of the socioreligious forces its policies were unleashing. Determined in its early years to prevent any revival of organized Muslim politics, the regime's policies had the unintended effect of bringing about just such a revival. Intent in the late 1980s on creating a pliant conservative Islam, the regime stimulated the growth of prodemocracy Islam. Soeharto's habit of playing different religious communities against one another stands in striking contrast to his professed interest in depoliticizing Islam and creating an "ideology of tolerance."[34] Soeharto's official statements did indeed emphasize *Pancasila* tolerance, but his actions spoke louder than his words. Again and again he pitted ethnoreligious groups against one another in a high-stakes game of divide and conquer. The repoliticization of religion and ethnicity and the systematic drain on Indonesia's social capital of tolerance and civility was to be the most tragic of Soeharto's legacies.

FROM LIBERAL SOCIALISM TO SECULAR MODERNISM

From the perspective of the fin de siècle West, one of the more unusual aspects of Indonesian political history is the fact that democratic socialists, not market liberals, were the primary carriers of the liberal-democratic ideals of freedom and equality to the Indonesian public. Viewed from the vantage point of Indonesian history, this fact appears less anomalous. As Feith and Castles have noted in their compendium of Indonesian political thinking from 1945 to 1965, the term *liberalism* in pre–New Order times was closely linked with the image of an unbridled and monopolistic capitalism.[35] This identification is in fact still widespread today. The association of liberalism with exploitation is not accidental, of course, but reflects the fact that the capitalism introduced by Europeans in nineteenth-century Indonesia was not that of market equality and fair play but a race-conscious colonial capitalism in which the state guaranteed European control of the commanding heights of the economy. Against this background it is not surprising that the idea of liberalism was tainted with the image of colonial domination.[36] Conversely, until the regime transition of 1965–66, socialism was universally acclaimed as the economic system most fitting for Indonesia. In the 1950s "few spokesmen of any political tendency would have failed to declare themselves both democrats and socialists."[37]

Rather than by way of liberal democrats, then, notions of freedom, universal citizenship, human rights, and enlightenment made their way into Indonesian political thought in association with democratic socialism. The association began in the period between the two world wars. During those years urban educated circles witnessed a proliferation of "study groups," a civic activity that to this day plays an important role in Indonesian public culture. Writers and intellectuals in these groups grappled with the big questions of modernism, such as how to balance tradition with modernity, the proper relationship of individualism to collectivism, and the difference between "Asia" and "the West."

One of the most influential political writers from this period was Sutan Takdir Alisjahbana, editor of the influential intellectual 1930s review *Poedjang-ga Baroe*. Alisjahbana was torn between his commitment to Enlightenment progress and emancipation and his pride of commitment to nationalism. Like later socialists, however, his commitment to the former values made him skeptical toward everything traditional. Indonesia had to change, he insisted, and this meant that Indonesians had to adopt many of the values and institutions of the West.[38] Since most of the native population was unprepared for these innovations, Alisjahbana argued that it fell to the artistic and intellectual avant garde to facilitate the transition from an immobile "tradition" to modernity. Years later, during the early New Order, these same attitudes of openness to the West, a belief in a stark divide between tradition and modernity, and an emphasis on the role of intellectual elites in modernization were promoted by secular modernists.

Indonesia's liberal socialists were most strongly influenced, however, by the remarkable founder of the Socialist Party, Sutan Sjahrir. Sjahrir embodied all the contradictions of this ambiguous political tradition. He was a democrat and an elitist, an anti-imperialist and an admirer of the West, and a Marxist with a liberal commitment to individual freedom.[39] Before the war, Sjahrir had had contacts with Alisjahbana and had published an article in the *Poedjangga Baru*. In it he argued that Indonesia had to follow a course of social evolution like that of Europe. For Sjahrir, this meant that Indonesia had to develop a "modern" and "rational" culture. Although Muslim by birth, Sjahrir was more of a secularist than his mentor and fellow Minangkabau Mohammad Hatta, Indonesia's first vice president. With his belief in the necessity of a break with tradition, he also held himself aloof from the Muslim community. This reluctance deprived him of the support enjoyed by populist liberals like Hatta and was to remain an enduring vulnerability of his movement.[40]

Unlike Soekarno and Hatta, Sjahrir did not collaborate with the Japanese administration during its occupation of Indonesia, fighting instead in the underground resistance. It was in part a result of his credentials as an anti-Japanese fighter, and someone who (it was hoped) would be acceptable to the British and Americans, that Sjahrir was chosen Indonesia's first prime minister, a post he occupied from November 1945 to June 1947.[41] During these same years Sjahrir's relationship with the Communist Left deteriorated, culminating in his break with Communist-sympathizing socialists in February 1948 and his formation of the PSI. Although some in the new party wanted to transform it into a mass organization, Sjahrir insisted that the party should emphasize the training of "cadres of convinced socialists, who understood the meaning of socialism and its application to Indonesia, rather than seek to build up an amorphous mass party of nominal socialists who would blindly follow the orders of their leaders."[42] Although the decision reflected Sjahrir's anxieties concerning the great divide between tradition and modernity, it was also influenced by his awareness that PSI appeals did not resonate with much of the public.

On these and other points, the New Order's secular modernizers shared much of Sjahrir's vision, as well as his political vulnerabilities. Many of the secular modernizers had begun their careers in the ranks of Sjahrir's PSI. After Soekarno banned the party in 1960, most withdrew from formal political activity but continued their dialogue with liberal Muslims, Christian democrats, and, most significant, reform-minded members of the military.

Some of these refugees from Indonesian socialism were Muslim, others Christian; a few were Hindu or agnostic. Having lived through the political turbulence of the late 1950s and early 1960s, most were convinced that mass politics in a still traditional society was dangerously destabilizing. Indeed, like most of the military command, the secular modernizers blamed parliamentary democracy for the chaos of the Soekarno era. In its place they advocated the formation of an American-style, two-party system. Like Sjahrir, too, the modernizers felt that in the absence of a well-developed middle class, the state and its experts should play a larger role in economic development than had been the case in the early modern West. Finally, sharing Sjahrir's ambivalence toward mass democracy, the secular modernizers argued that full and effective democracy would have to await the maturation of the Indonesian public. This cultural maturation required that the public be educated by an enlightened leadership. Only years later, after many had stopped collaborating with the New Order regime, did the secular modernizers realize that this mixture of progressive idealism and elitist avant-gardism was an invitation for authoritarian abuse.

The secular modernizers also differed from Sjahrir in their attitude toward Marxism. While Sjahrir had drawn on a liberal reading of Marx to develop his ideas on modernization, the secular modernizers put Marx aside in favor of Western modernization theory. Invoking Lucien Pye, S. Eisenstadt, W. Rostow, and (the young) Clifford Geertz and Herbert Feith, they argued that modernization required that Indonesia develop "autonomous" social structures, in which politics was conducted on the basis not of unreflective "primordial" solidarities but of rational and negotiable self-interest.[43] Theirs was a secular and modernist understanding of religion and politics. As mainstream modernization theory prescribed, the secular modernizers believed that progress required that religious ideology be removed from public politics so as to become, above all, a matter of personal piety (chapter 1). Politics after religion's privatization would be conducted not on the basis of primal solidarities but of rational discussion among actors committed to the inexclusive ideologies of citizenship and nation.

Writers associated with the secular modernizers introduced the notion of "primordial solidarities" (*ikatan primordial*) and the related distinctions of *santri* (practicing Muslim) and *abangan* (nominal Muslim of Javanist persuasion) into the nation's official political vocabulary. All three terms were borrowed from the writings of Western analysts, especially the American anthropologist Clifford Geertz. In the secular modernist view, primordial solidarities were deep but essentially nonrational commitments to region, ethnicity, and, most important, religion. In the Soekarno era, these primitive social allegiances had been drawn into national politics. In so doing, the primordialisms had added an irrational and violent element to national politics. The New Order regime cited these alleged precedents to justify its assaults on the party system and its efforts to depoliticize Islam. After 1983 it invoked these same precedents to justify its demand that all organizations accept the *Pancasila* as their sole ideological foundation (*asas tunggal*, chapters 5, 7).

Although many among the secular modernizers had expected that the New Order might rehabilitate the Socialist Party, the government maintained the ban imposed by Soekarno.[44] Although a similar restriction applied to Masyumi, modernist Muslims were allowed to form a new party, the Partai Muslimin Indonesia (chapter 5). Regime strategists calculated that although they had to make concessions to the modernist Muslim community, the PSI was weak enough to be ignored. At the same time, however, some planning agencies in the regime openly recruited PSI intellectuals into their bureau. The people in which the regime was most interested, however, were specialists of technocratic modernization, not political liberals committed to a balance of powers, individual rights, and the rule of law.

From Center to Margins

The secular modernizers' relationship to the regime underwent a rapid and dramatic evolution during the first years of the New Order. The change illustrates how New Order officials drew on the intellectual resources of their civilian advisers, while at the same time excluding them from real power.

The American political scientist R. William Liddle has rightly noted that the secular modernizers were not a unified group, and, "indeed, one of their hallmarks has been their inability to unite organizationally."[45] For a brief period, however, there was one core group among the secular modernists, a network of activists, writers, and intellectuals linked to one of the most remarkable journals of the early New Order, *Mahasiswa Indonesia* [Indonesian student], or *MI*. The subject of a highly original study of New Order ideology and politics by the French historian François Raillon, *MI* was founded on June 19, 1966, by intellectuals associated with anti-Soekarnoist student action fronts. *MI*'s editor-in-chief, Rahman Tolleng, was one of the most brilliant thinkers from the generation of '66. Tolleng was a twenty-nine-year-old Muslim Buginese who had been active in the Socialist Student movement (Gemsos). After the PSI was banned, he and his student associates remained active by maintaining ties with the Siliwangi officers. Based in West Java, the Siliwangi division had the highest percentage of secular-modernist officers in its ranks. Tolleng and the *MI* obtained offices and printing facilities for their newspaper with the help of the outspoken Siliwangi general (and virulent anticommunist) Dharsono and Brigadier General Sudhandi, a director of information and publications in the armed forces.[46]

Over time, the cordial relationship between *MI* and the Siliwangi modernizers gave way to guarded collaboration and, eventually, open conflict. Less than a year after its founding, *MI* launched a media campaign known as "operation crush corruption" (*operasi ganyang korupsi*), in which the newspaper invited disgruntled readers to report instances of corruption to the press. The campaign irritated the paper's military supporters but was not prohibited outright. A few months later, in early 1967, the newspaper escalated its criticism by attacking several of its former colleagues from the student action group KAMI. While making these criticisms, however, the paper was careful to express support for Soeharto. A year later Tolleng was named a member of the parliament (DPR) and the People's Consultative Assembly (MPR).

By 1969, however, the secular modernizer's relationship to the government was again becoming troubled. The election law passed in that year represented a major setback for secular modernizers. The law maintained the ban on the PSI, preserved the system of proportional representation rather than the district system supported by *MI* (which they felt would make politicians more responsive to local constituents), and stipulated that 100 of the parliament's 460 seats were to be filled by presidential appointment.[47] On all these points the government went against *MI*'s and other secular modernizers' recommendations.

Events after 1970 only worsened the relationship between *MI* and the regime. That year saw renewed student protest, as activists tried to revive the (by then disintegrating) student action groups through campaigns against corruption and price increases. Prominent among the protestors were individuals who in later years became some of the most principled democratic critics of the New Order: Arief Budiman, Sjahrir, Marsillam Simandjuntak, and the poet W. S. Rendra. Although sympathetic to the student demands, the *MI* group at first supported the government. Indeed, to the dismay of student reformists, some among its staff even went over to the government party, Golkar. These gestures of loyalty to the government were rewarded in 1971 with the appointment to the cabinet of economic advisers thought broadly sympathetic to *MI*'s views. The appointees included the later architects of the

New Order's market-oriented fiscal policies, including Emil Salim, Widjojo Nitisastro, Sadli, and Professor Subroto.[48]

Events were soon to demonstrate, however, that the imperatives of technocratic modernization could at this point be easily separated from human rights and the rule of law. Even as Rahman Tolleng was set to join the government party, student groups close to him launched fierce attacks on the president's wife, Ibu Tien Soeharto, because of her plans to solicit donations for a theme park of Indonesian culture to be built outside Jakarta. Inspired by the First Lady's trip to Disneyland, Taman Mini Indonesia ("The Park of Mini-Indonesia") was to be built around pavilions modeled on enlarged and idealized versions of ethnic houses found across Indonesia.[49] The project was to be financed in part by regional officials, from whom Madam Tien invited "voluntary" contributions.

Coming just after the president had appealed to citizens to fight waste and dedicate themselves to economic development, the First Lady's project incited lively public criticism. In an unusually blunt editorial, *MI* suggested that the project was "beyond the prerogatives of a presidential spouse" and likened Taman Mini to the ostentatious projects sponsored by former President Soekarno. Soeharto was outraged by this comparison. There followed a tit-for-tat exchange between the secular modernizers and the government, all of which diminished the former group's role in the New Order coalition. The government responded to the Taman Mini debate by establishing a parliamentary commission which eventually recommended that the state provide no more aid for the project. But government hard-liners would not let the matter end there. Unhappy that secular modernizers had been drawn into the ruling coalition in the first place, the hard-liners saw an opportunity to strike. In short order several of the most prominent leaders of the protest groups, including Arief Budiman, H. J. Princen, and T. Mulya Lubis, were arrested. Shortly thereafter the hard-line minister of the interior Amir Machmud[50] suggested that the protestors had been in collusion with "PSI" liberals and imposed new limits on the heretofore open press. He also banned student activists from engaging in political activities in the countryside. In justifying this last restriction, Machmud cited the concept of the "floating mass" (*massa terapung*). This was the doctrine that barred political parties from the countryside during all periods except national elections (held once every five years). Originally the prohibition had been intended to ensure that the masses would not be "distracted" from economic development. Ironically the doctrine of the floating mass had been introduced into Indonesian political discourse by activists associated with *Mahasiswa Indonesia*. The incident provided a poignant illustration of how the secular modernizers' ideas could be used for authoritarian ends.

Despite the government's crackdown, *MI* and the secular modernizers kept up their criticism. For the remainder of 1972 *MI* boldly promoted a campaign for a free press and vigorous defense of human rights. A longtime friend of *MI* and prominent activist from the generation of '66, Adnan Buyung Nasution went one step further, establishing Indonesia's first legal aid society, the Lembaga Bantuan Hukum (LBH). In the 1980s and 1990s the LBH became the nation's leading legal spokesperson for human rights. The social democratic activist Arief Budiman also joined with MI at this time in a campaign to defend the rights of former Communist prisoners, the first of whom had just been released back into society.

The interior minister responded to this defiance by escalating his repression. He forbade the newly established legal aid institutes from operating in the countryside and attacked what he referred to as "thirty extremists in the parliament"—a clear reference to, among others, liberal socialists and secular modernizers.[51] Despite these measures, the MI leadership did not back down. It criticized the government's mishandling of rice stocks after the poor harvest of 1972; blasted the director of the state oil firm, Ibnu Sutowo, for corruption; and accused the government of turning the government political party into a vehicle for military power.

One line of criticism more than any other, however, sealed, MI's fate. In early August 1973 the paper published an editorial warning that a social revolt was possible if the concerns of ordinary people continued to be ignored. The story appeared just before a wave of protests spread across Indonesia. The first of these was an anti-Chinese riot in Bandung; it was followed in October and November by widespread student and Muslim criticisms of the president's personal assistants, Ali Moertopo and Sujono Humardhani. On November 30 intellectuals and politicians supportive of the student protests released what was the first major manifesto against the New Order. This event marked a turning point in democratic Muslim and secular modernizers' opposition to the regime.[52]

Officially the government blamed these disturbances on the Communist Party. But government reports also hinted that secular modernizers linked to disaffected segments of the military might be involved as well. When the anti-government demonstrations first began, General Soemitro, the commander of the state's most powerful security organization, set out on a nationwide tour to meet the protestors face to face. In his meetings he acknowledged the legitimacy of the protestors' complaints and agreed that the government needed to take a new direction. Others in the New Order elite, including the president's personal assistant, Ali Moertopo, rejected these conciliatory gestures, implying that Soemitro was disloyal. At first Soeharto stayed aloof from the fray, allowing the dispute to drag on. On January 2, 1974, however, the president revealed his hand, with a decisive show of support for Moertopo. General Soemitro was forced to climb down. He made a humiliating public appearance with a beaming Ali Moertopo. Soemitro and the regime reformists had been decisively beaten.

Less than two weeks later, on January 15 and 16, Jakarta was shaken by fierce demonstrations on the occasion of a visit by the Japanese prime minister

Tanaka. Officially nine demonstrators were killed and twenty-three wounded; unofficial accounts put the toll higher. In the aftermath of this violence, which came to be known as the "Malari" affair, there were widespread arrests of young Muslims, former leaders of the PSI, human rights activists, and secular modernizers, including Rahman Tolleng of MI. Ali Moertopo alleged that the incident had been masterminded by the PSI and Masyumi. Tolleng countered that much of the violence had been instigated by agents provocateurs under Moertopo's command.

There has been much speculation as to the precise cause of these intra-elite disputes. Harold Crouch has argued that the disagreement was above all a military rivalry, pitting senior commanders close to the president against a new generation of professional officers from the military academies. In contrast, François Raillon has suggested that the disagreement originated in rivalry between a moderately liberal, pro-American faction, on the one hand, and a more conservative, Japanese-oriented group, on the other.[53] Both accounts correctly highlight that, rather than a unified bloc, the New Order elite was rife with factionalist rivalries and competing cliques. More ominous yet, there was evidence that, as in the late Soekarno era (chapter 3), political rivalries had led some in the elite to exacerbate tensions in society so as to weaken their rivals.

The Malari affair dealt a decisive blow to the secular modernizers and the controlled liberalization for which they had hoped. Although the regime adopted a few of their ideas on party simplification and economic restructuring, these policies were applied in a selective manner that retained none of the modernizers' concern for transparency and the rule of law. Moreover, as government revenues rose in the aftermath of the worldwide oil crisis in 1973 (which gave the state unparalleled revenues), even the technocratic portion of the secular modernizers' program was scaled back. Flush with new revenues, the elite expanded its patronage and launched a new and inefficient program for state-owned enterprise.[54]

Secularism Sidelined

The secular modernizers' marginalization was also evident in the government's policy on Islam. Although the secular modernizers included Christians in their ranks, the majority came from Muslim backgrounds. Rahman Tolleng, the editor in chief of *Mahasiswa Indonesia*, was himself a devout Muslim who in his early years had had ties with the modernist Muslim Pupils Organization (*Pelajar Islam*) as well as the PSI. Under his direction, however, *Mahasiswa Indonesia* became outspoken in its support for a greater separation of religion and state. In late 1968 a portion of his editorial staff quit to establish a rival journal, *Mimbar Demokrasi*, the key feature of which was its greater commitment to Muslim politics.[55]

More than other secular nationalist groupings, MI emphasized that responsibility for religious piety and education should be taken not by the state but by private individuals and civic associations. Challenging the government's subsidies for religious education, MI editorials insisted that the state should limit itself to providing general lessons on comparative religion. Indeed, several early MI editorials portrayed religion as a source of intolerance and tyranny. A controversial article in 1967 referred to religion as a cause of bloodshed in Europe; the article's remarks seemed a none-too-veiled reference to the Indonesian killings of 1965–66. MI also questioned the need for the Ministry of Religion. MI editorials suggested that some in the ministry sought to revive the Jakarta Charter and pressure mystics into Islamic conformity.[56] In this and other instances, the secular modernists sought to build an alliance with *abangan* (nominally Islamic) Javanese and other religious nonconformists.

No single development so clearly illustrates that New Order strategists were not uncompromising secularists or simple-minded Javanists than the failure of MI to convince government strategists of the wisdom of these policies. However much some in the inner circles of the government might have wished to implement secularist policies—and however much Western observers have been inclined to believe that they did—the government always steered clear of real political secularization. The Department of Religion not only survived under the New Order but saw its staffing and programs expand enormously.

This expansion reflected the influence of legislative committees in the parliament and Provisional People's Consultative Assembly (MPRS) in the years leading up to the clampdown of the early 1970s. In 1966 the MPRS made religious instruction compulsory in both public and private schools, from primary school to university. During these same early years (1967–71) the Department of Religion expanded its staff by an astounding 60 percent, transforming itself into the largest state ministry. As Donald K. Emmerson has noted, this was "by far the highest rate of growth of any comparable department during this period."[57] During these same years, the departments of religion, education, and the interior sponsored a series of programs for cultural "building up" (*pembinaan*) in which ex-PKI strongholds, purged of their Communist cadres, were targeted for religious indoctrination. In West Java, southern Sulawesi, and a few other areas, local officials went even further, introducing the Jakarta Charter into their regulations, thereby making the state responsible for the implementation of Islamic law, even among nominal Muslims who wanted nothing of it.[58]

At times, however, the early New Order's policy on Islam was buffeted by contrary winds. Responding to what it saw as Muslim defiance, the government during 1972–73 distanced itself from its main Muslim allies. It made clear, for example, that it supported religious indoctrination but felt that the regional initiatives applying the Jakarta Charter went too far. In 1973 the People's Consultative Assembly responsible for formulation of guidelines for state policy over the next five-year development period backed away from the MPRS's characterizations of religion as the foundation of development, a clear slap in the face of organized Islam.[59] Not coincidentally, Muslim representation in the new MPR had fallen significantly from the levels seen in 1966–68.

In 1973 the MPR seemed to take this opposition to organized Islam one step further. It presented proposals designed to give religion and "belief" (*keper-cayaan*)—meaning, in this instance, the mystical religion practiced by some citizens, and regarded as heterodox by many Muslims—equal standing in the eyes of the state. That same year the government introduced legislation for a new marriage law that proposed to "unify" all legal regulation of marriage and divorce. The new regulations would impose sweeping restrictions on polygyny, give women greater rights in divorce than recognized under Islamic law, and move most of the authority for marriage and divorce out of Islamic courts. These proposals caused great consternation among Muslim groupings.[60] But the bill's provisions were welcomed by secular women's groups, who, in 1957 and 1967, had supported efforts to move jurisdiction over Muslim marriage from Islamic to state courts.

Seen from the vantage point of these measures, the New Order appeared to be moving away from its early position toward a secular modernist posture. Indeed, as will become clearer in the next chapter, the period from 1973 to 1985 was a low point in Muslim-government relations. However, the govern-ment's reaction to the protest inspired by the marriage law provides a glimpse into how the New Order elite established its policy priorities and shows why these actions did not, over the long run, work to the favor of either secularists or Javanists. Principle always played second fiddle to power politics. Bypassing the secular parliamentarians who had sponsored the marriage bill, military officials took charge of the negotiations with Muslim representatives over the marriage law. They negotiated directly with representatives from Nahdlatul Ulama and the state-created Islamic political party, the PPP. It was only after the text of an agreement was worked out between army officials and Muslim representatives that parliamentary deputies were invited back into the discus-sions, essentially to rubberstamp a finished agreement. Press reports indicated that people in the government party, Golkar, were unhappy over the govern-ment's handling of the affair. However, as Leo Suryadinata has observed, in this instance military interests prevailed over civilian. And the military's interest lay in muting popular protest and depriving organized Muslim groupings of an excuse to mobilize against the government.[61]

The example illustrates what would be a recurring theme of government policy on Islam. Although some officials espoused a less conciliatory line, and although it launched fierce offensives against specific Muslim organizations (see below), the government never made secular modernist or Javanist values a high priority. Secularist and Javanist voices were heard in the regime's inner circles, but they were ignored when they contradicted basic regime inter-ests. Soeharto's preoccupation with power above all else prevented him from adopting a consistent position on religious matters. His unprincipled opportunism wreaked havoc with the efforts of those in the military and government interested in building a pluralist nationalism (chapter 7).

Although, in the first years of the New Order, Javanists still represented a significant constituency in the country, the secular nationalists remained as they had always been: a well-educated and intelligent elite without any significant mass base. Writing in 1973, R. William Liddle made the perspicacious observation that by rejecting the religious loyalties and beliefs dear to so many Indonesians, secular modernizers had "lost the ability to come to grips" with forces important to the nation's politics.[62] In the absence of a mass constituency, he added, the secular modernizers placed their hope in the armed forces. Initially they believed that the military could be a force for progressive modernization. By the early 1970s, however, it was clear that military reformers had been outmaneuvered by conservative rivals.

In the last years before its banning, *Mahasiswa Indonesia* renounced its earlier enthusiasm for the West and began to criticize the unregulated influx of imported cultural objects. In an article written by a brilliant young author, Goenawan Mohamad,[63] the newspaper bemoaned the uncritical thirst for foreign consumer goods, as well as the proliferation of nightclubs, massage parlors, gambling casinos, and pornographic films. The modernizing elite had not played the role its supporters had hoped. Instead, the article observed, modernization had allowed the ascent of yet another undemocratic elite.[64] In this and other statements, *MI* turned away from its earlier fascination with modernization theory and appealed for an endogenous development model.

This plaint has remained a recurring theme of liberal and social-democratic criticism in Indonesia. However, although *MI*'s secular modernists proclaimed their commitment to a bold "new syncretism" based on indigenous values rather than foreign modernity, they were unable to devise the terms for such an entity. There *was* one group of public intellectuals that shared these concerns about the influx of foreign values: modernist Muslims. They had less difficulty identifying a constituency for their ideas. With a clear social base and secure cultural identity, their chances for becoming a major political force were to increase as those of the secular modernists declined.

JAVANISM AND THE STATE

The complex play of interests in the early New Order shows that it is too simple to say, as many observers have, that the regime was consistently hostile to Islam. During the 1970s and 1980s it was a shibboleth in some Indonesian studies circles that the tensions between organized Islam and the Soeharto regime reflected age-old cultural conflicts. "Soeharto and the generals on whom he relies were brought up in a Hindu-Javanized milieu that made them more nominal (*abangan*) than practicing (*santri*) Muslims."[65] Even in the late 1990s, after twenty years of Islamic revival and ten years of regime courtship of conservative Islam, a handful of researchers continued to utter this refrain, as if nothing in Indonesian politics had changed and its central dynamic were really the perennial struggle of "Hindu" Javanists against *santri* Muslims.[66]

However, as the regime's relationship with secular modernizers has indicated, the religious policies of the early New Order were always guided by varied interests. The practice of power mandated inconsistency of principle. This tendency was equally apparent regarding the second of the two groupings discussed in this chapter, the nominally Muslim practitioners of Javanist Islam known as *abangan* or *kejawen* "Javanists."

It is well known that throughout his career President Soeharto has relied on Javanese spiritual advisers commonly referred to as *dhukun* (J., "specialist in esoteric arts"). One of the president's two personal aides during the early years of the New Order, Sujono Humardani (now deceased), was a leading patron of Javanist organizations and a master of the mystical arts himself. Sujono is said to have been a tireless spokesperson for Javanist interests before the president.[67] He was also the president's spiritual mentor in matters of mystical power.

However close Sujono and Soeharto's relationship, the president's range of spiritual interests underwent an important adjustment in the early 1980s. While continuing his mystical exercises, the president hired a Muslim preacher previously active in the armed forces to serve as his personal instructor in Islamic devotion. Accompanied by several of his children, the president studied Arabic-language passages from the Qur'an and hadith, and developed a respectable mastery of basic Muslim greetings, prayers, and devotion. As news of the president's piety spread in the early 1990s, many progovernment Muslims pointed out that in his youth Soeharto had briefly attended Muhammadiyah schools, where he was exposed to modernist views. The suggestion was that the president had always had modernist sympathies, and these were now only becoming more pronounced.

Neither this early schooling nor his devotional training in the 1980s, however, dimmed the president's enthusiasm for power-oriented mystical magic. Confronting the most serious political challenge of his thirty-two-year rule in 1997, the president is known to have consulted *dhukun* specializing in political arts. In 1998 the president is rumored even to have recruited a West African magician renowned for his political magic. Whatever the truth of this story (which, if true, is evidence of a most unusual "globalization" indeed), Soeharto has repeatedly demonstrated that he sees no inconsistency between Islamic piety and elite mysticism.

New Order history shows, then, that one should not make too much of the former president's Javanist predilections, since these were always but one influence on the regime's religious policy. Indeed, although well disposed to elite variants of the mystical arts, it was clear even in the early years of the New

Order that Soeharto had little sympathy for the populist variants of Javanist religion that had flourished in the Soekarno era. These folk Javanisms were too independent, too popular, and too left-wing for the architect of New Order authoritarianism.

The folk Javanist community had provided the bulk of support for both the Indonesian Communist Party and the left-wing of the Nationalist Party in the final years of the Soekarno era. In the aftermath of the destruction of the PKI, one of the first ambitions of the Soeharto regime was to destroy or neutralize left-wing associations among Javanists, and win that community back to conservative nationalism. In its first two years, the New Order banned more than one hundred left-wing mystical organizations, including all those linked to the Communist Party or openly anti-Islamic in their ideology.[68] These measures were intended in the first place to placate conservative Muslims who were demanding that all mystical sects be banned. Equally important from the regime's perspective, however, the policy had the welcome effect of making the remaining Javanist organizations dependent on regime protection. From an outside perspective, this policy might appear "pro-Javanist," as has often been argued. However, in the 1990s, when political realignments dictated a new policy, the regime did not hesitate to reverse itself, embracing conservative Islam while sacrificing popular Javanism (chapters 6, 7).

Over the long term, then, the big losers under the New Order era were not *santri* Muslims but populist Javanists. Although Soeharto pretended to be their patron, he did so on the condition that they be tethered to a tight state leash. Their villages were subjected to government-mandated programs of religious "building up" (*pembinaan*). Their children were required to receive instruction in a state-stipulated Islam. And any Javanist organization that attempted to promote its tradition as an explicit alternative to Islam was banned.

Not surprisingly, then, by the 1980s anthropologists and journalists were reporting that normative Islam was making great progress in many former strongholds of secular nationalism, while public Javanism was in decline.[69] The institutions of *public* Javanism were hit particularly hard. In most of the countryside, for example, the lavish communal rituals (*slametan desa*) celebrated by Javanists at village spirit shrines (*dhanyang*), so vividly captured in Clifford Geertz's *The Religion of Java*,[70] had disappeared by the late 1980s. Where they survive, most operate as private celebrations no longer sanctioned by local authorities.[71]

In this sense, New Order policies succeeded in bringing about what devout Muslims had long advocated: a relegation of Javanist spirituality to the sphere not of religion (*agama, din*) but of personalized religious belief (*kepercayaan*). Unlike some contemporary Western views (chapter 1), religion in mainstream Islam is not a matter of inner belief or personal conviction alone but of divinely enjoined commandments to which one "submits" as a believer. Religion (A., *din*, I., *agama*) is first and foremost what *God* commands, not what an individual feels, desires, or holds dear. The prioritizing of religious experience in normative Islam works contrary, then, to religion in individualistic liberalism. God's commands are what is essential, and it is this august example to which individual belief and feeling should conform. From this perspective, the Western liberal idea that inner belief is the essence of religion errs in shifting emphasis away from a properly religious attitude of humble surrender to the divine toward an immodest affirmation of the self.[72]

Javanists and Muslim mystics have often rejected this normative understanding of religion in favor of a more gently relativist view. Javanists in particular often point out that the commands of Islam enjoy no more privileged epistemological status than mystical experience. In the mystic's eyes, the things that pious Muslims called divine law or commandments are, in the end, just one more product of human "experience" (*rasa*). The normative Muslim's emphasis on the objectivized immutability of *shariah* is the same: just one more interpretation among many. *Kepercayaan* "belief," then, is the equal of *shariah* commands because, notwithstanding normative Muslim claims to the contrary, everything is in the eye of the beholder. This argument underlay Javanist demands that *kepercayaan* belief be made the equal of state-recognized religions.

By outlawing or crippling independent organizations, the New Order government made it difficult for Javanists to promote their beliefs as a public alternative to normative Islam. Javanists were left with Soeharto as their first line of defense, but Soeharto was a fickle friend indeed. There was no clearer illustration of the painful ironies of the mystics' dependency than Soeharto's public pronouncements on Javanist mysticism in the late 1980s, as he began his celebrated policy shifts on Islam. In a speech presented in late 1988, for example, Soeharto urged members of mystical organizations to return to their religion of birth (*agama induk*). Mysticism, he said, should not be an alternative to one's birth religion, but its complement. Although many mystics rejected this proposal and insisted that their organizations would still admit people from all religions, some of the most prominent national organizations—especially those controlled by Soeharto cronies—went along with the president. Some began to identify themselves as Islamic and to define their mystical practices as personal "belief" within Islam, not an alternative "religion." When, in 1989, the national congress of Indonesian mystical associations declined to accept a chairman recommended by the regime, Soeharto responded by refusing to recognize the organization itself. The result was a disaster for mystics. After 1989 they were never again allowed to hold a national congress, and their already limited influence in government circles declined precipitously.

Nahdlatul Ulama and the Politics of Islam

The third and final group I examine in this chapter is Nahdlatul Ulama, the association of "traditionalist" Muslim scholars established in 1926.[73] As with other organizations in the early New Order, NU had a complex and shifting relationship to the Soeharto regime. At first NU had expected to be a privileged partner of the government. Since the Soekarno era the NU leadership had regarded itself as the primary representative of the Muslim community to the government and the military, and it felt all the more confident of this role in the early New Order. Unlike the modernist Masyumi (chapter 5), no faction in Nahdlatul Ulama had gone over to the side of the rebels during the regional rebellions of 1957–60. Indeed, identified as these rebellions were with modernist Islam and anti-Javanese sentiment, the NU leadership had been openly hostile toward the rebels. While Masyumi was tarred as a traitor to the nation, NU presented itself as a loyal ally to the president and the armed forces.

NU expressed its opposition to the rebellions not from outside Soekarno's Guided Democracy government but from within. From 1959 to 1965 Nahdlatul Ulama was a central, though often unhappy, player in Soekarno's NASAKOM government. When Soekarno had first proposed a return to the Constitution of 1945 and the establishment of a "Guided Democracy," NU, along with the other Muslim parties, had rejected the idea. Eventually, however, the NU leadership relented and supported the president.

The gesture was typical of NU's relationship with Soekarno and other nationalist leaders. However much they railed against secularism and communism and spoke in favor of an Islamic state, the NU leadership consistently showed itself more willing than the modernists to make concessions to the Soekarno government. The party's accommodationism has often been dismissed by critics as simple opportunism, inspired by the leadership's desire to maintain its staffing monopoly in the Ministry of Religion (which it had enjoyed since the early 1950s). The ministry was indeed an important patronage resource for NU. Based as it was in the countryside among the poorest segment of the Muslim community, NU enjoyed few of the advantages of the modernist Muslim middle class. Employment in religious administration was one of the few avenues of upward mobility for NU's associates.

Although there was an economic calculus to NU's accommodationism, then, NU was not guided by crude economism alone. Despite his flirtation with nationalist Marxism, the NU leadership had long held Soekarno in high regard. His popularity in NU circles was apparent as early as 1940. In that year Soekarno published a series of articles in which he praised the Turkish secularist leader Mustafa Kemal Ataturk for having brought progress to Turkey by effecting a separation of Islam and state. He blamed much of the backwardness of the Muslim world on the tendency of traditionalist Muslims to reduce Islam to matters of traditional jurisprudence (*fiqh*).[74] Despite these criticisms, in June 1940 a closed-door meeting of the NU leadership voted 10 to 1 in favor of Soekarno over Mohammad Hatta as the future president of an independent Indonesia. They did so despite evidence that on religious matters Hatta was considerably more pious than Soekarno.

The incident is interesting because it shows that even before independence there was a pattern to NU's political behavior which had less to do with economic opportunism than with a potent mix of nationalism, Javanese ethnic pride, and multi-interest pragmatism. In general, in fact, NU has always been a less "ideological" organization than its modernist rivals. The organization's center of gravity lay not in ideology, least of all of an abstractly systematized sort, but in a way of life associated with the religious scholars (*ulama*) who comprised the party's core. Each religious leader has his followers. Each also has an array of social and economic enterprises on which his spiritual and educational enterprise depend (chapter 3). These day-to-day involvements have a "logic of the concrete" which ensures that NU's leaders are rarely guided by abstract principles alone. Their job is to defend a community and a way of life. The needs of that community required not ideological purity but a complex balancing of multiple interests.

One of the few Western observers to have grasped the contextual logic of NU's practice was the American political scientist Allan A. Samson, who studied NU during the early years of the New Order. Comparing NU with the modernist Masyumi, Samson observed that NU was less a "goal-centered political party as . . . a religious welfare association primarily concerned with the defense of traditionalist Islam and the retention of religious and personal interests."[75] During debates in the Constitutional Assembly from 1957 to 1959 NU's political leaders joined with the Masyumi in advocating the establishment of an Islamic state. But Samson remarks wryly that NU's leaders were "never wholly committed . . . to this attempt."[76]

In these and other matters NU's behavior also showed the influence of the organization's unusual leadership structure. Since its founding in 1926 the organization had a dual leadership, divided between, on the one hand, its Tanfidziyah, or executive body, and its Syuriyah, or council of religious scholars. The former tended (and tends still today) to be dominated by Jakarta-based politicians, pragmatic and cosmopolitan in their dealings with outsiders. Although they intervene in party affairs on only select occasions, the members of the Syuriyah board are, in principle, the organization's preeminent leaders. Comprised of prominent *ulama* recruited from across Indonesia (especially Java), the Syuriyah makes sure that party policies are in accord with Islamic law, especially the Shafi'i school of law to which NU adheres.[77]

The relationship between NU's two administrative bodies was formalized at the time of the organization's founding in 1926. It took on a special importance, however, after the tumultuous changes of 1952. In that year NU withdrew from Masyumi, which had operated as a pan-Islamic political federation uniting traditionalists and modernists since 1945. The NU leadership withdrew from Masyumi in protest over what they regarded as the party's domination by modernist Muslims, particularly those linked to the Persis leader Mohammad Natsir (chapter 5). Having withdrawn from the Masyumi, the NU leadership was faced with the formidable task of organizing its own political party. Lacking well-educated cadres, the NU responded to this challenge by recruiting politicians who had no previous association with the NU.[78] Once again, this action showed that the Syuriyah board was unbothered about collaborating with "secular" politicians. The board was well aware that politics is the art of the possible and that this art requires that one balance an array of interests rather than just one. The creation of the party also reinforced the dualized structure of authority in the organization, shifting management of daily affairs into the hands of men prone to an instrumental view of politics. As long as the politicians defended Muslim interests and NU's role in the Department of Religion, the Syuriyah board granted them great latitude.

Indonesian commentators on Nahdlatul Ulama sometimes compare the organization's internal dynamics to those of traditional Qur'anic boarding schools (*pesantren*). Historically those schools were organized around the charismatic personality of a senior religious leader (*kyai*). The *kyai* would delegate authority for certain matters to some of his own family members and senior students. Otherwise, however, the school was loosely organized, with no formal lists of students, fuzzy boundaries between class levels, and a variety of loosely coordinated activities over the course of the day. Seeking special varieties of religious knowledge (*ilmu*), advanced students came and went, the best among them traveling from *pesantren* to *pesantren* in search of specialized religious knowledge (*ilmu*).[79]

Under different circumstances, NU's decentralized structure and its level-headed pragmatism might have become significant resources for a contextual and empirical reinterpretation of Muslim politics. The history of democratization in the West shows us again and again that democratic habits often begin when actors put aside unworkable idealizations and recognize that their efforts to realize absolutist goals do more harm than good. In sixteenth- and seventeenth-century Europe, Protestants and Catholics agreed to stop killing each other, not because of some sudden theological enlightenment but because decades of bloodshed had led them to the realization that post-Reformation wars of religious purification were unwinnable and a greater evil than religious diversity.[80]

For compromises like these to have an enduring political impact, however, at some point they must be elevated above immediate self-interest and mere political expedience. It is not hard to imagine that a shift from momentary expedience to principled pluralism could have taken place in the Nahdlatul Ulama of the Soekarno era. We know that even in the late 1950s some among the NU leadership had begun to formulate principles whereby the pluralistic compromises of the Soekarno era were legitimated on grounds other than narrow self-interest. As early as 1957, in fact, a bright young religious scholar from East Java, Achmad Siddiq, wrote an article in which he took issue with most of his colleagues, arguing that Islam does not require the establishment of an Islamic state. He went on to assert that Muslims should accept the pluralism embodied in the *Pancasila*.[81] (In 1984 Siddiq worked with Abdurrahman Wahid to urge NU to accept the government demand that the organization recognize the *Pancasila* as its sole ideological foundation; see chapter 7). In these and other instances, and as is still the case today, NU displayed an uncanny ability to generate highly original and tolerant thinkers. The organization did so in part because, however conservative its masses, its scholars were confident of their identity as Muslims and the juridical grounds for rejecting superficial and unrealizable essentializations of "Islam." For them, Islam was this-worldly as well as transcendent; it was too directly implicated in the welfare of believers to be reduced to utopian abstractions. Beyond all the talk of "opportunism" and the charisma of its leaders, then, NU possessed an intellectual culture rich with the potential for a principled and empirical reconceptualization of Muslim politics.

But this was the tragedy of Muslim politics in the Soekarno era. Under the harsh political regimen of Guided Democracy, there was little chance that this pluralist potential might blossom into an enduring institutional form. NU was the weakest of the three groupings officially united under Soekarno's NASAKOM alliance of nationalists, Muslims, and Communists. During the final years of his rule, Soekarno preferred to work with the Communists more than with NU. Equally unfortunate for any principled pluralism, the Communist Party was intent on its own utopian abstraction, centered on a revolutionary program of mass mobilization. That campaign brought them squarely into confrontation with NU. In these uncivil circumstances, the prospects for a principled legitimation of pluralism became slim indeed. Rather than enunciating the joyous terms for a new Muslim politics, NU prepared itself for war.

In the face of the growing power of the PKI and the growing reliance on extra-constitutional politics, NU's strategy seemed clear. Its mainstream leadership began an offstage collaboration with the army (chapter 3). The relationship evolved through several stages. In the early 1960s NU joined forces with ABRI (Indonesian Armed Forces) to oppose the joint PNI-PKI legislation on land and sharecropping reform. In 1963 the NU leader Idham Chalid was alone among party leaders in defending the army's efforts to establish a labor organization as an alternative to the PKI-dominated labor federation, SOBSI (*Sentral Organisasi Buruh Seluruh Indonesia*). In fact Chalid went further, calling for cooperation with the army's labor federation.[82] The army's SOKSI (Central Organization of Indonesian Socialist Workers) recruited most of its membership from laborers employed on army-controlled enterprises and estates. During 1965–66 this union's membership joined with NU in the campaign to wipe out the PKI.[83] In all this there was little likelihood of NU strengthening its habits of the democratic heart.

From Collaboration to Confrontation

Having cooperated with the military during 1965–66, NU expected to benefit from the altered political climate of the early New Order. Again, unlike Masyumi, the traditionalists had managed to bring their political organization into the New Order more or less intact. And unlike the PNI, NU was not tainted by its ties to President Soekarno or accusations of leftists in its ranks. In August 1966 Achmad Sjaichu, NU's second vice president, compared NU's alliance with the army to the relationship between "two brothers."[84]

At first it seemed that NU was to be rewarded for its loyalty. In May 1966 Sjaichu was elected president of parliament. That same year the most famous of NU's Jakarta-based politicians, Z.E. Subchan, was elected vice president of the Provisional People's Consultative Assembly, a position he held until 1971. Officially a fourth vice president of NU, Subchan was the kind of brilliant eccentric only imaginable in the NU. Still today in Jakartan circles he is remembered for his taste for alcohol, dance, and nightclubs, as well as his notably un-Javanese habit of speaking his mind. While the leader of the NU Syuriyah board, Idham Chalid, had defended President Soekarno during the Guided Democracy period, Subchan had been an outspoken critic. While Idham sought to work with the president in the NASAKOM government, Subchan forged closer ties with the army commander, General Nasution.[85] While Idham continued to express his support for Soekarno after September 30, 1965, Subchan worked with anticommunist Catholics and modernist Muslims to bring Soekarno down. With Harry Chan Silalahi of the Catholic Party and Mar'ie Muhammad of the HMI, he founded the first anticommunist action group, the "Action Front to Crush the Counterrevolutionary Thirtieth of September Movement."[86] This group was the first to sponsor mass rallies against the PKI, the first on October 4 and the second, which turned violent, on October 8.

Subchan's ties to the military dated from the revolutionary era when he, a successful businessman, had helped purchase arms in Singapore.[87] When anticommunist groups had mobilized on campuses and in the capital in the early 1960s, Subchan developed ties not only with fellow members of the NU but with Chinese Catholics and modernist Muslim students.

Subchan had expected that in the aftermath of the coup a reformist wing of the army, under the direction of General Nasution and the Siliwangi modernizers, would become the dominant force in the new government. But Nasution was a Sumatran and a pious moderate Muslim in a military dominated by Javanists and secular modernizers. Worse yet, Nasution had a cool relationship with the man who had directed the campaign against the coup leaders, General Soeharto. In 1959, when he was army chief of staff, General Nasution had relieved Soeharto of his command of the Central Javanese Diponegoro Division. General Nasution was said to have been unhappy with the extent to which Soeharto was involved in "fund-raising."[88]

In the weeks after September 30, 1965, it became increasingly clear that Soeharto and his associates, not General Nasution, were the real powers-to-be. In the months to come, it became even clearer that the NU leadership had serious differences with the government over matters of religious policy. In early 1966, even before President Soekarno's full fall from power, there was a sharp exchange between government officials and Muslim representatives over Muslim plans to revive the Jakarta Charter and, with it, government enforcement of Islamic law. Over the next few months the NU backed away from the hardline demands of some modernist Muslims, insisting that what it sought was the application of *shariah* within a *Pancasilaist* state. This vague formulation seemed to signal NU's agreement with the military's refrain that only the *Pancasila* could serve as the basis for the nation. But the formulation left notably unclear just how *shariah* was to be enforced. Would penalties be imposed on those who refused its application? Would the many ex-Communists now converting from Islam be subject to prosecution or death? In statements at this time, Muslim supporters of the Jakarta Charter took care to reassure Christians that non-Muslims would be spared the provisions of *shariah* law. But *shariah* supporters provided no such reassurances to Javanese mystics or nominal Muslims.

The debate over the Jakarta Charter continued for the first two years of the New Order. In early 1968, however, NU changed its tack. It expressed full support for the *Pancasila* state but added that, under the terms of the agreement reached in 1959, the source of the *Pancasila* itself was the Jakarta Charter. The NU leadership thereby claimed that the *Pancasila* was not only compatible with *shariah* but required its implementation. Other Muslim groups soon joined the chorus demanding the application of *shariah* and insisting that such an action did not violate the *Pancasila*.[89] Breaking with his own government, the minister of religion, Kyai Dachlan (affiliated with the NU), expressed support for this reform, calling those who objected to the Jakarta Charter hypocrites.

Faced with this controversy, armed forces representatives finally stepped in and demanded an end to all discussion of the Jakarta Charter. Military spokespersons insisted that there be no return to the divisive ideological debates of the late Soekarno era. Undaunted, Subchan and his colleagues pressed forward with calls for other radical reforms. Fearful that early elections would work to the benefit of Muslims, the army urged a delay in the scheduling of the vote. NU demanded they be held in 1967.[90] In 1969 NU also objected to the government's demand that the government be allowed to appoint 20 percent of the deputies to national and regional parliament.[91] The NU press also criticized the regime's foreign policy, demanding a harder line on Israel. NU representatives also called for limits on foreign investment, protection for Muslim textile firms threatened by Japanese investment, and limits on Chinese enterprise in the countryside.[92]

Few of these efforts significantly impacted government policy, but they did seal NU's political fate. By the mid-1970s Nahdlatul Ulama had moved from being the closest of the government's Muslim allies to its strongest critic. The government responded to this and other defiance by hardening its stance toward NU and the entire Muslim community. A 1968 reorganization of the parliament saw the number of Muslim deputies drop from the 42 percent who had sat in the 1955 parliament (the last one freely elected) to 28 percent. In the cabinet announced shortly thereafter, only four of the twenty-four ministers appointed were from Islamic parties.[93] With these actions Soeharto showed that those who defied his demands could expect to be barred from government patronage.

CONCLUSION

Despite its repression of Muslim political initiatives, the New Order government continued to make significant concessions to NU and other Muslim organizations on matters of religious education and "building up" (*pembinaan*). In fact, the scale of New Order subsidies to religious programs was like nothing ever before seen in Indonesian history. In 1985 a French and an Indonesian researcher commented on the impact of government religious programs in one of the most frequently targeted provinces, East Java. They observed that Islamic bureaus for the propagation of the faith were "present in all thirty-seven districts of East Java and in permanent contact with agents for the transmission of Islam. . . . Being a total of approximately sixty-five thousand people, a number that represents a well-implanted network in rural society and therefore a line of transmission quantitatively equal to those that the army, Ministry of Interior, or national education dispose."[94]

The shifting alliances of the early New Order demonstrate, of course, that its support for Islamic predication in no way diminished the regime's opposition to Muslim political autonomy. Nonetheless it is important not to interpret retrospectively and assume that everything in the New Order's religious programs was contrived from the start. An unsteady coalition, the early New Order had no master plan for Islam. In their first years Soeharto and his military supporters explored relationships with a diverse array of allies, including secular modernizers, Javanists, and Muslims. Having strengthened its hold on power by 1969, however, the regime's attitude toward its coalition partners hardened, as did its policy on Islam. The regime rid itself of the more troublesome elements of its anticommunist coalition. Determined to prevent the emergence of independent social organizations, it eviscerated the very associations it had earlier exploited to destroy the PKI. Organized Islam was pushed out of the ruling coalition but in a way intended to guarantee that it would never again become an effective claimant to state power.

It is important to remember, however, that the purge of New Order allies was not limited to organized Islam. Military reformists were also silenced. Popular

Javanist associations that longed for ideological independence were banned. Secular modernizers were accepted only on the condition that they emphasize technical modernization and leave aside their concern for the rule of law. Since they operated on the margins of formal politics, it took longer to get student activists in line, but by 1974 they, too, were being smothered by state controls. The logic of Soeharto's rule was not blind opposition to political Islam but a determination to centralize power and destroy all centers of civil autonomy and non-state authority.

The organizations that presented the biggest threat to the regime's monopoly of power were the political parties. Among them, Nahdlatul Ulama posed the greatest challenge. Its leaders felt that the regime was in their debt, and they defiantly insisted that it make good on its promises. In the end, however, there was a steep price to be paid for this defiance. In the aftermath of the 1971 elections NU lost the one ministry it still controlled, the Ministry of Religion. The post of minister went to a new and relatively unknown man, Mukti Ali. Ali would prove a serious and decent minister—a modernist with *pesantren* experience and progressive ideas on matters of Islamic education, law, and inter-religious dialogue. But the loss of the ministry was a great blow to NU, stripping it of employment opportunities and prestige.

Although all Indonesia's political parties were crippled by New Order restrictions, NU was the biggest loser. Among all the parties it had best weathered the New Order storm, but in the end it had little to show for its efforts. The lesson seemed clear: The New Order government was determined to block political Islam's advance. Amid the labyrinth erected to confine, however, other Muslims were about to discover an unexpected path forward.

Chapter Five

THE MODERNIST TRAVAIL

THE NEW ORDER regime presented modernist Muslims with challenges even more daunting than those faced by Nahdlatul Ulama's traditionalists. The final years of the Soekarno era had not looked kindly on believers in the compatibility of Islam and modern civilization. From 1956 on, the modernists' primary political organization, the Masyumi, was excluded from governing coalitions. In the late 1950s Masyumi leaders were the subject of Communist Party campaigns portraying them as stooges of the U.S. Central Intelligence Agency. Finally, in the aftermath of regional rebellions outside Java, on August 17, 1960, President Soekarno, backed by the military high command, ordered Masyumi officials to dissolve their party or be banned.

Over the months that followed, most of the senior Masyumi leadership, including many who had had nothing to do with the regional rebellions, were imprisoned. Although they avoided outright dissolution, Masyumi allies in the youth and student community, including the Muslim Student's Association (*Himpunan Mahasiswa Islam*) and the Muslim Pupils (*Pelajar Islam*), also became the target of fierce Communist propaganda. Barred from government contracts and ravaged by the nation's economic crisis, business leaders associated with the party also saw their fortunes decline. With these and other setbacks, an organization that in the early 1950s had been among the most optimistic of Indonesia's political parties, sank into bitterness and despair. The confidence of its leadership in the consonance of constitutional democracy with Islam had been shaken, for some irreparably.

Against this background, it is not surprising that the Masyumi leadership greeted the New Order regime with high hopes. They looked to the military-dominated government to restore their party to Indonesian political life. They hoped that the changed national environment would allow them to revive their campaigns for a heightened state commitment to Islam.

For the majority of modernists, this last concern was the most compelling. Since the independence struggle of the mid-1940s, the Islamization of state had been a rallying cry of Muslim political activism. In debates in the Constituent Assembly (1956–59) Nahdlatul Ulama, Masyumi, and the other small Muslim parties had united against secular and communist nationalists to demand that the constitutional bases of the nation become Islam.[1] Beneath the appearance of unity, however, there were already great divides. Although it sounded like the most tangible of issues, the Islamization of state was an ideological hall of mirrors. Muslim leaders could not agree on what such a program entailed. Did it require, as most Nahdlatul Ulama leaders insisted, the establishment of a Council of Ulama to ensure that all laws and legislation conform to Islamic law (*shariah*)? Which scholars and which school of law? Nervous about the traditionalist views of NU scholars, Masyumi leaders agreed that governmental legislation should conform to Islamic law, but they were less eager to specify how that law might be interpreted, and by whom.

By the beginning of the New Order these disagreements over the role of Islam in state had created deep divides, not only between traditionalists and modernists but among modernists themselves. Having suffered the slings and arrows of Soekarno's final years, some modernists were determined to press forward with the campaign to Islamize the state. Others were convinced that political circumstances made any talk of such a campaign foolish. Still others had concluded that the Islamic state was an ideological mirage.

The legacy of the late-Soekarno era added to the modernists' difficulties. In the face of Soekarno's dissolution of the Constituent Assembly in 1959, the disastrous participation of some Muslim figures in regional rebellions, and the ferocious violence of 1965–66, most Muslim leaders realized that the time was not right to revive the campaign for an Islamic state. For the moment the Indonesian military was the preeminent power, and it was, to say the least, little interested in revisiting the matter of an Islamic state.

During the ten years leading up to the New Order, the military had slowly expanded its power by, among other things, doing battle against what it called forces of the "extreme Left" (Communists) and the "extreme Right" (Muslim separatists). The regional rebellions of the late 1950s had allowed the armed forces to purge themselves of officers sympathetic to Islamic causes;[2] the violence of 1965–66 had allowed a purge of the Left. By the beginning of the New Order the armed forces command was more ideologically unified than ever. It was also deeply skeptical of civilian politicians. Military leaders were convinced that they alone could defend the country's ethnic and religious minorities against Muslim majoritarianism. Although the military leadership had eagerly mobilized Muslim forces in the campaign against the PKI, it was no secret that some officers worried that the alliance might have only raised false hopes.

During these same years, the state's appropriation of Dutch properties (nationalized between 1957 and 1959) gave the military control of substantial economic assets. Management of these took the military onto a collision course with labor unions and the Communist Party.[3] The economic decline of the 1960s wreaked havoc with military budgets, making the military all the more dependent on extracurricular income. Both activities reinforced the military leadership's commitment to its "dual mission" (*dwifungsi*) of external defense *and* internal security.

Although, for the moment, military dominance made it difficult to contemplate reviving the question of an Islamic state, then, most Muslim modernists still expected the government to restore the good name and legality of their

party. After all, the party that had most stridently supported Masyumi's dissolution, the Communist Party, lay in ruins, and the Nationalist Party was also
crippled. The modernist leadership was convinced that if Masyumi could be
revived and elections held soon, the party might yet achieve its goal of taking
power through the ballot box. Even if a fully Islamic state were not possible,
a deeper Islamization of state and society seemed well within reach.

It soon became clear, however, that even the most modest of these goals
were not to be realized. As the dust settled from 1965–66, Soeharto's advisers
signaled that they were opposed to concessions to anyone who had had anything to do with Masyumi. As the strength of the regime's opposition became
clearer, the modernists' euphoria gave way to confusion, disbelief, and anger.
Determined not to acquiesce in the face of a second marginalization, the senior
Masyumi leadership resolved to pursue politics in a different form, through an
ambitious program of religious predication or *dakwah* ("appeal," especially to
Muslims for a deeper profession of faith). *Dakwah* was to be the senior modernists' preferred weapon of resistance.

In principle, of course, Islam enjoins all Muslims to engage in *dakwah* as a
basic religious duty. During the party campaigns of the 1950s, *dakwah* had
been used for explicitly political programs, as when Masyumi and Nahdlatul
Ulama used devotional meetings (*pengajian*) to mobilize electoral support. The
earlier precedent in mind, the Masyumi leaders concluded that a vigorous program of predication was the best solution to their predicament. Direct confrontation with the authorities was out of the question. By taking the high road of
predication, it was said, the Masyumi community would eventually become so
strong that the regime would be unable to ignore it. Then Islam would have
to be given its rightful due.

There was another, younger group of Muslim modernists, however, who
were weary of the party conflicts of the 1950s and viewed the subordination
of predication to political ends as dangerously short-sighted. Although the
young modernists were ideologically varied, the most outspoken among them,
and the best-known in Indonesia today, were those associated with the movement of Islamic revitalization known by the Indonesian term for renewal, *pembaruan*.[4] Unlike their elders, the renewalists rejected any linkage of predication
to the struggle for state power. They did so not because they believed in a full
separation of religion and politics (as conservative Muslim critics claimed) but
because they felt that the subordination of Islamic ideals to the needs of party
politics distorted religious teachings and Muslim politics itself. Party politics
would achieve nothing unless there was a profound change in Indonesian culture. In the junior modernists' eyes, the party-based competitions of the 1950s
and early 1960s had led the senior leadership to confuse means with ends.
The leadership had neglected mass education and social welfare programs so
as to devote all their resources to the struggle for state power. It was time to
rediscover what was essential in Muslim politics, the renewalists argued, and

replace the petty distractions of party politics with the high politics of Islamic justice and democracy.

Although no one could have foretold it at the time, the rivalry between these two visions of Islam and nation was to become one of the defining events of the New Order. When it first became public in the late 1960s, the dispute appeared to be little more than an intramural spat among a few marginal Muslims—representatives of movements that, in the eyes of the New Order's conservative nationalists, were about to dissolve like sand beneath the great wave of modernization.

However, the debate among Muslim modernists did not diminish in importance in the 1970s and 1980s but took on greater public importance. During those years the ranks of the educated middle class expanded dramatically, new Muslim print media flourished, and the nation witnessed a remarkable Islamic resurgence. No one in the New Order leadership had anticipated the resurgence, and the initial reaction of some in the Soehartoist elite was to demand its suppression. By the late 1980s, however, all players on the national scene recognized there was no going back; the revival had decisively altered the rules of the political game. From now on, the struggle to capture Muslim allegiances was to be a key feature of national politics.

ASPIRATION AND DENIAL

From the first days of the New Order there were signs that all was not well in Masyumi's relationship with the new government. Although most Indonesians had expected New Order officials to move quickly to free the Masyumi leaders imprisoned by Soekarno, the latter were not released until July 1966. The government cited legal complications to justify the delay. But it was no secret that the effort had been impeded by opposition from high-ranking members of the military. Army officials still blamed Masyumi for the many lives lost in suppressing regional rebellions a few years earlier.

After the senior Masyumi leadership was finally freed, the modernist community moved quickly to organize a campaign for their party's rehabilitation. In August 1966 sixteen modernist organizations gathered in Jakarta to form a Coordinating Body for Muslim Good Works (BKAM). Its purpose was to lobby for Masyumi's legalization. This meeting was followed on August 15 by a large rally to welcome the freed Masyumi prisoners at the great Al-Azhar Mosque in the elite southern suburb of Kebayoran Baru. Additional meetings of the "Big Family of the Moon and Stars" (*keluarga besar Bulan Bintang*), as the Masyumi alliance was known, took place in late October 1966. One notable achievement of these latter meetings was that the usually cautious Muslim Students Association finally lent its support to the campaign.

HMI's gesture was taken as a sign that the rehabilitation campaign was making headway. Although HMI had been spared Masyumi's fate in 1960, the student organization and its alumni association were linked to Masyumi by close fraternal ties. Equally significant, in early 1966 a small number of HMI alumni had begun to work for the government. Most entered the bureaucracy under the auspices of Widjojo Nitisastro and Sumitro Djohadikusumo in the national planning agencies. Sumitro had been an intellectual supporter of the Indonesian Socialist Party and had cooperated with leaders from the progressive wing of Masyumi in the 1950s and early 1960s before both parties were banned. His recruitment of Masyumi Muslims showed that some government bureaucracies were open to moderate modernists.[5]

HMI support was also seen as auspicious because most modernists believed that politically connected HMI alumni could lobby the New Order government. No sooner had the Masyumi initiative gotten under way, however, than some in the New Order's inner circles made clear their reservations about the campaign. On December 26, 1966, the armed forces headquarters released a "December Declaration" (*pernyataan Desember*) in which it stated its unequivocal opposition to the rehabilitation of any group that had deviated from the *Pancasila* and 1945 constitution. The armed forces statement singled out the Communist Party as one such deviationist. To the dismay of Masyumi leaders, however, the statement also put Masyumi and the PSI in the same category. The former general secretary of Masyumi, Prawoto Mangkusasmito, a Masyumi moderate, crafted a politely worded letter protesting this slighting of the Masyumi legacy. Published on March 30, 1967, his letter pleaded that Masyumi should not be equated with the PKI, because the Muslim party had been a victim of the political abuses of the Old Order. Soeharto's advisers ignored Prawoto's appeal.

Desperate to keep their campaign on track, in April 1967 the leaders of the BKAM resolved to lend their support to efforts to organize a new modernist party rather than one that bore the Masyumi banner. In the weeks before this announcement, the Soeharto government had signaled that it would look more favorably on this option than it would the rehabilitation of Masyumi itself. At first, regime spokespersons seemed to respond positively to the BKAM proposal. Once again, however, military leaders intervened to clarify to Soeharto that no such body should be approved if its leadership included anyone from Masyumi—even moderates who had had nothing to do with the regional rebellions. After weeks of discussions, on October 24, 1967, Mohammed Natsir sent a letter to the president indicating that he would not be involved in any new party. Modernists hoped that this concession would open the way for the founding of their new party, which they were already calling Partai Muslimin Indonesia or, simply, Parmusi.[6]

On February 20, 1968, President Soeharto legalized Parmusi. In accordance with the government's demands, two figures from the Muhammadiyah who were regarded as having cordial ties with the government, Djarnawi Hadikusumo and Lukman Harun, were appointed interim chairman and secretary general, respectively—posts they were to hold until Parmusi's first national convention in November. The modernists were not yet out of the political woods, however. As the November conference approached, regional supporters of the Masyumi urged the leadership to challenge the government prohibition on Masyumi leaders by allowing one moderate figure to assume a leadership role in the party. At the November convention these regional activists carried the day, electing the former foreign minister Mohamad Roem chairman of the new party. Anxious not to appear confrontational, Roem declared that he would not accept the appointment unless Soeharto gave his blessing. Few of the convention delegates were prepared for what followed. A few hours before the convention's close, delegates were stunned by the news that Soeharto's cabinet secretary, Major General Alamsjah Ratuprawiranegara, had telegrammed to say that the government would not accept Roem's election. At this late hour, it was impossible to select a different leader; the delegates left in confusion. Despite a later appeal from Masyumi supporters, the military held firm in its opposition.[7] Roem stepped down.

This was but the first in a series of government measures restricting the independence of the new Muslim party. Aware of tensions between accommodationists and independents in Parmusi, over the months that followed Soeharto strategists engineered another split in the already crippled Parmusi leadership. First, the government arranged the election of two rival leaderships, each of which denied the legitimacy of the other. (Years later, in 1996, the same tactic would be used against Megawati Soekarnoputri and the Indonesian Democratic Party; see chapter 7). Having provoked this crisis, the government then intervened to "restore order" by appointing a leader supported by neither of the two sides, H.M.S. Mintareja. A strong accommodationist, Mintareja did not object to the government's striking of Masyumi names from the candidate lists for the 1971 elections.

In light of its compromised conception, it is not surprising that when the elections were finally held in 1971 Parmusi's share of the vote fell far short of the figure achieved by Masyumi in the 1955 elections. Although the neotraditionalist Nahdlatul Ulama managed to capture a percentage of the vote almost identical to its 1955 showing (18.7 percent versus 18.4 percent in 1955), Parmusi's share of the vote tumbled from Masyumi's earlier 20.9 percent to a mere 7.36 percent. For the time being, it seemed, the modernist road to political rehabilitation was not to pass by way of a revived party organization.

STATE AGAINST POLITICAL SOCIETY

At first, most political observers regarded the government's policies as directed not against the Muslim community as a whole but specifically against Masyumi. We know that military officials close to the president had an especially strong dislike for Masyumi leaders. It was not too long, however, before many began to suspect a broader regime bias against Islam itself. Two years after the 1971 elections the government announced its intention to "simplify" the electoral system by fusing the nine parties still operating into two; one of these parties was supposed to represent Muslims. In principle, of course, the simplification applied equally to all political parties. However, the biggest loser under the policy was the Muslim community, which earlier had seemed poised to make great electoral gains.

The restructuring program had three components. First, the government fused the nine surviving political parties into two broad party alliances. The first of these parties, known as the Indonesian Democratic Party (*Partai Demokrasi Indonesia*), was intended to represent the interests of the Nationalist Party, Catholic and Protestant parties, and several small nationalist groupings. The Indonesian Nationalist Party was regarded as the PDI's core constituency. In the two years following the events of September 30, 1965, the PNI had experienced a disastrous decline, as its left wing was purged and it lost access to government patronage. The newly created PDI, therefore, was no more than a shadow of the former PNI. Indeed, the PDI was the weakest of the state-organized parties until the mid-1990s, when its leadership passed into the hands of the daughter of Indonesia's first president, Megawati Soekarnoputri (chapter 7).

The second of the two parties, the Party of Unity and Development (*Partai Persatuan dan Pembangunan*, or PPP), was intended to represent people previously associated with the four Islamic parties. The most important of these Muslim parties were the modernist Masyumi (now regrouped under the Parmusi) and the traditionalist Nahdlatul Ulama. Soeharto's personal aide, Ali Moertopo, was the architect of the electoral reforms. He was convinced that unless the government took direct action, the Muslim parties would reap the benefits from the destruction of the Communist Party and the Nationalist collapse. Moertopo also understood, however, that modernist and traditionalist leaders were famously incapable of getting along. He was certain, therefore, that the fusion of the disparate Muslim parties would weaken, rather than strengthen, the Muslim vote. The 1977 elections demonstrated that his assessment was correct.

The second component in the government's restructuring of the party system was its imposition of far-reaching restrictions on party campaigns. The government was determined to prevent any recurrence of the mass mobilizations of the late 1950s. Consistent with its understanding of the politics of "primordialism" (chapter 4), its long-term goal was to deconfessionalize politics and encourage people to express their political allegiances in a manner free of ethnic or religious passions. With these goals in mind, the state forbade political parties from having branches at the subdistrict or village level. At the same time, however, the government party, Golkar, was allowed to operate in villages and towns the entire year. This showed that depoliticization was less the goal than political control. Government regulations also barred the two parties from holding rallies or recruitment drives at any time other than one month before elections. Each party also had to submit a list of candidates to security officials, who had the right to strike any name to which they objected. Party officials had no right of appeal. Through these and other measures, the Soeharto government transformed Indonesia's once vibrant electoral system into an empty shell.

The third element in the government's restructuring of the electoral system was, as mentioned earlier, its establishment of a government party, *Golongan Karya* or Golkar.[8] The party's name, the "Association of Functional Groups," was intended to convey the impression that it served the national interest rather than the sectional interests of class, religion, or ethnicity. But Golkar's actions demonstrated that there is no more sectional interest than state power itself. Denying the voluntarism essential to civil democracy, the government required all state officials to swear their "singular loyalty" (*monoloyalitas*) to Golkar. Officials who refused had to resign their posts. This requirement posed particular problems for officials in the Department of Religion. Since the republic's founding, this was the one government ministry that had recruited heavily from the ranks of Muslim parties. During the first year and a half following the party fusion, department officials were exempt from the requirement to join Golkar. After this brief grace period, however, they, too, were subject to the principle of "singular loyalty."[9]

In subsequent years Soeharto's aides repeatedly intervened to rewrite party platforms, alter candidate lists, recall legislative delegates, or, when necessary, imprison critics. Even Golkar was not exempt from these state controls. In the early 1990s, when there was much talk of a new "openness" (*keterbukaan*), some in the government party argued that the time had come to transform Golkar into a political force independent of the president. Giving Golkar greater autonomy, it was said, would allow the party to develop the leaders required to sustain the New Order legacy after Soeharto was gone. To the surprise of most of the Golkar leadership, however, the president's operatives flatly rejected these proposals. Golkar was to remain subordinate to the state, and the state was subordinate to the political and economic interests of Soeharto.

CIRCUMNAVIGATING THE STATE

In the face of this repression, the modernist Muslim leadership split over its stance toward the government. Senior figures loyal to the Masyumi head, Mohammed Natsir, concluded that the best strategy was one of principled non-cooperation. Younger modernists, including moderates and the renewalists, settled on a strategy of constructive engagement and societal reform. The junior modernists argued that the Muslim community should emphasize education and social welfare because, over the long run, changes in society were the best way to make political progress. Even while hoping for a transformation of the state, however, the junior modernists rejected the senior leadership's demands for a fuller "Islamization" of the state, insisting that Muslim politics in no way requires an Islamic state. This disagreement was to become one of the central divides among Muslims in the 1980s and 1990s.

However fixed their political vision, clearly the senior leadership had been left with few options. During 1966 and 1967 Natsir and his associates had carefully avoided confrontation with the government, hoping that their re-peated gestures of good would allay military suspicions. The crowning moment in these efforts was Natsir's letter of October 24, 1967, in which the Masyumi leader declared openly that if a modernist party were established, he would not be among its leaders. But Soeharto and his advisers responded to this concession by only ratcheting up their pressures, determined to prevent any modernist Muslim organization from becoming a force in Indonesian politics.

In hamstringing the Masyumi leadership in this manner, the government aggravated tensions long latent in the modernist community and reinforced the conservative drift of the Masyumi leadership (chapter 4). In the early 1950s, just after the Nahdlatul Ulama withdrew from the party, Masyumi was a complex and unsteady alliance between, on the one hand, Muslim constitu-tionalists, committed to a procedural democracy and the rule of law, and, to borrow Marshall Hodgson's phrase, "*shariah*-minded" Islamists, more con-cerned with abstract principles than uncertain experimentation with constitu-tional government.[10] All Masyumi's major groupings agreed on the importance of expanding the role of Islam in state and society. Beyond this vague formula, however, few agreed on just what Muslim politics meant for the day-to-day management of the economy, state, and society.

During the first years of the independence era, Natsir had skillfully mediated between the conservative and constitutionalist camps in Masyumi. Natsir him-self claimed to be a supporter of democracy but qualified his endorsement by insisting that Islamic democracy differs from what he called liberal democracy. In describing the two political systems, he emphasized that Islamic democracy could not allow everything to be subject to the will of the people. Ultimate sovereignty lies with God, and the ethical imperatives provided by God in *shariah* must take precedence over man-made legislation.[11]

This is, of course, a familiar argument in Islamist discourses on democracy, one that in no way identifies its exponent as conservative, moderate, or pro-gressive. For solidarity building and the mobilization of the Muslim masses, the very vagueness of the formula can be useful. The appeal to Muslim solidar-ity shifts attention away from potentially divisive policy issues toward the sim-ple affirmation that, somehow, Islam must be at the center of social life. Like Mom and apple pie for Americans, this vague notion is one to which few pious Muslims object. When it comes to the daily management of a modern state, however, this little message causes big problems, since it provides few real clues as to how the state should be organized.

Dutch-educated and well-read, Natsir was familiar with the history of Western and Muslim political thought. Natsir's understanding of Muslim politics had been influenced by his collaboration in early adulthood with the founder of the strict modernist organization, Persatuan Islam (Persis, *"Muslim Unity"*), Ahmad Hassan.[12] Through Hassan, Natsir was introduced to the works of the great Pakistani political writer Sayyid Abdul A'la Maududi, a modernist conservative and critic of "Western" democracy.[13] Although his early writings demonstrate that Natsir had the intellectual capacity to engage the central questions of Muslim politics, in the end he never went beyond this early reading. Pressed by the independence struggle and later competition with secular nationalists, Natsir retreated to writing sloganistic appeals for mass mobilization. He never formulated a coherent theory of modern Islamic government. Nor did he encourage his supporters to engage in the critical rereading of Muslim politics required to do so.

The political hardships Masyumi experienced contributed to this failure. As Masyumi was turned into a political pariah, the balance of power in the organization shifted to its conservative wing and away from activists interested in rethinking Muslim politics.[14] The constitutionalist wing of the Masyumi community never entirely disappeared. But its influence in the "big family of the moon and stars" declined drastically, in a manner that had serious implications for the modernist community's future.

Other events in the early New Order reinforced Masyumi's increasing conservativism. The government's fierce persecution of Masyumi activists discouraged moderate Muslims from joining the Natsir group. Conversely, from the late 1960s on, those who lashed themselves to the Natsir raft were more conservative and unoriginal in their thought than their counterparts of the 1950s. This transformation was particularly apparent in the social profile of youthful recruits to the Natsir movement. As the Soeharto regime escalated its repression in the late 1970s, many young Muslim idealists were driven out of universities and professional employment. Many of these activists had begun their careers with brightly democratic views. Barred from the mainstream and hardened by repression, many turned to the Natsir group for solidarity. What they encountered there, of course, were decidedly conservative readings of Muslim politics. In this way, political marginalization reinforced a process of ideological essentialization, further diminishing the chances of a creative reinterpretation of Muslim political thought.

Two other developments reinforced this conservative turn in the neo-Masyumi community—one international, the other domestic. Masyumi's leadership had always been committed to an internationalist understanding of Islam. Its news media consistently devoted more attention to the larger Muslim world than did other Muslim media. Yet the Muslim world to which Natsir and his followers looked underwent profound changes in the 1960s and 1970s. One important aspect of this change was a hardening of attitudes toward the United States.

Unlike the European powers, the United States had never had a colonial presence in the Muslim world, and in the 1950s Muslim modernists in many countries showed a sympathetic interest in American democracy. Nowhere was this truer than in Indonesia. Indonesian Muslims shared Americans' fierce opposition to communism, and, at first at least, appreciated U.S. efforts in Vietnam. This gave the United States a special status in the eyes of many Indonesian Muslims—something of a partial exception to the Western imperialist rule.

In the years following Masyumi's demise, however, the image of the United States in the Muslim world underwent an unhappy transformation. After the 1967 Arab-Israeli war the United States came to be identified with the humiliating occupation of Muslim lands and with an uncompromising commitment to Israeli military superiority. Even liberal Muslims found it hard to defend these American actions. During these same years, the image of America in popular media underwent an equally startling transformation. To put the matter a bit simplistically, if the United States was previously seen as the land of cowboys and scientists, both of whom excited a grudging admiration, by the late 1970s these icons had been displaced by troubling images of pornography, violence, and drugs. More generally, the counterculture that swept the West in the 1960s and 1970s offered a modernity more difficult for Muslim modernists to understand or admire than earlier Western achievements in education and technology. To many Muslims, it seemed that what the West now offered was no longer disciplined excellence but sexual hedonism and do-your-own-thing individualism.

In Indonesia there was a media dimension to the American mutation. The globalization of cinematic marketing that began in the late 1970s and 1980s converged with ruthless marketing policies by Indonesian film distributors to bring about a near-total collapse of the domestic film industry in the late 1980s.[15] In its place, the country saw an influx of foreign action films and sexual dramas. Less visible but equally dramatic, the 1980s saw the illegal importation of American, European, and East Asian pornography, an event that made hard-core pornography available even in remote corners of the archipelago. These and other events—the expansion of tourism, alcohol and drug abuse, AIDs, and the growth of the Southeast Asian sex industry—left ordinary Muslims deeply confused about the values for which the West stood. Some Muslims began to feel that the real threat from the West was less political than it was a pernicious subversion of public morality.

The second and final influence on the Masyumi group's ideological evolution was domestic and had to do with the organization's changing class base. In the 1950s Masyumi had a brightly urban orientation, one consistent with the middle-class profile of its core base. But the 1950s and 1960s laid waste to the wealth of the merchants and small industrialists who had provided the lion's share of Masyumi funds. The economic collapse of the old *santri* complicated the Natsir group's efforts to maintain a mass base.[16] Its middle-class support waning, the organization moved down market in its appeals, turning for support to the poor and lower middle class of urban Indonesia.

By the mid-1980s a new *santri* middle class was taking shape. It was concentrated not in independent enterprise but in education, bureaucracy, and government-dependent business. Employed as they were in state-related enterprise, however, the new *santri* were reluctant to voice their opinions in ways that might jeopardize their ties to the government. Compared to the *santri* of the 1950s, then, the new Muslim middle class was less political, emphasizing piety and morality rather than party politics or the struggle for the state.

Herein lies an additional clue to the rivalry that eventually pitted the senior modernists around Natsir against the junior modernists. Hardened by political persecution, driven to emphasize bare-bone essentials, and pushed toward a poorer and less-educated market segment, the Natsir group came to emphasize not merely the *shariah*-mindedness of Masyumi conservatives but the strict and anti-cosmopolitan Islamism of the urban poor and lumpen–middle class. The consequence of all these trends was that by the mid-1980s Natsir's modernist group tended to have a more uniform ideological profile than in the 1950s. The constitutionalist and cosmopolitan wing of the community had declined or departed. In ideological terms, the Natsir group now resembled the stiffly sectarian *Persatuan Islam* (Persis) of the 1930s and 1940s more than the inclusive Masyumi of the 1950s.

Persis was a small modernist organization founded in Bandung in 1923. In the 1930s and 1940s this organization achieved a reputation for its fierce diatribes against secular nationalists, including the young nationalist leader, Soekarno.[17] Ideologically Persis resembled the Islamic Brotherhoods (*Ikhwan Al-Muslimun*) of the Middle East and Maududi's Jama'at-i Islami more than other Indonesian organizations. Persis writers regularly attacked Christian beliefs and warned of plots to Christianize Indonesia. Unlike Muhammadiyah writers, Persis authors also advocated the literal application of *hudud* laws for criminal punishment, including the amputation of hands and feet for theft.[18]

On matters related to women, the Persis position was that men and women were equal under Islam but also different in a manner that required gender segregation. The most critical traits separating men from women, Persis authors insisted, were those of a God-given nature. Women are sweet and soft, men strong and more intelligent. In creating these differences, God has also indicated that women's realm is the family and household, whereas men's is the nation and religious community. However effective her leadership in female affairs, no woman should serve as a religious judge, mosque *imam*, or party leader.

One of the most celebrated of Persis's writers was a gifted, Dutch-educated gentleman who wrote under the pseudonym A. Muchlis. A. Muchlis's birth name was Mohammed Natsir—the very man who was to become the leader of Masyumi. The young Natsir, it should be noted, was one of the more open-minded of Persis writers. Compared to his well-known colleague Isa Anshary, he was reluctant to call his Muslim critics apostates (*murtadd*). Although he shared Persis views on women, the law, and Christian missions, he was also one of the writers most committed to the ideal that Christians are not a devia-tionist sect but a "people of the book" who must be accorded rights and protec-tion as specified in the Qur'an and Sunna.

Like other Persis writers, however, Natsir's perspective on Islam was not drawn from an appreciation of Muslim civilization nor a reflection on the mod-ern age but from an Islam of idealized canon. The way Natsir justified the argument that *shariah* should be applied in Indonesia illustrates his unempiri-cal view of Islam. Criticizing secular nationalists, Natsir argued that 90 percent of all Indonesians are Muslims. For Natsir, this demographic fact meant that it was unfair and undemocratic that the "minority 10 percent" should impose its will through the creation of a secular or nonconfessional state. As with other Persis writers, the ostensibly democratic logic of this argument was grounded on what was, in fact, an undemocratic refusal to recognize that the single largest constituency opposed to the establishment of an Islamic state consisted of Java-nists and democratic Muslims. Natsir regarded the aspirations of these Muslims as less legitimate than supporters of an Islamic state. This habit of linking ostensibly democratic principles (the commitment to majority rule) to a bla-tantly undemocratic avant-gardism (Muslim supporters of *shariah* should be able to decide what is best for their unenlightened brethren) was to remain a troubling blind spot in the Natsir group's political vision.[19]

THE POLITICS OF PREDICATION

Faced with New Order persecution, Natsir and his associates resolved to put party politics aside in favor of an intensive program of religious predication (*dakwah*). Contrary to government ideas on religious "building up," however (chapter 4), Natsir viewed his *dakwah* initiative *not* as a purely spiritual matter but as political struggle in a new form.[20]

The clearest indication that the senior leadership's predication campaign did *not* involve a shift from the political to the narrowly spiritual was that rather than joining with already existing *dakwah* organizations, Natsir and his associ-ates opted to organize an entirely new predication group, the Indonesian Coun-cil for Islamic Predication or DDII (*Dewan Dakwah Islamiyah Indonesia*). At the time of the DDII's founding, Indonesia already had several distinguished *dak-wah* organizations. The most important of these, and the one theologically

closest to the Natsir group, was the fifty-year old *grande dame* of Islamic predication, Muhammadiyah.[21] In the 1990s, that organization was estimated to
have twenty-five million followers, only several million fewer than the Nahdlatul Ulama. NU had a predication organization of its own, and there were several
other national organizations as well.

Thus there was no shortage of predication organizations when Mohammad
Natsir invited preachers, teachers, and political leaders to meet in the Tanah
Abang region of Central Jakarta in February 1967 to announce plans for a new
dakwah counsel. The new organization, the DDII, was formally launched several months later, on May 9, 1967. In choosing *not* to join forces with the
Muhammadiyah, Natsir and his colleagues signaled that their program was to
be more boldly political than its modernist predecessors. Not only did they
not wish to hide the organization's ties to the earlier Masyumi, their hope was
that the DDII would provide a public forum for the party's leaders during their
long winter of discontent. The political relationship between Masyumi and the
DDII was apparent in other ways as well: in the domination of the DDII leadership by two former Masyumi leaders (Natsir and Anwar Harjono); in the use
of Masyumi symbolism, such as the image of the moon and stars; and in the
DDII's access to Masyumi facilities, such as its national headquarters on Kramat
Raya Street in central Jakarta.

The political nature of the DDII's program was also evident in the social
target of the group's predication. One of the organization's expressed aims, for
example, was to respond to what DDII officials regarded as religious calamity of
horrendous proportions: the conversion of large numbers of nominally Islamic
Javanese to Hinduism and, most alarming in DDII eyes, Christianity. In retrospect, the actual numbers of Javanists leaving Islam at this time was not nearly
so great as Muslims feared. In the early 1970s, however, the triumphalist declarations of a few missionaries implied that the movement into Christian ranks
was massive.[22] Although the rates of conversion seen in the early New Order
would not continue, no one could have been certain of this at the time. What
was clear was that the majority of the converts came from former PKI strongholds in East and Central Java. This seemed to imply that the scale of conversion could rival that of the PKI's earlier membership.

The Christian community was well positioned to take advantage of this crisis. Since independence, most of the clergy in Christian churches had been
indigenized, diminishing the identification of Christianity with European identity. Even before the violence of 1965–66, then, rates of conversion to Christianity had been on the rise. Between 1953 and 1964 the number of Roman
Catholics in Java almost doubled. A few Protestant sects had achieved annual
growth rates of almost 20 percent, much of it based on recruits from urban
Java.[23] Ironically Christian efforts to proselytize in rural Java were impeded not
just by Muslim opponents but by Communists who saw the evangelicals as
agents of Western imperialism.[24]

Having indigenized their clergy and consolidated their organization, the churches in Java were better positioned than at any time in their history to benefit from the crisis among Javanist Muslims caused by the anticommunist killings. Although individual Christians participated in the violence, many denominations forbade their members from joining in. They did so at a time when Islamic organizations called loudly for violence against Communists. On October 7, 1965, the NU daily, *Duta Masyarakat,* called for the "annihilation" of the party and all accomplices in the Thirtieth of September Movement. In November 1965 a religious ruling (*fatwa*) issued by the Muhammadiyah referred to "extermination" of PKI members and other "neo-colonial imperialists" as an "obligatory" (*wajib*) religious act and "nothing less than a HOLY WAR."[25]

Although at a local level some Muslims welcomed ex-Communists to their services,[26] the contrast between the statements of Muslim and Christian leaders was not lost on survivors of the killings. Christian groups were also far more active helping families who had been shattered by the violence. During this same period much of the Muslim leadership continued to voice suspicions of ex-Communists. When, in 1968, the first PKI prisoners were released back into society, NU officials reacted not by attempting to proselytize but by protesting that the detainees should not have been released so soon. Even as late as 1969 the organization's executive committee in Jakarta issued instructions stating that people previously associated with "banned parties or organizations" should not be accepted as new members.[27]

Against this backdrop—of years of *santri-abangan* rivalry, of massive bloodletting in ex-Communist communities, of continued hostility in Muslim circles toward ex-Communists, and of the passage of church leadership into native hands—it is not surprising that a number of Javanists converted from nominal Islam to Christianity. The total number of converts was about 3 percent of the entire Javanese population, or 1.5 percent of Indonesia's population as a whole; figures for Javanese conversion to Hinduism were less than half this number. Over the next two decades the number of Christians in Java increased by another two million, a rate three to four times that of simple population growth.[28]

The Muslim leadership was caught off guard by this rapid Christian advance. An American political scientist residing in Indonesia during these years observed, "Both traditionalist and modernist Muslims feel as threatened by Christian missionary efforts as they did by the expanding activities of the Communist Party before 1965."[29] Worse yet, as far as Muslim leaders were concerned, a tiny minority among the Christians refused to abide by instructions from the Department of Religion prohibiting door-to-door proselytizing in Muslim regions. In late November 1967, in the aftermath of church burnings in Aceh and Sulawesi, President Soeharto convened an inter-religious conference to discuss the ground rules for proselytizing.[30] At the urging of Muslim delegates, the conference formulated a statement of principles affirming that "no religious community will be targeted for the dissemination of religion by another."[31]

Although it looked at first as if all participants in the conference had agreed to the statement, the Protestant delegation ultimately balked. Later they explained that they could not accept the declaration because it is the duty of all Christians to evangelize.

This, then, was the context in which Mohammed Natsir and his colleagues founded the Dewan Dakwah Islamiyah Indonesia. The DDII sought to respond directly to the threat of large-scale diversion from Islam. The organization also chose to work in regions where it competed directly with Christian missionaries.[32] Not coincidentally, in the years following its establishment, government officials barred the DDII from some areas, such as new convert communities in south-central Java. This policy changed abruptly, however, when Soeharto began to court conservative Muslims in the 1990s. One of the least noted of the president's many concessions at this time was his instruction that the DDII be allowed to operate in villages in Central and East Java where, a generation earlier, nominal Muslims had converted to Hinduism and Christianity.[33]

ANTI-LIBERAL ISLAM

Another difference was apparent between the DDII and existing *dakwah* organizations. The DDII was far more preoccupied than its modernist counterparts with forging strong ties with international Muslim organizations and with using *dakwah* to heighten Muslim awareness of international issues. Earlier, in the 1950s, Masyumi had already shown an internationalist consciousness greater than other Indonesian Muslim organizations. But the internationalist emphasis increased after the DDII's founding.

In part, of course, this emphasis reflected changes in global Islam in the years following the organization's founding. Having been established in 1967, the DDII became operational after the 1967 Arab-Israeli war and before the oil boom of 1973. These latter years coincided with an increase in international Islamic assistance to Muslim groups in Indonesia, from which the DDII benefited. The DDII established ties with donors in Saudi Arabia, Kuwait, and Pakistan. Its media organ, *Media Dakwah*, also featured favorable commentaries on social and intellectual developments in those same countries.

There was a domestic reason for the DDII's internationalist emphasis as well. Barred from the national political stage, the DDII used international issues to voice indirect criticism of domestic actors, including Christians, secularists, feminists, and Muslim progressives. Years later, in 1987, this mobilizational technique took a new turn when Ahmad Sumargono, Lukman Harun, and others in the most conservative wing of the DDII established an affiliate organization, the Indonesian Committee for Solidarity with the Islamic World, or KISDI (*Komite Indonesia untuk Solidaritas dengan Dunia Islam*). KISDI was originally established to heighten Indonesian sympathy for the plight of the

Palestinians. Although genuinely concerned with Palestinian suffering, the KISDI leadership knew well that the Palestinian cause could be used as a wedge to underscore differences between Muslims and the West. The campaign proved to be a brilliant recruitment strategy. Although most Muslim youth had long since lost interest in Masyumi, many were deeply moved by the Palestinians' plight. In promoting this issue, then, KISDI was able to introduce the younger generation to the senior modernist cause.

In the 1990s KISDI launched other, equally effective campaigns in support of Muslims in Bosnia, Indian Kashmir, France, and Algeria. A theme in all these campaigns has been the treachery of the West (especially the United States) and Western hypocrisy in the enforcement of human rights. When Soeharto intensified his courtship of conservative Islam in the early 1990s, he borrowed directly from KISDI's critique of human rights and liberal democracy. Through his aides, Soeharto also appealed to KISDI to aim its critique of human rights not only at Western powers but at the domestic prodemocracy movement.

From the DDII's perspective, the timing of these events was felicitous indeed. In the 1970s and 1980s DDII officials were unhappy with the quality of instruction in government-run religious schools. Although they welcomed the government's policy mandating religious instruction from grade school to university, they objected to what they regarded as a liberal bias in the State Islamic Institute Colleges (IAIN) and in the Department of Religion. In June 1995 DDII officials told me they regretted that under the leadership of the minister of religion Munawir Sjadzali (minister, 1983–93),[34] the government in the 1980s sent young scholars to universities in the United States and Western Europe rather than the Middle East. DDII anxieties seemed confirmed when some among those recent Ph.D.s, such as Nurcholish Madjid and Harun Nasution, returned home preaching variants of Fazlurian neomodernism and Mu'tazilah rationalism that DDII scholars regarded as too tolerant, too humanistic, and too theologically liberal.[35] Even worse in DDII eyes, some of these individuals went on to receive important appointments in the Department of Religion. In calling for a "contextualization" of Islamic doctrines, Sjadzali himself was seen by DDII officials to have moved out of the role of arbiter and become an advocate of a moderate renewalist Islam.

Faced with these challenges, the DDII took advantage of Masyumi's internationalist reputation and solicited scholarships for study in the Middle East; they obtained funds for domestic programs as well. Through these initiatives, the DDII has been able to send hundreds of students to centers of learning in the Middle East. In so doing, the organization helped to maintain a cadre of activists committed to an internationalist and fiercely anti-liberal variant of reformist Islam.

Media Islam

Nowhere is the DDII's internationalist consciousness more apparent than in its official publication, *Media Dakwah*.[36] This magazine's history illustrates keenly the broader, and increasingly illiberal, evolution of the DDII under the New Order.

Originally *Media Dakwah* was not a monthly magazine, as it is today, but an intermittent series of stenciled offprints produced for limited distribution among DDII supporters. In fact, at first the publication was used almost exclusively to circulate speeches and policy statements from Natsir and other DDII figures. In the late 1960s and early 1970s the government prevented the publishers of *Media Dakwah* from selling the magazine to the general public by refusing to give it the general publication license (SIUPP, *Surat Izin Usaha Penerbitan Pers*) required for mass publication.[37] Weakened by the ban on Masyumi and barred from mainstream media, these inexpensive offprints were vital to the DDII's cultural survival. But their dissemination was largely limited to an urban network of activists and preachers.

The DDII's media difficulties worsened after 1974. In January of that year there were street battles in the capital on the occasion of a visit by the Japanese prime minister to the capital. In the aftermath of the riots, official statements placed full blame not on the elite rivalries clearly implicated in the disturbances (chapter 4), but on what were described as underground elements of the Masyumi and the Socialist Party. Even worse as far as DDII Muslims were concerned, the regime took advantage of the incident to crack down on the heretofore outspoken national press. Among the newspapers it banned was *Harian Abadi*, a daily identified with Masyumi interests. The closing of *Abadi* deprived the modernist Muslim community of its last mass-circulation daily.

Making the DDII's exclusion all the more bitter was that the late 1970s were years of unprecedented growth in the mass media, driven by sales of print publications to the growing urban middle class. Remarkably, the most successful print media at this time tended to be nonconfessional, and some of the most widely read among these were also Christian owned. The most respected newsweekly of this period, *Tempo* (banned in June 1994 for its critical investigations of Minister of Research and Technology Habibie; see chapter 6), illustrated the trend. *Tempo*'s owners and staff came mostly from Muslim backgrounds. But the paper's reporting took an unequivocally nonconfessional line, consistent with the cosmopolitan tastes of its readership as well as the iconoclasm of its brilliant editor in chief, Goenawan Mohamad. (In the early 1970s Goenawan had briefly worked for the nationalist *Mahasiswa Indonesia*; see chapter 4).[38]

During these same years the Catholic owned Kompas-Gramedia Group began its ascent to its dominant position among the country's print media. In the mid-1990s this media conglomerate dominated the publishing industry, owning all or part of some twenty-three magazines and six newspapers, as well as the country's largest publishing house. This is a remarkable achievement for a Catholic-owned media conglomerate in a majority-Muslim nation. For some Indonesians, the Gramedia group's success has been a source of pride, testifying to the nation's tolerance. Against the memory of their own marginalization—and their allegation that *Kompas* had political ties to "Chinese Catholics" close to the government—DDII Muslims bitterly resented this media success.[39]

Editors associated with *Tempo* and *Kompas* point out that their publishing success was the result not of government engineering but their own ability to respond to the fast-changing tastes of the urban middle class.[40] These publishers have indeed shown a genius for combining quality reporting with brilliant marketing. The best of their media easily match the finest American mass publications for their seriousness and breadth of coverage (although the Gramedia group publishes tabloid newspapers as well). In their editors' eyes, an additional element in their success has been their attempt to downplay exclusivity in their reporting. Religious issues are regularly featured in the *Kompas* group's publications, but, as with *Tempo*, the authors featured tend to be ecumenical. Invariably DDII authors and other anti-Christian ideologues are rarely among those invited to write.

After 1974, then, Masyumi modernists lacked a national newspaper, and the heretofore limited-purpose *Media Dakwah* assumed an even heavier propaganda burden. In 1976, under the leadership of the respected and moderate Mohamad Roem, the publication changed its format from an intermittent offprint to a monthly newsmagazine. Still published on inexpensive newsprint, it evolved over the next four years into its present format, which includes newsprint-quality photos and occasional glossy inserts. Like religious media in many parts of the world, *Media Dakwah* blends moral and religious critiques directly into its reporting. What distinguishes the magazine in the Indonesian context—beyond, of course, its identification as heir to the Masyumi mantle—is that its articles present their appeals to vigilance and struggle in a manner that is accessible and uncompromising. The magazine avoids intellectualist writing and strives for a kind of middle-brow advocacy. Although the magazine publishes articles of a serious and even specialized nature, the editors ask authors to write in a clear and forceful prose. Muslim critics of the magazine sometimes refer to its writing as "dry" (*kering*) and "harsh" (*keras*), and dismiss it as lowbrow and inflammatory. The magazine never features the intensely introspective essays so prominent, for example, in *Ulumul Qur'an*, Indonesia's most respected journal of civil-Islamic renewal for most of the 1990s. Also absent is the latter journal's sympathetic reflections on non-Islamic religion, its extended excursions into Western and Islamic philosophy, and its multisided dialogues on controversies in contemporary Islam (feminism, the idea of the Islamic state, human rights, etc.). *Media Dakwah* is adamantly anti-humanist. Disdainful of speculative philosophy, it emphasizes the uncompromising superiority of Islam and the threats posed to Muslims in a world dominated by darkly anti-Islamic powers. In all these respects the magazine illustrates clearly the gulf between the harsh conservatism of today's DDII and the ideological ecumenicism of the 1950s' Masyumi.

Through *Media Dakwah* and their predication efforts, the DDII succeeded at keeping their vision of Islam in the public arena during the difficult years of the late 1970s and 1980s. They even managed to attract new recruits from the ranks of disaffected student radicals. Among this youthful rank and file, moreover, was a marked increase in conservative militancy during the 1980s and 1990s. This reflected the New Order's persecution of the DDII and the party's evolution toward an austerely conservative Islamism. Elsewhere in the modernist Muslim community, however, a new generation of leaders was coming to the fore, one with very different ideas on religion and politics.

PROGRESS THROUGH CULTURAL RENEWAL

From the first days of the New Order there were other modernist Muslims who chose to operate within the confines of the New Order system even while working for change. There were, for example, the Masyumi moderates recruited to government planning agencies. There were also religious scholars from Muhammadiyah and Nahdlatul Ulama who went to work in the departments of religion and education, where they quietly labored to improve Muslim relations with the government.

Outside those in government employment, however, was another group of young Muslims from the ranks of the generation of '66 who sought to strike a balance between criticism and constructive engagement. Like the modernist recruits to the planning agencies, the most influential of these individuals came from the ranks of the modernist student organizations, the Islamic Students Association and the Indonesian Muslim Pupils. These young modernists were neither technocrats, economists, nor politicians. Most were public intellectuals working in academia, nongovernmental organizations, or Muslim social organizations. Working outside government, these young writers and activists were freer than the Muslim technocrats to speak frankly. Unburdened with the responsibility of a mass organization, the junior modernists were also better able than the senior leadership to experiment with new strategies for Muslim progress.

In the late 1960s the leading figures among the junior modernists included such young intellectuals as Usep Fathudin and Utomo Danadjaja from the PII; Ahmad Wahib, Dawam Rahardjo, and Djohan Effendi from the "limited group" discussion circle in Yogyakarta; and Nurcholish Madjid from the Jakarta head-quarters of the HMI. Most of these young men came from modernist theological backgrounds and at some point in their lives had had contact with the Masyumi leadership. During the first two years of the New Order, most supported the effort to revive Masyumi. However, as it became apparent that this effort was doomed, the young modernists broke ranks with the senior leadership and advocated a different strategy for social change.

There was a larger reason for the junior modernists' ambivalence toward Masyumi and a party-based politic. Many had watched with dismay as the parliamentary system of the late 1950s politicized religion, drove nominal Muslims into the arms of the Communist Party, destroyed the PSI and Mas-yumi, and ended in a bloody massacre of hundreds of thousands of Indone-sians. As with their youthful counterparts in the Socialist Party, this experience had left many of the young modernists ambivalent about mass politics. Al-though few were willing to invite official wrath by expressing their concerns publicly, some also had deep misgivings about the killings of 1965–66. To many, the "low" politicization of Islam seemed only to have corrupted Islam's high political ideals.

The young modernists were also confident that the New Order would im-prove if Muslims worked with it rather than against it. This attitude had been shaped by the young modernists' experience during the difficult years of the early 1960s. From 1960 on, the Masyumi and the PSI were banned and much of their leadership imprisoned. During the same period the Communist Party established itself as the nation's most powerful party, and set one of its priori-ties as the dissolution of the HMI and PII. In these desperate circumstances military officers in many parts of the country had secretly provided resources and protection for modernist Muslim youth (chapter 4). On the basis of this earlier collaboration, many young Muslims were convinced that they could work with reformist members of the New Order leadership.

There was also a generational logic to the junior modernists' ambivalence toward party politics. As alumni of the student movement of 1965–66, the young modernists were neither dependent on nor committed to the party orga-nizations of the 1950s. Indeed, the political parties represented a sphere in which the junior leadership were always certain to play second fiddle to their elders. Better educated than the latter, and less enamored of their stiffly hierar-chical ways, the Muslim youth chafed at this subordination. In the face of the New Order's restrictions on political parties, then, the junior modernists found it easy to distance themselves from mass politics and, in its place, promote revitalization through the social and intellectual skills they owned. The renew-alists were also convinced that any long-term revitalization had to allay military concerns about the loyalties of Muslims.[41]

The young intellectuals who devised this strategy at first did so indepen-dently, working out of discussion groups in Jakarta, Bandung, and Yogyakarta.

Discussion groups had been a focus of nationalist activity during the final years of Dutch colonialism (chapter 3), and many of the New Order groups modeled themselves on these earlier associations. The discussion group model, however, also reflected the pivotal influence of the Indonesian Socialist Party in the early years of the New Order. Like the socialists, the young modernists were convinced that the chaos of the 1960s showed that what the country needed was quality cadres, not mass mobilization.

Although the modernist students had several discussion groups, the man whose name has come to be most widely associated with events at this time was Nurcholish Madjid. A Javanese raised in the traditionalist stronghold of Jombang in East Java, Madjid had been twice elected leader of the HMI during the tumultuous years of 1966–71. In a series of bold public presentations in the late 1960s and early 1970s Madjid asserted that the Muslim community bore some of the responsibility for its failure to achieve influence under the New Order. The party organizations that Muslim politicians were attempting to revive, Madjid argued, had in the 1950s already demonstrated their inability to capture the hearts and minds of most Indonesians. Rather than repeating the mistakes of that period, Madjid said, the Muslim community should develop new organizations capable, above all, of winning the moral allegiance of all Indonesian Muslims. Only through such a revolution in values could Indonesia escape the debilitating polarization pitting Muslims against secular nationalists.[42]

As in his writings still today,[43] Madjid's style of argument in these presentations was not based on the jurisprudential cadences of Islamic traditionalism or the abstract idealism of Islamic modernism. Madjid's writing was representative of a new genre of Muslim scholarship that combined Qur'an-inspired commentary with practical political analysis and sophisticated social theory. As the range of his prodigious scholarship expanded in the 1970s and 1980s Madjid mined the resources of classical Muslim thought, demonstrating more firmly the grounds for renewalist values in earlier movements for Islamic reform. His dissertation in Islamic studies at the University of Chicago, for example, focused on the scholarship of Ibn Taymiyya, the great fourteenth-century reformer popular among Islamist conservatives. Madjid's analysis demonstrates that there was a wellspring of pluralist values even in Taymiyya's work, particularly regarding relations with non-Muslims.[44]

Although a few Muslim authors had experimented with boldly eclectic writing of this sort in the 1950s, its dispassionate sensibilities were out of step with the mobilizational struggles of the time. The New Order replaced Soekarno's revolutionary rhetoric with the key words of *modernity* and *modernization*. Even the best of regime ideologues, however, could provide little clarification as to what these terms really meant. What is modernity, and what does modernization require? Must one become culturally "Western" to be truly modern? Must religion follow the course outlined by modernization theorists for Christianity in the West? Must religion become no more than personal belief?

It was questions like these that young Muslim intellectuals debated across Indonesia in their study groups and publications. At first many of the young modernists were influenced by secular modernizers associated with *Mahasiswa Islam* (chapter 4). Unlike the *MI* activists, however, junior modernists like Madjid, Dawam Rahardjo, and Ahmad Wahib were convinced that there was a middle road between secular liberalism and the senior modernists' ideologized Islam.[45] Even while rejecting what they called the "mythology" of the Islamic state, the junior modernists felt that Western liberalism's high wall between religion and state went too far. Religion, they insisted, could be a force in public life without degenerating into the simplistic idealizations of the 1950s. Slowly but surely, the terms were being crafted for a civil Islam.

Secularism versus Secularization

The influence of early New Order debates on Madjid's scholarship was also evident in the fact that one of the first topics he chose to take from his discussion group out into the public arena concerned the thorny issue of secularization. One could hardly think of a more provocative point from which to launch a career as a Muslim intellectual. The idea that modern social development is inherently secularizing, in the sense that it requires the abolition or (at the very least) "privatization" of religious conviction, was a lynchpin of postwar modernization theory (chapter 1). Conservative intellectuals in the Muslim world were convinced that if they conceded this point, they would also have to renounce one of modernist Islam's most cherished ideals, namely, that Islam, unlike Christianity, is *din wa-dawla*, that is, personal spiritual devotion *and* public politics.[46] For these Muslims, secularization and secularism were the antithesis of Islam's most hallowed truth. Modernist leaders like Mohammed Natsir argued that Islam is a "total" system intended to regulate the whole of human life. To concede the idea that Islam cannot control all social spheres implies a renunciation of Islam's holism.[47]

Madjid aimed his argument squarely at the terms of this conservative modernist argument. In a series of stunning public presentations during 1970 and 1971 he accused his fellow Muslims of having misunderstood what was essential in Islam, by "sacralizing" things actually profane. Among the mis-sacralizations Nurcholish identified were Muslim political parties and the idea of an Islamic state (*negara Islam*). Noting, quite correctly, that there is no Qur'anic injunction for an Islamic state, Madjid asserted that Muslim leaders had confused a man-made imperative with a divine one. The proper course of action in the face of this error, Madjid argued, is to "secularize" the political while preserving what is truly sacred in Islam.

According to Madjid, this effort at desacralization or "secularization" is necessitated by the most central of Muslim doctrines, *tauhid*, belief in the uncompromised oneness of God. "Islam itself, if examined truthfully," Madjid wrote, "was begun with a process of secularization. Indeed, the principle of Tauhid represents the starting point for a much larger secularization."[48] This commitment to *tauhid* requires a never-ending effort to distinguish the divine from the merely human in Islamic tradition. In so doing, Madjid argued, *tauhid* also implies a commitment to reason, knowledge, and science, all of which can be understood as acts of devotion to a creator whose majesty is immanent in the natural laws of the world. "Thus modernity resides in a process, a process of discovery of which truths are relative, leading to the discovery of that Truth Which Is Absolute, that is Allah."[49]

From a theological perspective, Madjid's comments on *tauhid* lay broadly within the tradition of Islamic modernism and neo-modernism, with their emphasis on the unity of God and the compatibility of science and progress with Islamic revelation. Where Madjid disagreed with his modernist elders, however, lay in his insistence that, while paying lip service to these ideals, Muslim leaders had done little to effect their realization in practice. Rather than taking steps toward social and intellectual renewal, Madjid implied, Muslim leaders had wasted their time on ideological bickering. By subordinating Islam's high ideals to low political intrigues, Madjid asserted, Muslims had failed to develop the "psychological strike force" required for the new era. The quest for state power had created a fetishistic emphasis on the Muslim community's "quantity" rather than its cultural "quality."[50]

The cumulative result of this failed strategy, Madjid argued, was that Muslims were left unprepared to compete with more modernized groups in Indonesian society. Surveying the New Order scene, Madjid took note of the preponderance of Chinese, Christians, and Western-oriented technocrats in private and state enterprise. Rather than condemning this as evidence of a government bias against Muslims, Madjid implied that it was in part the fault of Muslims. If Muslims continued to invest in bankrupt political initiatives, they would only marginalize themselves further from their fast-changing society.

Enunciated as it was in the face of the government's suppression of Muslim political activity, the senior modernist leadership concluded that Madjid's argument was little more than an opportunistic ploy for government favor.[51] But Madjid's long involvement in Muslim affairs and his role in the 1980s and 1990s as a distinguished spokesperson for democratic reform show that the accusation of opportunism was spurious. Often described in the Muslim media in the late-1960s as the heir apparent to Mohammad Natsir, Madjid was well aware that confronting the Muslim establishment might imperil his career. Yet he was convinced that the Muslim community was reacting to the New Order in a self-defeating manner. What was required, he felt, were bold words to shock the leadership into new ways.

In the months following his well-publicized broadsides, the risks implicit in his initiative seemed confirmed. Madjid was denounced by such formidable modernist leaders as H.M. Rasyidi, Hamka, and Natsir himself.[52] Supporters of Madjid in other youth organizations, such as Utomo Danadjaja and Usep Fathudin from the Islamic Pupils (*Pelajar Islam*), were expelled from their organizations. To many observers, it seemed that Madjid's career was over.

As is often the case in Islamic debates, the theological, not just the political, elements in Madjid's argument excited some of the most furious criticism. Madjid's qualified support for secularization provoked special outrage. Critics argued that this idea amounted to a Westernized interpretation of Islam. By understanding *tauhid* as the desacralization of all but God's oneness, it was said, Madjid and his friends ignored the recorded example of the Prophet. This record, critics said, provides clear norms for how society should be organized. As one Malaysian critic asserted,[53] to deny this precedent is to rid Islam of its sociological wholeness, transforming it into a mere "spiritual personalist ethical system" akin to what Christianity has become in the West. This may be conveniently accommodating to New Order interests, critics said, but it contradicts Islam's claim to provide an integrated way of life.

The subtlety of Madjid's argument was lost in the sound and the fury of the subsequent debate. Although he and his colleagues were accused of being secularists, they consistently distinguished secularization, understood as the desacralization of domains wrongly valorized as sacred, from secularism, a Western ideology advocating a total separation of religion from politics and social life. They condemned the latter while insisting that the former was demanded by Islamic monotheism. In the aftermath of the controversy, however, Madjid himself expressed misgivings at his choice of terms, commenting publicly that his reference to "secularization" had invited misinterpretation.[54]

One point made by Madjid's detractors was technically correct. Critics argued that Madjid's understanding of secularization drew on Western sources, citing as it did the work of social-liberal thinkers like the American sociologist Robert Bellah and the Protestant theologian Harvey Cox. Rather than expressing uncritical enthusiasm for the West, however, Madjid's appeal to these authors was illustrative of the way he and his colleagues felt that Muslims should be open to scientific and religious literature from outside Islam. Madjid's affirmation of an inclusive and humanitarian approach to other religions and other thinkers has remained a central feature of his thought to this day. It is a theme he pursued in his dissertation under Fazlur Rahman at the University of Chicago from 1978 to 1984 and one that he has refined in a series of widely read books in the 1980s and 1990s, all of which have consolidated his support among the educated middle class.[55]

This effort toward inter-religious and inter-cultural ecumenicism was a general characteristic of Indonesia's young modernists in the 1970s and 1980s. Rejecting the scholasticism of classical jurisprudence, these writers kept

Qur'anic knowledge at the center of their arguments. But they struggled to contextualize this knowledge through an eclectic exploration of other traditions and new intellectual paradigms. Western social science, classical Islamic scholarship, Indonesian history—these and other sources were drawn into the effort to create a new Muslim discourse of civility and pluralism.

In the early 1970s, however, the detail of this message was lost amid the sound and the fury of the conservatives' campaign. For Muslim conservatives, secularization meant secularism pure and simple, and secularism implied the relegation of Islam to political impotence. Although conceding that his choice of terms had caused confusion,[56] Madjid held his ground and continued his call for an open and inclusive Islam. He is important in the history of modern Indonesian Islam not merely for these ideas but because he spoke to something larger than himself: the disillusionment of many Muslims of the generation of '66 with party politics and the growing conviction among many that Muslims could progress only by renouncing the mythology of the "Islamic" state. In this sense, young modernists like Madjid, Dawam Rahardjo, and Djohan Effendi, as well as reform-minded traditionalists like Abdurrahman Wahid of NU (chapter 7), legitimated the efforts of nonparty activists to move beyond the "low politics" of party building to the high politics of education, science, and civil debate. Commenting on Madjid's impact, Fachry Ali and Bahtiar Effendy make the point that Madjid's understanding of Islamic renewal encouraged a more "empirical" attitude toward Islam.[57] Rather than quibbling over abstract doctrines or formulating a one-size-fits-all ideology, these new initiatives acknowledged the particularities of Indonesian culture and history, and from there devised their strategies for a high politics of cultural renewal.

NEW SANTRI

In sociological terms, the rise of the young modernists signaled the arrival on the national stage of a new class of Muslim activists and public intellectuals. Unlike earlier Muslim leaders, this new class had no reverential titles and only nominal ties to political parties or Qur'anic schools. They were more likely to have been trained in Islamic history or Western social science than traditional Islamic commentary or scripture. Although committed to modernization, they rejected the notion that development was merely a technological or economic process that could succeed without a cultural and moral foundation.[58] Although there were a handful of uncompromising Islamist movements in Indonesia during the 1980s,[59] the really notable feature of the period was the patient effort of moderate Muslims to promote Muslim education and social advance.

The cultural temperament of the resurgence also reflected the nature of the educational changes taking place in Indonesian society. Between 1965 and 1990 the percentage of literate Indonesians jumped from 40 percent to 90 percent of the total population.[60] The increase in the percentage of people completing senior high school was equally dramatic, rising from approximately 4 percent in 1970 to more than 30 percent today.[61] These changes were accompanied by an explosion in the market for Muslim books and magazines.[62]

The political temperament of the resurgence was also affected by the slow but steady movement of Muslims into government, a process that gradually muted the stark opposition between a military-dominated state and Muslim society. Even in the early New Order, of course, pious Muslims had worked as government officials. They had operated behind the scenes to promote a relaxation of tensions between Muslims and the state. In 1972–73, for example, they advised the government to tone down initiatives in the People's Consultative Assembly on marriage and on Javanist "belief" (*kepercayaan*) so as to moderate legislation regarded by devout Muslims as anti-Islamic (chapter 4).[63] If these early gestures looked like no more than government retreats in the face of fierce protest, the Department of Religion's Decision No. 70 in 1978 reflected a more deliberate overture to organized Islam and a more significant triumph for the state's Muslim advisers. The decision banned missionizing by the members of any one religion (Christians being the main target) among citizens who already professed, however nominally, another government-recognized religion. Christians protested that many Javanese are Muslim in name only and thus should not be subject to the stricture. But the government brushed these objections aside. Indeed, in 1979 the departments of religion and home affairs joined forces to strengthen the restrictions with their joint decision No. I/1979. As the Indonesian anthropologist Bambang Pranowo has observed, "The Islamic groups enthusiastically welcomed these decisions, for they were directed especially toward the Christian missionaries actively carrying out religious propagation amongst the Muslim community."[64] Conversely, Christian missionaries I interviewed in East Java in the late 1970s and the 1980s lamented that these restrictions had a disastrous impact on their missions. Although at the time few Western scholars had noticed, a fundamental change in New Order religious policy had occurred.

Another program to which Muslim leaders point as evidence of a change of attitude on the part of the government was the expansion of the State Islamic Institute Colleges (IAIN). Between 1979 and 1991 the academic staff at these institutes more than doubled to twenty-two hundred. The total number of students almost quadrupled, from twenty-eight thousand to one hundred thousand. Today student enrollment in Indonesia's fourteen IAIN comprises 18 percent of the student population in higher education.[65]

These efforts in higher education were accompanied by an equally impressive program of infrastructural development sponsored by the Department of Religion, focusing on the construction of mosques, prayer halls (*musholla*), and Islamic schools (*madrasah*), especially in areas regarded as weakly committed to Islam. The construction of mosques in East and Central Java reveals the unrelenting progress of this program. In East Java the number of mosques increased from 15,574 in 1973 to 17,750 in 1979, 20,648 in 1984, and 25,655 in 1990. In comparison, during the same seventeen-year period, the number of Catholic churches increased from 206 to 324. Protestant churches (including many small, evangelical meeting halls) increased from 1,330 in 1973 to 2,308 in 1984. In the face of stricter government controls, the number then declined to 1,376 in 1990. A similar program of mosque construction occurred in Central Java, where, between 1980 and 1992, the number of mosques almost doubled from 15,685 to 28,748.[66] There was a smaller but much-publicized program under the auspices of one of President Soeharto's many foundations, the Amal Bakti Muslimin *Pancasila*. The Amal Bakti program constructed 400 mosques and posted 1,000 Muslim proselytizers (*dai*) to areas of the country deemed devotionally weak.

In all this, the young modernists saw confirmation of the wisdom of their policy of political nonconfrontation. But the road ahead was still hazy.

ISLAM POLITICIZED

This cultural progress was not matched, of course, in the political arena. The early 1980s saw the government escalate its ideological campaign requiring all social and political organizations to acknowledge the "Five Principles" (*Pancasila*) as their "sole foundation" (*asas tunggal*). Even religious organizations had to change their charters, acknowledging the *Pancasila* as their foundation. The government's campaign caused great resentment among Muslims *and* Christians. In the case of Muslims, however, the policy had an especially devastating impact. The already fractured leadership splintered further as fierce disputes erupted over how to respond to the new regulations. Some Muslims were convinced that the real goal of the "sole foundation" policy was the final destruction of their organizations.[67]

In the electoral arena the government campaign dealt a severe blow to the Islamic Party of Unity and Development, and decisively enhanced Golkar's electoral advantage. This was especially apparent after 1984, when Nahdlatul Ulama withdrew from the PPP and announced that it was returning to its original 1926 charter. By the terms of this agreement, NU was to be an organization for social and religious welfare, not politics (chapter 6).[68] With NU's defection, Muslim support for the PPP plummeted. At the same time, the government party, Golkar, increased its share of the Muslim vote. Election observers decried what they regarded as blatant regime manipulation of the party system. To many, Islam seemed finished as an organized political force.

Some observers have described these government actions as reminiscent of the earlier Dutch colonial policy of tolerating Islamic religion but ruthlessly repressing all forms of political Islam.[69] There is a measure of truth to the analogy.

What it obscures, however, and what the young modernists seemed to have sensed, is that the Dutch never provided the massive support to Islamic piety that the New Order did. Equally important, the Muslim leadership understood that Islamic piety is not so easily quarantined from the public and the political. Despite their setbacks in the formal political arena, then, Muslim leaders today look back on the 1980s as a decisive turning point, not only for the cultural fortunes of the Muslim community but for its political capital as well.

In fact, by the late 1980s, the great majority of Muslim leaders believed that their acceptance of the *asas tunggal* policy had the unintended consequence of strengthening Muslim political influence. Once Islam was no longer identified with any single party, all the political parties began to advertise their commitment to Islam. This "greening" (green being a symbol of Islam) of the campaign process was dramatically evident during the 1992 and 1997 electoral campaigns, and received widespread comment in the national media. Lukman Harun, a Muhammadiyah leader and founding member of the ultraconservative Indonesian Committee for Solidarity with the Islamic World, summarized the general view of Muslim intellectuals in the late 1980s:

> Yes, we compromised in accepting the *Pancasila*, and there were many people who disagreed. But at first we didn't really understand what the consequence of this would be. Before, there was one party identified with Islam. But look at what has happened. After being depoliticized, suddenly Islam is no longer confined to any one party but is promoted by all of them.[70]

There was another dimension to this change. In Java, where the nominally Islamic Javanist community had long resisted Islamic reform, media and academic reports in the 1980s noted that many former strongholds of Javanist Islam were beginning to take on a more pious face.[71] The type of Islam adopted in these cases, it should be emphasized, owed more to a politically moderate "neo-*santri*" Islam than to the party-based Islam of the 1950s. Nonetheless, the growth of devotionalism in areas previously renowned for their Javanist heterodoxy was welcomed by Muslim leaders. The change also did not escape the attention of the president's advisers (chapter 6).

On all these points, the contrast with the first ten years of the New Order government could not be more striking. Whereas those early years had been marked by a small but controversial movement of Javanese from Islam to Hinduism and Christianity, by the 1980s there was clear evidence of Islamic revival and Javanist decline. In the 1990s field reports suggested that some of the earlier converts to Christianity and Hinduism were returning to Islam, as the revival reached into the very heartlands of Javanism.[72] The cultural progress of Islam was also leading to renewed debates over political Islam.

The Quest for the Middle Class

It was in the booming metropolitan regions of Indonesia, however, that the evidence of Islam's social progress was most visible. In large cities a new middle class was taking shape, even as the gap between rich and poor increased.[73] Not surprisingly, universities were at the forefront of this trend. In the 1950s and early 1960s Indonesia's national universities had been bastions of secular nationalism, and the *santri* community was the weaker of the factions in the student body. But the late 1970s saw a rapid growth of the so-called Salman movement (*gerakan Salman*) and similar Muslim student groups on state campuses. Salman students rejected the scholastic arguments of traditionalist scholars (*ulama*) and the harshly exclusive styles of the modernist elite. They adopted relaxed forms of dress and interaction while encouraging strict adherence to Muslim morality and devotion.

The model for this campus devotional movement was developed at the Salman Mosque at the Bandung Technological Institute, under the guidance of Imaduddin Abdulrahim, a charismatic intellectual who, a few years later, would play a key role in the founding of the Association of Indonesian Muslim Intellectuals (chapter 6). In its religious outreach, the Salman Mosque Committee invited pop bands to play, sponsored seminars on religion and development, published a small journal of culture and economic affairs, and developed economic programs for poor residents living near the campus.[74] Salman was the new Muslim activism par excellence. By the early 1980s Salman-inspired outreach had become a feature of campus life at almost every university in Indonesia.

Eventually the movement for Islamic revival reached beyond the university and touched the lives of the urban poor and the middle class. A decade earlier, in the 1970s, few Indonesians could have imagined such a development. Those years had witnessed a rapid expansion in urban wealth and an infusion of Western and East Asian consumer styles into elite circles.[75] Night clubs proliferated, alcohol consumption was widespread, and rebellious youths affected permissive lifestyles that shocked their elders. Urban society was becoming more moneyed, and many people were worried about elite youths' callous disregard for traditional mores.

In an article on cartoons and the media during this period, the political scientist Benedict Anderson captures well the ambivalence the new middle class felt toward these changes. Anderson's discussion focuses on the unease of elite Javanese in the face of their own children, as privileged youth abandoned the hierarchical etiquette of their parents. Far removed from their own cultural background, the senior generation awoke to find their offspring dismissing their values as quaintly obsolete. Hence the elite's anxiety:

Such events suggest to Indonesia's rulers that the future threatens to elude them, and so the past is summoned to their aid. Most of them are deeply aware of the far journey they have made in their lives from the rural townships of late colonial Java to the metropolitan pomp of the "cosmopolitan" Jakarta they now enjoy. . . . Their past has also not prepared them morally for the lives they now lead. Most of them grew up in the sphere of provincial Javanese society, and the norms and values of that society have left powerful residues at the core of their consciousness.[76]

It was against a less privileged but otherwise similar background that many middle-class Muslims came to speak out against what they regarded as the "privatization" (*pribadisasi*) of moral concerns during the 1970s. Unlike the Javanist officials of Anderson's description, however, these new Muslim urbanites carried a less amorphous "residue" from their early years. Rather than with existential anxiety and invented Javanese tradition, many in the new Muslim middle class responded to the anomie of urban life with calls for stricter adherence to Islam.

One need only compare Anderson's portrait to that of Kuntowijoyo in the epilogue to his *Paradigma Islam: Interpretasi Untuk Aksi* (Islamic paradigms: Interpretations for action) to realize that, however similar their anxieties, the new Muslim intellectuals were not plagued by the existential vagueness of Anderson's elite. A Yale-educated historian from Gadjah Mada University, Kuntowijoyo describes the moral crisis among urban youth in terms strikingly similar to those of Anderson and attributes it to similar causes. "Apparently social changes since 1965 have given birth to a new social class, a middle class, one which is almost without roots to any prior historical period."[77] But Kuntowijoyo's analysis goes on to describe a social dialectic different from that portrayed by Anderson. Alongside the indulgent hedonism of privileged youth, Kuntowijoyo observes, there is an emergent counterculture of principled criticism. This new culture is not based on traditional Javanese notions. Indeed, Kuntowijoyo (referring to Anderson's earlier writings on Javanese traditions) insists that the new public criticism rejects Javanism in favor of an unhierarchical reinterpretation of Muslim politics.

When the New Order government brought this new middle class into existence, Kuntowijoyo writes, it expected it to be "faithful" (*mempunyai kesetiaan*) to its policies. But among those making the pilgrimage from village to city, there were some who brought an Islamic ideology contemptuous of the elitist values of government bureaucracy. In Kuntowijoyo's view, then, this neo-*santri* tradition acts as an anti-hegemonic subculture, quietly subverting the New Order from within:

The process of decolonizing and detraditionalizing consciousness has already gone so far that the bureaucracy cannot assume [popular acceptance of] a concept of power like that of a magical source radiating invulnerability. . . . The social and moral basis of the authoritarian bureaucracy is finished.[78]

This theme of Muslim subversion of elitist Javanism was common in the critical Islamic literature of the 1980s. In an age when the voices of critical nationalism and the moderate Left had been silenced, this public Islam was one of the last remaining discourses of social resistance. Kuntowijoyo's confidently assertive tone is also characteristic of this writing, distinguishing it from the tentativeness seen in 1970s' Muslim literature. Muslims have joined the ranks of government and business, Kuntowijoyo proclaims, and they are prepared to Islamize not only the peasantry but the middle class and political elite.

Not surprisingly, by the early 1990s a now middle-aged Nurcholish Madjid was at the forefront of this critical and public Islam. In 1986 Madjid established an association for urban proselytization known as Paramadina (from the Spanish word *para*, "for," and the Arabian city of Madinah). Zifirdaus Adnan has wryly observed that although the Paramadina officials "explained that the target of the *dakwah* (missionary activity) was the middle-class people who have not received sufficient understanding of Islam," the presence of four high government officials at the organization's inaugural celebration indicates that the "the target is not only the middle class but also the elite class."[79] The organization counted no fewer than eight cabinet members on its advisorial board.

But all is not a matter of elite Islam. An additional feature of the Islamic advance has been the emergence of a new kind of revivalist proselytizer (*dai*). Many of these pop revivalists come from backgrounds in film, music, and other mass media rather than Muslim schools. They use deeply emotional accounts of their conversion rather than complicated doctrinal exegesis to move people to a deeper faith. Their prominence testifies to a dispersion of religious authority beyond the ranks of traditionally trained Islamic scholars, a trademark of the new Muslim activism in all majority-Muslim countries (chapter 1).[80]

Despite the regime's fierce ideological offensive, then, by the late 1980s Muslim activists showed a new confidence. It is this attitude that is so apparent in Kuntowijoyo's article, with its open contempt for the Javanism of the ruling elite. By itself, the critical tone of this article is, again, not unusual, as it was a regular feature of the new Muslim criticism. What was more distinctive about Kuntowijoyo's broadside, however, was not its message but its medium. The paper was originally presented at the inaugural meeting of the Association of Indonesian Muslim Intellectuals (ICMI, *Ikatan Cendekiawan Muslim Se-Indonesia*) in Malang, East Java, in early December 1990. It was then reprinted in the published proceedings of the conference, alongside more cautious articles by government intellectuals.[81] ICMI was a Soeharto-sponsored association designed to mobilize Muslim support at a time when segments of the military were challenging the president. The president also hoped to use ICMI to take the wind out of the sails of Indonesia's fledgling prodemocracy movement by dividing it along religious lines.

But Kuntowijoyo's essay provides a hint of just why the president's tactic was to run into trouble. Inaugurated to the beat of the president's drum, some of the ICMI membership wanted to dance to a different drummer. From the start, there was tension in the organization between those who wished to work for the regime and those who hoped to work for democratization. This tension would become even more apparent in the months following the Malang symposium, fueling as it did a renewed debate about the proper relationship of Muslim politics to democracy.

CONCLUSION

There were other Muslim actors and movements during the first years of the New Order. But the rivalry between the junior and senior modernists illustrates clearly the changing nature of Muslim politics at this time. The two groups were not distinguished by the fact that one promoted political Islam and the other a privatized spirituality. What separated them were their contrasting visions of just what Muslim politics should be. The Masyumi Old Guard insisted that there could be no proper politics without something akin to an "Islamic" state and state enforcement of Islamic law. The junior modernists countered that the Islamic state was an illusion the pursuit of which only impedes Muslim renewal and a high Muslim politics. The senior leadership accused their junior colleagues of paring down Islam's totalizing truth, imposing a Christian model on Islam. The junior modernists rejected this charge. They insisted that they, too, believed there could be no easy separation of Islam from politics; a purely privatized Islam was unthinkable. Unlike the Masyumi Old Guard, however, the young modernists felt that the claim that Islam is inherently *political* only makes more urgent the question of how politics is to be conducted. This was an issue on which the junior modernists already had ideas in the early 1970s. Their views would evolve further as the New Order progressed.

What was clear from the beginning, however, is that the junior modernists were skeptical of the idea of the "Islamic state." This idea, they claimed, had become a political mirage leading Muslims away from the struggle to achieve a balanced relationship between state and society. In the words of one of the most respected young modernists, Aswab Mahasin, the "mythology" of the Islamic state only undermined efforts to devise a genuinely Muslim politics.[82] It was this effort not to repudiate politics (as their critics charged) but to recraft the relationship between religion and politics in a *civil pluralist* manner, that made the renewalists' efforts so important.

By the late 1980s the cultural terms for a civil-democratic reformation of Muslim politics were widely available. There was also growing public support for a democratic reform of national politics. The very strength of the Islamic resurgence, however, drew the attention of Soeharto and his advisers. The regime had no interest in tapping Muslim energies to support democratic reform. Faced with growing opposition from former military allies, the president concluded that he needed a new base of support. As he began to cultivate Muslim allies, his actions caused great controversy in the Muslim community. But the matter did not end there. As he drew ultraconservative Muslims into his strategy for dividing and conquering his opposition, Soeharto also reintroduced bitter sectarian divides into a military and a bureaucracy earlier purged of religious divisions. Through these and other efforts, Soeharto forced the peaceful proponents of civil Islam to confront the cold realities of power. He was to be as surprised as they by the result.

Chapter Six

ISLAM DEFERRED:

REGIMIST ISLAM AND THE STRUGGLE FOR THE MIDDLE CLASS

W HEN, on December 6, 1990, President Soeharto beat a large mosque drum (*bedug*) to open the first national conference of the Association of Indonesian Muslim Intellectuals, he shattered in one fell swoop one of the most enduring stereotypes of New Order politics. Here, after all, was a man long regarded as a staunch defender of Javanist mysticism and *Pancasila* pluralism giving his blessing to an elite Muslim organization openly dedicated to the Islamization of Indonesian society. Most observers were aware that the president had made a few concessions to Muslims in the late 1980s. But no one had expected Soeharto to depart so boldly from the ground rules of New Order politics by sponsoring a Muslim lobby in the state. With this action, it was said, the president was doing more than increasing Muslim participation in elite politics. He was "playing the Muslim" card against those in the military and prodemocracy movement who had begun to challenge his rule. New Order politics would never be the same.

In 1990 few observers could have predicted that ICMI was to become the most significant new Muslim organization of the whole New Order period. ICMI's ascent provoked deep tensions in the ranks of the military, confused and frustrated the country's fledgling (and proudly multiconfessional) prodemocracy movement, and unleashed fierce debates in the Muslim community itself. In the months following ICMI's founding, the reform-minded leader of Nahdlatul Ulama, Abudurrahman Wahid, distinguished himself as ICMI's most ardent critic. In a vocabulary not unlike that Soeharto might have used six years earlier to attack Islamist opponents of the *Pancasila*, Wahid denounced ICMI as a "sectarian" organization that was "reconfessionalizing" politics and society. Wahid's attacks on the association, and his none-too-subtle hints that Soeharto was betraying the hard-fought achievements of Indonesian pluralism, deeply angered the president, and Wahid would pay dearly for his criticism. Although in the mid-1980s Wahid had been among the Muslim leaders Soeharto courted, after his critical comments Wahid was deemed a Soeharto foe. Soeharto strategists launched secret campaigns to slander Wahid and remove him from the leadership of NU (chapter 7).

During most of the 1990s, then, ICMI was at the center of the storm in Indonesian religious politics. No organization illustrates more clearly the radical shifts of the late Soeharto regime; none provides a better vantage point on the political dilemmas of Indonesian Islam. In this chapter, then, I want to examine the circumstances of ICMI's founding and its operation until the regime crisis of 1997–98. In the next chapter I examine the role of ICMI and the larger Muslim community in the political battles of Soeharto's final years.

These events provide insight into the changing nature of elite attitudes on Islam in the New Order era and counsel against the long-held view that Soeharto was deeply committed to Javanism or *Pancasila* pluralism. The ICMI legacy suggests a less generous conclusion: that Soeharto's religious policies were animated less by an enduring commitment to Javanism or *Pancasila* tolerance than by cold calculations as to what was required to defeat opponents and remain in power. The shifting opportunism of the president's religious policies, and his playing of different groups against one another, wreaked havoc with those who hoped the state might work with civil Islam rather than against it.

For the comparative study of Muslim politics, the ICMI example also sheds light on the dilemmas faced by Muslim democrats where Islamization is embraced by an authoritarian regime. In such difficult circumstances, ruling elites often play the interests of Muslim reformers against those of secular democrats. Inevitably this divide-and-conquer strategy has an effect not unlike that here in Indonesia, unleashing fierce debate in the Muslim community about the relative importance of democracy to Muslims. It was just such a debate that marked Soeharto's final years. But the issue did not end there. Attempting to trap political Islam, Soeharto became tangled in his own snare, not least of all by a Muslim community that proved more concerned with democracy and justice than the New Order master had imagined.

Old Beginnings

Media reports on ICMI's genesis often portray it as the spontaneous creation of five students from the Universitas Brawijaya in Malang, East Java.[1] The five students, the story goes, were devout but otherwise unexceptional youth who yearned to bring Muslim intellectuals of all persuasions together to talk about the future of the *ummat* and the nation. To do so, in early 1990 they came up with the idea of organizing a national conference of Muslim intellectuals to which leaders from all major Muslim associations, as well as the government and media, were to be invited. It was hoped that this meeting would in turn lead to the creation of a permanent association of intellectuals that might help to diminish the factionalism plaguing the Muslim community. What was most needed to revitalize Islam, the students explained, was unity.

Having come up with the idea in early 1990, the students then approached the rectors of the state-run Brawijaya University and Malang's Muhammadiyah University. Under the leadership of its reform-minded rector, Malik Fadjar,[2] in the late 1980s the Muhammadiyah University had earned a reputation as the bravest of Indonesia's Muslim universities, and a center for research on Islam and democracy. In public, the rectors of both universities responded favorably to the students' proposal but expressed reservations about the symposium's expense. Privately the rectors also voiced concern that security officials would not tolerate such a bold effort to unite Muslim thinkers.

It was no secret, after all, that as recently as January 1989 military authorities under the direction of the Catholic commander of the armed forces, General Benny Moerdani, had staged a show of force to close down a gathering of Muslim intellectuals in the town of Kaliurang near Yogyakarta, central Java. (Although today Moerdani is blamed by conservative Muslims for actions like these, insiders insist that he acted at the behest of Soeharto.) That meeting, too, had been organized to discuss plans for a national organization of Muslim intellectuals. The sponsors of this abortive initiative were two respected alumni of the Association of Muslim Students, Imaduddin Abdulrahmin and M. Dawam Rahardjo. Imaduddin and Dawam had invited fifty intellectuals to the meeting; forty came. On the second day, however, police showed up as well, and the meeting was forcibly closed.

Earlier, in 1984, there had been another attempt to create an association of Muslim intellectuals, at a meeting near Bogor in West Java. That meeting had been sponsored by the Council of Indonesian Ulama (MUI), a government-managed assembly of Islamic scholars, and Dawam Rahardjo's Institute for Religious and Philosophical Studies (LSAF) in Jakarta. At the meeting, Rahardjo expressed the view that the time seemed right to create a nonpolitical association of Muslim intellectuals. Representatives from the MUI balked, however, fearing government disapproval, and the plan was shelved. The effort was revived in 1987, again by Rahardjo and his friends. This time the organizers appealed to the upper reaches of the New Order elite, asking Alamsyah Ratu Perwiranegara, a Soeharto confidant, to act as a sponsor for the organization. Alamsyah agreed, but security officials squelched the initiative nonetheless, citing concerns that the organization violated the *Pancasila*.[3]

Undeterred by these setbacks, in early 1990 the five Malang youths set out at their own expense to visit centers of Islamic education in Java in order to promote their idea and to raise funds for the conference. In the course of their travels they met with prominent Muslim intellectuals, including, not coincidentally, Imaduddin and Dawam. Both men urged the students to think bigger than a mere symposium and promote the formation of an association of Muslim intellectuals, like the one they had attempted to found a few years earlier.[4]

Even on the basis of these few details, it is clear that press reports on the role of the five Brawijaya students in ICMI's founding hid what was, in fact, a more complex history. From the start, prominent Muslim intellectuals were directly involved in the effort. For political reasons, however, these senior intellectuals chose to distance themselves from the publicity surrounding ICMI's founding. Indeed, the Malang meeting in early 1990 at which the five Brawijaya students were supposed to have come up with the idea for a national symposium was not an ordinary student affair but had taken place in the context of a visit to the campus by none other than Dr. Imaduddin. It was he who had urged the students to sponsor a national symposium. Not coincidentally, the rector who had approved Imaduddin's visit to Brawijaya University—at a time when Imaduddin was still barred from most Indonesian campuses—was an alumni of the Muslim Students Association, of which Imaduddin himself had been a member in the late 1960s.

What the media account of the students' role correctly underscores, however, is that, at least in the first instance, the effort to establish an association of Muslim intellectuals did originate within the independent Muslim community. However much it was to be drawn into Soehartoist intrigues, the original idea for ICMI was not just something engineered by the regime, as has often been claimed. Rather than being the brainchild of five anonymous students from a provincial university, however, the plan for the association originated with well-known public intellectuals. Some of those intellectuals had reputations with the security forces that might have compromised efforts to establish the organization had their names been featured too prominently. Imaduddin openly acknowledges this, noting that his familiarity in security circles might have diminished the organization's chances had he been too directly involved in early discussions.[5]

In Search of Patron

One of the rules of the New Order political game was that for any organization to survive it had to receive official government approval. The surest way to win government approval was to secure the patronage of a well-placed regime official. With this model in mind, Imaduddin proposed that the students invite the minister of the environment, Dr. Emil Salim, and the minister of research and technology, Dr. B. J. Habibie, to act as co-chairmen of the national conference.

The choice of these two figures was revealing. Emil Salim was one of the architects of the New Order's fiscal reforms and its export-oriented industrialization policies. A soft-spoken gentleman with a twinkle in his eye, Salim was a well-regarded member of the so-called Berkeley mafia, liberal economists trained at the University of California, Berkeley (many under the sponsorship of the Ford Foundation) who, in the late 1960s and early 1970s, had urged the government to adopt market-oriented policies.[6] Salim was also one of the mid-level bureaucrats who in the late 1960s and 1970s had sponsored the admission of development-minded Muslims into government agencies, at a time when pious Muslims in government were few (chapter 4). In the 1980s

Salim had developed a reputation as a gentile proponent of clean government and improved relations with Muslims.

Habibie's public image was different. He was regarded not as an elite reformist but as one of Soeharto's most trusted and docile lieutenants. He was one of the few cabinet officials who could walk in and have a meeting with the president at almost any time, and one of the few with whom the reserved Soeharto had regular conversations. Habibie made no secret of his special relationship to the president. In public, he proudly identified himself as a "child" (*anak buah*) of Soeharto and a "student" of his political ways. However great his dependence on the president, however, Habibie's real passion was not politics, as such, but high technology. His most cherished dream was to make Third World Indonesia a manufacturer of that most First World of products, airplanes.

Soeharto had recruited Habibie to government service in 1974, when Habibie was working in West Germany. A few years earlier Habibie had earned a doctorate in engineering from the Technical University in Aachen, graduating summa cum laude. He went on to work in the German aircraft industry specializing in aeronautic design. Serious, pleasant mannered, and quick to learn, Habibie was soon elevated to the position of vice president and director of applied technology at Messerschmitt-Bolkow-Blohm, an aircraft manufacturer. No foreigner had ever achieved such an elevated position at Messerschmitt.

It was the promise of putting this passion for technology to work in Indonesia that lured Habibie back to his homeland. Soeharto's invitation to Habibie came by way of Ibnu Sutowo, the head of the giant state oil firm, Pertamina, in a meeting with Habibie in Dusseldorf in 1973. The year was one of great tumult in world oil markets, as Middle Eastern oil producers reduced their exports and the price of quality crude skyrocketed. As an oil exporter, Indonesia benefited from this rise in oil prices, and government revenues soared. The revenues captured Soeharto's imagination. After several years of hard work to stabilize finances, restore infrastructures, and expand farm production, the president was now dreaming of more ambitious projects.

After returning to Indonesia, Habibie worked for several months out of Sutowo's office, during which time he had no specific charge and no clear authority. An energetic man with a strong task orientation, Habibie was at first unhappy with his lack of institutional responsibility. Nonetheless he used the months with Sutowo to familiarize himself with Indonesia's bureaucratic culture and to devise plans for new state industries. Finally, in 1976, Habibie got the break he was waiting for. He was given control of a major state enterprise with his appointment to the directorship of the newly established Nusantara Aircraft Industry (IPTN). Two years later he was appointed state minister of research and technology in the Third Development Cabinet. Shortly thereafter he was also made director of Indonesia's "strategic industries," state-owned firms responsible for everything from aircraft and armaments to shipbuilding.

Few stars in Soeharto's inner circle had risen more quickly. The dreamy technologist had acquired an industrial empire.

By the time of ICMI's founding in 1990, Habibie had become the regime's leading proponent of state-supported industrialization. In this sense he was heir to the mantle of Lieutenant General Ibnu Sutowo, the former head of Pertamina. In the early 1970s Sutowo had used Pertamina's oil revenues to bankroll wildly unprofitable enterprises. Woefully ill managed, these had run up debts of more than ten billion U.S. dollars in just seven years.[7] Sutowo was removed from his post in February 1976, but he was never charged with criminal misconduct. Nor, despite Sutowo's failure, did Soeharto give up on his own plans for state-sponsored industrialization. As director of the state's strategic industries, Habibie became the spokesperson in the state administration for this side of Soeharto's personality. Habibie was never given funds on the titanic scale of Ibnu Sutowo, and his personal lifestyle was less ostentatious. But his strategic industries nonetheless absorbed hundreds of millions of state dollars each year. Despite repeated appeals by cabinet economists, the amounts of these subsidies were never disclosed and never allowed to become a topic of public discussion. The only person to whom Habibie ever had to present a balance sheet was Soeharto.

Chastened by Sutowo's failure, Habibie gave his strategy of state-subsidized industrialization a distinctive twist. He believed that the state should not try to do everything but concentrate its investment in a few select industries. Unlike the state's economists, Habibie believed that most state investment should go not into employment-generating, labor-intensive industries but into "value-added" high technology. By investing in industries of this sort, Habibie argued, Indonesia would not be doomed forever to remain a producer of poor-quality goods. It could leap-frog directly into the ranks of the advanced economies.

This curious industrial strategy reflected Habibie's own professional preferences as an aircraft engineer. But it also revealed what was to be an enduring blind spot in his economic thinking. His proposals took no account of the nature of global markets or comparative advantages. After all, even Japan had long hesitated to enter the aircraft market, recognizing that the industry was so competitive and technology-intensive that latecomers faced great risks. But Habibie was convinced that if the government invested in training and capital goods the resulting industries would eventually pay for themselves. Using technologies licensed at great cost from European firms, Habibie eventually managed to get several planes into the air. But none of his aircraft ventures ever came even vaguely close to breaking even.

It was not the market, however, that was critical in determining whether Habibie went forward with his plans. The realization of his technological dreams depended on the approval of one man alone, President Soeharto. And Soeharto found Habibie's ideas dazzling. Having restored Indonesia's economy and revitalized agriculture, the aging Soeharto hoped to crown his achievements as the

"Father of Development" (as he had had the National Assembly designate him) with the creation of First World industries. Habibie was the technologist of Soeharto's dreams.

Although both Habibie and Salim were regarded as members of the Muslim wing of the New Order elite, then, in many respects the two could not have been more different. With his privileged access to Soeharto, Habibie was the ultimate insider, though a bright and personally engaging one by New Order standards. In contrast, Salim, with his squeaky-clean commitment to good government, was always in danger of falling into the ranks of the regime's critics. (During the crisis of 1997–98, Salim became one of the first elite politicians to demand that Soeharto step down.) Further, Salim was known to disapprove of Habibie's management of the strategic industries and was also concerned about reports that Habibie was using his office to create cronyist businesses for his brother, wife, and son.

People who knew Habibie in Germany in the late 1960s and early 1970s say that he was never a particularly pious Muslim. His passion was technology, not piety, and he is said to have had a genuine affection for German science, culture, and cuisine. Friends report that when he returned to Indonesia in January 1974, Habibie experienced reverse culture shock. He was torn with doubts as to whether he could adapt to life back in Indonesia and whether he had made the right decision in relinquishing his position at Messerschmitt. He was especially preoccupied with the question of what he, a European-trained engineer, could possibly accomplish in backward Indonesia. After several months of uncertainty Habibie emerged from this personal crisis with a renewed sense of himself and his public charge. He chose to highlight two features in his personal profile. The first was the one he had emphasized in Germany: that he was a passionate builder of airplanes and missionary of high technology. Here was a role to which he could lay more effective claim than anyone else in Soeharto's inner circle.

The second strand in his new public persona, Habibie concluded, was that he would teach Indonesians how to be both modern and Muslim. Habibie's Islamic modernism had nothing to do with the complex legalisms of *shariah*. Although he was not comfortable with the phrase, his was essentially a *Protestant* Islam, inspired in part by the Christian Protestantism with which he had been intrigued back in Germany. For Habibie, Islam resembles German Protestantism in that it demands a spirit of hard work and scientific excellence, not turgid legal exegesis or, least of all, radical political ideology. This is not to say that Habibie's was not a deeply felt religiosity; on the contrary, after returning to Indonesia he developed a growing interest in pietistic dimensions of his faith. In the late 1970s Habibie performed his daily prayers faithfully; twice weekly he also fasted from both food and drink from the first light of day to sunset, on the model of the Prophet. At the same time, however, he emphasized that the most essential of contemporary Islam's demands is that one use one's mind and master modern technology.

Soeharto, too, changed in the 1980s in a way that reinforced his special relationship with Habibie. As it became clear that Indonesia was in the midst of a Muslim resurgence, and that all major Muslim organizations had agreed to his demand that they accept the *Pancasila* as their "sole foundation" (*asas tunggal*), Soeharto's attitude on organized Islam softened. Reassured that there were no more serious threats to the *Pancasila*, Soeharto began to study the Qur'an and Arabic language with a military chaplain (chapter 5). Many among Soeharto's confidantes were unaware of his new interest, but Habibie was. The president appreciated Habibie's interest in Islam and, as the Islamic revival gained force in the 1980s, sometimes shared his thoughts on religion with Habibie. When, in the late 1980s, Habibie began to make public statements about Islam's importance for national development, many in the Muslim community correctly concluded that these were not simply Habibie's opinions, but Soeharto's.

HABIBIE TAKES CHARGE

In his meetings with the Malang students, Emil Salim agreed to attend the national symposium but declined to play a leadership role in any organization that might emerge from its deliberations. He cited personal reasons, insisting he was "too old" and that Habibie would make a more energetic chairman. Privately, other Muslims said that there was no way the president would allow Salim to assume a leadership post in an organization from which he might be tempted to criticize the government. The Malang students therefore invited Habibie to lead the proposed organization which, at Nurcholish Madjid's suggestion, had tentatively acquired the title ISMI—*Ikatan Sarjana Muslim Indonesia* (Association of Muslim Indonesian Scholars).

Even at this late moment, however, Habibie was not entirely sure how far to go with the students. He wanted a clearer statement of their political loyalties, and a broader indication from the Muslim community, particularly its modernist leadership, that they would support him. Habibie's concerns reflected his own political dilemma. Up to this point, Habibie had had no independent political base; he owed all his political influence to the president. At the same time, however, it was no secret that he had high political ambitions. His prospects for realizing any such aspirations, however, depended on his ability to develop a mass following. The only conceivable group to which he might look for support, he felt, was modernist Muslims. Like him, they placed great emphasis on science, progress, and education. More important, aside from the democratic left (which no Soeharto confidants could dare embrace), the modernists were the one mass constituency that still had no effective voice in the regime. The Malang students' initiative offered Habibie a bridge to a constituency of which he had long dreamed.

Contacted by letter and through telephone appeals, Habibie at first made it look as if he was too busy to meet with the students. According to public accounts deliberately leaked by his aides, Habibie protested, "How can I do it? I am an engineer and a builder of airplanes, not an Islamic scholar!" Friends report that he was determined not to go forward until he made absolutely sure that he had the president's full support. Soeharto was still holding his political cards close to his vest; in particular, it was not yet clear whether Soeharto's overtures to the modernist Muslim community were any more than a strategem to build popular support for the 1992 elections, after which the concessions might end. Habibie had no interest in sacrificing himself for a temporary electoral strategy.

It was only after Habibie was contacted by the former minister of religion and close Soeharto confidant, Alamsyah Ratu Perwiranegara, that he agreed to meet with the students. Soeharto had instructed Alamsyah to confirm the seriousness of the invitation by contacting Habibie. This was the sign for which Habibie had been waiting. Although a well-known Soeharto loyalist, over the course of his career Alamsyah had maintained contact with moderate Muslims. To Habibie, the president's recruitment of Alamsyah underscored the seriousness of the ICMI initiative for Soeharto. It also sent a message to another constituency about which Habibie was concerned, the military leadership. Most of them made no secret of their dislike for Habibie and the ICMI initiative. With General Alamsyah's recruitment, the president had signaled that the high command should stand back and let Habibie proceed.

On August 23, 1990, the students, accompanied by Imaduddin, Dawam Rahardjo, and M. Syafii Anwar (a Rahardjo friend and respected journalist), traveled to Habibie's office on Thamrin Avenue to present their request to the minister. Habibie was solicitous but uncharacteristically quiet during the students' initial presentation. The meeting ended with Habibie asking the students to draw up a petition and circulate it among prominent Muslim intellectuals to express support for him and the organization. The petition was intended to impress upon the president and the nation that the students' appeal enjoyed broad public support.[8] Habibie also asked for an outline of the association's organization and goals, which he promised to present to the president. "I am a servant of the president," he said (according to the reports of those present at the meeting), "so I must go to him to request permission to work with you." The petition was seen by most observers as a tool with which Habibie could legitimate his ascension to a position of leadership in a Muslim community in which he had no prior involvement.

Over the next week, Imaduddin, Dawam Rahardjo, and Nurcholish Madjid—all members of the independent Muslim community—drew up a document outlining the organization's goals and expressing support for Habibie's chairmanship. They then circulated the document among prominent Muslim intellectuals in Jakarta, Bogor, Bandung, and Yogyakarta. Several leading intellectuals, such as the historian and Soeharto critic Deliar Noer refused to sign it. Noer insisted that Habibie had never done anything for the Muslim community and that the organization's real purpose was to rally support for Soeharto's reelection. Eventually, however, forty-nine individuals signed the document. In the meantime, too, Habibie talked with several of his colleagues in the cabinet, soliciting their advice on the wisdom of his leading the organization. It is interesting to note that most were not yet aware of the president's intentions and urged Habibie to decline the invitation, on the assumption that Soeharto would disapprove. One, Dr. Saleh Afiff (minister of national development planning), advised Habibie not to turn down the request but to seek Soeharto's counsel directly. Habibie agreed and arranged an appointment with the president, sending him the petition and outline of the organization's goals.

Only Habibie and Soeharto were present during their meeting but later the president's handlers circulated an idealized account of the exchange to cabinet officials and the media. According to this now mythic account, Habibie began the meeting by repeating his disclaimer that he is an engineer, a maker of airplanes, and unqualified to lead an association of Islamic intellectuals. Then, more quietly, he turned to the president and said, "Also, if I lead this organization, maybe I will be separated [*terpisah*] from Bapak [lit., "Father," "Sir"]. Perhaps my and Bapak's understanding of Islam differ?" Lacking an independent political base, Habibie always took care to demonstrate his unswerving loyalty to the president. However contrived, the official account of Habibie's meeting with the president reflected Habibie's very real concern that he not be given a task that might jeopardize his political future.

The mythic account of the meeting reports that President Soeharto responded without hesitation to Habibie's query, saying, "This is good, you can do it." Then, in a demonstration of his own mastery of Islamic knowledge, the president told Habibie to take a pen, open his notebook, and record what follows. Over the next two hours, the official account claims, the president "dictated" (*mendikte*) a long discussion of the basic principles of Islam, including the meaning of the *Sunnah*, obligatory prayer (*sholat*), and passages from the Qur'an. Again the image was that of Soeharto the "Bapak" (Father) instructing a favored if somewhat naive son. At the end, the president said, "Now you understand what I know." It was no accident, of course, that details of the president's demonstration of Islamic expertise were immediately leaked to the press. The story was supposed to underscore that the president's knowledge of normative Islam was great and that it was this religious knowledge, not some political instrumentality, that had led him to support the formation of this Islamic association.

After this, Habibie went to work to mobilize support for ICMI in elite circles. He invited several ministers and Muslim intellectuals to his home, where he described ICMI and invited them to assist in its establishment. Of the ministers in attendance, Minister Rudini, an ex-military man known for his nationalist and reformist leanings, initially expressed reservations about the organization. In a gesture that was to be repeated by hundreds of other government officials in months to come, however, upon learning of the president's support Rudini immediately agreed to join the organization.

Now with full presidential support, Habibie, on September 27, again met with the students and their supporters, informing them that the plan had the president's blessing. As a final condition of his agreeing to become chairman, however, Habibie asked that he be allowed to bring some of his staff from the Agency for the Assessment and Application of Technology (BPPT) to work in ICMI's administration. This was a delicate moment in Habibie's negotiations with independent Muslims involved in the ICMI effort. Up to this point, most Muslim activists had assumed that the organization they were founding was to be self-managed, even if titularly headed by Habibie. Habibie's appointment of loyalists to strategic posts in ICMI indicated that the organization was not going to enjoy the autonomy the independents had hoped for.

Among the aides Habibie proposed to bring to ICMI was Dr. Wardiman Djojonegoro, an engineer and close assistant to Habibie at the BPPT. After 1990 Wardiman would become Habibie's right-hand man in ICMI; in 1993 he was named minister of education and culture. A Madurese of aristocratic background, in the 1980s Wardiman had a reputation for enjoying the good life and having decidedly "nationalist" views on matters of Islam. In his years at the BPPT, however, Wardiman had also demonstrated managerial skill and unfailing loyalty to Habibie. His appointment to the steering committee of ICMI was a clear indication that in selecting his aides Habibie aimed to put loyalty above devotion to the Muslim cause.[9] Habibie's appointment of loyalists was also intended to reassure the armed forces that he intended to control independent activists in the new organization, and not provide them with a platform for political Islam. In his public pronouncements, Habibie repeatedly emphasized that ICMI was not political but techno-scientific and educational.[10]

At the same September meeting, Habibie suggested that the organization's first national symposium be held at the beginning of December on the campus of Brawijaya University in Malang. Three teams were set up to coordinate plans for the symposium. With the president's blessing, preparations for the December meeting now proceeded apace. During October and November 1990 officials from the state-sponsored Council of Islamic Scholars were drawn into the preparations, as were staff from the ministries of religion and information. What had begun as a grass-roots effort by a few Muslim students and independent intellectuals had indeed become a top-heavy and regime-controlled initiative.

BUREAUCRATS, INTELLECTUALS, ACTIVISTS

As this brief history indicates, it was clear from the beginning that ICMI was not going to become the independent body its student and activist supporters had dreamed of. Soeharto was intent on using the organization for his own ends; Habibie was determined to ensure that his allies controlled its leadership. For Soeharto, ICMI was but the latest in a series of organizations he had created to co-opt support and contain opposition. For Habibie, however, ICMI was a new political adventure, rich with possibilities but also fraught with danger. Military critics were waiting in the wings, and if ICMI became too independent, it would be the end of Habibie.

Despite the domination of its leadership posts by regime loyalists, ICMI was never just an instrument of presidential or Habibie ambition. Although Soeharto and Habibie exercised ultimate control, there were several constituencies in ICMI's ranks, each with its own ideas of what ICMI should become. The first and most powerful of these internal groupings was the one so apparent in the preparations for ICMI's founding, government bureaucrats close to Habibie. After 1993 the ranks of this first grouping were swelled as other officials rushed to join the organization. In sheer numerical terms, state bureaucrats always comprised the ICMI core.

The second group in the new organization consisted of independent scholars and intellectuals. Unlike the bureaucrats, most ICMI intellectuals were unhappy with Habibie's domination of the organization. Most also opposed the crude politicization of ICMI, whether in the service of Habibie or statist Islam. Although never the dominant force in ICMI, the independent intellectuals were not marginal to the organization's day-to-day affairs. On the contrary, to the Indonesian public and in their own eyes they were the "real ICMI" (*ICMI sejati*). It was they who had taken the lead in ICMI's creation. They were also the ones who were most keen on working out a new relationship between Muslims and the state.

The third and last of ICMI's groupings, the independent political activists, was the most heterogeneous. Although often portrayed as pro-Soeharto, the activists' attitudes on Soeharto and democracy were, in fact, extremely varied. Some in this group were unswerving Soeharto loyalists; others counted themselves among the president's most uncompromising critics. Although disunited, ICMI's activist factions played a decisive role in shaping ICMI's internal organization and its relationship with the Soeharto regime.

Viewed as a whole, the acrobatics of these three groups provide insight into Muslim politics in the late New Order and its attempted degradation at the hands of Soeharto.

Bureaucratic Elites

The cream of the crop among the ICMI elite, the government bureaucrats at first consisted of officials from Habibie's strategic industries and his Agency for the Assessment and Development of Science and Technology. Most of these officials were uninterested in Islamic ideology, especially of an activist sort. Like Habibie, they were also opposed to ICMI's becoming the nucleus for an independent political party. The ICMI bureaucrats were already members of the state party, Golkar; some played key roles in its operations. Rather than wanting ICMI to become an independent organization, then, these people hoped to turn ICMI into an elite lobby in Golkar and the state.

For self-interested reasons, at the very least, many in the bureaucrat group *were* interested in effecting change in the New Order regime. In particular, most hoped that ICMI would help bring about a heightened state commitment to Muslim enterprise and Muslim representation in the state bureaucracy. Inasmuch as this group was concerned about reform at all, then, the type they had in mind was best expressed in the Indonesianized English phrase popularized by ICMI, *proporsionalisme*. *Proporsionalisme* in government and the economy was to become one of ICMI's most lasting contributions to Indonesian political discourse. For elite Muslims like Habibie, the slogan had an alluring ideological appeal. It clothed their rivalry with secular nationalists for the spoils of state in the garb of a populist struggle for Muslim civil rights.

The central demand of the proportionalist argument was that the state had to do more to bring Muslim representation in government, the military, and business into line with Muslim numbers in society as a whole. Proportionalists were particularly concerned with what they regarded as two irregularities in the national landscape. The first concerned Christians. Although they comprise just under 10 percent of the national population, Christians have long been disproportionately represented in the professions and middle class. The primary reason for this imbalance is that during the colonial era Christians had greater access than Muslims to higher education and state resources. In the military the purge of Muslim officers involved in the 1950s' rebellions also contributed to a disproportionate Christian representation in the officer corps. For hard-line conservatives like the *Dewan Dakwah Islamiyah Indonesia* (chapter 5), these imbalances were not merely the unfortunate effects of political history but the conscious product of a sinister plot by domestic and international forces to "Christianize" Indonesia. Few in ICMI's bureaucratic elite took such charges seriously. But many bureaucrats were convinced that the Muslim public's belief in such conspiracy theories was symptomatic of imbalances that the New Order regime had to address.

As great a concern as Christians to ICMI's elite bureaucrats was the economic dominance of Sino-Indonesians. Their prominence in the Indonesian economy was not new, of course. During the 1950s, when the divide between Chinese and *pribumi* (lit., "sons of the soil," i.e., native, non-Chinese) was burdened with a less religious freight than it was in the 1990s, government circles were already talking of the need to diminish Chinese economic dominance. The government launched several affirmative-action programs during those years to address the problem. Plagued by corruption and cronyist patronage, the programs had little positive impact.[11] In the years since the New Order's founding, the Sino-Indonesian economic advantage had, if anything, only increased. The remarkable expansion of overseas Chinese capitalism in East and Southeast Asia during the 1970s and 1980s created a transnational network for trade, credit, and information superior to anything commanded by the region's native entrepreneurs.[12] Another reason big Chinese businesses thrived in New Order Indonesia, however, was that during its first two decades the Soeharto regime preferred working with Chinese rather than the native (and largely Muslim) middle class. Lacking full political rights, Chinese were unlikely to protest when subjected to the patronal exploitation for which Soeharto cronies were famous.

For these and other reasons, most observers estimate that by the 1990s Sino-Indonesians controlled about 65 percent of Indonesia's nonfarm private enterprise. Their position in the economy as a whole was less decisive, because the agricultural sector is quite large and state firms account for 30–35 percent of Indonesia's GDP. Enterprise in both these spheres is *pribumi*-dominated.[13] Nonetheless, as the Muslim middle class grew restless in the 1980s, a central issue it became concerned with was Muslim underrepresentation in business. This notion was then picked up by elite bureaucrats like Habibie. They understood that proportionalism could put populist winds in their careerist sails.

A second wave of bureaucrats flooded into ICMI after Soeharto's announcement of his new cabinet in March 1993. This group consisted less of Habibie loyalists than Muslim officials with a keen sense of changing factional winds in the bureaucracy. After the 1993 cabinet was announced, it became clear that ICMI was not a passing phenomenon but a growing bureaucratic presence. From this point on, Muslim officials aspiring to upward mobility could not afford to overlook the benefits of getting onboard the ICMI bus.

It had not always been this way. When ICMI was first established in December 1990 its professional benefits for Muslim bureaucrats were far from clear. In its early months, ICMI was the target of repeated criticism by high-ranking military authorities and nationalist-inclined politicians, and many people predicted that the organization would be short-lived. Indeed, before 1993 critics like Abdurrahman Wahid of Nahdlatul Ulama had forecast that Soeharto, once reelected in 1993, would allow ICMI to languish. Wahid was certain that ICMI was just a momentary electoral ploy. And when Soeharto announced his cabinet in March 1993, some observers felt that this pessimistic prognosis had been confirmed. Although the number of non-Muslims in the cabinet (four of forty ministers) had diminished to a proportion roughly equivalent to their percentage in society—a clear concession to ICMI proportionalism—all the ICMI sympathizers in the new cabinet were from the ranks of Habibie's elite bureaucrats, not ICMI's independent scholars or activists.[14] The "real ICMI" had gained little ground at all.

Although Soeharto excluded independent ICMI scholars and activists from his cabinet, he did not exclude them from government as a whole. On the contrary, by some estimates,[15] more than three hundred Muslims of a loosely ICMI complexion were appointed to the thousand-member People's Consultative Assembly, making them the single largest nonmilitary constituency in the body. It was a well-known fact that membership in the MPR facilitates heightened influence in government and business.

It was ICMI representation in the MPR more than the composition of the cabinet, then, that caught the attention of ambitious Muslim officials. The result was a veritable sea change in bureaucratic culture between the installation of the sixth development cabinet in March 1993 and the ICMI national congress in December 1995. Fearful of aligning themselves with the wrong faction, most Muslim bureaucrats in 1991–92 had hesitated to join the government-sponsored organization. After 1993, however, this hesitation vanished and mid-level Muslim bureaucrats rushed to join ICMI. This second influx insured that pro–status quo bureaucrats were the largest of ICMI's core constituencies.

The growing participation of government bureaucrats had implications beyond ICMI itself. After 1993 fierce struggles erupted in state bureaus and universities across the country, as ICMI members sought to take control of offices and budgets. On European and American campuses with large Indonesian populations, student organizations were similarly polarized between supporters and opponents of ICMI.[16] In commenting on this rivalry in discussions with this author, the ICMI leadership typically referred to their anti-ICMI rivals as Christians and "nationalists." However, the ideological complexion of the ICMI opposition was actually more varied. It included secular nationalists; Golkar traditionalists; military nationalists; Christians, Buddhists, and Hindus; secular modernizers; opponents of Habibie's industrial policies; and, most of all, democratic Muslims uneasy with what Abdurrahman Wahid and others regarded as the "reconfessionalization" of Indonesian society.

Although few foreign observers had noticed, the struggle between these two piecemeal alliances, ICMI and the "nationalists," marked a new phase in New Order cultural politics. The change touched on something few would have thought possible in the heat of the ideological campaigns of the early 1980s: the return of sectarian factionalism to the ruling elite itself. From the 1970s through the mid-1980s the Soeharto regime had been unrelenting in its efforts to force all social and political organizations to recognize the *Pancasila* as their sole foundation. Now, the symbols of Muslim mobilization long suppressed

by the Soeharto regime had reappeared—in, of all places, the government bureaucracy. More astounding yet, this sectarian divide had reemerged with full
presidential blessing. ICMI was the beginning of a "new" New Order indeed.

Muslim Intellectuals and the Public Sphere

If bureaucrats constituted the largest and most powerful of ICMI's subgroupings, they never controlled all aspects of the organization. In fact, as
far as many in the media and Muslim community were concerned, the "real"
membership of ICMI consisted not of government bureaucrats but of the organization's two other groupings: Muslim intellectuals, including many of a civil
democratic complexion, and activists interested in using ICMI to promote political change. These two groups were not mutually exclusive; many people
combined the roles of scholars and activists. Complicating matters further,
each subgroup was not ideologically unified, least of all in their attitude toward
Soeharto. Some in each subgrouping were pro-Soeharto; others were not.

In terms of their numbers, the independent intellectuals were the smallest
of ICMI's three core constituencies. Nonetheless their moral influence in ICMI
and the Muslim public at large was the greatest. The single most influential
figure in this group was Nurcholish Madjid, the former student leader who, in
the 1970s, had gone on to promote a civil-democratic vision of Islam that had
great appeal in the new Muslim middle class (chapter 5). In some accounts[17]
Madjid is thought to have played a minor role in ICMI's establishment, and
then distanced himself from the organization after 1993 as ICMI was drawn
into elite politics. But Madjid himself views his role otherwise. Yes, he told me
during our annual meetings between 1991 and 1998, he liked to keep his
distance from the bureaucrats and regime-oriented ICMI activists. While criticizing ICMI's politicization, however, Madjid remained a key player in the
organization until the overthrow of Soeharto in May 1998. It was Madjid, after
all, who drafted the document in mid-1990 that outlined ICMI's goals and
organizational structure. And it was Madjid more than any other person who
regularly intervened to protect reform-minded activists when their actions provoked regime censure. Madjid was unstinting in his criticisms of those who
would reduce ICMI to a vehicle of Habibie ambition. But he never severed his
ties with the organization because he recognized that the bureaucrats and regime activists were not its whole. Much of the public agreed with Madjid, and
regarded him, not Habibie, as the organization's spiritual leader.

Madjid was convinced that most of the Muslim middle class believed, with
him, that Islam must influence politics and public life, but in a way that rejects
the subordination of high principles to regimist ploys. Long before Amien Rais
(the Muhammadiyah leader) popularized the phrase, Madjid's was a "high politics" of political civility and principled pluralism. In 1991–92, as conservatives

were mobilizing to use ICMI against Christians and "nationalists" in the bureaucracy, Madjid made repeated appeals for inter-religious tolerance. In a celebrated and courageous presentation on October 21, 1992, he insisted that the Qur'an was revealed to confirm and protect the truth of prior revelations, especially but not exclusively those of Judaism and Christianity.[18] This meant that the details of these other revelations were still valid except if explicitly abrogated by the Qur'an. Inasmuch as this is so, Madjid insisted, believers in these other revelations should be recognized as brothers and sisters within an "Islam" understood as including everyone who has surrendered (*pasrah*) to God's will. In this broader sense of the term, then, "Muslims" include not just believers in God's revelation to the Prophet Muhammad but Christians, Jews, and others.[19] This interpretation was greeted with outrage in conservative circles like the Dewan Dakwah Islamiyah Indonesia (chapter 5). In Jakarta, Yogyakarta, and several other cities, threats were made against Madjid's life.

But this controversy did not lead Madjid to retire from public life or give up his role in ICMI. In 1993–94 he was at it again, speaking out on the importance of free speech and public criticism for democracy and society. That same year he risked Soeharto's ire by calling for a genuinely democratic multiparty system. In 1994 he publicly challenged one of the ideological tenets of the New Order, insisting that Islam does not merely require "consultation" and "consensus" but principled political opposition. In 1996–97, as Indonesia experienced growing ethnoreligious violence (chapter 7), Madjid again spoke out on the importance of civility and tolerance for democracy. A true civil society, he wrote, requires a "common platform" across which religious, ethnic, and political differences can be managed with civility and respect. During the last months of the Soeharto regime, finally, Madjid risked everything by going public with his opposition to Soeharto's rule. He was moved to speak bluntly as it became clear that some among the president's supporters were attempting to recruit ultraconservative Muslims to a hateful campaign against Chinese and Christians (chapter 7). The man long thought opposed to the "politicization" of Islam, then, repeatedly demonstrated that he was not against religion in politics per se but to the subordination of Islam's high ideals to low regimist ploys.

There were other intellectuals in ICMI, and, in general, its center of gravity on matters of religious law and doctrine was less consistently pluralist than Madjid. On questions of Muslim politics, in particular, ICMI intellectuals had strong disagreements. Although the majority accepted the idea that democracy is rightly based on the principle of popular sovereignty, a few (e.g., Jalaluddin Rahmat, Ismail Suny) continued to present arguments similar to those elaborated by Mohammad Natsir in the 1950s, to the effect that ultimate sovereignty lies with God, not humans.[20] Similarly, although most of ICMI's intellectuals embraced the concept of the nation-state and citizenship, a few (Amien Rais, Ali Yafie) insisted that Muslim law requires that government distinguish Muslims from *dhimmi* (A., "protected minorities"), at least in the sense that the presidency be reserved for a Muslim.[21] Finally, although the great majority of ICMI intellectuals emphasized the importance of equal rights for women, most rejected the bold recommendations concerning women's roles that were made by the former minister of religion Munawir Sjadzali (minister, 1983–93). Among other matters, Sjadzali had argued that the Qur'an's message on female inheritance, specifying that a daughter's share be half that of a son's, be abrogated on the grounds that the economic situation of women in Indonesia is different from that in the time of the Prophet Muhammad.[22] Indonesian women are co-partners in the household, Sjadzali said, and, as such, their daughters should receive shares equal to sons.

Although they disagreed on details of Islamic law, the great majority of ICMI's independent intellectuals agreed with Madjid on the importance of democracy, civil society, and tolerance. The majority did not lament ICMI's intellectual pluralism but celebrated it. For these people, ICMI's worth lay not in advancing Habibie's career or taking one more step down that golden road to a magical Muslim unity but in providing an arena in which Muslims could have a dialogue in a free and civil manner. Put in the vocabulary of contemporary democratic theory (one that intellectuals like Madjid used), the primary utility of ICMI was as an open *public sphere* for discussion and exchange.[23] That this discussion did not bring a settled consensus was no problem as far as most of ICMI's intellectuals were concerned. Free speech and civil discussion were *democratic* goods in their own right.

For many Western observers, and for some Indonesian critics, the idea that independent intellectuals saw ICMI primarily as a forum for free discussion invites disbelief. After all, such a tepid program pales in comparison with the big-power plays of Soeharto and Habibie. But one has to remember that the political repression of the late Soekarno era and New Order had effectively barred modernist Muslims from public discussion and debate. However restrictive the larger system of the 1990s, ICMI gave Muslim intellectuals the impression that they were again a respected partner in the national dialogue.

The question remained, nonetheless, as to whether this Muslim public sphere would merely be narrowly self-serving, or, as Madjid hoped, promote the democratic rights of people of all faiths. The achievement of this latter goal was far from guaranteed.

Activists Disunited

The third and last of ICMI's three groupings, the political activists, was always the most controversial. The activists have been accused of everything from being Soeharto's lackeys to being his enemies. Ironically, to some degree all these charges are true, in the sense that some activists displayed each of these attitudes. But the truth is that ICMI's activists never shared a cohesive political vision. They were divided into three rival groupings: pro-Soeharto but anti-military populists; anti-Soeharto reformists; and pro-Soeharto *regimist* Muslims.

The pro-Soeharto but anti-military populists were under the leadership of ICMI's most controversial activist, Adi Sasono. Adi started his political career in the early 1960s as a member of the Muslim Students Association. During 1965–66 he played a minor role in the student action groups that helped to bring Soekarno down. In the early New Order Adi's ideas on politics and modernization were influenced by socialist intellectuals, especially Rahman Tolleng and the secular modernizers of *Mahasiswa Indonesia* (chapter 4). In 1968, however, Adi and Dawam Rahardjo broke with Tolleng to create a new journal, *Mimbar Demokrasi. Mimbar* was to be democratic and modernizing like Tolleng's publication, but it was also intended to reach out to a broader Islamic public. Well before the Islamic revival of the late 1970s, Adi had decided that he would make Islam his vehicle for political ambition.

At a personal level, Adi was less well known for expertise in Islam than for his interest in grass-roots development through nongovernmental organizations (NGOs or, in Indonesian, LSMs, *Lembaga Swadaya Masyarakat*). In the late 1960s and early 1970s Sasono aligned himself with proponents of NGO-based small-scale enterprise, "appropriate technology," people's credit schemes, and cooperatives. Even in these early years there were indications that Adi hoped to put these organizations to grander use. Friends who worked with Adi in the 1970s recall his having little patience for the tiresome labor of educating the urban poor or training villagers. Activists at a Jakarta-based NGO where Adi worked in the early 1980s remarked that in the course of a big development project in Qur'anic boarding schools (*pesantren*), Adi seemed less interested in the *santri* students than in using the project to mobilize political supporters.

Adi's appetite for political networking was handicapped, however, by the fact that he lacked a steady patron. In the early 1970s Adi allied himself briefly with the popular mayor of Jakarta, Ali Sadikin, and received funds for several small programs. In the 1980s he worked closely with a Jakarta-based NGO, LP3ES.[24] From there he set out to establish his own development institute, appealing to foreign sponsors like the German Neumann Stiftung and the Ford Foundation. Having heard of his limited management skills, however, most donors declined, and Adi remained a bit player in the big world of Jakarta NGOs.

In addition to his reputation as an inconsistent manager, Adi's profile was complicated by an ideological factor. Although, since the early 1960s, he had sought to present himself as a Muslim activist, Adi's reputation in Jakarta was not primarily as a Muslim thinker but as a representative of that more exclusive club of those who try to combine Muslim modernism with antiestablishment politics. The language of social justice and egalitarianism that Adi invoked in his public statements was that of progressive Muslims and socialist democrats, not the mainstream Muslim leadership. Adi's reputation had been reinforced by his celebrity in the early 1980s as one of Indonesia's leading proponents of a Latin American–style dependency theory, complete with its critique of metropolitan capitalism and the West. Adding to his socialist image, in the mid-1970s Adi joined with secular nationalists and democratic Muslims to create a nongovernmental organization designed to ease the integration of ex-PKI prisoners back into society. The parolees were encountering hostility in their home villages, and this organization sought to address their plight.

When Adi spoke of building a Muslim mass movement in his early years, then, his statements were often hard to distinguish from those of left-leaning progressives. He stressed issues of workers' rights, economic equality, and social justice, not Muslim economics or devotion. In the late 1980s Adi did begin to pepper his speeches with Islamic phraseology. Despite these efforts, as Adi became a force in ICMI in the 1990s the oft-heard crack was that he was a "watermelon Muslim"—"green on the outside, red on the inside."

ICMI's establishment in December 1990 provided Adi with the structure and resources he had always lacked. With them, Adi came into his own. Just a year after the organization's founding, Adi had catapulted himself into Habibie's inner circle. By 1995 he was the number-two man in the organization, pushing aside even Habibie's close aides. Adi's efforts to win Habibie's confidence were aided by the fact that, unlike the staff from Habibie's institutes, Adi was popular among urban Muslim activists. Equally impressive as far as Habibie was concerned, Adi was a well-known figure in NGO circles, the leadership of which shared his enthusiasm for cooperatives and small enterprise. These populist credentials gave Adi a mass appeal which Habibie hoped to draw on.

In the course of his ascent into the ICMI leadership, Adi also moderated his views on capitalism, though in a manner that raised eyebrows among his prodemocracy friends. Rather than speaking generally of the evils of international capital, as he had before, Adi now focused his criticisms on ethnic inequalities in the economy. Whereas a decade earlier Adi had implied that the New Order regime was a comprador of international capital, he now took care to avoid criticizing Soeharto and the indigenous, *pribumi* wealthy. When asked what could be done to address the imbalance between Chinese and *pribumi*, Adi responded by stressing the importance of cooperatives, much as he always had. But from 1992 on, he also spoke of the need for the state to sponsor *pribumi* businesses and to maintain its hold on state-owned enterprise so as to counter the Chinese. Populist economics had converged with regime interests indeed.

In the years following ICMI's founding Adi also became a close ally of Probosutedjo, the wealthy stepbrother of the president, regarded by many as one of the masters of New Order cronyism. Probosutedjo was well known for his criticisms of Chinese; his enemies called him a racist.[25] Unlike his reserved elder brother, Probosutedjo took to ICMI with a missionary zeal. He spoke passionately of the need for *proportionalism* in the economy and government, became a staunch advocate of Islamic banking, and made statements supportive of Adi's work with cooperatives. Adi's networking had indeed caught a big fish.

Careful not to contradict Habibie, Adi continued to differ with his boss on the critical question of what ICMI was to become over the long term. Habibie's views on the matter were well known: He wanted ICMI to support Golkar and, eventually, his own campaign for president. In contrast, consistent with his earlier populism, Adi spoke of the need to transform ICMI into a mass-based movement for structural change. Although he was careful not to express the view too openly, it was no secret that Adi also believed that Indonesia could only be transformed by returning the military to its barracks. If the first wing of Adi's populist Islamism was proportionalism, the second and more startling was anti-militarism.

Most in ICMI's activist wing were unwilling to go so far as Adi in this criticism. Most felt it dangerous to risk the military's ire when ICMI was still so weak. A small number took even greater issue with Adi, insisting that his opposition to the military was stupid and unnecessary. Linked to a regimist-Muslim faction in Golkar (see below), these pro-military activists felt that there was no need to challenge the military establishment, since eventually it would realize the wisdom of making common cause with conservative Muslims.

Among those activists who shared Adi's anti-militarism, however, most also agreed with his arguments as to what should be done with Soeharto. Like Adi, they emphasized that Soeharto was no longer just a military man but had become an independent political force all his own. He alone in the Indonesian political firmament, they insisted, has the power to take on the military. In private conversations, most of Adi's supporters admitted that they had no illusions about Soeharto as a person. They conceded that he was incorrigibly corrupt and had done great harm to Muslims in his first years of rule. But, they added, Soeharto will not rule forever. In the meantime, they argued, ICMI-ites should take aggressive advantage of the opportunity Soeharto has provided. In Adi's eyes this meant that ICMI should move quickly to build as large a nonmilitary presence in government as possible. ICMI-ites need to infiltrate the bureaucracy, win control of ministries, and build a force that can search out and neutralize "secular nationalist" supporters of military rule.

But it was not just the bureaucracy that Adi's supporters hoped to control. They also devised bold plans for mass mobilization. Building on his earlier work in the NGO community, in the 1990s Adi positioned himself as *the* elite spokesperson for Indonesia's cooperatives; he also had his allies appointed to leadership posts in the government-controlled Federation of Cooperatives. It was as a result of these efforts that Adi was named minister of cooperatives in the "reformation" cabinet announced by Habibie after Soeharto's resignation in May 1998. When, in 1992, ICMI began to develop a national network of Islamic "people's credit bureaus," Adi's allies were also there, securing appointments to key posts.

For Adi's military rivals, however, the most alarming of his mass initiatives was that undertaken in 1994 and 1995, when his operatives attempted to win leadership positions in the government-controlled national labor federation (SPSI). Adi's agents spoke openly of the need to "bring ICMI to labor." During most of the New Order, local military officials supplemented their incomes by offering security services to businesses and factory owners; services offered included labor discipline and strike breaking.[26] Adi's operatives were aware of these cozy deals, and, in appealing to workers, made a point of criticizing collusion between the military and big business (much of which is Chinese). News of these appeals quickly reached military intelligence, which had penetrated every level of the labor movement.[27] The military moved quickly to block Adi's labor program. By 1996 military officials had removed Adi's aides from the few leadership positions they had won and warned his labor supporters to cease associating with him. For military officials, the entire episode confirmed their suspicions that Adi was a dangerous opponent willing to take on the military on their own turf.[28] For many in the military, Adi had become a threat as sinister as Habibie himself.

Most in ICMI's second activist wing, the reform activists, disagreed with Sasono, hoping that heightened Muslim presence in state and society would eventually bring about a new compromise with the military.[29] Although the reformists felt that the military had overstepped its authority, they were resigned to the idea that populist mobilization against the military was foolish. Rather than pushing the military into a corner, then, these activists hoped that the simple pressure of social change would relax tensions, diminish the military's political role, and allow a gradual increase in representative democracy.

With their resigned realism, this second group, the reform activists, could at times sound accommodating to Soeharto. The reform activists took pains to applaud the president for what he had accomplished in the economy and for his support of Islam. In the election campaign of 1992, the ICMI leadership was pressured to make public statements supporting Soeharto for president. Most reform activists went along with ICMI's bureaucratic wing and made these gestures. Like Amien Rais, the outspoken leader of Muhammadiyah (and an ICMI reformist), however, most also made clear that they hoped that during the next round of elections in 1997–98 there would be more candidates and fairer electoral procedures. Reform activists like the University of Indonesia professor Sri Bintang Pamungkas, went even further. They spoke out openly against corruption, called for an end to the military's role in politics, and regularly demanded that Soeharto step down.

A third and final grouping among the ICMI activists, whom I shall call the *regimists*, had an entirely different perspective on these questions of democracy, the military, and Soeharto. This group included Din Syamsuddin, head of the youth wing of Muhammadiyah and, from 1991 on, a top-ranking Golkar strategist;[30] Amir Santosa, an associate professor of political science at the University of Indonesia who, in the 1980s, had switched from the nationalist camp to regime Islam; and more shadowy figures like Fadli Zon and Eggy Sudjana. Sudjana was a former Muslim student activist who in the early 1990s had been recruited to work at Adi Sasono's Center for Information and Development Studies (CIDES). Although Adi had his own political agenda, the behind-the-scene activities of Sudjana showed that there were points on which the Sasono populists and the regimists collaborated. Not the least of their mutual interests was their support for Soeharto.

From the beginning, Din, Amir, Fadli, Eggy, and others in the regimist group stated publicly that Muslims should not oppose but should work with the government, on the grounds that Soeharto was doing much good for the Muslim community. In this and other statements the regimists spoke little about democratization. Some were openly skeptical about the compatibility of democracy with Islam or Indonesian culture.[31] While advocating a heightened role for Islam, then, the regimists were staunch supporters of the Soeharto status quo. Unlike Sasono, the regimists also advocated cooperation with pro-regime segments of the military. Just as the government had become more accommodating toward Islam, the regimists argued, over time the military will develop a collaborative relationship with Muslims. Inasmuch as this is so, the regimists asserted, there is no reason to push the military into a corner.

On the question of the government party Golkar, the regimists were closer to Habibie and the ICMI bureaucrats than they were to the Sasono populists. Like Habibie, the regimists argued that the central institution through which a new accommodation between government, military, and Muslims will be achieved is not ICMI but Golkar. In their eyes, ICMI was just a taxi for the ride up the road to Golkar and the state. In taking this position, the regimists advocated the "Islamization" of Golkar and the bureaucracy. They were adamant that there was no need for broader changes to the system. Muslim proportionalism was vital. But proportionalism did not require an upending of any of the key elements in the status quo: Soeharto's rule, military involvement in politics, *Pancasila* as the sole foundation, or big-power patronage in business.

Although they agreed with the ICMI bureaucrats on the questions of Soeharto and Golkar, the regimists disagreed with the bureaucrats on the critical issue of Habibie's political role. The regimists saw themselves as first and foremost allied to Soeharto and conservative members of the military. The regimists also had ties to Soeharto's children, several of whom contributed generously to a regimist think tank set up in 1994 (see below). Inasmuch as Habibie served the interests of Soeharto, the first family, and the military, then, the regimists were ready to work with him. But if and when their interests diverged, the regimists made clear that they would side with Soeharto and the military.

Although at first this strategy seemed clear, its implementation after 1995 was to prove difficult. In that year, factionalism in elite circles became so bad that it reached into the ranks of the military. Splits in the "Muslim" wing of the military forced individual regimists to choose one military sponsor over another; eventually ICMI's regimist clique split in two (chapter 7).

In 1994, however, there were few signs of this impending elite factionalism. On the contrary, in that year there was much to suggest that the changes which Din and Amir had forecast, promising closer collaboration between regimist Muslims and the military, were under way. In 1994 President Soeharto replaced several of the most prominent critics of ICMI in the military command with figures sympathetic to regimist Islam. The controversial Catholic minister of defense (1988–93) and head of the armed forces, Benny Moerdani, was forced into retirement. The head of the armed forces' powerful Bureau for Social and Political Affairs (Sospol), Lieutenant General Harsudiyono Hartas, a strong ICMI critic, was replaced by Lieutenant General Hartono. Hartono was known to be sympathetic to ICMI and, not coincidentally, hostile toward Nahdlatul Ulama's Abdurrahman Wahid. Hartono also had close personal ties to several of the president's children; in February 1995 he was made army chief of staff. The new armed forces commander, General Feisal Tanjung, was also seen as a supporter of regimist Islam.[32] So, too, was the president's son-in-law, Major-General Prabowo Subianto, who, though young, was rapidly moving up the ranks of the military command.

Together, these four officers—Feisal Tanjung, Hartono, Syarwan Hamid, and Prabowo—comprised the ascendant "Islamic" wing of the armed forces. It cannot be overemphasized, however, that the "Islam" they supported was not that of Nahdlatul Ulama, Muhammadiyah, or the majority of Indonesian Muslims, but Soeharto-dependent regimist Islam.[33] It should also be noted that Soeharto's removal of the anti-ICMI commanders in 1994 did not reflect a general warming of ties between "ABRI" and "Islam." By 1994 neither of these two entities was sufficiently united on the question of Soeharto and Islam to allow their characterization in unitary terms. On Soeharto and democracy, ICMI was split. In ABRI, too, factional tensions were growing, especially between the "green" (regimist Islam) wing and a "red-and-white" nationalist wing. The "greens" were animated as much by personal political ambition as any ideological conviction. The "red-and-white" group included in its ranks many pious Muslim officers deeply concerned by what they regarded as the subordination of Islam to Soeharto interests.

There were good reasons for these concerns. Just after Soeharto announced his changes in the ABRI high command, Feisal, Hartono, and Prabowo joined with several of the president's children to create a well-endowed think tank for Din, Amir, Fadli, and several other ICMI regimists. The think tank was known by its English name, the Center for Policy and Development Studies or, simply, CPDS. The CPDS's sponsors had ambitious plans. The center was intended to become the leading think tank for regimist Islam and to serve as the bridge between ICMI regimists and military "greens."[34] As such, it was also intended to marginalize intellectuals and reform activists in ICMI who still dreamed that the organization might be used to promote democratic reform.

After 1994 the CPDS leadership moved quickly to position their think tank as the main policy and strategy center for ICMI. A few years earlier, most people had assumed that Adi Sasono's Center for Information and Development Studies was to play this role. But CIDES had continued to sponsor conferences on human rights, sustainable development, and equitable growth. In the face of such independence, the regime slashed its funding for CIDES. In contrast, the CPDS received generous donations from the presidential first family. The regime's lavishness allowed the CPDS to hold its weekly meetings in a private room in one of the capital's most expensive hotels, the Jakarta Hilton.

The regimists' ascent was further evidenced with the appointment of Din Syamsuddin in 1994 to the directorship of the powerful Research and Development (Litbang) Bureau in Golkar. The Litbang Bureau devises programs to strengthen party support and to target and attack Soeharto enemies. Din had been working with Litbang since shortly after completing his Ph.D. degree at the University of California, Los Angeles, in 1991, and his influence in the organization was apparent from the start (chapter 7).[35] As director, however, he enjoyed a vastly expanded authority.

Although at the time few observers took note of Din's appointment, it was an event of far-reaching importance in New Order religious politics. It showed that Soeharto, having grown disenchanted with ICMI independents, had decided to move his Islam policy away from exclusive reliance on Habibie and ICMI toward less public "Muslim" actors. Soeharto now supported the ascendance of a regimist Muslim faction in Golkar itself. Given the complexity of Muslim politics, it is a mistake to describe this as the "Islamization" of Golkar. The ascent of the CPDS was indicative not so much of a change toward Muslims as a whole but of a tilt toward ultraconservative Islam. With these changes, Soeharto also turned his back on his policies of the early 1980s, when he had promoted the *Pancasila* in opposition to religious sectarianism. After 1994 Soeharto openly encouraged the factionalization of the elite along "religious" lines, on a scale never seen in New Order history.

As its three core groupings show, ICMI never became a cohesive political organization. Whether on questions of Soeharto and the military or Habibie and reform, the organization was racked with fierce disagreements and irresolvable contradictions. Some in ICMI had concluded that Soeharto was an important political asset and should not be challenged. Others, a smaller but influential minority, still hoped to use ICMI to promote democratization and economic justice. Rather than diminishing over time, the tensions between these groupings only intensified as Soeharto refined his policy on Islam and increased his reliance on regimist Muslims.

CORPORATISM AND INDEPENDENCE

ICMI's umbrellalike organization illustrates a pattern of corporatist control that, as Benedict Anderson and David Reeve[36] have shown, has long character-ized authoritarian government in Indonesia. The corporatist tradition was not a New Order invention. In the late 1950s, as President Soekarno turned his back on parliamentary democracy (chapter 3), he and the military spoke of the need for new, corporately organized political associations. The most elaborate outlines of this new political format were provided in the armed forces' state-ments on *integralism*, which began well before the Soeharto era.[37]

Whether in politics (as seen in the fusion of political parties), business orga-nization,[38] or religion, the basic principles of integralism, as practiced in the New Order, have always been clear. Competing interests and social organiza-tions are urged toward mutual "consultation" and "consensus" through their incorporation into a forced union. Once inside this administrative corral, the association's members are prevented from exercising any real initiative. As with Habibie in ICMI, the state decides who is to lead the organization. And it is the leader's job to make sure that association members do not stray too far from state guidelines. Independent-minded associates are barred from leadership positions. Those who continue to challenge the system are expelled, harassed, or, when necessary, imprisoned.

This, then, was the model for the Soeharto regime's efforts to organize and control independent Islam through ICMI. If seamless control was the ideal, however, the corporatist model nonetheless encountered serious resistance from the beginning. At the founding meeting attended by Soeharto in early December 1990, intellectuals and reform activists displayed what was, by New Order standards, a surprising boldness in their papers and speeches (chapter 5). The critical tone of several papers convinced many independents in the organization that there might yet be room for member initiative. Events during ICMI's initial months seemed to confirm this hope. In the months after the Malang conference, for example, Muslim activists who had previously been banned from public forums found that they now enjoyed unprecedented freedom of movement and access to the press. Almost overnight, the media began to feature stories on Islamic discussions of politics and development, discussions that, just a few months earlier, would have been viewed as "anti-*Pancasila.*"

Here again, the experience of Imaduddin Abdulrahim provides a telling il-lustration of the change. In interviews in August 1992 and June 1993 Dr. Imaduddin noted that before he joined ICMI he was regularly barred from giving public lectures. After he became part of the association, however, all this changed. He traveled freely around the country, "from Aceh to Java," as he put it, and did not once have to secure police permits. For him, this was proof that, whatever the president's motives in supporting ICMI, an important change had occurred:

> No, it wasn't just an effort on the part of the president to court Muslim support so as to outflank his rivals in the army. Of course, there is a measure of politics of that sort, but I am not so cynical. I think President Soeharto has eyes; he sees what is happening, and he realizes that 90 percent of his people are Muslim and they have to be given a role in national life. It's a genuine opening. It's the first time in twenty-seven years that we have been brought into the political life of the country, and we have to take advantage of it.[39]

By this time, of course, Imaduddin had distinguished himself as one of the most prominent ICMI independents to have defected from the ranks of Soe-harto critics to Soeharto supporters. That he might have enjoyed greater free-doms, then, should come as no surprise. At least until 1993, however, even critical intellectuals and activists, like Haidar Bagir, Dawam Rahardjo, and Nur-cholish Madjid, stated their belief that Soeharto was relaxing his controls and ICMI might further that change. Independent intellectuals bristled at the re-ports of Western journalists that the Muslim community was "euphoric" and self-deluding about Soeharto. Haidar Bagir, operations director at *Republika* (the ICMI newspaper) and editor in chief at the Muslim publishing house, Mizan, expressed what was a widely held opinion among ICMI independents at this time:

> Some people in the Western media make it seem as if we are so full of emotion with recent developments that we don't understand the motives of certain government officials. But that's just not true. Democratic politics is bargaining. ICMI may not be a full realization of our aspirations. And yes, some people will be co-opted by the bureaucracy. We know that. We know, too, that many in government supported ICMI for reasons that had nothing to do with religion. But politics is not a matter of Muslims winning and others losing everything. Muslims and non-Muslims are getting lessons in democracy. It's not everything we want. But it's a real opening.[40]

Haidar and other independents also pointed out that ICMI's establishment had allowed the Muslim community to launch important welfare initiatives. These included the establishment of an Islamic Bank, the Bank Muamalat; the cre-ation of a scholarship fund for Muslim students; and a program of foster par-entage and educational support for Muslim poor.[41]

In a similar manner, independent activists and intellectuals credited ICMI with having had a visible influence on the devotional piety of the middle class. "ICMI has made bureaucrats who were previously afraid to perform the Friday prayers proud to do so," said one ICMI official in 1992. Nurcholish Madjid echoed these sentiments. Whatever its long-term political impact, he said,

ICMI has deepened Islamic devotion among the middle class and government officials. "This," he added, "is a valuable achievement in itself."

Nonetheless it was impossible not to notice that the room for political maneuver in ICMI was far less than independent Muslims had expected. From the beginning, democratic reformers in ICMI were barred from strategic positions in the organization. For example, in early 1991 it was widely expected that Dawan Rahardjo was to be made the ICMI general secretary. Unlike other independent Muslims, Dawam had never been regarded by security forces as an extremist or antigovernment activist. He had an impeccable reputation as a modernist Muslim with strong ties to the NGO community. He had also distinguished himself as a development theorist (his academic training was in economics), which seemed to provide him with the pragmatic credentials Habibie was looking for. In the end, however, the post of general secretary and all other strategic positions in the organization went to Habibie loyalists.[42] Rahardjo was given a purely symbolic position in the ICMI leadership, and his journal, *Ulumul Qur'an*—a well-respected mouthpiece of civil-pluralist Islam—was given a small subsidy. After just two years, however, the subsidies were eliminated—one more sign that Soeharto's strategists were shifting their patronage resources away from Muslim independents to conservative, regimist Muslims.

Other incidents in the months following ICMI's founding revealed the tensions in the organization between reform-minded activists and Habibie aides. In May 1991 Emha Ainun Najib, a popular Javanese writer and the director of ICMI's Cultural Discussion Bureau, tried to have ICMI sponsor a small conference on the Kedung Ombo Dam in Central Java. In the mid-1980s this dam project had generated great controversy, as it displaced thousands of farmers but provided little compensation. The dam had become a cause célèbre in prodemocracy and Muslim democratic circles. By putting Kedung Ombo on the ICMI agenda, Emha sent a clear message that he was determined to have ICMI do more than just bolster the images of Soeharto and Habibie. As the day for the conference approached, however, Najib received a notice from an ICMI higher-up demanding that the event be canceled. Eventually it was, and Emha resigned from ICMI.

Other incidents revealed much the same tension between reform-minded activists and ICMI bureaucrats. On May 2, 1992, ICMI independents attempted to hold a one-day conference on human rights issues to which they invited several prominent human-rights advocates, some of them Christian. As the event's opening address was concluding, ten uniformed officers appeared and asked to see the conference permit. The ICMI audience protested that no permit was needed because the seminar was being held at ICMI's headquarters. The police insisted that all meetings of more than five people anywhere in the country require a permit and demanded that the meeting be brought to a close. The organizers relented, and the meeting ended.[43]

Several weeks after the failed May meeting, in September 1992, Adi Sasono joined with several other ICMI independents to establish the Center for Information and Development Studies. Adi was determined to make CIDES the primary bureau in ICMI for research and policy formulation. His hope was that, with the government changing its policy on Islam, CIDES would eventually assume the advisorial role for the government played in the 1970s and 1980s by Ali Moertopo's Center for Strategic and International Studies (CSIS). However much he was willing to support Soeharto, however, Adi, at this point, was still determined to show some independence. In December 1992 he took what was, in light of the abortive May meeting, the bold step of sponsoring a one-day seminar on human rights at ICMI's annual national meeting. That this was the first national event CIDES chose to sponsor raised many eyebrows. Despite rumors of possible police action, the meeting took place and included presentations by prominent human rights activists from outside ICMI.[44] Equally remarkable, in February 1993 CIDES launched an academic journal, *Afkar*. The first issue surprised even many ICMI independents by reprinting papers from the human rights meeting, several of which contained unusually blunt criticisms of government policy. In private, Habibie warned Sasono that if he continued with such foolish initiatives Sasono would compromise both their political careers.

These incidents show that during ICMI's first years some intellectuals and activists in the organization exhibited a genuine desire for independence. But the influence of this independent-minded wing declined dramatically after 1993, for three reasons. First, the president and his family were angered at what they regarded as Habibie's inability to curb independents in the organization; this led to dramatic cuts in funds for ICMI programs like the Center for Information and Development Studies. The second reason was the rush of government bureaucrats into the organization in 1993, in the aftermath of the cabinet and MPR appointments of ICMI Muslims. The third and most decisive influence on the decline of the ICMI independents, however, was Soeharto's and the "green" generals' sponsorship of the regimist think tank, the Center for Policy and Development Studies (CPDS), which was to prove itself a more effective instrument for regime interests than the ICMI independents.

MILITARY AND MUSLIM OPPOSITION TO ICMI

Factionalized from within and manipulated from without, ICMI inspired fierce opposition from other quarters of the Indonesian political universe. The two most important of its critics were, first, the "red-and-white" (after the colors of the Indonesian flag) or "nationalist" armed forces leadership and, second, the outspoken leader of the Nahdlatul Ulama, Abdurrahman Wahid.[45]

The nationalist officers were a loosely organized group, united more by their opposition to ICMI than by any coherent program. They included reform-minded officers like Sumitro and Rudini, as well as conservative integralists like Harsudiyono Hartas. The strength of the opposition to Soeharto among the nationalist military command also varied. Some were convinced that as a result of his pique with the former Catholic commander of the armed forces, Benny Moerdani, Soeharto had momentarily lost his senses in making his appeal to Islam. They expected the president to restore his relationship with the armed forces sometime soon. Other members of the red-and-white military, however, were critical of Soeharto and convinced that the nationalist tradition, as well as ABRI's reputation, could only be restored by Soeharto's removal.

The ideological heterogeneity of the nationalist military command made it difficult for Wahid to establish a stable relationship with them. Wahid was convinced that his vision of a pluralist and democratic Islam was the best for Indonesia. He also felt that for democratization to occur the prodemocracy community had to reach a peaceful accommodation with the military. In both statements and actions, Wahid sought to reassure the nationalist military command of his good will, in the hope that they would realize that his program of pluralist Islam and gradual democratization offered a brighter future than that promised by Soeharto and Habibie. A few military officers, like the retired reformist general Soemitro, did rally to Wahid's side. A few other active officers provided protection for Wahid when he was under threat, as was increasingly the case after 1994 (chapter 7). Although most in the red-and-white military approved of Wahid's nationalism, however, they were put off by his commitment to democratization. However great their opposition to ICMI, and however valiant Wahid's attempts to convince them otherwise, the red-and-white faction of the military was caught in its own contradictions concerning nationalism and democratic reform. They were nationalists, yes, but conservative nationalists. Discussions of democracy made them uneasy. This ambivalence undermined the efforts of civilian and military nationalists to create a pluralist alternative to conservative Islam and Soeharto.

ABRI and the Evisceration of the Nationalist Center

Although Soeharto and military commanders had had disagreements at at other times during the New Order era, none had ever reached the proportions seen in the late 1980s.[46] One had to look all the way back to the pre-Soeharto era in the early 1960s, to the conflict between President Soekarno and the military (ABRI), to find a breech between government and military of similar proportions.[47] A number of developments had contributed to this chilled relationship. By the end of the single-foundation (*asas tunggal*) campaign of 1983–85 Soeharto had so effectively neutralized opposition to his rule that he had turned himself into Indonesia's paramount ruler, and "the influence of ABRI on the national stage [had] declined considerably."[48] Earlier, at the beginning of the New Order, Soeharto had always been the leading figure among several military commanders. By the mid-1980s, however, the Soeharto-dominated military coalition had given way to Soeharto's paramount rule.

The other development affecting ABRI's relationship with the president during these years was that for the first time in New Order history the president's children were becoming major players in the national economy. Never shy about using the family name, Soeharto's children helped themselves to lion's shares of contracts and business partnerships available in Indonesia's fast-developing economy.[49] The scale of the first family's cronyism raised eyebrows among even the most loyal of Soeharto commanders. The resentment was heightened by the fact that the modest liberalization of the economy that took place in the 1980s altered the balance between private and state enterprise. Privately held enterprise began to lead the way in the economy, while the state-owned industries in which many military retirees found employment began to decline. Marginalized from the regime's inner circle and hurting economically, some in the ABRI began to rethink their relation to Soeharto.

For most of his career, the Catholic commander of the armed forces in the 1980s, Benny Moerdani, was known as a fierce Soeharto loyalist and uncompromising opponent of liberal reform. In the mid-1970s he had been one of the architects of the Indonesian seizure of East Timor. Commander of the armed forces from 1983 to 1988, Moerdani had also assumed responsibility for neutralizing Muslim opposition to the single-foundation campaign. By the end of his tenure as commander of the armed forces, however, Moerdani was said to have been so dismayed by the cronyist abuses of the first family that he appealed to the president to control his children's avarice.[50]

Most accounts of the meeting in which this exchange occurred indicate that Soeharto reacted to Moerdani's appeal with stony silence.[51] Soeharto was never one to take affronts to his authority lightly, however, and over the next four years he moved carefully but ruthlessly against Moerdani. At the end of February 1988 Soeharto replaced Moerdani as armed forces commander in chief and assigned him to the less influential post of minister of security and defense. As Adam Schwarz asserted, "it was a classic case of Soeharto trying to weaken ABRI politically by removing one of its main political thinkers."[52] In 1993 Moerdani was removed from even this ministerial post. That same year Soeharto replaced Harsudiyono Hartas (a fierce critic of ICMI and a Moerdani ally) as head of ABRI's Social-Political Department. The next year he dismantled BAIS, a powerful intelligence agency linked to Moerdani.

Others in ABRI, including many officers not allied to Moerdani, had quietly lent their support to the campaign against Soeharto. In 1988 the ABRI command had attempted unsuccessfully to block Soeharto's choice for the vice presidency, Sudharmono. Although a retired military officer, Sudharmono was regarded as having been insufficiently loyal to ABRI when, as state secretary, he awarded contracts for state businesses. Sudharmono had also provoked Moerdani's ire by attempting to make Golkar more independent of the armed forces. Despite ABRI opposition, Soeharto managed to have Sudharmono appointed vice president. In 1993 the military again challenged Soeharto over the issue of the vice presidency. This time, by announcing its choice of candidate well in advance of the MPR congress (at which the president and vice president are chosen), ABRI got its way. ABRI's candidate was Try Sutrisno, a respected if uninspiring East Javanese general. Although pious in matters of Muslim devotion, in his early career Try had been close to Moerdani. He was also one of the officers present during bloody military crackdowns on Muslim protestors in Lampung, South Sumatra, in 1989, and Tanjung Priok, Jakarta, in 1984.

The military's defiance angered Soeharto, and he was determined to teach its leadership a lesson. Most Indonesian observers regarded the president's ICMI initiative as punishment of the ABRI leadership for its actions, as well as an effort to balance the president's loss of support among the military with a new base among Muslims.[53] This playing of one elite faction against another has long been a trademark of Soeharto leadership.[54] But it had been a rule of the Soehartoist game that neither the political left nor Muslim mass organizations should ever be drawn into these intrigues. That rule had now been decisively broken.

The simmering tension between the president and the military helps to explain the ABRI leadership's reaction to ICMI. From the first, high-ranking military officers counseled against legalizing the organization. In the days before the meeting in which the president approved ICMI's formation, no less a figure than Vice President Try Sutrisno urged the president to reject the proposal. Eventually, as it became clear that ICMI had the president's backing, the military command stopped its public sniping, and Try Sutrisno himself attended the Malang meeting.[55]

Despite this apparent accommodation, military criticism of ICMI continued. Rather than attacking the organization as a whole, however, military critics warned of factions within ICMI who wanted to use the organization for political ends. In a widely publicized speech presented on June 18, 1993, Try Sutrisno, without mentioning names, warned that there were signs that some people were using Islam as an "instrument of legitimation."[56] Earlier, in April 1993, several months after the installation of the People's Consultative Assembly packed with ICMI sympathizers, the vice president had given his blessing to an even more direct challenge to ICMI. Openly breaking with Soeharto, Try helped to sponsor the establishment of an Association of Nusantara Intellectuals (ICNU). Clearly the armed forces leadership lay behind ICNU. The leadership hoped to send the message that intellectuals should organize on the basis of multireligious nationalism, not exclusive religious allegiances. Despite this ABRI support, however, ICNU foundered and eventually collapsed. Military-dominated as it was,

ICNU sparked little interest among independent nationalists. In 1994 and 1995 there were similar efforts to launch "nationalist" alternatives to ICMI, but all suffered ICNU's fate.

ICNU's failure was indicative of a broader problem faced by the red-and-white military leadership. Since the collapse of the alliance of Javanist and secular modernizing generals in the early New Order (chapter 4), most of the military command had aligned itself with Soeharto and shown little interest in cultivating a nationalist base in society. After their brief and ultimately abortive collaboration with secular modernizing intellectuals in the late 1960s, the military's attitude toward civilian allies hardened. The ABRI command drew back from contacts with civilian nationalists. Indeed, "when Benny Moerdani was ABRI commander . . . , he discouraged contacts between junior officers and civilian intellectuals because the latter were 'too Westernized and a destabilizing influence.' "[57] The senior command put itself squarely behind Soeharto's policy of bulldozing all remaining outcrops of civic independence.

Whether with Javanist mystics, secular modernizers, socialist democrats, or Muslim nationalists, the armed forces had unwittingly undermined the organizational basis for the centrist nationalism that, now, in the early 1990s, some felt they should revive. During 1990 and 1991 the armed forces leadership, supported by Moerdani, gave its blessing to parliamentarians' efforts to assert their independence from the president. As with the ICNU initiative, however, the effort was seen by civilian nationalists as too little too late.

Faced with the military's attempt to enhance its influence in parliament and Golkar, Soeharto counterattacked. The campaign reached its fateful climax in October 1993, when Soeharto arranged to make B. J. Habibie chairman of the annual Golkar party congress, and Habibie had his ally, Harmoko, appointed party chairman.[58] With these achievements, Golkar was securely back in Soehartoist hands. The "old man" (as Soeharto was known in military circles) had again outwitted the red-and-white military leadership.

Abdurrahman Wahid and Pluralist Islam

It was precisely because conservative nationalists in ABRI had helped to eviscerate their most likely constituencies that some among the armed forces leadership regarded the reform-minded leader of Nahdlatul Ulama, Abdurrahman Wahid, as their last best hope. NU had displayed solid nationalist credentials since Wahid's father, Wahid Hasyim, led the way in 1945 in the compromise that allowed the establishment of the republic (chapter 3).[59] In collaboration with the respected NU scholar, Achmad Siddiq, in 1983–84 Wahid had led NU to accept the Pancasila as its "sole foundation." The Muslim legal arguments Wahid and Siddiq invoked to justify embracing the national ideology served as a model for other Muslim organizations' acceptance of *Pancasila*.[60] Wahid won high praise for his efforts from the then minister of religion, Munawir

Sjadzali, and for the next four years Wahid enjoyed a cordial if distant relationship with Soeharto. The president provided funds for the construction of a mosque in front of Wahid's home in Jakarta's southern suburbs, and NU businessmen were allowed to compete for government contracts. By the late 1980s, however, as Soeharto flirted with less mainstream Muslims, Wahid began to wonder whether his vision of pluralist Islam was quite what the president had in mind.

Wahid had had doubts about the president's intentions even before Soeharto launched ICMI. In 1988, while inviting Muslim scholars to participate in the composition of new laws on religious education and on Islamic courts (laws passed in 1989), Soeharto had surprised Wahid and the NU leadership by reaching over their heads into the ranks of conservative Muslims when selecting scholars to advise the government on the law. This was one of the earliest indications that the president's "opening to Islam" was going to be selective. Wahid and his followers received a greater shock a year and a half later, in the course of what came to be known as the *Monitor* affair.[61] In October 1990 the mass tabloid *Monitor* published the results of a readers' poll in which president Soeharto was ranked the most admired figure among the paper's readership, and the Prophet Muhammad the eleventh (below even the flamboyant Catholic editor of *Monitor*, Arswendo Atmowiloto). Besides having a Catholic editor, *Monitor* was part of the Catholic-owned *Kompas-Gramedia* conglomerate, whose dominance of the media market has long irritated conservative Muslims (chapter 5). The *Monitor* poll outraged these conservatives. The Dewan Dakwah Islamiyah Indonesia and its ally, KISDI (chapter 5), quickly organized fierce demonstrations. The minister of information, Harmoko, a Soeharto loyalist and Habibie ally, responded by revoking *Monitor*'s publishing license. Under the government's harsh restrictions, the revocation could not be appealed in the courts.

Six months later Arswendo was convicted of blasphemy, a punishable offense under Indonesian law. He was sentenced to the maximum penalty of five years in prison; he would be released after four. Wahid was also outraged by the affair but for reasons different from those of the conservatives. He regarded the government's refusal to press its case against *Monitor* through the courts as an affront to the rule of law, and saw the refusal of the Muslim leadership to defend the right of free speech and legal process as a setback for democracy.[62] Wahid also knew that behind the scenes the *Monitor* campaign had been coordinated by the new leadership of Golkar's Research and Development Bureau, who were intent on using the incident to signal Soeharto's born-again commitment to conservative Islam. The message the government sought to send through the *Monitor* affair was that the New Order's old alliance with Javanists was over. Henceforth the president would act as champion of conservative Muslim interests against Javanists, Christians, and other minorities.

In the mid-1980s, when Wahid had begun his effort to transform the NU into a vehicle of grass-roots development and pluralist tolerance, he had hoped to win the president to his vision of civil Islam. By the late 1980s, as Soeharto's rivalry with the military intensified, Wahid's confidence began to be shaken. By 1990–91 his hopes lay in tatters, as Wahid realized that the president was not interested in the Muslim community as a whole but only in regimist conservatives. The change was no more blatantly apparent than in Soeharto's sponsorship of the *Monitor* affair.

As his hopes for a changed Soeharto faded, Wahid looked for allies in the military. Wahid had no illusions about the armed forces' democratic instincts. He regarded the military as a complex organization, with a tendency toward authoritarianism but with the possibility of reform.[63] He was critical of military obsequiousness to Soeharto but felt that, if not cornered, some in the armed forces leadership might support democratic reform.

In the aftermath of the *Monitor* affair, Wahid launched a two-pronged initiative to shore up his standing in the Muslim community and to assist the cause of pluralist nationalism. In March 1991, just four months after ICMI's establishment, he and forty-four other prominent intellectuals from varied religions joined together to establish the Democratic Forum (*Forum Demokrasi*, or Fordem). As the leader of Indonesia's largest mass organization, Wahid immediately became the forum's chief spokesperson. He took pains to underscore that the forum was not a mass movement, nor even a protest group, but a nonconfessional discussion group intended to encourage reflection on democracy and pluralism. Although Wahid denied any intention to discredit Habibie's organization, the contrast with ICMI was striking.

Equally impressive, however, was the difference in the government's response to the forum. Although Soeharto had beaten the drum that inaugurated ICMI, he went out of his way to beat down the Democratic Forum. Meetings of the little discussion group were broken up by force. Government officials demanded to know what need there was for a prodemocracy organization in a country that had already achieved a "*Pancasila* democracy."[64] The repression of the Democratic Forum reached a fever pitch in early 1992, in anticipation of the June 1992 elections. Members of the organization were warned not to hold open meetings nor to comment publicly on their discussions. By late 1992 the group many had hoped would become an engine for democratic reform had run out of gas.

If the Democratic Forum was Wahid's attempt to build a democratic-nationalist alliance, a rally he sponsored on March 1, 1992, sought to strengthen his role in the Muslim community. As Douglas Ramage has noted,[65] Wahid's "Great Assembly" (*Rapat Akbar*) was the biggest rally by a nongovernmental organization in twenty-five years. In my interviews with Wahid a month after the event, Wahid commented that he had hoped to attract one million people to the rally. As a result of police actions taken at the instructions of the president, however, less than one-fifth of the expected number of participants appeared. The permit for the rally was delayed, and, on the day of the event, buses were turned back en masse outside Jakarta. Unwilling to ban the rally outright (since it was ostensibly in support of the *Pancasila*), Soeharto was determined that it should not succeed in its goal of showing mass support for Wahid's inclusivist Islam.

The Great Assembly was supposed to have celebrated the anniversary of NU's founding and the organization's commitment to *Pancasila* pluralism. But Wahid also intended the rally to serve as a protest against Soeharto's ICMI policy. In speeches, he decried ICMI as dangerously sectarian and warned that the organization had fundamentalists in its ranks.[66] In conversations with supporters, he was even blunter, warning that the president's courtship of conservative Muslims could lead Indonesia down the path of sectarian violence like that in Algeria.

Although in its aftermath Wahid declared that his rally had been a great success, in private he was shocked and angered by government actions against him.[67] In my interviews with him, he placed full blame for the repression on Soeharto and expressed fear that Soeharto's flirtation with "fundamentalist Islam" could set back Indonesian democracy for years. Wahid was also dismayed to see the ease with which the president had outflanked military officers sympathetic to Wahid's initiative. For the time being, he said, no force in state or society seemed able to stop the president's flirtation with ultraconservative Islam. He was worried that a revival of the sectarian violence that had plagued Indonesia in the late 1950s and early 1960s was imminent. He also expressed concern that, this time around, the religious sectarianism might take an ugly anti-Chinese turn.[68] History was to prove him right.

The Great Assembly marked a turning point in Wahid's relationship with the president and the president's relationship with organized Islam. The Soeharto regime had turned its back on Wahid and NU. It had flooded ICMI with government bureaucrats to ensure that the organization did not show too much independence. Most shocking of all, the president had begun to recruit hardline Muslims to his cause, for use against the democratic opposition. The groundwork had been laid for an even fiercer attack on Wahid and his allies. The much-promised era of "openness" had come to an end. The struggle to construct a civil and democratic Islam was about to be put to an awful test.

CONCLUSION: ICMI AND THE LIMITS OF OPENNESS

As can be seen from this history, ICMI was never a unitary organization and never had a unified position on the questions of Soeharto and democratization. Organized during a momentary convergence of interests between the president and elite Muslims, the organization declined as soon as Soeharto realized that some in its scholarly and activist wings were unwilling to play by his rules.

ICMI managed to survive largely because it continued to provide legitimacy for Soeharto and served as a vehicle for Habibie's ambitions. Its independent wing was vitiated, however, as the regime promoted an influx of government bureaucrats into the organization and barred independent Muslims from leadership roles. The long-awaited flow of state funds to ICMI bureaus and think tanks also never materialized. In contrast, there was no shortage of funds for regimist Muslims at the Center for Policy and Development Studies.

The armed forces leadership had at first been united in its opposition to ICMI. Threatened by ICMI's ascent and disturbed by the president's interference in their affairs, the ABRI command seemed a natural ally for the independent-minded Abdurrahman Wahid. From mid-1990 to late 1991 there was a flurry of reform activity among some military representatives in parliament. This suggested that some in the military were trying to make common cause with Wahid. Alarmed by Wahid's prodemocracy statements, however, most in the military declined the NU leader's invitation to join him in strengthening pluralism through gradual democratization. The more common attitude among the military command was expressed by the head of ABRI's Social and Political Affairs Bureau, Harsudiyono Hartas. Hartas denounced ICMI as sectarian for its elevation of Muslim interests above the national good. But Hartas also denounced Wahid's Democratic Forum for advocating "liberal" ideals incompatible with *Pancasila* democracy. By retreating to a conservative defense of the status quo, the military command undermined efforts to establish a multireligious middle ground in Indonesian politics. Having done his dirty work against Wahid, Hartas was replaced in March 1994 by an officer sympathetic to ICMI.

At the same time, too, Habibie's growing prominence in national politics posed new problems for ICMI independents. In his role as director of Indonesia's strategic industries, Habibie had become the leading regime proponent of subsidies to state enterprises. Economists critical of his efforts argued that the industries under Habibie's direction receive subsidies totaling hundreds of millions of dollars each year. In April 1994 the minister of research and technology was also criticized in the press for secretly "borrowing" three hundred million dollars from government reforestation funds and plowing them into his capital-hungry industrial projects. These and other incidents undercut the image Habibie hoped to project as a regime insider supportive of reform. In the eyes of ICMI independents, it began to look as if he were just another Soeharto crony.[69]

For economic reasons, however, Habibie continued to enjoy some support among mainstream Muslims. Many saw Habibie as one of the few government leaders speaking to the problem of the marginalization of Muslims in the national economy. The economic liberalization of the late 1980s had unleashed a new wave of enterprise, but, aside from Soeharto's children, Muslims and non-Chinese Indonesians remained secondary players in it. Although his ideas were criticized as elitist and wasteful, Habibie's impassioned discourses on technology and "value-added" industry appealed to members of the Muslim middle class who feared that the low-wage, export-oriented industrialization, favored by economic technocrats, would provide low-paying jobs for the poor but nothing for them. From this perspective, Habibie's efforts to present himself as an economic nationalist, willing to bend the rules of the market to support the indigenous majority (or at least its representatives in government and big business), made good tactical sense, however little these efforts helped the Muslim populace as a whole.[70]

Habibie's critics' worst fears seemed confirmed on June 21, 1994, when the government, with clear presidential support, banned three news magazines that had been at the forefront of investigation into Habibie's dealings. The three weeklies—*Tempo, Editor*, and *DeTik*—were among the most distinguished of Indonesia's mass weeklies. Journalists and political observers disagree as to whether Habibie was directly responsible for the ban, or whether, as his defenders insist, the action was taken by the president.[71] But Habibie never expressed regret over the ban, even when speaking with reform-minded supporters. Worse yet, hard-line conservatives in the Dewan Dakwah Islamiyah Indonesia rallied to Habibie's defense, in what was one of their first public expressions of support for the regime. Lukman Harun, a Muhammadiyah leader and hard-line member of KISDI (chapter 7), summed up the DDII position on the ban:

> *Tempo, DeTik, Editor*—why should we do anything for these magazines? What have they ever done for us? They are not Muslim publications. We Muslims have to be realistic about who our friends are and what we should support. Don't speak to us about democracy and freedom. We have been held outside of power for more than twenty-five years. Now we have a chance to come in. Now more than ever we have to look clearly and understand what our interests are.[72]

Although some in its rank and file doubted the wisdom of the new course, DDII opposition to Soeharto was giving way to opportunistic collusion.

The press closings marked a little-noted turning point in late New Order politics. Although most independent observers had long been convinced that the era of "openness" was over, the banning of the three weeklies indicated that the era was not just over but had ushered in a new regime alliance. The most notable group in the ranks of the regime's new supporters were conservative Muslims previously critical of Soeharto. The logic of the new arrangement was clear in the government's actions against the weeklies. The restrictions were imposed in the aftermath of criticisms of Habibie, the man most directly responsible for implementing presidential policy on Islam. The bans indicated just how central regimist Islam had become to Soeharto's new strategy.[73]

In 1990–91 some in the independent Muslim community had believed that things had changed and that the time had come for Muslim intellectuals to put some of their high political ideals into practice. Committed as he was to a more thorough separation of Muslim and state power, Abdurrahman Wahid had been skeptical of this possibility from the beginning. In the end, his skepticism proved well founded. Soeharto not only limited ICMI's room for movement, but, irritated with ICMI independents, he shifted his patronage to Muslims of a regimist cast. The antidemocratic consequences of Soeharto's hardened position on Islam, and, in particular, of his decision to channel resources to Muslim ultra-conservatives, were to become tragically apparent in the regime's final years.

Chapter Seven

UNCIVIL STATE:

MUSLIMS AND VIOLENCE IN SOEHARTO'S FALL

T HE CRACKDOWN on the press in June 1994 marked the end of Soeharto's experiment with limited liberalization and the beginning of a
dangerous new policy on Islam. The timing of the two policy shifts was
not accidental. The new policy on Islam was based on the idea that the president could best neutralize the growing prodemocracy movement by mobilizing
conservative Muslims to his side. The "turn to Islam," begun in the late 1980s,
had thus entered a new and final phase. Rather than attempting to co-opt
mainstream Muslims, the president now concentrated his energies on conservative Muslims willing to trade his patronage for their assistance in containing
the democratic opposition. The divide-and-conquer strategy, long central to
Soeharto's rule, had taken an ominous turn indeed.

It is important to remember just how much this new policy differed from
earlier regime gestures toward Muslims. The New Order's "Islamic turn" began
in the aftermath of the single-foundation (*asas tunggal*) campaign of 1983–85;
in its early phase the effort was directed at Nahdlatul Ulama. Under the leadership of the great reformers Achmad Siddiq and Abdurrahman Wahid, Nahdlatul Ulama had been the first Muslim mass organization to accept the *Pancasila*
as its ideological foundation. That Siddiq and Wahid had provided this leadership stood them in good favor with the New Order leadership. That their organization was also the largest in Indonesia reinforced government strategists'
conviction that NU was the regime's best choice of Muslim partner.

Developments in the months leading up to the 1987 national elections at
first seemed to confirm the wisdom of Soeharto's strategy. After its withdrawal
from party politics in 1983–84 the NU leadership impressed on its membership that they were no longer obliged to vote for the Muslim PPP but could
lend their support to any party. The Soeharto administration was delighted
with this policy, but some in the traditionalist organization were not. A significant minority in NU was linked to the former executive chairman, Idham
Chalid (a Wahid foe), and those in this group were still loyal to the Muslim
Party of Unity and Development (PPP). They did not want to use the PPP to
oppose the government outright. They did, however, wish to defend the party
and patronage structure on which their own careers depended.

The pro-PPP faction in NU soon felt that they had additional grounds for
complaint. In their view, Wahid had not simply pulled NU out of party politics

but had begun to campaign against the PPP in favor of Golkar and the Indonesian Democratic Party. Their grievance had some validity. In the months leading up to the 1987 elections, Wahid made several appearances with Golkar and PDI leaders at well-publicized rallies around the country. He made no joint appearances with figures from the PPP; indeed, his public statements expressed nothing but contempt for the party's leaders. Many observers interpreted these actions as Wahid's taking revenge on the PPP leadership for having marginalized NU in the organization.[1]

Whatever Wahid's motives, NU's withdrawal from the PPP had a disastrous impact on the party's electoral performance. In the 1987 elections the PPP's share of the vote fell to just 16 percent of the national total, down from 27.8 percent in 1982. Meanwhile, the share of the Muslim vote to Golkar increased. Golkar officials were delighted with this result, viewing it as confirmation of the wisdom of their courtship of NU. Following the elections, in what many observers saw as a "thank you" to the NU leader, Soeharto appointed Wahid to the People's Consultative Assembly as a delegate from Golkar.[2]

Four years after the NU's decisive "withdrawal" from politics, then, Wahid and NU seemed not less involved in politics but more so. The politics in which the leadership was engaged, however, consisted of carefully hedged support to the Soeharto regime. After Wahid's appointment to the MPR, many of his critics in NU accused the executive board chairman of hypocrisy for turning against the PPP and violating the very terms of political withdrawal he had earlier promoted.

We now know, however, that there was a more complex logic to Wahid's actions than the accusation of opportunism implied. As Martin van Bruinessen and Andrée Feillard have both shown,[3] the NU leadership's decision (agreed on in December 1983, and finalized a year later) to withdraw from politics had been supported by NU's varied factions for different reasons. Some in the NU leadership wanted to teach the PPP leadership a lesson for marginalizing NU representatives in the party. NU-affiliated businesspeople wanted to end the confrontation with the government so that they could once again get state contracts. Following the example of Nurcholish Madjid, youthful activists in the organization were convinced that NU could make greater progress if it put electoral concerns aside in favor of social and educational development. Many senior *ulama*, finally, felt that the Jakarta-based leadership of their organization had become too independent and that it was time for the *ulama* to reassert their power by diminishing NU's involvement in politics.

Wahid himself appears to have agreed with most of these reasons. But he also supported the withdrawal from formal politics because he knew that government repression was driving down membership rolls and threatening NU's survival. Contrary to what some Indonesian and foreign commentators have implied, Wahid did *not* base his actions on the conviction that Islam and politics do not mix. On the contrary, he regarded his organization's withdrawal from the electoral arena as a strategic move that would allow NU to concentrate its energies in those spheres of informal political activity where the organization might yet have influence.[4]

At NU's national congress in November 1989 Wahid's critics mounted a fierce effort to remove him as chairman of the NU executive board. Wahid presented a spirited defense of his actions, however, and managed to assemble a coalition of senior *ulama*, businesspeople, and youthful activists sufficient to ensure his reelection as chairman of the executive board (Tanfidziyah).[5] Some among Wahid's critics, however, continued to accuse the embattled leader of being too close to Soeharto. By all accounts, even some in the military felt this way. Benny Moerdani, the powerful minister of security and defense, secretly supported those opposing Wahid's reelection, on the grounds that Wahid was too close to Soeharto. These were the years, of course, when Moerdani was locked in a bitter struggle with the president, and Soeharto's triumph was not yet assured. Soeharto attended the 1989 congress and was warmly applauded by the delegates, especially after he beat a mosque drum and pronounced Islamic greetings in a way that convinced delegates that he was a kindred spirit with traditionalist Islam. A noted observer of Nahdlatul Ulama present at the congress described the president's achievement:

[The president] left an impression that he was a person culturally close to NU. His previous image as an anti-Islamic follower of mystical groups was effectively erased, and the memory of his [previous] confrontational attitude toward the Muslim community . . . was fully forgotten. If the people's support was to play a role in all future power competition, it was clear that Soeharto would at least be able to draw on the support of the NU membership.[6]

The convergence of interests between Wahid and Soeharto was only temporary, however, and gave way to open conflict after the formation of ICMI in December 1990. Wahid's refusal to support the new organization infuriated the president. Wahid's leadership of the Democratic Forum led Soeharto's advisers to declare Wahid Soeharto's enemy number one. In March 1992 Soeharto had his son-in-law, Prabowo Subianto, carry a warning to Wahid that the NU chairman had overstepped the bounds of their agreement; the message threatened unspecified actions if Wahid continued to oppose the president.[7]

During 1993 and early 1994 the president's strategists kept up pressure on the embattled NU leader, unleashing a campaign of slander and innuendo in the Muslim community. Aides to Minister Habibie warned journalists at *Republika*, the ICMI newspaper, that reporters were giving the NU leader too much favorable publicity and demanded that they restrict their coverage to reports critical of Wahid.[8] Independent ICMI leaders, like Nurcholish Madjid, made clear their dissatisfaction with the government campaign by deliberately including Wahid in public events. But the barrage of anti-Wahid slander was fierce.[9] On December 2, 1994, *Republika* published a story in which it misquoted the

Japanese anthropologist Mitsuo Nakamura so as to make it sound as if he were urging Wahid to step down.[10] Modernist Muslim intellectuals in Jakarta told me, in 1994, that they had been instructed to circulate rumors claiming that Wahid no longer fasted during Ramadhan or performed his daily prayers, that he was an ally of Benny Moerdani, and that his kind words for Chinese were the result of bribes from business leaders. Wahid's ecumenicism was being made to appear a tawdry fraud.

Wahid responded to the president's pressure with calm defiance. In mid-1994 he made public statements in which he referred to the growing disenchantment in Muslim circles with Golkar and the Muslim party, the PPP. He went on to hint that the NU leadership might well throw its support to the Indonesian Democratic Party in the next elections. Wahid's comments on the possibility of an NU-PDI alliance only deepened the president's anger. The remarks also set off alarms in the ICMI-linked leadership of Golkar's (Litbang) (Research and Development) Bureau. The careers of the regimist Muslims that headed that bureau depended on their ability to make good on their promise to deliver a Muslim vote larger than that of the 1992 elections. Already in 1994 Soeharto had hinted that he was planning to run for a seventh term of office in 1997–98. Even if health problems made this impossible, Soeharto wanted to be sure that *he*, not the military, would choose his successor. Although she had many political enemies, Soeharto's daughter, Siti Hardiyanti Rukmana (known in the mass media as "Mbak Tutut"), was among the candidates he was known to favor.

The report that Wahid might collaborate with the Indonesian Democratic Party in the next elections cast a dark cloud over all these plans. The PDI was no longer the third-string organization it had been for most of the New Order. Muslim disenchantment with the PPP had convinced many voters that there was no point in voting for the party. Growing numbers of voters, even devout Muslims, were looking to the PDI as an alternative to the regime's paltry offerings. In the Muslim student community, resentment against ICMI and regimist Islam was leading many liberal activists to make common cause with prodemocracy nationalists. For the first time in a generation, activists were beginning to talk of a "red" (social democratic) and "green" (Muslim) alliance against Soeharto.

The PDI's fortunes seemed to be on the rise after the party's national congress in December 1993. That meeting had seen the election of the daughter of former President Soekarno, Megawati Soekarnoputri, to the role of party chairperson. Megawati's victory was said, by many observers, to have been made possible by the support she received from nationalist or "red-and-white" faction in the military leadership. Although they had varied opinions on Soeharto and democratization, the red-and-white commanders were united in regarding Habibie and ICMI with alarm. Few among them were interested in supporting a full-blown prodemocracy movement or promoting Megawati to the presidency outright.

They hoped simply that Megawati's leadership might allow the PDI to win a sufficient share of the 1997 vote so as to impress upon Soeharto that his Islam policy was mistaken. On the basis of this electoral performance, it was hoped that the president might return to his senses and initiate modest reform.

Although a plain speaker, Megawati's gritty determination and her identification as heir to the mantle of Soekarnoist nationalism made her a lightning rod for public disaffection. Worse yet, as far as regime strategists were concerned, Megawati was a personal friend of Wahid. This made it all the more conceivable that Wahid and Megawati might indeed be able to do what many in New Order Indonesia had long thought impossible: unite the Muslim NU with PDI nationalists in the struggle against Soeharto. This was regime strategists' worst nightmare.

By mid-1994 the CPDS-linked Muslims who worked as strategists in Golkar's Research and Development Bureau had concluded that there was a strong possibility that Wahid and Megawati might unite their forces. In secret documents circulated among strategists,[11] they referred to the "red-and-green alliance" of Megawati and Wahid as the single greatest threat to Soeharto since the mid-1960s. The scuttling of this alliance, the document said, must become the top priority of all the president's supporters.

Invoking Clifford Geertz's categories of *abangan* and *santri*,[12] the documents made a coldly compelling analysis of the vulnerabilities of the Wahid-Megawati alliance. They observed, for example, that traditionalist and Javanist Muslims were still deeply suspicious of each other over the role of NU in the 1965–66 killings. They implied that these tensions were a resource the regime could draw on to worsen ties between supporters of Wahid and those of Megawati. In the near term, however, they argued that the best way to scuttle the red-and-green alliance was to oust Wahid from leadership of NU.

PLAN ONE: TOPPLING WAHID

The campaign to unseat Wahid moved into full gear in the months leading up to NU's twenty-eighth national congress in Cipasung, West Java, in December 1994. By this time Wahid was aware that he had been targeted by government strategists. In a feint that showed his gift as a political prize fighter, a few weeks before the congress Wahid threw off his opponents by hinting that he might not seek the chairmanship again, especially if NU's "nonpolitical" orientation could be protected. At the same time, however, he scoured the countryside meeting with leading *ulama* in an effort to defend his policies and improve his chances for reelection.

Opposition to Wahid inside NU came from several sources.[13] Supporters of the PPP and those who wanted NU to show more independence accused him of collaborating too closely with the government. Business people criticized

Wahid for being too much in the opposition and spoiling what they had hoped would be a lucrative rapprochement with the state. Although the "Anyone But Gus Dur" (*Asal Bukan Gus Dur*) campaign included people of varied ideological persuasions, its leadership eventually fell into the hands of a noted NU entrepreneur, Abu Hasan.

Although a political novice, Hasan was one of Nahdlatul Ulama's wealthiest business supporters. Active in trade, construction, and shipping, he had long been a generous contributor to NU projects. Hasan's role as a leading NU donor had allowed him to establish a patronage network among the cash-strapped NU membership. Equally important, as a successful businessman Hasan had close ties to the first family, especially the president's daughter, Mbak Tutut. Mbak Tutut was a close ally and personal friend of the head of the armed forces Social and Political Affairs section (Sospol), Lieutenant-General Hartono. Hartono had been the commander of the East Javanese Brawijaya Division when ICMI was founded in Malang, East Java, in December 1990. Through this and other activities, Hartono had come to be identified in the press as a "pro-Muslim" and "pro-Habibie" general, and he was regularly involved in government initiatives with regimist Muslims, as in Abu Hasan's campaign against Wahid.

By late 1994, however, tensions were growing in Jakarta's regimist Muslim community, and it was clear that the characterization of the handsome Madurese general as "pro-Habibie" was too simple. It was no secret that the president's children had developed an intense dislike for Habibie. Mbak Tutut, in particular, resented Habibie's privileged relationship with her father, not least of all because she saw him as a rival to succeed the president. Mbak Tutut also resented Habibie for failing to rein in intellectuals and activists in ICMI. Among those she particularly disliked was the NGO-activist-turned-Habibie confidant Adi Sasono. It was for this reason that she had joined with the "green" generals Hartono, Feisal Tanjung, Syarwan Hamid, and Prabowo Subianto to establish the Center for Policy and Development Studies (CPDS) as a think tank rival to Sasono's CIDES (chapter 6). Tutut and Hartono supported the regime's outreach to Muslims, but they wanted to make sure that the Muslims who were mobilized were of a sufficiently regimist stripe.

Supported by Tutut and Hartono, then, Abu Hasan's campaign against Wahid was to be the CPDS's first real trial by fire. Although some details remain vague,[14] CPDS officials advised Abu Hasan throughout his campaign. The CPDS also provided funds and coordination for other members of the anti-Wahid movement in NU and in the Muslim mass media. Although at this point the CPDS leadership saw itself as competing with Adi Sasono's CIDES, their relationship was not yet so antagonistic to preclude collaboration. Sasono worked behind the scenes to whip up anti-Wahid spirit in the sometimes reluctant Muslim mass media. Although in public Wahid decried what he called an

"ICMI" campaign against him, in private he said that the CPDS, Sasono, Tan-jung, and Hartono were his real antagonists.

When the five-day congress finally began in early December, it was still unclear whether Wahid had the votes to prevail. President Soeharto opened the congress, but he sent a pointed message concerning his own preferences for the NU leadership by refusing to greet Wahid or sit in his company. The armed forces commander and CPDS-patron, General Feisal Tanjung, also ad-dressed the assembly, and worked behind the scenes against Wahid. But not all the Jakarta elite wanted to bring Wahid down. Vice President Try Sutrisno, also present at the NU congress, was a Wahid supporter. Another who disap-proved of the anti-Wahid effort was Minister of Defense General Edi Sudrajat. Over the years to come Sudrajat was to intervene at critical moments to block anti-Wahid initiatives by other military commanders.

In the end, after several days of speeches and lobbying, Wahid was reelected to the chairmanship. Reports later indicated that the anti-Wahid effort back-fired because leading *ulama* were angered by the state's unprecedented interfer-ence in their affairs. Equally interesting, several local military commanders, instructed to mount a show of force against Wahid outside the meeting hall, opted at the last moment to deploy their troops away from the site. On the day of the vote, one officer made a point of taking off to play golf rather than mass his forces.

In public comments after the congress, Wahid blamed ICMI for the cam-paign against him. In private he was more specific, saying Din Syamsuddin and Amir Santosa (both of the CPDS) had joined forces with Adi Sasono in the campaign to unseat him. Although he was well aware of the support provided by Feisal Tanjung, Hartono, and Mbak Tutut to Hasan's initiative, Wahid made a point of *not* mentioning their participation. To attack Mbak Tutut would invite the wrath of the president. To attack Feisal or Hartono would violate the armed forces' first commandment: that no matter how great the tensions be-tween its various factions, military laundry should never be aired in public. Wahid's identification of ICMI as the force behind the campaign allowed him to fend off his attackers without degrading his relationship with the president or alienating fence-sitting members of the armed forces.

Having failed to oust him, regime strategists sought to keep up the pressure on Wahid by provoking a split in the NU executive board. They urged Abu Hasan to constitute a rival executive body, known as the Central Coordinating Executive (Koordinasi Pengurus Pusat NU). At first, Hasan appeared to have succeeded in his efforts to recruit prominent *ulama* and political leaders to the rival body. But these efforts were hurt when several of those alleged to have allied with Hasan denied ever having agreed to join. Although Hasan continued his campaign into 1997, it never became a serious threat to Wahid.

But there were other ways to pressure Wahid. Promoted to army chief of staff in March 1995, General Hartono launched a media blitz to demonstrate that under his leadership and that of the armed forces commander, Feisal Tanjung, Muslims were no longer marginal to the regime but were its central concern. Over the course of 1995 and early 1996 Hartono made repeated visits to NU *pesantren* providing financial grants to *ulama* willing to challenge Wahid's leadership. The president's daughter and Hartono ally, Mbak Tutut, did the same, dispensing gifts and contracts to *ulama* willing to oppose Wahid.

The ranks of Wahid's opponents in NU, it should be said, included many decent individuals with motives other than those of supporting Soeharto. Some were upset by what they regarded as Wahid's willingness to sacrifice NU's social and economic interests for an unwinnable political cause. Others disliked what they perceived as the liberal or secular bias of his political views. However varied the motives of Wahid's opponents, the overall result of their actions was the same: a severe deterioration of Wahid's relationship with Soeharto and great pressures on the rank and file to break with their embattled leader. The autonomy of NU, long the most independent of Indonesia's Muslim organizations, was in jeopardy.

The campaign against Wahid had originally escalated, of course, after he had hinted that he wanted to join forces with the nationalist leader, Megawati Soekarnoputri. While keeping the heat up on Wahid during 1995 and 1996, the regimist camp also turned its attention to Megawati and the nationalists. Her forces, too, were about to feel the effects of the government's turn to regimist Islam.

Plan Two: Javanists to the Margins

Strategists at the CPDS and the Litbang Bureau were embarrassed by their failure to leverage Wahid's fall. There was a competitive logic to their embarrassment. The CPDS leaders saw themselves in rivalry with other Muslim strategists hoping to win Soeharto's favor. In particular, they were determined to distinguish themselves from Adi Sasono's Center for Information and Development Studies (CIDES). ICMI and CIDES, the CPDS leadership argued, were incapable of delivering the strike force required by the Soehartoist camp. The reason for this inability, they insisted, was that ICMI was too poorly managed and too full of Muslims unsympathetic to the president. Because of ICMI's and CIDES's weaknesses, CPDS officials argued, Soeharto should rely on their think tank to get the job done. CPDS strategists would not waste time with Muslim moderates and civic democrats but would concentrate their attention on conservative hard-liners.

Unfortunately for the CPDS strategists, the think tank had flunked its first test by failing to oust Wahid. Some in the pro-government Muslim community predicted that the CPDS's career would be brief as a result. But the CPDS's strategy for the president was based on more than neutralizing Wahid. It also involved undermining Megawati Soekarnoputri and, equally important, eliminating the chances for a Wahid-Megawati alliance against the president. While urging the government to restrict Wahid's movement during 1995, then, the CPDS and its sponsors turned their attention to the other partner in the fledgling red-and-green alliance, Megawati's Democratic Party.

Megawati's rising popularity baffled the CPDS strategists. Like many foreign observers, regimist Muslims had long dismissed Megawati as a lightweight who lacked the skills to lead a mass organization. Overshadowed for much of her adult life by her photogenic artist-brother, Guruh Soekarnoputra, Megawati only emerged as a serious candidate for national leadership after the 1993 national elections. Despite a wooden speaking style and quiet Javanese reserve, Megawati's statements on social justice, economic reform, and an end to political and religious bullying touched a deep chord in the nationalist public. To the consternation of her enemies, Megawati's the-world-is-too-much-with-me manner only seemed to make her more attractive to the long-suffering nationalist public. They saw in her sweet suffering a symbol of their own long isolation.

Well read in the anthropological and political-science literature on religion and politics in Indonesia, the CPDS strategists realized from the beginning that they had an effective card to play against Megawati's and Wahid's red-and-green alliance. The card was the memory of the killings of 1965–66 and the bitterness they had left between Muslim traditionalists, especially in NU, and the Javanist Muslims who were an important part of Megawati's base. Wahid and Megawati were also aware of this legacy, and both understood that it might be exploited by their enemies. For Wahid, the memory of the killings was of particular concern because he knew that NU cadres had played a central role in one of the worst areas of violence: East Java. From the beginning of his career, one of Wahid's unstated but deepest ambitions had been to ensure that NU would never again allow itself to be used in state-sponsored killing.

But the regime's strategists had no such scruples, and it was with this vulnerability in mind that they set out to instigate a divisive religious controversy in March 1995. The controversy concerned a charmingly eccentric mystic, Soekarnoist, and commentator on public affairs, Permadi Satrio Wiwoho, S.H. A lawyer and low-level aristocrat from Solo, Central Java, Permadi specialized in Javanese mysticism and paranormal skills, including foretelling the future. As is the case with many Javanese spiritualists, Permadi had a light-hearted, ironic speaking style that sometimes made it difficult to determine whether he was attempting to be serious, sarcastic, or simply humorous. In the New Order period, most Javanist mystics remembered well that some of their brethren had been banned, imprisoned, or executed during 1965–66, and they took care to avoid criticism of the Soeharto regime. But Permadi was different. He did not shy away from making public comments and regularly offered his views on everything from consumer affairs (at one time he served as president of the National Consumer's Union) to Soeharto's abuses. For most of his career

Permadi's good looks, light manner, and aristocratic pedigree had helped him to avoid the wrath of New Order censors. Cassette recordings of his speeches and spiritual reflections were available in music shops across Java. In March 1995, however, Permadi was to discover that since the press closings of 1994 the limits of allowable speech had narrowed.

The campaign against Permadi began on March 9, 1995. On that day Permadi was summoned to the armed forces' Central Java headquarters in Semarang by the regional commander, Lieutenant General Soeyono. Although he fell from their favor after the events of July 27, 1996 (see below), in 1995 Soeyono was an ally of the pro-Habibie generals, Syarwan Hamid and Feisal Tanjung; he was made army general staff head in late 1995. Soeyono called Permadi to Semarang to explain remarks the mystic had made a year earlier, first in a radio broadcast and then again in a seminar at Gadjah Mada University in April 1994. Edited versions of these remarks had circulated on cassette tapes in spiritualist and nationalist circles, and these had caught the attention of security officials.

In later public statements, Soeyono explained that he was particularly concerned about what he regarded as political comments on Permadi's tapes. By the tightly controlled standards of the New Order, the remarks in question were bold indeed. Among other comments made on the tapes, Permadi stated that Golkar was as bad as the Indonesian Communist Party, that President Soeharto would fall from power in a bloody confrontation during 1997 or 1998, and that Megawati Soekarnoputri was likely to be the republic's next president. Permadi had also dared to say what many other political observers suspected: that many lower-ranking members of the military leadership were disgusted with Habibie's domination of Golkar and were preparing to shift their support from Golkar to Megawati's PDI.

Although Permadi's encounter with Soeyono was reported in the press,[15] early stories on the affair made no mention of anything related to Islam. In fact, the case generally did not catch the public's attention. What public reaction there was tended to be hostile to the government, because the incident was seen as one more example of the regime tightening the screws on independent speech.

One week later, however, the Permadi affair took a new and more dangerous turn. On March 17 Din Syamsuddin—director of the CPDS *and* the Research and Development Bureau of Golkar, former head of the youth wing of the Muhammadiyah (1989–93), and a bright young Ph.D. (1991) in Islamic Studies from UCLA—brought the Permadi matter to the attention of the Muslim community by releasing a statement to the Muslim-oriented newspaper, *Pelita.* Din's statement repeated the allegations made earlier by Lieutenant General Soeyono. But Din also highlighted something new. He charged that Permadi not only had insulted Soeharto and Golkar but had slandered the Prophet Muhammad. While Soeyono's allegations had caused little stir, Din's were about to have a huge impact.

Slander is a legal offense in Indonesia, and the slandering of a religion is taken especially seriously. Din, of course, knew this very well. It was he, after all, who in October 1990 had mobilized the Muslim community against another person accused of slandering Islam, Arswendo Atmowiloto, the editor of the tabloid newspaper *Monitor* (chapter 6). Din's statement and subsequent interviews alleged that Permadi's misstep was even more serious than Arswendo's. Permadi's insensitive remarks, Din claimed, were one more example of an impious secularist thumbing his nose at Muslims.[16]

Din did not deny that his complaint against Permadi had political motives, but he insisted that those motives were thoroughly principled. In an interview after his public complaint, he said that, in Islam, "religion and politics cannot be separated," and it was on the basis of the need to defend religion by intervening politically that he had taken action against Permadi and Arswendo. Din took particular exception to Permadi's statements allegedly referring to the Prophet Muhammad as a benevolent dictator. Permadi had described the Prophet in this manner in response to a question from the floor at the Gadjah Mada University seminar a year earlier. The question had come up in response to observations from another panelist, Adnan Buyung Nasution, to the effect that the problem with the state's "integralist" ideology is that it can degenerate into dictatorship. On hearing this remark, Permadi jumped up to say that the problem in Indonesia was not really dictatorship. After all, he said, there have been people in history who have enjoyed near-dictatorial powers but have used their power for good. Illustrating the irreverent eclecticism for which he is famous, Permadi then cited Pope John Paul II and the Prophet Muhammad as two examples of people who had used dictatorial powers benevolently. Later, in the question-and-answer period, Permadi added a second observation. He remarked that although the Prophet had the purest of motives, he had never succeeded in creating a just or peaceful society, since the political system he built was plagued by factional warfare.

At the original Gadjah Mada seminar, Permadi's remarks provoked little audience reaction, although some Muslim officials later claimed that they had tried to challenge Permadi's remarks but had been hushed. (During Permadi's trial in August 1995, however, these claims were effectively rebutted by defense witnesses.) Permadi's remarks were made in the context of a public discussion of Soeharto's rule, and the audience seemed to understand that rather than impugning the Prophet Permadi was really rebuking the president. Taken out of context, however, Permadi's comments were made to look as if they were directed against the Prophet. Unlike Soeyono's charges, Din's were guaranteed to provoke a public furor.

Just in case Din's statements failed to reach their mark, however, other regimist Muslims had been lined up to join the anti-Permadi campaign. The same day that Din Syamsuddin's statement was published, the head of the government-sponsored Council of Indonesian Ulama, (MUI), K. H. Hasan Basri, called a press conference in which he denounced Permadi's statements as slander (*fitnah*) against Islam and demanded that the government take legal action against the nationalist mystic.[17] Basri is a conservative modernist with close ties to the Dewan Dakwah Islamiyah Indonesia (DDII) (chapter 5). His appointment to the chairmanship of the MUI in 1993 had been widely seen as further proof of the regimist turn of Soeharto's policy on Islam.

In an interview with the weekly *Tiras* two weeks later, Basri admitted that he had not actually listened to the cassette of Permadi's statements but relied on a transcript provided him by Din Syamsuddin. Weeks later, as Din was accused of having engineered the entire Permadi controversy, Din denied ever giving Basri a copy of the Permadi transcripts, insisting that the MUI scholar had obtained them on his own.[18] But Basri's earlier statement showed that the two men had worked together.

Coordinated in this manner by the regimist leadership, the campaign against Permadi quickly turned ugly. Several days after Basri's remarks, the chief of the Muslim Party of Unity and Development, Ismail Hasan Metareum, described Permadi's comments as a "duplication of Salman Rushdie's statements in the *Satanic Verses*." A short time later, an East Javanese scholar, K. H. Syansuri Badawy, was quoted in the *Jawa Pos* as saying that under these circumstances "the shedding of blood is allowed" (*halal*). Demonstrations by Muslim youth against Permadi soon took place across Indonesia. The fiercest were coordinated by the DDII and its ally, KISDI.[19] As the campaign escalated, nationalists began to worry that Permadi's life was in danger. Sensing the threat, Permadi left Solo for Jakarta, where he surrendered himself to police for interrogation and protection.

In the end, the campaign against Permadi lost momentum. From the beginning, democratic Muslims and secular democrats appealed for calm, arguing that the whole matter should be resolved in court. Democratic Muslims pointed out that the timing of the accusation was suspect. Although Din Syamsuddin claimed to have received a copy of the Permadi cassette just days before releasing his statement to *Pelita*, his critics countered that Permadi's views on the president and Golkar were nothing new and that his observations on the Prophet Muhammad, although insensitive, had clearly not been directed at the Prophet but at Soeharto. Moreover, as reporters looked into Permadi's comments, they discovered that portions of the original speech had been excised from the transcripts circulated by Permadi's accusers in a manner that made his statements harsher than they had actually been.[20]

Critics of Permadi's accusers charged that the timing of the whole affair was no accident. The allegation was made, after all, in the aftermath of the failed campaign against Wahid and the continuing anxieties in regimist Muslim circles about a possible alliance between Wahid and Megawati. Journalists observed that the Permadi campaign was political theater at its worst, designed to antagonize Muslim relations with Javanists and rally conservative Muslims to Golkar in the 1997 elections.[21] Other critics noted that the attack may have had a secondary purpose: to embarrass Amien Rais, the head of Muhammadiyah. A strong critic of Soeharto, Rais was present at the seminar in which Permadi made his comments. Rais also has long been a bitter rival of Din Syamsuddin in the Muhammadiyah. As chairman of the Muhammadiyah, Rais had made clear that he intended to steer the modernist organization in the direction of pro-reform activism. This was exactly the opposite of the pro-regime policy advocated by Rais's two biggest rivals in the Muhammadiyah, Syamsuddin and Lukman Harun. During 1995 and 1996, when Muslim conservatives linked to the DDII and KISDI were lining up to support the Soeharto regime, Amien and his followers placed themselves squarely in the ranks of the regime's critics. By attacking Permadi, it was said, Din, Harun, and the CPDS were attempting to humiliate Amien. Anti-Amien innuendo circulating in Jakarta asked: If Amien were present at Permadi's talk, why didn't he challenge Permadi's statements?[22]

In the end, Permadi was convicted of slander and sentenced to eight months in jail. By the time the verdict was delivered, however, Permadi had already been in detention for eight months, so he was allowed to go free. His relatively light sentence was seen by many observers as proof that high-ranking government officials, including some in Soeharto's inner circle, had been upset by the crudely politicized nature of the campaign. Indeed, according to some reports, the president's wife, Bu Tien (who had relatives in the Solo court), was personally upset by the case against Permadi and had let her opinions be known.

In retrospect, the regimist Muslim campaign against Permadi was clearly a qualified success at best. The initiative at first provoked outrage among conservative Muslims. Eventually, however, this protest was overshadowed by the efforts of mainstream leaders in the Muhammadiyah and NU to ensure that the protest did not create the hysteria that had marked the *Monitor* affair. In fact, the only major Muslim organizations to join fully in the Permadi campaign were the ultraconservative DDII and its affiliate KISDI. In a series of publications and public statements, the DDII endorsed every item in the Golkar-inspired case against Permadi. The DDII's flagship publication, *Media Dakwah* (chapter 5), published a detailed report on the affair, which it used not only to attack Permadi but to expose the "collapse of mysticism in Indonesia."[23] Never before had the DDII so vigorously participated in regime-sponsored provocation. The once proud DDII had defected into the Soeharto camp.[24]

The Permadi affair also provided an important political lesson for mainstream Muslim leaders like Amien Rais, leaders who were moderately conventional on theological matters but democratic in matters of governance and public policy. In the 1980s Amien had developed a reputation as a leader quick to respond to perceived threats to Islam. He had long been a bitter critic of "Christianization" and phrased his criticisms in terms that echoed the Dewan Dakwah. According to friends and advisers, however, the Permadi affair impressed on

Amien that the Soeharto regime would not hesitate to play regimist Muslims against democratic reformers.

Another audience had also watched the Permadi affair from the sidelines and reached an even sadder conclusion; these were the Javanist members of the ruling elite. Although Soeharto had been campaigning for several years to win the support of organized Muslims, he still included in his inner circle figures regarded as nominal Muslims or even Javanists. Indeed, one of the president's most important ministers, State Secretary Moerdiono, was known to be a Javanist nationalist with a personal affection for Abdurrahman Wahid.[25]

Elite nationalists like Moerdiono were especially shocked by the Permadi affair. For the first time they realized that the president's turn to conservative Islam had serious implications for the balance of power in Golkar itself. If they had not understood that point before, they did now—not least of all because regimist Muslims in the president's inner circle put them on notice that this was the case. According to the testimony of a friend who disagreed with his actions, Din Syamsuddin himself explained to colleagues that one of his goals in provoking the Permadi affair was "to send a message to all those old *abangan* in Golkar that times had changed; they no longer enjoyed the president's sympathy. They had better change or get out."[26] CPDS strategists had long since identified Moerdiono as one of the most influential of these "old *abangan*," and they were mobilizing sentiment in elite circles against the influential state secretary. The cancer of religious sectarianism was spreading into the body of the political elite.

From the perspective of the CPDS and regimist Muslims, the Permadi affair was not a success. But it had a profound impact on national political realignments. Faced with a growing opposition, government strategists had played the regimist Muslim card with a fury. Now it was time to take aim at the main target.

PLAN THREE: DEMOLISHING MEGAWATI

The effort to isolate Megawati Soekarnoputri began well before the Permadi affair in mid-1995. Obstacles had been placed in the way of Megawati's leadership immediately following her election to the position of PDI chairperson in December 1993. Her main rival for the PDI leadership at that time, Soeryadi, was a popular and often outspoken figure who had helped to increase the party's share of the vote during the national elections in 1987 and 1992. Ironically, it was Soeryadi's willingness to criticize the government that led to his fall from regime favor and ouster in 1993.

The government had forced Soeryadi out on the expectation that his replacement would be Budi Harjono, a quiet man regarded as more accommodating toward the government. Having engineered Soeryadi's removal, however, the government unwittingly opened the way for Megawati's ascent to the leadership post. She was reportedly helped in this effort by military commanders upset with Golkar, Habibie, and the president's turn to conservative Islam. These nationalist officers believed it necessary to revitalize the PDI so as to counter the growing power of the Habibie group. The person best able to bring about that revitalization, they felt, was Megawati. She was appointed chairwoman of the party in December 1993 and ratified as leader in January 1994.

No sooner did Megawati assume the PDI chair, however, than pro-Habibie figures in the military and government mounted a counter campaign to undermine her authority. In mid-1994 one of the smaller parties that make up the PDI (fused into the party during the party "simplification" of 1973), the Association of Supporters of Independence (*Ikatan Pendukung Kemerdekaan Indonesia*, or IPKI), voted to withdraw from the PDI. Although a small organization, IPKI enjoyed considerable influence in the PDI because its ranks included retired Soekarnoist military officials—precisely the constituency Megawati had to maintain if she was to mount an effective challenge to the government.

This was the first of many problems for Megawati. In regional branches of the PDI during 1994, rival executive boards were established by military and civilian leaders intent on undermining Megawati's leadership. Many of these regional executives consisted of no more than a few members of the local PDI; indeed, in a few instances appointees included people with no prior PDI experience. Despite the contrived nature of these rival executives, governors across the country refused to recognize the Megawati-appointed leadership, innocently claiming that they could not do so until the local PDI made peace with the government-sponsored rebels.

The most serious of these challenges took place in the heartland of Megawati support, East Java. In that province, the governor refused even to allow Megawati to make public appearances until two rival provincial executives had "agreed to unite." Meanwhile, behind the scenes, government strategists were advising the PDI rebels on how to take measures ensuring that no such reconciliation was possible. In this and other cases, the government attempted to present itself as a neutral arbitrator for an "internal" party affair. Political observers understood well, however, that the government was actually behind the campaign.[27]

The campaign against Megawati escalated further on December 29, 1994, with the formation of a "Reshuffled National PDI Executive." Under the leadership of Yusuf Merukh, this new PDI executive sought to replace Megawati's national board with people loyal to the dissident PDI and Soeharto. The reshuffled executive was greeted with dismay among PDI rank and file. But the mere existence of the rival executive allowed the government to claim that the PDI's problems were caused by Megawati's inability to unite her party's factions.[28]

Once in place, the rival leadership moved quickly to tighten the screws on Megawati supporters. In January 1995 Merukh released reports summarizing allegations he had made two months earlier. Merukh charged that more than three hundred members of Megawati's provincial executives had had ties to the Communist Party. Merukh then demanded that Megawati step down so that he could lead the effort to cleanse the party of its tainted cadres.[29] A few weeks later, in February 1995, Merukh made his attacks more personal, alleging that Megawati's husband, Taufik Kiemas, was himself a "Class C" Communist supporter who as late as March 1966 had engaged in actions against Muslim activists in South Sumatra.[30]

Government-instigated attacks on Megawati continued without letup from 1995 into 1996. The campaign succeeded in scuttling Megawati's plans to revitalize the regional leadership by replacing government cronies with PDI loyalists. Ironically, however, the government's crude repression only increased public sympathy for the modest Javanese woman, transforming her into a hero of the pro-reform movement.

Golkar strategists realized that their efforts might be backfiring in late 1995, when the party's Research and Development Bureau conducted a secret poll in Central and East Java to determine the breadth of support for the suffering PDI leader. To these officials' amazement, the poll revealed that, were elections held at that time, Megawati would beat Golkar in both Central and East Java.[31] With the two most populous of Indonesia's provinces in jeopardy, Golkar and CPDS strategists now realized that they could no longer afford just to handicap Megawati's leadership. They urged the government to take firmer action, so as to remove Megawati from her post before the 1997 elections.

At this point, responsibility for the campaign against Megawati moved away from the CPDS and Golkar's Research and Development Bureau into the hands of the pro-Habibie military leadership under the command of General Feisal Tanjung and Syarwan Hamid. In early 1996 Feisal arranged a luncheon between the former head of the PDI, Soeryadi, and President Soeharto at the president's residence in Menteng, Jakarta. According to people close to Soeryadi, the president and Soeryadi, during their luncheon, did not explicitly address the crisis in the PDI. Having been pushed out of the PDI by the president's supporters two years earlier, however, Soeryadi was led to understand that the president was having second thoughts about Soeryadi's removal.

Time was running out, however, and the effort against Megawati had to move forward quickly. In the days following Soeryadi's lunch, a plan of attack was presented to him and the reshuffled executives. The plan called for the anti-Megawati group to convene an emergency meeting of the PDI leadership in Medan, Sumatra, on June 20, to discuss the crisis caused by "popular" opposition to Megawati. It was made clear, of course, that the meeting should be convened in such a manner that the mainstream PDI leaders would refuse to participate, which of course they did. At the emergency congress, Soeryadi would be elected the new PDI chairman, and provincial boards would be given the choice of either assenting to Soeryadi's leadership or being replaced with "reshuffled" provincial leaders.

As can be seen from this history, the tactics used against Megawati resembled those used against Abdurrahman Wahid after the NU national congress in December 1994. The key feature in both efforts was the government's provocation of dissent in the organization, followed by the creation of a rival executive to undermine the legitimate leader's authority. But regime strategists had also learned from the failure of their NU initiative. To take over the PDI, they realized, they had to promote a leader distinguished enough to serve as a credible alternative to the party's legitimate leader. For the PDI, the one man capable of assuming that role was the party's former chairman, Soeryadi.

Preparations for the Medan congress were rumored to have been coordinated by two unlikely allies: Adi Sasono's CIDES and Sofyan Wanandi, a wealthy Chinese conservative businessman and backer of the Center for Strategic and International Studies. Closely linked to Soeharto in the 1970s and early 1980s, the CSIS had fallen out of favor with Soeharto in the late 1980s, as he began his courtship of conservative Muslims. The ideological complexion of the CSIS had always been varied, and by the 1980s it included in its ranks moderates and supporters of constitutional reform. Having long played by the rules of the New Order game, however, Wanandi's vision of politics remained Soeharto-centered. Friends said he viewed the crisis in the PDI as a chance to regain lost influence with the president. With this goal in mind, Wanandi is said to have contributed about U.S.$270,000 to finance the Medan congress. Prominent among conservative Catholics, Wanandi is also said to have lined up a small group of Catholics to assume leadership roles in Soeryadi's reshuffled executives.

Wanandi had no influence among the Muslim membership of the PDI, however, who, by 1995, comprised about 80 percent of the party's rank and file. The task of mobilizing Muslim members of the PDI to the anti-Megawati cause was therefore assigned to Adi Sasono's CIDES. Adi had a disciplined network of supporters across the country, recruited from the ranks of Muslim student activists, Muslim laborers, and the cooperative movement. His earlier association with the NGO movement also gave him credibility in some PDI circles. It was because he had this credibility and network of supporters that Adi was seen as a better partner for the PDI project than his rivals in the CPDS, Din Syamsuddin, Fadli Zon, and Amir Santosa. Din, Fadli, and Amir were flush with funds, but the only mass organizations in which they had supporters were the Dewan Dakwah Islamiyah and a tiny wing of the Muhammadiyah. Given its conservative and anti-Christian reputation, the Dewan Dakwah had absolutely no influence in the PDI. The Muhammadiyah was no better as a prospective ally; it was led by Din and Amir's bitter rival, Amien Rais, a strong critic of the Soeharto government.

Adi Sasono's operatives had no such difficulties. Although the idea of collaborating with their long-hated rivals in the CSIS struck several of the younger CIDES recruits as distasteful (as one of them told me), they viewed their collaboration as a sign that they had indeed come of age. Power politics requires that one look the other way on matters of principle.

Megawati had supporters in the armed forces as well, especially in the Marine Corps, which had a history of nationalist sentiment reaching back to the Soekarno era. In fact, during June and July 1996 one marine commander is said to have kept Megawati updated on the preparations being made against her. But this modest assistance from a few military figures could not prevent Soeryadi's Medan conference from taking place in June 1996 or the subsequent establishment of rival PDI executives across the country. In late June and July Megawati's supporters mounted fierce campaigns to challenge these rival executives whenever they gathered for meetings. Slowly but surely, however, Soeryadi managed to get his rival executives up and running. In several instances, Soeryadi supporters forcibly seized control of PDI offices, driving out Megawati's supporters.

In anticipation of an attempted takeover of the national headquarters in central Jakarta, in late June 1996 Megawati supporters began holding all-day vigils at the party headquarters. With each passing day the vigils attracted more and more supporters. As the crowds grew larger, Megawati and her supporters grew bolder. They proclaimed the grounds in front of the headquarters a free-speech forum (*mimbar bebas*) open to all who wished to speak. They criticized not only Soeryadi but the cronyism and violence of the Soeharto regime as a whole. Soon the forum had a momentum greater than the PDI cause itself. Critics of the government with no historical ties to the PDI began to make visits there, giving speeches in which they expressed their support for Megawati and called for sweeping reform. In early July Jesse Jackson from the United States made an unscheduled stop at the PDI forum during a visit to Jakarta. People across Indonesia began to wonder whether, as Megawati's supporters proclaimed, the protest was the beginning of a "people's power" movement capable of toppling Soeharto.

According to the government advisers I interviewed in January 1997, the turning point in the regime's policy on the PDI protest occurred when growing numbers of Muslim leaders came to express their support for Megawati. Abdurrahman Wahid was in their ranks from early on, of course. But so, too, were dissident Muslim retirees from the military. More surprising yet, modernist Muslims with historical antipathy toward the political left, such as Ridwan Saidi (a former member of the PPP), also came forward to place themselves in the ranks of the prodemocracy campaign. Gestures of solidarity like these showed that despite two years of government repression the long-feared "red-and-green" alliance was alive and well. The possibility that this collaboration might escalate into a full-blown challenge to the regime forced its hand.

State Terror

The government attack on the PDI headquarters began at 5:30 a.m. the morning of July 27, 1996. The event marked a return to the hard-line tactics of the early New Order and baptized Megawati as the leader of a revitalized prodemocracy movement. Although at first it caused great confusion in the ranks of Indonesian democrats, the July 27 incident marked the beginning of the end of the Soeharto regime.

The capture of the PDI headquarters required two waves of attack. Each consisted of eight hundred Soeryadi supporters rushing the headquarters, peppering it with a barrage of stones and other projectiles (dutifully trucked in by government organizers), and then beating whomever among the defenders they could with heavy metal rods. Megawati's defenders suffered the most serious injuries, but there were casualties on both sides.

In the two weeks preceding the attack, Soeryadi's supporters had been trained at a camp outside Jakarta by military advisers from the Indonesian special forces, under the direction of the most notorious of the "green" generals, Major General Prabowo Subianto (Soeharto's son-in-law).[32] Even with these hardened personnel, the government thugs were surprised by the courage of the Megawati defenders. After a half hour of pummeling, Soeryadi's forces turned back, bloodied and confused. In discussions of the violence in the weeks that followed, government strategists admitted that they had underestimated the dedication of Megawati's supporters. The strategists blamed their miscalculation in part on their inability to secure the cooperation of military intelligence bureaus. Military advisers to the attackers had been reluctant to draw intelligence agencies into their plan because they knew that most security officials wanted nothing to do with the anti-Megawati campaign.

Having failed the first time, the second assault began two hours later, at 7:30 a.m. This time the Soeryadi supporters were backed up by members of the army special forces (out of uniform) under the command of General Prabowo. This second attack succeeded in its aim; the assailants captured the headquarters and arrested many of its defenders. Initial reports from the scene of the battle indicated that about forty people died in the assault. However, the Indonesian Human Rights Commission (founded in 1994)—a government body distinguished for its fairness, courage, and integrity—indicated in its report on the violence in October 1996 that it could confirm the deaths of only five people, though it acknowledged that several dozen more had disappeared.[33] It has yet to be determined how many of those who disappeared were killed and how many simply could not be located or went into hiding.

Having captured the party headquarters, the security forces closed off the streets around the office. In the hours that followed, PDI supporters made several unsuccessful attempts to recapture the headquarters. Eventually some of the demonstrators spread out into the city, where they were joined by residents of Jakarta's slums. Some among this enlarged group then attacked and burned government offices and buildings owned by individuals linked to Soeharto.[34] The two days of rioting that followed were the worst the capital had seen since 1974.

In the aftermath of the violence, Megawati urged calm, appealing to her supporters to await the outcome of her court suit against the government and Soeryadi. At the same time, however, her rank and file continued to challenge Soeryadi whenever he attempted to visit his provincial executives. Although neither these protests nor her court appeals (which were eventually dismissed) succeeded in restoring Megawati's leadership in time for the 1997 elections, they thoroughly discredited the Soeryadi group. Soeryadi became so unpopular that many in government had second thoughts about the wisdom of supporting him and urged Soeharto to reconcile the two PDI factions. Ultimately, however, regime strategists decided against this course of action. Government persecution had made Megawati so popular that they felt they had no choice but to drive her from politics entirely.

Surprised by the courage of Megawati's supporters, the government escalated its propaganda campaign by blaming the violence of July 27 on a little known new-left organization, the People's Democratic Party (Partai Rakyat Demokrasi, or PRD). The PRD was an attractive scapegoat. It had gone public with its party platform only several days before the assault on the PDI, on July 22, 1997. Although the PRD was committed to multiparty democracy, its analysis of Indonesia's political crisis placed primary responsibility for New Order policies on global capitalism and the capitalist class. Its political vocabulary was of an unreconstructed *Marxisant* Left. So unusual was the coincidence of the PRD's founding on the eve of the PDI attack that some observers speculated that the organization had been infiltrated by government operatives intent on creating a leftist scapegoat for the violence of July 27.[35] In the days following the July 27 disaster, government officials described the PRD as the "mastermind" of the violence and the Indonesian Communist Party as the "master" of the PRD.

Indonesia's Muslim organizations responded in different ways to the government's allegations. The national leadership of the Nahdlatul Ulama was openly skeptical. Rather than accusing the government of lying, however, the NU leadership politely requested that government officials offer proof. Reaction in the modernist community was more varied. Nurcholish Madjid, now a member of the government-sponsored Human Rights Commission (Komnas HAM), was at first polite when he learned of the government's claims that the PRD and Communists were behind the July 27 violence. In a surprisingly blunt rejection of the government account, however, Madjid later insisted that the allegation of Communist subversion was "an old language" that hid the real cause of the violence, namely, that legitimate avenues of political expression had been blocked by the state. Madjid urged Muslim and other democrats to remain calm but to hold to their long-term strategy of creating a civil society strong enough to counterbalance the power of the state.[36]

Others in the mainstream modernist community, however, were less critical in their reaction to the government claims. The Muhammadiyah leadership had been startled by the rapid ascent of the PDI and the unexpected reappearance of the political Left. Although, under Amien Rais, the Muhammadiyah leadership was firmly committed to democratic reform, most were still fiercely anticommunist and allergic to anything associated with the Left. Although they understood that the government had engineered the attack on the PDI, many nonetheless believed that there might be some truth to the charge of left-wing infiltration of Megawati's PDI.

In what many observers regarded as one of the most serious mistakes of his political career, Amien Rais, the Muhammadiyah head and Soeharto critic, voiced qualified support for the government's charge that Communists were behind the July 27 violence. "The discovery of Molatov cocktails, explosives, and gasoline," he said, "shows that there probably was an intention to destabilize the country in a dangerous way."[37] Rais went on to advise that "Megawati has to learn from this incident"; he made no such mention as to what the government should learn. Adding insult to injury, Amien then observed that charges that the military had overreacted in the July 27 disaster were patently false. It was obvious, he said, that the armed forces had used "persuasion" rather than violence to quell the uprising. Amien failed to mention that the government was responsible for the assault on the PDI or that its agents provocateurs might well have provoked subsequent riots. Unlike Nurcholish Madjid, Rais also did not mention the government's failure to provide channels for democratic participation.[38]

Muslim ultraconservatives were even more unqualified in their support of the government. Ahmad Sumargono, the leader of the hard-line Committee for Solidarity with the Islamic World (KISDI), declared that he was sure that the PKI was behind the July 27 disturbance because "violence is the PKI's way." Hussein Umar of the DDII spoke in a similarly pliant manner, declaring: "Their process of infiltration, underground activity, psychological warfare, sabotage and strikes—these are their tactics. It's all communist doctrine."[39] The cover of the August issue of the DDII magazine, *Media Dakwah*, made the same point. It showed a bald devil (the PKI) riding the symbol of the PDI, a wild bull; above it was written, "What Is Behind the Bald Devil?" *Media Dakwah*'s September issue had a more complete and provocative analysis of the July 27 violence. The magazine cover showed a fist smashing a hammer and sickle, above which were written the words, "Crush the Communists: Muslims Are the First Against the Communist Party!" In private, however, some younger members of the DDII were disturbed by their organization's regimist turn. One member told me that he felt Mohammad Natsir would never have engaged in such immoral collaboration.[40]

Two weeks after the July violence, on August 11, 1996, some forty thousand Muslims rallied at the Senayan stadium in Jakarta in support of the government's claim that the PRD and Communists were the instigators of the July 27 incident. There was a broader political logic to the Muslim show of support. In the weeks following the July 27 disaster, the government pressured Muslim leaders to condemn the People's Democratic Party and declare their support for the government. Organizations that refused were treated to a barrage of bureaucratic threats. They had difficulties securing permits for public meetings, found their members called in for interrogation, and saw business supporters threatened with loss of contracts. In the face of this repression, most Muslim organizations complied with the government's demand. Although Abdurrahman Wahid and the senior NU leadership refused to do so, even a few of NU's junior affiliates joined the government chorus.[41]

As on previous occasions, Wahid was made to pay for his independence. In August and September 1996 government-sponsored slander against Wahid intensified in Muslim circles. The usual allegations were made that Wahid does not pray, does not fast, and supports "Christianization." To these familiar charges was now added a more bizarre claim: that Wahid had joined the Baath Party in Iraq while studying there in the 1960s and, because of this alleged socialist background, had aided in the establishment of the People's Democratic Party.

However ridiculous these allegations, Wahid was worried that Muslim public opinion was turning against him. He was convinced that his old nemesis, Adi Sasono, aided by Eggy Sudjana of CIDES, had masterminded the rumor campaign against him (a charge I was never able to confirm). In September 1996 he responded to the rumormongering by alleging that it was in fact Adi Sasono who had had ties to the People's Democratic Party. Adi vigorously denied these charges and fired a barrage back at Wahid. If Wahid is so upset by the events of July 27, Adi charged, where was he during the killings of Muslim protestors at Tanjung Priok in 1984? Had he not invited the man responsible for the Tanjung Priok violence, Benny Moerdani, to visit Qur'anic schools in the aftermath of the killings? Where, in fact, are Wahid's allegiances?[42]

By late 1996 these charges and countercharges had created confusion in the ranks of Muslims and secular democrats. Whatever the truth of Sasono's and Wahid's recriminations, to many observers it seemed that government hardliners had triumphed. They had smashed Megawati, rallied ultraconservative Muslims against the specter of communism, and demoralized the democratic opposition. As 1996 drew to a close, the pro-reform community looked weaker and more factionalized than at any time since the late 1980s. In the words of the human rights lawyer, Adnan Buyung Nasution, the events of 1996 had left the prodemocracy movement thoroughly "disoriented" and "without any idea as to what to do next."[43] Worse yet, July 27 was but the beginning of a more dreadful cycle of violence.

WAHID'S CHOICE

As 1996 came to a close, the loneliest voices in the Muslim community were those of its two greatest leaders, Abdurrahman Wahid and Nurcholish Madjid. Each man had dedicated himself to a long-term strategy of democratization premised on civic organizations and a middle class capable of counterbalancing the power of the state. The slogan "civil society" or, as it is known among Southeast Asian Muslim scholars, *masyarakat madani*,[44] had captured the imagination of Muslim democrats frustrated by the reversals of 1994 but hoping to avoid a slippery slide into violence. The idea of civil society seemed to offer a kinder and gentler road to democracy, one that avoided confrontation with the state by emphasizing an incremental expansion in civic power.

As with proponents of civil society in other parts of the world, however, Madjid and Wahid had both assumed that, in response to gentle urgings from society, the state would gradually move in a civil and accommodating direction. But Soeharto's violent reaction to the prodemocracy movement illustrated the general truth that, in the end, there can be no genuinely civil society without a civilized state. The regime's repression left the proponents of peaceful democratization disheartened. To many, their movement seemed to have collapsed.

Hard-liners in KISDI and the DDII dismissed Wahid and Madjid's talk of civic independence and citizen initiative as the dreamy idealism of political juveniles. KISDI and DDII leaders argued that Muslims had long been kept out of power by an unholy alliance of Christians, Javanists, and secular modernizers. Now that Soeharto realized that he needed Muslims there was no point to forging an alliance with the democratic opposition—especially an opposition that included Christians and secularists. After all, DDII leaders told me in January 1997, what had that opposition done for Muslims during their long and cruel cold winter? The most appropriate course of action, the KISDI and DDII leadership argued, was to accept the president's invitation and reap the benefits of collaboration. The rush of Muslim leaders to declare their support for the July 27 crackdown showed that the state's strategy of undermining the prodemocracy opposition by mobilizing regimist Islam was making progress.

The political crisis presented Abdurrahman Wahid with an awful choice. More than Nurcholish Madjid, Wahid had to concern himself not merely with promoting high principles but attending to the socioeconomic welfare of NU's vast membership. In the course of his activities with the Democratic Forum and his struggle to defend his chairmanship, Wahid was made to realize that every act of political independence had its price. The price was regime attacks on his rank and file. However much his core ideals converged with those of Madjid, Wahid was obliged to factor the welfare of his membership into his evaluation of the costs and benefits of democratic action.

By late 1996 government restrictions on his rank and file were exacting so high a cost that Wahid's chairmanship of the NU was in doubt. Wahid understood this well. At the beginning of the year he had thrown himself behind Megawati's democratic campaign. In late July that campaign had collapsed in the face of state terror. More alarming yet, in August and September 1996 Wahid received reports from intelligence advisers indicating that he was about to become the target of another government attack. The reports were not clear as to what kind of action was planned against the NU leader. They merely indicated that with Megawati out of the way the regime was going to provoke some kind of incident to discredit Wahid's claim to speak for the Muslim community.

Against this backdrop of suspicion and violence, on October 10, 1996, fierce anti-Christian and anti-Chinese riots swept through the town of Situbondo on the northeast coast of East Java. Over the course of twelve hours, in a ninety-square-kilometer area around the town, twenty-five Christian schools and churches were destroyed, five people were killed, and dozens of Chinese stores were damaged or destroyed. Situbondo's population is largely made up of immigrants from the island of Madura off the north coast of East Java. The Madurese in this region are well known for their fierce allegiance to NU and traditionalist Islam. Poor and undereducated, however, they are also known to be more socially conservative than Wahid. Situbondo, one might say, was where the tension between Wahid's enlightened leadership and the NU mass was dangerously apparent.

News of the riot stunned Wahid's supporters. Could their worst fears have been realized? Was this the event that many had forecast, the one intended to demonstrate that Wahid couldn't control his supporters, and all this talk of NU as an agent of pluralism and tolerance was a fraud? As in the months before the September 30 coup in 1965, rumors often play a central role in Indonesian politics, and they can exercise a critical influence on political judgments. The information circulating in NU circles after the Situbondo riots heightened anxieties among Wahid supporters. Reports from the shattered town—confirmed by journalists who visited Situbondo—indicated that most of the rioters were not local people but provocateurs ferried in aboard three trucks from outside town. In crisp black ninja uniforms the rioters moved around town unimpeded for four hours before security officials finally appeared. Their leaders blew whistles directing their troops to their targets; a truck dispensed gasoline for petrol bombs. By the time the police arrived, the rioters had moved on to neighboring towns, where they carried out a similarly well-planned program of terror against Christian churches and schools.

The chronology of events leading up to the violence added to suspicions that it had been engineered. Tension had arisen in Situbondo about a month earlier, when a poor rural migrant named Saleh made inflammatory comments about Islam. Saleh was a janitor at one of the town's mosques. A self-taught student of Islamic mysticism, Saleh claimed to have developed a special religious knowledge (*ilmu*) that led him to heterodox conclusions. He believed that Allah is not almighty but merely a being like any other, that the Prophet Muhammad is not a true prophet, and whether one performs the daily prays is of no importance. Saleh also made comments deprecating the spiritual abilities of one of Situbondo's most esteemed Muslim scholars, KH As'ad Syamsul Arifin (deceased).

From the beginning, questions were raised about Saleh's mental state. People familiar with him described the solitary migrant as so simple-minded as to be retarded; others thought him emotionally disturbed. In light of this information, Muslim leaders in Situbondo were surprised when they heard that government prosecutors had taken Saleh's ramblings so seriously. Muslim leaders in the town agreed that there was no need to take the hapless Saleh to trial. For reasons no one could understand, however, local prosecutors disagreed. On September 12, 1996, Saleh was formally charged with religious slander in the Situbondo district court. After Saleh was convicted on October 3, Situbondo's two most prominent Muslim scholars asked that his sentencing be postponed three days beyond the scheduled date of October 10, because they were to be out of town on that day. The authorities ignored their request.

On the morning of October 10 a crowd gathered in front of the courthouse. Upon learning that Saleh had been sentenced to five years in prison, someone in the crowd shouted, "Kill him," and urged the crowd to seize the detainee. Saleh and the judge fled the courthouse through a back door. Mysteriously, however, someone in the crowd then shouted, "He's in the church," and the crowd surged forth to attack and burn a nearby church. Although the number of rioters was not great, they moved unimpeded through town, burning churches and schools. Local townspeople looked on in amazed terror.

The scheduling of the trial, the ease of the provocation, the trucked-in demonstrators (who appeared after the rioting began), and the ease with which the rioters moved from Situbondo to nearby cities raised suspicions that the violence had been engineered. Even President Soeharto remarked that he felt that the violence had been orchestrated by a mysterious "third force." (He meant to give the impression, of course, that this force was the long defunct Communist Party.) Because Situbondo is an NU stronghold, the evidence of outside provocation aroused special concern among Wahid's advisers. In an emotional statement three days after the Situbondo violence, Wahid apologized to the Christian community, expressing deep regrets that some of the people involved in the rioting had ties to the NU.[45] He also established a commission in NU to investigate the riots. Although never published (and though, for political reasons, its existence was eventually denied by NU leaders), the results of this investigation were summarized in what later became known as the "Situbondo White Book." The report indicated that the violence had indeed been directed by agents provocateurs from outside Situbondo. But the book stopped short of saying just who had hired them for their services.

The Situbondo mystery did not end there. During October and November 1996 information began to emerge from East Java prisons that several NU youths, arrested for participating in the unrest, were being tortured; one man eventually died in detention.[46] Equally surprising, the reports of torture were leaked under highly suspicious circumstances. There were even tape-recorded interviews with Ahmad Siddiq, the detainee eventually killed in prison, in which he spoke of being tortured by army officials he called Christians. NU officials in the region were convinced that this information had been released so as to heighten anti-Christian sentiment among the NU rank and file. They suspected that that unrest was intended to show that Abdurrahman Wahid could not control his membership and that Wahid's claim that NU was a force for tolerance and democratization was a fraud.

Among the people advising Wahid, these incidents were taken as proof that the dirty-tricks bureau responsible for ousting Megawati was still active and was now targeting him. During late 1996 repeated reports were heard from around Central and East Java of further provocations—including (false) rumors of mosques being burned, of young NU women being raped, and so on. NU officials mobilized their full resources to prevent further outbreaks of violence. Members of their youth corps, Ansor, were placed on guard around Christian churches. A network of individuals, linked by cellular phones, was established to report suspicious activities. For most of late 1996 East and Central Java remained calm.

But the cycle of violence had not yet ended. On the night of December 27, 1996, Indonesia was rocked by still another riot. This incident took place in the West Java town of Tasikmalaya after a policeman assaulted a respected Islamic teacher. As rumors circulated that the teacher had died in police custody (he had been injured but had not died), rioters attacked police stations, churches, and Chinese stores and residences. Tasikmalaya, although not an NU stronghold, is regarded as a *santri* (pious Muslim) city. The decline of the textile industry in the district a few years earlier had fueled popular discontent.

Suspicions as to the possibility of outside provocation were heightened, however, when it became clear that—just as in Situbondo—several of the youths arrested and charged with leading the riots happened to be members of NU's student organization. Once again, Wahid supporters were informed by their intelligence operatives that the riot had been orchestrated by anti-Wahid agents. These reports alleged that the NU detainees were affiliated with a small prodemocracy organization that had been infiltrated by dirty-tricks operatives who had encouraged the membership to engage in violence.

Shortly after receiving these reports, Wahid went public with his accusation that agents linked to ICMI were responsible for both the Situbondo and Tasik-malaya violence. He pointed his finger at Adi Sasono and Sasono's chief lieutenant, Eggy Sudjana, from ICMI's Center for Information and Development Studies. What Wahid did not mention in his public accusation was that this same intelligence information indicated that certain "green" generals close to Habibie had provided logistical support to the rioters. To have made this point would, again, have violated one of the basic rules of New Order politics: that civilians should never highlight divisions in the military.

Adi Sasono denied all these allegations. He and his supporters insisted that Wahid singled him out not because he had anything to do with the riots but because he was the chief assistant to Habibie. Whatever the truth of these charges, they were indicative of the downward spiral of rumor and violence into which Indonesian politics had plunged. The antagonism did not pit a unified "government" against a nongovernmental democratic movement. The tensions were now reaching into the ranks of the political elite itself, including the military, where supporters of Habibie and ICMI were facing off against a heterogeneous alliance of "nationalist" officers opposed to Habibie and conservative Islam.

Many Indonesians suspected that Soeharto had masterminded this cycle of violence, utilizing his familiar tactic of playing rival claimants for power off one another. Others, however, felt that things were not quite that simple. Rivalry among factions in the ruling elite had taken on an incendiary momentum all its own. Whatever Soeharto's actual responsibility, he was about to be caught in his own game.

ACCOMMODATION AND RESISTANCE

Escalating tensions among the political elite catalyzed an astonishing political realignment in late 1996 and early 1997. The central element in this realignment was Abdurrahman Wahid's (temporary) withdrawal of support for the democratic movement and his apparent reconciliation with President Soeharto. Although Wahid provided the president with gestures of support, he continued to criticize Habibie. Indeed, as his reconciliation with the president progressed, he grew even bolder in his criticisms. Equally surprising, he also challenged the most basic ground rule of New Order politics, not to criticize the armed forces leadership. Wahid asserted that certain army generals were using conservative Islam for political ends. Although he did not single out individuals by name, the leaders he had in mind were primarily the pro-Soeharto "green" generals, Feisal Tanjung (commander of the armed forces), Syarwan Hamid, Sjafrie Sjamsuddin, and Prabowo Subianto. That Wahid felt confident enough to make this accusation indicates that he felt he was voicing an opinion shared by the anti-Soeharto military. Wahid's change of heart was not really a "reconciliation" with Soeharto, then, but evidence of the escalating rivalry between the "nationalist" coalition, on one side, and pro-Soeharto Muslims, on the other.

The curious drama of Wahid's accommodation to Soeharto began with the president's unexpected attendance at a national meeting of one of Nahdlatul Ulama's affiliate organizations, the Rabithah Ma'ahid Islamiyah (RMI) in Probolinggo, East Java, on November 2, 1996. There had been no prior announcement of Soeharto's visit. But Wahid was fully prepared for the visit. When Soeharto arrived, Wahid was waiting at the front of the conference hall; he greeted the president by grasping his hand warmly and drawing him to his side. Soeharto returned the uncharacteristically emotional gesture, walking hand-in-hand with Wahid to the front of the hall.[47] One day after this encounter, Abdurrahman Wahid astonished the nation by declaring that Nahdlatul Ulama would support Soeharto for another presidential term in 1998.[48]

For most Indonesians, this news was too bizarre to believe. For two years the president had refused even to meet with Wahid. By the terms of New Order protocol, a meeting with the president is necessary if the elected leader of an organization is to be seen as legitimate. The NU rank and file were delighted by Soeharto's visit, then, hoping that their confrontation with the regime was finally over. Wahid's prodemocracy friends were dismayed, however, wondering whether Wahid had defected from the cause.

Conservative Muslim strategists in ICMI and think tanks associated with the regime were also stunned by news of Wahid's meeting. Since the overthrow of Megawati, these people had operated on the assumption that their charge was to subvert Wahid's authority in advance of the May 1997 elections. By late 1996 they were confident that their campaign was getting the better of Wahid and he would soon have to step down. Suddenly, however, Wahid had played *his* cards and done so to a remarkable effect. He had implicitly offered to deliver his constituency to Golkar *if* the president made gestures of reconciliation with NU. By coming to Probolinggo, Soeharto provided just that gesture—and did so in an uncharacteristically dramatic way. Thus the president signaled that he considered Wahid and NU vital players in the national scene. Consistent with his preference for playing political rivals off one another, Soeharto also implied that he was having second thoughts about his collaboration with Habibie and ICMI. By this time it was no secret that several of the president's children despised the outspoken minister.

Wahid was aware that his meeting with the president gave him a momentary advantage over his opponents. He was convinced that NU was under violent siege, and he was determined to turn the tables and show Habibie, the regimist generals, and KISDI hard-liners that they had underestimated him. His counterattack did not end with his meeting with the president in Probolinggo. A few days after the meeting, Abu Hassan—the dissident NU businessman promoted by the regime as an alternative to Wahid—announced that he and Wahid had "reconciled" (*rujuk*).[49] More astounding, on November 14 Wahid traveled to Situbondo to meet with General Hartono, now chief of staff of the army. Hartono just happened to be in town to attend a meeting of NU-affiliated scholars. The Madurese general had helped direct the campaign against Wahid during 1994–96. Yet, like Soeharto, here he was suddenly traveling to East Java to meet with the NU leader.

Hartono was, of course, one of the putatively "green" generals who had helped to establish Din Syamsuddin and Amir Santosa's CPDS. Linked as he was to the president's daughter, Mbak Tutut, however, Hartono had always been something of an outsider among the regimist generals. This outsider standing was reinforced by his dislike of Habibie (an antipathy he shared with Tutut), his suspicion of Prabowo, and his disdain for Feisal Tanjung. Hartono's public reconciliation with Wahid placed these generals, and the CPDS think tank they sponsored, in a difficult position. In public statements after the Probolinggo meeting, representatives from the CPDS spoke vaguely but politely of Wahid's "change of heart." They were painfully aware, however, that their own political future was now in question. The Wahid realignment was about to send CPDS into bitter factional crisis.

During this same period in late 1996, the president's daughter, Mbak Tutut, was also hoping to reconcile with Wahid. She was chair of the East Java wing of Golkar and, as such, had a special interest in mending her ties with the popular NU leader. Wahid had the ability to deliver an enormous vote to Golkar, and such a shift in the electorate would speak well of Tutut's leadership skills. But it was not just Golkar that underlay Tutut's interest in Wahid. It was no secret that her father had hinted that he might well support her for president after his last term in office, in 2002–2003. It was understood, however, that Soeharto would only back Tutut if she could demonstrate an ability to mobilize support equal to or greater than that of her main rival for the presidency, B. J. Habibie. For Mbak Tutut, there was no better way to demonstrate this capacity than by reconciling with the most powerful of Habibie's enemies, Abdurrahman Wahid. A high-stakes reconfiguration was in the works indeed.

Golkar insiders say that Mbak Tutut had wanted to accompany her father to Probolinggo for the first meeting with Wahid. But Wahid knew that he had Tutut in a position of weakness, and he wished to impress upon her his displeasure with her earlier actions against him. So Wahid insisted that she not accompany her father. The meeting of Wahid with Tutut's friend, General Hartono, was a first step in her own reconciliation. But Wahid wanted a more significant concession before meeting directly with Tutut. His demand was simple: He believed that the regimist Muslims at the CPDS had masterminded the worst attacks on him since 1994. And he knew that Hartono and Mbak Tutut were major benefactors of the CPDS. Tutut and Hartono were thus made to understand that a condition of full reconciliation with Wahid was their withdrawal of support from the CPDS.

In late December 1996 Hartono and Tutut indicated that they no longer wanted the CPDS to oppose Wahid. The CPDS head, Amir Santosa, went along with this policy, and the institute's role as the headquarters for the anti-Wahid campaign came to an end. However, the think tank's other benefactors—Feisal Tanjung, Syarwan Hamid, and Prabowo Subianto, all allies of Habibie—rejected the truce with Wahid. They quickly established a rival think tank, the Institute for Policy Studies, and made Din Syamsuddin and Fadli Zon its directors. In taking this position, Feisal, Syarwan, and Prabowo signaled their continuing commitment to Habibie over Tutut. To change course and reconcile with Wahid would have only hurt Habibie's chances for the presidency. Unable to agree on post-Soeharto leadership, the ruling elite was cracking.

The Muslim public greeted Wahid's varied reconciliations enthusiastically. Not grasping the logic of the realignment, several mainstream Muslim intellectuals called for Wahid to take the next logical step: reconcile with Habibie and his chief lieutenant, Adi Sasono.[50] But these appeals misread Wahid's moves entirely. The NU leader was not interested in making amends with the New Order leadership as a whole but only with Soeharto so as to outflank his primary rivals—Habibie, the regimist generals, KISDI, and Sasono. Further, he believed that, for the time being, Megawati's challenge was stalled, and the regimist generals and their think tank advisers were about to mount another campaign against his rank and file. With the democratic movement in disarray, Wahid was determined at the very least to defend his organization. Survival would require compromise. In his heart, however, Wahid suspected that the realignment might ultimately create unintended consequences and a new political crisis. History would prove him right.

FROM SOEHARTO TRIUMPH TO REGIME COLLAPSE

At first sight, the political realignment of late 1996 and early 1997 seemed a brilliant Soeharto triumph. The president had driven Megawati to the margins, played rival claimants against one another, and reminded everyone that they had to play by his rules. And play by those rules they did, at least until the May 1997 elections for the National Assembly (DPR). Having reconciled with the president, in early 1997 Wahid seemed to go one step further, making none-too-subtle expressions of support for the president and the government party, Golkar. For members of the democratic opposition, Wahid's actions took on an even more surreal quality when, in the run up to the May elections, Wahid made several well-publicized trips around the country in the company of Mbak Tutut. Going further, he described Tutut as a "figure in Indonesia's future"—a wonderfully vague reference that seemed to hint that he supported her effort to succeed her father but really only meant that she was intent on trying to do so.[51]

However mysterious his declarations on Tutut, Wahid's actions were greeted in prodemocracy circles with a mixture of resignation and anger. Wahid's defenders insisted he had no choice; events had forced him to put aside his democratic engagements so as to protect his NU base. If he failed to secure that base, they argued, he had no political future whether in NU or the prodemocracy movement. Those less generous in their criticisms, including many reform-minded modernists, insisted that Wahid's democratic credentials had always been weak and that he had always pursued his own narrow interests. The alliance with the Soeharto family only made this opportunism more apparent.

The elections of May 1997 demonstrated just how thoroughly the government's policy on Soeryadi's PDI had been discredited. Golkar increased its share of the vote to almost 75 percent of the total, and the Muslim PPP won 22.4 percent. But the puppet PDI earned its lowest share ever, a mere 3.07 percent of the national vote. No one among Soeryadi's supporters had anticipated so total a collapse. The party's dismal performance was evidence of the depth of public disapproval of the government's actions against Megawati's PDI. In the aftermath of the elections, even Lieutenant General Syarwan Hamid, the mastermind of the strategy against the PDI (and a close aide to Habibie), conceded that the government had overplayed its hand. Facing criticism from ABRI colleagues, he noted that the armed forces was "concerned" about the PDI collapse.[52]

Even in this moment of regime triumph, however, there were surprising signs of resistance. In the last two weeks of the election campaign, a spontaneous movement arose to get Megawati supporters to shift their vote to the Muslim PPP. The leadership of the PPP did not welcome this effort since it seemed to place them in league with Megawati. Government officials condemned the initiative as illegal. Megawati was at first noncommittal about the movement. Rebuffed by the PPP leadership, however, she eventually declared that she did not support the alliance with the Muslim party and would abstain from voting in May. Although the Megawati-PPP collaboration fizzled, then, it indicated that the "green-and-red" alliance of which Megawati and Wahid once dreamed still captured the public's imagination.

In the aftermath of the election, national politics shifted away from the issue of Soeharto's succession toward the question of whom Soeharto would pick for vice president in March 1998. The three candidates deemed most likely for the post were General Hartono, Minister of Information Harmoko, and Habibie. The "nationalist" leadership in Golkar and the military was said to prefer that the president maintain the existing vice president, Try Sutrisno. But Try enjoyed little support among regimist Muslims, and, for the moment, that wing was ascendant in the ruling elite.

Of the three main rivals, Hartono and Habibie attracted the most attention. Hartono, once a Habibie supporter, was now seen as a bitter opponent of the minister of technology. Suspicion that Hartono was positioning himself to challenge Habibie for the vice presidency increased when, in mid-June 1997, the president announced a cabinet reshuffle, appointing Hartono minister of information. Shortly thereafter Hartono indicated that he wanted to join the Association of Indonesian Muslim Intellectuals (ICMI). Suspicion that Hartono was doing so as to challenge Habibie for the ICMI leadership increased when Hartono announced that he was "willing" to become the organization's chair if, for some reason, Habibie were "unable" to serve.[53]

In sum, by July 1997 Indonesian politics looked as if it had been purged of its oppositionist turmoil and reduced to a simple game of intra-elite rivalries. The last of the regime's really powerful critics, Abdurrahman Wahid, had been beaten into silence. This might well have remained the case had Indonesia not experienced a sudden economic downturn in August and September 1997. The crisis was sparked by currency problems in Thailand a month earlier and a rapid loss of investor confidence in banking and finance throughout East and Southeast Asia.

Over the next six months the Indonesian rupiah lost almost 70 percent of its value relative to the U.S. dollar. The collapse of the rupiah drove up the cost of servicing government and private debt, much of which was denominated in dollars. This, in turn, meant that in the final months of 1997 most Indonesian firms were defaulting on their loans. As banks failed to receive payments on outstanding loans, the banking system froze. Interest rates soared, and lending institutions refused to make additional loans. This, in turn, caused factories to default on payments to suppliers and workers, causing upstream suppliers to default on their loans, prompting further drops in production and more layoffs. The resulting downward spiral of financial gridlock, factory closure, unemployment, and investor flight had, by early 1998, created one of the most dramatic economic contractions the world had seen in the postwar era. Indonesia's poverty rate, having fallen to less than 14 percent of the population in early 1997, edged toward 40 percent in late 1998.

The government reacted to the financial crisis with greater decisiveness than its counterparts in Thailand and South Korea.[54] The macroeconomists who advised the government on fiscal policy had always been the best of the government's policy makers; sound fiscal policy remained one of the New Order's real achievements. But the scale of the crisis dwarfed the measures the macroeconomists were able to devise. By late 1997 the economic collapse had turned into the worst political crisis of the New Order era.

The crisis breathed new life into Megawati's campaign for far-reaching political reform. From September 1997 on, her demands for political reform again were featured prominently in the national media. Megawati was not alone in calling for reform. Emil Salim, a long-time member of the reformist wing of the government (chapter 6), moved fully into the ranks of the anti-Soeharto opposition, saying that simple economic reforms would not succeed unless they were accompanied by political reform at the top.

Abdurrahman Wahid also moved to place himself at the forefront of those demanding reforms. Friends of Wahid say he was determined to clear his name and correct the impression that he had bolted from the prodemocracy camp. Having moved earlier in the year to mend his relationship with Megawati, in October he met with her to demand that the president initiate economic reforms. In December 1997, a month before Wahid suffered a stroke (which he survived but that sidelined him from political events during the first months of 1998), he joined with Megawati in what was, by Indonesian political standards, an unprecedented move: the call for Soeharto to step down. Indirectly, the campaign also aligned Wahid with Amien Rais, the outspoken Muhammadiyah leader. In public, however, Wahid refused to consecrate his alliance with Rais with a joint declaration, maintaining the chill that had marked their relationship since Rais's comments on the violence of July 27, 1996, and his remarks on the need for Muslim "proportionalism" in politics and the economy in early 1997.

In late September 1997 Rais had spoken out even more boldly than Wahid against Soeharto, announcing his intention to run for the presidency.[55] Adi Sasono and other Habibie supporters in ICMI quickly chastised their former colleague, as did Habibie's military supporters, Syarwan Hamid and Feisal Tanjung. But these attacks only heightened Rais's standing and breathed new life into campus demonstrations spreading across the country. Ironically, Soeharto himself had helped Rais's ascent to a position of leadership in the opposition. In March 1997 Soeharto had arranged Rais's removal from ICMI's Board of Experts (*dewan pakar*). The president had been angered by Rais's comments concerning first-family cronyism and sweetheart deals with foreign multinationals.[56] Rais's expulsion from the Board of Experts embarrassed Habibie, since it again demonstrated ICMI's subordination to presidential whim.[57] Rather than silencing Rais, however, his removal only emboldened him to speak out even more firmly against first-family corruption. Soeharto had unwittingly consolidated the ranks of the opposition just before the economic crisis of 1997. For the first time, that opposition now united Wahid's NU, Megawati's nationalists, and the reform-minded modernists around Rais.

During the first months of 1998 the campaign against Soeharto hung perilously in balance. The public seemed to hesitate in the face of political uncertainties and the country's economic decline. Student activists on campuses around the country, however, held mass demonstrations demanding that Soeharto step down. In March, public attention shifted from the campus battles to Jakarta and the question of whether Soeharto might satisfy calls for political change by appointing reformists to his new cabinet in March 1998. There was a sense that Soeharto was to appoint Minister Habibie as vice president and at least a few ICMI moderates to his cabinet.

In the end, Habibie was appointed vice president. But in what can only be regarded as an astounding miscalculation, Soeharto chose not to appoint any ICMI (or other) moderates to the cabinet, opting instead for loyalist cronies. The slighting of ICMI pointed to what had become a growing tension in the Soeharto camp. When they learned that ICMI staffers (including Sasono) might be appointed to the cabinet, Soeharto's children lobbied their father to strike these names from his list. The first family's dislike of Habibie had intensified in late 1997. Soeharto's daughter, Mbak Tutut, continued to view Habibie as her main rival for the presidency. The Soeharto family also blamed Habibie for failing to control ICMI activists opposed to Soeharto. The president is said to have been especially angry at Amien Rais and his supporters in the Muslim media, including the ICMI-linked newsweekly, *Ummat*. Since the monetary crisis erupted in August 1997, the weekly had been at the forefront of those demanding democratic reform. In the end, Soeharto heeded his children's counsel and excluded the ICMI moderates.

This was a tactical blunder of enormous proportions. In one bold move, Soeharto galvanized moderate Muslim opposition to his rule. With Wahid sidelined by a stroke, leadership of the Muslim wing of the anti-Soeharto movement now passed to Amien Rais. Since July 1996, Rais had been regarded with suspicion by secular-minded nationalists. Despite his brave statements against Soeharto in 1997 and 1998, many democrats remembered that, a few years earlier, Rais had made caustic statements concerning Chinese business; on several occasions he had even participated in events sponsored by KISDI.[58] He had also joined the attack on government policies that, he claimed, had unfairly benefited Christian segments of the Javanese population. Similarly, in the aftermath of the assault on the PDI headquarters in July 1996, Rais had chosen not to criticize the government, focusing his remarks instead on Megawati (chapter 6).

The worsening political crisis, however, gave Rais his first opportunity to act as a national leader, rather than the head of a specifically Muslim organization. Aided by two advisers known for their democratic sensibilities, Syafi'i Anwar (of *Ummat*) and Syafi'i Maarif (a University of Chicago–trained Ph.D. and subsequent chairman of Muhammadiyah), Rais responded to the challenge with great courage and skill. In early 1998 he called for an alliance with Wahid and Megawati against Soeharto. Wahid again declined to join formally with Rais, but the two leaders coordinated their actions sufficiently that each reinforced the other.

By April 1998 opposition to Soeharto was again gaining momentum. Student demonstrations on campuses across the country were growing. Equally remarkable, these demonstrations saw extensive collaboration between secular social democrats and Muslim student groups. Only in Jakarta, where the Soehartoist KISDI had its base, were some conservative Muslim students unwilling to collaborate with secular democrats.

The press was also increasingly bold in its opposition to the president. The cronyist composition of the new cabinet stiffened the resolve of mainstream reformists to throw their lot in with the anti-Soeharto opposition. At the same time, however, there was widespread anxiety among civilians and reformist members of the military that the president might be preparing to unleash further violence. The well-publicized kidnapping and torture of two dozen student activists in early 1998 suggested that the escalation had begun.

SOEHARTO'S VIOLENCE

One figure in the Soeharto camp caused the democratic opposition particular concern, namely, the president's ambitious son-in-law, Lieutenant General Prabowo Subianto. It was widely reported that, when stationed a few years earlier in East Timor, Prabowo had reached over the heads of local military commanders and organized civilian vigilantes to commit acts of rape, torture, and murder against villages sympathetic to the pro-independence opposition. As noted above, Prabowo also directed the violence against rebels in Aceh after 1989. Political observers in Jakarta also knew that for the past several years Prabowo supporters had infiltrated the leadership of the country's largest martial arts association. Members who opposed Prabowo's efforts had been beaten up or expelled. Reports had it that Prabowo had already utilized some of these martial arts experts in acts of terror against Soeharto foes.

Prabowo had also become a patron of Ahmad Sumargono and his hard-line Indonesian Committee for Solidarity with the Muslim World (KISDI). With the help of activists from the Center for Policy and Development Studies, Prabowo had approached KISDI in 1995 and offered support for their programs. Having won KISDI to his cause, Prabowo then urged Sumargono to approach the leadership of the Dewan Dakwah Islamiyah Indonesia, asking them to give up their opposition to the regime. By mid-1996 both KISDI and the DDII had effectively allied themselves with the brash young general and with the regimist Muslim campaign against the prodemocracy movement.

On the evening of January 23, 1998, during the Muslim fasting month, Prabowo came to the military's special forces headquarters (KOPASSUS) outside Jakarta to break the fast with seven thousand of Sumargono's KISDI supporters. The rapid rise of Sumargono in Indonesian politics in the 1990s had astonished Muslim politicians, who were not used to seeing people in their circles rise to such prominence without the backing of an established Muslim organization. Many realized that Sumargono had a secret benefactor.

Sumargono also raised eyebrows because his public statements against Jews, Christians, Chinese, the United States, and other "enemies of Islam" were so strikingly out of character with the Indonesian Muslim mainstream. Equally serious, Sumargono did not limit his diatribes to non-Muslims. After the bloody attack on Megawati's PDI in 1996, Sumargono was at the forefront of the conservative Islamists' attacks on Muslims who refused to back the government's version of events. Such people, Sumargono said, were "pro-Communist" and "anti-Islamic." Sumargono had attacked not only the prodemocracy movement but also moderate segments of the Muslim community, such as the editors of *Republika*. In December 1996, for example, he and the DDII sponsored a fierce demonstration against the ICMI newspaper, complaining that its reporting on the July 27 violence had become too "leftist" and sympathetic to the People's Democratic Party.[59]

Among Muslim democrats it was understood that Sumargono's rise had been aided by the man with whom he broke the fast that January evening, Lieutenant-General Prabowo. Prabowo had cultivated ties among conservative Muslim politicians since the late 1980s. Well-known for his hatred of the Catholic General Benny Moerdani, by 1997 Prabowo had begun to speak openly in conservative Muslim circles of the need to free Indonesia of "minority tyranny." At the January meeting with Sumargono's supporters Prabowo had spoken with fierce emotion about the need to take action against Chinese and other "enemies of Islam." These statements raised concerns among Muslim democrats that Prabowo might be readying his allies for violence.

After the public ceremony with the KISDI activists, Prabowo met privately with a smaller number of ultraconservative leaders. In that meeting he distributed copies of a fifty-five-page booklet that purported to explain the logic of Indonesia's economic crisis and the country's ongoing negotiations with the International Monetary Fund (IMF).[60] Entitled "The Conspiracy to Overthrow Soeharto" (*Konspirasi Mengguling Soeharto*), the booklet painted a picture of a vile domestic and international conspiracy against Soeharto. The IMF, the United States, Israel, Indonesian-Chinese, and the pro-democracy movement were all united in this "Jewish-Jesuit-American-Chinese" effort. The reason President Soeharto had been targeted, the book explained, was that he was a Muslim, and he and his family were becoming too powerful for the cabal of Jews, Jesuits, Chinese, and CIA-Mossad agents who control international capitalism.

Although its cover bore no author's name, the conspiracy book had been written by individuals earlier affiliated with the CPDS and now active in its institutional successor, the Institute for Policy Studies (IPS). IPS funding was reportedly provided by the pro-Habibie generals—Feisal Tanjung, Syarwan Hamid, and Prabowo in alliance with the most politically active of the Soeharto children, Bambang and Mbak Tutut. Among the many absurd details provided in this book was the allegation that the death, one year earlier, of the president's wife, Bu Tien, was not a natural event. On the contrary, the document explained, Tien had been murdered by a Chinese doctor who had deliberately misled the president by giving his wife a clean bill of health just the day before she died. She had been killed on the instruction of secular-nationalists in the government, including State Secretary Moerdiono (a well-known Javanist and "red-and-white" nationalist), and "a Catholic extreme Jesuit clique" (*kelompok Katolik ekstrim Jesuit*) linked to the Center for Strategic and International Studies. After murdering the first lady, the two groups had hoped to kill the president and seize control of the state. The conspiracy had received support from "the CIA (Amerika), Mossad (Jews), the Vatican, and overseas Chinese."[61]

This astounding document reinterpreted the history of the New Order from a regimist Muslim perspective. It explained, for example, that, from the beginning of the New Order through 1988, "all political, military, and economic power was totally controlled by a Jesuit extremist power group with the full support of certain members of the military and the economic backing of Chinese."[62] These groups had taken advantage of the "good faith of President Soeharto" until the mid-1980s, when the president had "begun to be aware of their movement." Confronted as they were by the president's new determination to support Muslims and indigenous Indonesians (*pribumi*), this "extremist Jewish Christian clique and their Chinese conglomerate supporters" fought back to reverse their declining influence.

The final phase of this anti-Soeharto resistance, carried out with the "full support of the American CIA and the Jewish secret intelligence Mossad as well as the Vatican," was to create the economic crisis that swept Indonesia in late 1997. The crisis was not the result of crony capitalism or the president's plundering of fifteen to twenty-five billion dollars from the economy. Rather, it had been provoked by Chinese conglomerates, acting at the advise of their "*abangan and secular nationalist*" allies in government, intent on "destroying *pribumi* business and strengthening the domination of non-*pribumi* conglomerates."[63] The booklet concludes with a chilling message:

> Soeharto is increasingly aware that he has been betrayed by people close to him, people who have allied themselves with enemies who want to destroy Soeharto himself. . . . The Muslim community also has to become aware, aware that power in this country cannot fall into the hands of Zionist agents or groups who have a phobia toward Islam.[64]

It is important to remember that this booklet was not an obscure tract authored by some unstable marginal group. The document was composed by sophisticated and affluent intellectuals at a pro-Habibie think tank supported by Feisal Tanjung, Syarwan Hamid, Prabowo, and two of the Soeharto children. It was released to ultraconservative Muslim circles at a time when pro-democracy groups were uniting to blame Soeharto for Indonesia's economic crisis. The booklet's anti-Chinese and anti-Christian rhetoric was the most hateful the Soeharto regime had ever used.

The booklet was originally published in late November 1997, shortly after government reformers announced plans to close sixteen private banks burdened with nonperforming loans. Among the banks slated for closure was one owned by Bambang Soeharto, son of the president and an IPS supporter. Bambang reacted angrily to this news, filing suit against the two officials responsible for the decision, Bank Indonesia Governor Soedradjad Djiwandono (a "Christian") and Finance Minister Mar'ie Muhammad (a former HMI activist known for his opposition to cronyism and Habibie). Conservative Muslims linked to KISDI soon joined the clamor, speaking out against what they described as a 'Christian' conspiracy against the Soeharto family, and demanding Mar'ie's and Soedrajad's resignation.

During the last weeks of 1997 Soeharto negotiated a financial rescue package with the International Monetary Fund. During these same weeks, however, he appealed to Chinese-Indonesian business leaders to support him in a "love rupiah" campaign intended to reverse the currency's decline. Even after signing the IMF agreement in mid-January, the president continued to make statements contradicting the accord, indicating, for example, that some government monopolies were to be maintained. Soeharto also hinted that Minister Habibie was to be his choice for vice president. More ominously, he also spoke out against "currency speculators" intent on "ruining" the country; it was universally assumed he was referring to Chinese. In mid-January 1998 Soeharto had Feisal Tanjung telephone Chinese business leaders, demanding financial contributions for the rupiah campaign.[65] Following the example of Sofyan Wanandi of the CSIS, however, the business leaders refused, convinced that actions that might undermine the IMF reforms would only exacerbate the economic crisis.

Wanandi was soon to discover that Soeharto had increased the penalties for defiance. On January 18, 1998, a bomb went off in central Jakarta; its fabricator escaped. At the site of the bomb blast, however, police found a most unusual document: an e-mail message purported to be from Sofyan Wanandi to the People's Democratic Party (PRD), the same party the government had blamed for the riots of July 27, 1996. The message conveyed the astounding announcement that Wanandi was prepared to give the PRD funds for a bombing campaign to bring Soeharto down.

The agreement outlined between a conservative Chinese millionaire and a small band of new-left idealists is so implausible as to be laughable. But the message's sinister intent was all too apparent. The economic crisis shaking Indonesia is not the result of presidential cronyism or corruption, it implied, but a campaign financed by ungrateful Chinese and hateful pro-democracy activists. Soeharto's treacherous opponents were threatening violence; the clear implication was that the regime had to respond in kind.

Over the next few days the regime's verbal warfare against Chinese Indonesians took on a tone of racial hatred never before heard in New Order history.

On February 3, 1998, Lieutenant General Syarwan Hamid spoke at a rally of conservative Muslims at the huge Sunda Kelapa mosque. With him were Habibie's right-hand man, Adi Sasono, and Hussein Umar of the DDII and KISDI. Syarwan spoke in shocking terms of "these rats who take away the fruits of our national development and work for their own self-interest. Don't think the people don't know who these rats are. It's time to eradicate these rats." He did not tell his audience who these rats were, but their identity as Chinese Indonesians was apparent to all. The next day a previously unheard of group, the Twenty-first Century Islam Foundation, issued a statement asserting that the economic crisis ravaging Indonesia was the result of a conspiracy instigated by Sofyan Wanandi and others in the Sino-Indonesian business elite. The very same day Lukman Harun, a high-ranking official in KISDI and the Muhammadiyah (and an enemy of Amien Rais), echoed the refrain, calling openly for a campaign not against Soeharto but against all "rats" and "traitors" to the nation. Lukman went on to clarify that Soeharto is the leader not only of Indonesia but of all Indonesian *Muslims*. On February 8, 1998, this same message was carried on KISDI's website, in an article that ended with a shocking refrain:

> It's time for the Indonesian people and the Muslim community, which are both now suffering, to come to a basic conclusion: that, if necessary, we must drive evil people out of this Indonesia we so love. Even if we have to rebuild from nothing, we would begin from our own uprightness and the heroism we possess.[66]

The ideological ground was being readied for a full-scale assault on Chinese, Christian, and pro-democracy opponents of the regime.

The evidence suggests that these and other efforts to mobilize ultraconservatives were directed by General Prabowo and his allies. After the MPR session in March, Prabowo had been made commander of the strategic reserve (Kostrad). His close friend, Major-General Muchdi, was made commander of the special forces (KOPASSUS). These and other appointments gave Prabowo overwhelming military superiority in the Jakarta region. But even Soeharto did not entirely trust his ambitious son-in-law, so he also appointed ABRI independents to key posts in order to balance the power of the Prabowo group. Led by General Wiranto (made commander in chief of ABRI) and Bambang Yudhoyono (chief of staff for Social and Political Affairs in ABRI), the moderate officers feared that Prabowo was intent on taking advantage of the political crisis to catapult himself to power. In February Wiranto had already signaled his dissatisfaction with Prabowo by denouncing the anti-Chinese campaign as "garbage."

Remarkably, however, Prabowo's courtship of regimist Muslims only stiffened Muslim democrats' opposition to Soeharto. During my visit to Jakarta in March 1998 an ICMI independent, who had attended Sumargono's rally with Prabowo, told me he was so alarmed by what he had seen that he immediately reported it to his colleagues, alerting them to this dangerous escalation in regime rhetoric. Nurcholish Madjid, Amien Rais, and *Ummat* responded not by toning down their calls for peaceful reformation but intensifying them.

However hardened the resolve of the Muslim mainstream, the groundwork was still being laid for a campaign of violence and intimidation. Although the full logic of the violence of Soeharto's final days remains unclear, evidence indicates that forces linked to Prabowo were responsible for the sniper killing of four prodemocracy students at the Trisakti University in Jakarta on May 12. The murders triggered two days of violence in the capital and cities across Indonesia worse than any in the whole New Order era. In Jakarta, more than one thousand buildings were destroyed and thirteen hundred people were killed. Many of the dead were rioters trapped in burning malls, some of which had had their doors sealed shut when the hapless looters were inside. Chinese Indonesians were also singled out for grotesque acts of violence. According to the accounts of human rights workers (at first denied by the police),[67] more than one hundred Chinese Indonesian women were hunted down and raped. Other Chinese Indonesian women were stripped, and then paraded and beaten in public. An estimated 100,000–150,000 Chinese fled the country.

Although a full accounting of the violence has yet to be made, it is believed that the forces most directly responsible for maintaining law and order in the capital—the strategic reserve under Prabowo and the special forces under Major-General Muchdi—were evacuated from the city center at the start of the rioting. Eyewitness reports gathered by government investigators and human rights monitors confirm that during this time black-clad riot commanders moved about the capital in trucks, openly encouraging violence. As in Situbondo two years earlier, these troops moved largely unimpeded through the capital, although in a few places small squadrons of marines and police officers worked desperately to prevent violence.[68]

The consensus thus far among Indonesian observers is that this violence was intended to create the impression that the anti-Soeharto opposition was hateful and anarchic. The riots were also meant to create a crisis of such awful proportions that the president, in Egypt when the riots first erupted, would feel compelled to remove General Wiranto and, in his place, give Prabowo special authority to restore order. Whether Soeharto himself was fully aware of this plan is unclear. Whatever the case, after Soeharto's return from Egypt the armed forces commander, General Wiranto, confronted the president in his Cendana Street home. Although outgunned by Prabowo in the capital, Wiranto had worked carefully over several weeks to consolidate an anti-Prabowo alliance in the armed forces as a whole. When Soeharto returned, Wiranto presented him with a list of Prabowo's misdeeds and asked that Prabowo be removed from his command. Whether because he had never agreed to Prabowo's plan or because Wiranto left him no other option, Soeharto relented and Prabowo was stripped of his authority.

Nonetheless Prabowo remained at large for a few more days. Several days after the riots Prabowo aides are alleged to have warned Amien Rais that they would turn Independence Square in central Jakarta into a "sea of blood" if Amien went ahead with his planned demonstration of May 20 demanding that the president step down.[69] In the early hours of that day Rais called off the event after traveling to Independence Square and seeing that Prabowo had indeed positioned troops in full battle gear to block the event.

Evidence provided by prodemocracy Muslims also indicates that Prabowo, aided by IPS director Fadli Zon, provided the directives and funding for a KISDI rally against prodemocracy activists at the National Assembly on May 22. By the time the event was staged, however, it was too late to save Soeharto. He had resigned the day before, pressed by a professional military leadership outraged by the violence of May 13–14. He was also pressured by the defection of supporters, including Syarwan Hamid on May 18 and fourteen cabinet ministers on May 20. The terms of Soeharto's resignation were unclear, however, as is his complicity in subsequent violence.

Despite Soeharto's resignation, KISDI organizers went ahead with their demonstration on May 22. They switched the theme of the demonstration from supporting Soeharto to rallying for the president's successor, B. J. Habibie. Banners carried at the event indicated the new KISDI line, "Opposition to Habibie = Opposition to Islam." "Never have I been more ashamed," one Muslim democrat told me, "than when I saw those demonstrators abusing the brave prodemocracy students, even while those students prayed." Soeharto had fallen, but the struggle between regimist Islam and the forces of democratic reform was not yet over. It was to remain a central line of conflict in post-Soeharto Indonesia.

Conclusion: Indonesia in the Balance

The struggles of Soeharto's final days indicate that there was no seamless consensus among Muslims on democracy or pluralism. There was a dominant pattern, however. A handful of ultraconservatives supported the regime and coordinated their actions with Prabowo and other hard-liners. But the Soeharto supporters' appeal to ethnoreligious hatred only stiffened the resolve of the great majority of Muslim leaders to democracy, nonviolence, and the rule of law.

In his last days as president in May 1998 Soeharto called in a council of Islamic scholars to advise him on an appropriate course of action. But he was not really interested in their advice. He merely wanted to impress upon the nation that the Muslim community was his primary constituency and that he still enjoyed their support. At the urging of Nurcholish Madjid, however, the scholars rejected this ruse and urged Soeharto to step down. This courage in the face of great peril was typical of Muslim democrats' actions during

Soeharto's final days. Despite repeated threats of violence, Abdurrahman Wahid, Amien Rais, and Nurcholish Madjid held firm in their calls for "*Reformasi Damai*" (peaceful reformation). In the face of Prabowo's efforts to cloak the president in the garb of Islam, all but a few ultraconservatives rejected this vile abuse of their religion and demanded that the president step down.

The violence of Soeharto's fall revealed with shocking clarity the failed logic of his policy on Islam. Having earlier attempted an alliance with a broad segment of the Muslim community, beginning with Abdurrahman Wahid and NU, Soeharto realized, early on, that many in the mainstream community were interested not merely in political spoils but in democratic reform. Realizing his error, the president narrowed his scope, first to Habibie and ICMI, and then to a small group of regimist conservatives willing to trade support for presidential favors. In his last desperate days the president had elite think tanks unleash a barrage of anti-Chinese and anti-Christian propaganda that betrayed the *Pancasila* ideals for which Soeharto had once pretended to stand. That the bulk of the Muslim leadership rejected these antidemocratic feints bears eloquent testimony to their civil-democratic convictions.

This is not to say that the road to reform, or a consensus on just what Indonesian democracy should be, is going to be reached any time soon. The economic crisis Indonesia suffered from late 1997 to late 1999 was of a scale that would have strained even the most settled democracies. More important, although Soeharto stepped down on May 21, 1998, his regime did not. The cautious commander of the armed forces, General Wiranto, succeeded in having Prabowo removed from power. Over the remainder of 1998 he pursued a quiet program of armed forces consolidation, aimed at removing those who had abused their power by encouraging ethnoreligious hatred.

Wiranto's ability to promote a more aggressive consolidation, however, was limited by ultraconservatives in the Habibie coalition who were intent on preventing any investigation of the violence that accompanied Soeharto's fall. KISDI activists decried Wiranto's efforts as an attack by "secular nationalists" on Islam. They claimed that the action was being orchestrated by the retired Catholic general, Benny Moerdani[70]—a charge, of course, without the least merit. The two figures most responsible for the military consolidation, Wiranto and Bambang Yudhoyono, were well known for their Islamic piety, warm ties with Muslims, and determination to make sure that Islam was neither marginalized nor used as an instrument of regime terror.

These and other reforms were dogged, however, by ancien regime elements in the Habibie government. A year and a half after the May riots, there still had been no full prosecution of Prabowo or his supporters, nor of anyone responsible for the rapes and murders. When in June and July 1998 human rights workers issued reports documenting the May violence, KISDI's Ahmad Sumargono dismissed the activists as Zionists and "secularists" intent on bringing down the Habibie government. Although in early 1999 Sumargono temporarily broke with Habibie (after Habibie publicly criticized Prabowo), no one in the Habibie administration ever chided Sumargono for these outrageous claims. In early October 1998 a government-appointed, fact-finding team released its report which stated that rapes of Chinese women had indeed occurred in May. It also asserted that there was evidence indicating that Prabowo, Fadli Zon (of the IPS), and other individuals might have conspired to aggravate the violence. The commission called for an investigation.[71] KISDI again responded by claiming that the report was a "secularist" attack on Islam and Habibie. The Habibie administration never responded to the fact-finding commission's appeals, nor did it investigate allegations of criminal conspiracy.

Although blessed with a wit and technical intelligence his mentor lacked, Soeharto's chosen successor, B. J. Habibie, had spent most of his political life in Soeharto's shadow. He had long been silent on Soeharto's abuses. Lacking an independent base of power, he was deeply dependent on regime insiders inherited from the Soeharto regime. These included ultraconservatives intent on squeezing Chinese Indonesians out of the economy. In the months following Soeharto's resignation, some among these hard-liners made it clear that Habibie was to make *no* concessions either to prodemocracy reformers or the wounded Chinese community. In the face of growing international protest, on July 15, 1998, Habibie issued a general statement condemning violence against women. In an interview for the *Washington Post* in July 1998, however, he observed that if the one hundred thousand Chinese who had fled Indonesia after the May riots chose not return, "their place will be taken over by others."[72] On other occasions he denied the existence of discrimination against Chinese. Even as he made these statements, Indonesia, in late 1998, witnessed urban riots in which Chinese shop owners were again the target of mob violence.

During his year as interim president, Habibie went along with demands for press freedom, electoral reforms, and the staging of national elections on June 7, 1999. In all these measures he was pressured by the same reform movement that had brought down Soeharto. To his credit, in January 1999 Habibie agreed to hold a referendum in East Timor to decide the fate of that long-suffering people. He was helped in this policy decision by one of the last truly capable reformers among his advisers, Dewi Fortuna Anwar. Despite this progress, Habibie's government ignored calls to investigate the former president's riches, estimated at U.S.$15 billion. Indeed earlier, in mid-1998, Habibie fired his attorney general because the gentleman was taking his inquiry into the Soeharto wealth too seriously. In June 1999 the man who replaced the first attorney general stepped down when a watchdog agency reported that he had received half a million dollars in cash payments from friends of Soeharto.

Lacking a sufficient base of his own, Habibie was obliged to recruit to his cabinet Prabowo supporters and people regarded as complicit in the July 1996 assault on the PDI. Two of Prabowo's military allies—Feisal Tanjung and Syarwan Hamid—were awarded key ministerial portfolios in the Habibie cabinet.

These appointments made any serious investigation of Soeharto-era abuses highly unlikely. Regimist Muslims responsible for some of the most hateful propaganda of the late Soeharto period also remained at large and unrepentant.

Having been spared a public accounting, regimist Muslims continued to play a supporting role for Soeharto and Habibie. When bloody violence broke out between Christians and Muslims in Ambon, eastern Indonesia, during the first weeks of 1999, there were allegations that the ex-president's supporters had instigated the violence to distract public attention from ongoing investigations into Soeharto's wealth. True to form, KISDI officials responded by issuing a counterallegation claiming that the real cause of the violence was Christian rebels intent on an independent Ambon. When the Ambon violence escalated and consumed hundreds of Muslim and Christian lives, KISDI supporters called for a *jihad* (religious war) against all "enemies of Islam." Eggy Sudjana, a key aide to Adi Sasono (minister of cooperatives in the Habibie cabinet), joined in this scandalous betrayal of Indonesian nationalism by also demanding a *jihad* against fellow Indonesians.[73] Hoping to rally conservative Muslims to his own run for the presidency, Sasono made no move to scold his lieutenant. A few weeks later, KISDI announced that Sasono was someone they could support for president in 1999.

During the last months of 1998 and the first four months of 1999, Indonesia was gripped by growing ethnoreligious violence. In November 1998 an ugly clash erupted between Christian and Muslim gangs in Jakarta in which fifteen Christian gangsters were captured, tortured, and killed. Later, a little-known "Muslim" group circulated a flyer in mosques around Jakarta with a photo of one of the butchered Christians, claiming that he was actually a Muslim killed by Christians. The flyer's headline blared, "See what Christians do to Muslims." In Banyuwangi in late 1998 more than a hundred NU preachers and alleged *abangan* "sorcerers" were mysteriously killed. As with the Situbondo violence two years earlier, the executions were carried out by black-clad vigilantes, trucked in to remote locales to capture, murder, and dismember their victims. The pattern of violence, with its clear attempt to pit NU Muslims against *abangan* Javanists, resembled the earlier provocations in Situbondo. Many observers suspected that the goal of the violence was also the same: to worsen ties between NU Muslims and Javanists in order to reduce the chances of a Wahid-Megawati alliance.

A similar pattern of mysterious killings of Muslims and nominal Muslims emerged in West Java during the first months of 1999. The only difference here was that some of the victims were known to be critics of Soeharto. As if all this violence were not enough, on April 19 a bomb ripped through the bottom floor of the national Istiqlal Mosque in Jakarta. No group claimed responsibility, but the act was widely perceived as an effort to spoil relations between Muslims and non-Muslims in the run up to the national elections.

In the face of this brutal frenzy many observers concluded that hard-line Soehartoists were intent on scuttling the election of a reformist government. In January and February Abdurrahman Wahid himself voiced this opinion and, during visits to Soeharto's residence, appealed to the ex-president to restrain his followers. Soeharto ignored Wahid's appeal, and on March 20, 1999, Wahid announced that his mission had failed and he would no longer meet with Soeharto. Meanwhile, showing he had no intention of stepping back from the fray, in an interview with a Japanese newspaper in mid-April Soeharto repeated the charge made a year earlier, that he had been driven from power by an international cabal of "Zionists" opposed to him because he is Muslim.[74] Even this late in the game, Soeharto was intent on playing the regimist Muslim card.

In the end, however, these ploys failed to achieve their goal. Despite threats of violence, the June 1999 elections were a triumph of peace and moderation. They were also a stirring testimony to Indonesians' rejection of the politics of hatred and ethnoreligious polarization. Although forty-eight parties contested the race, five parties emerged the winners. They were, in order of prominence, Megawati's PDI-P (Indonesian Democratic Party–Struggle), Golkar, NU's PKB (Party of National Renaissance), the Muslim PPP, and Amien Rais's Partai Amanat Nasional (PAN). Megawati's PDI-P was by far the greatest vote getter, winning about 35 percent of the vote, almost twice the Golkar total. Together, the parties of Megawati, Wahid, Rais, and other reformers captured 60 percent of the vote.

Megawati's share of the vote was all the more impressive in light of Muslim conservatives' insistence, in the final weeks leading up to the elections, that the public could not accept the leadership of a woman. Four days before the elections, the government-linked Council of Indonesian Muslim Scholars (Majelis Ulama Indonesia) issued a religious edict (*fatwa*) in which it called on Muslims not to vote for parties headed by non-Muslims or by people unlikely to promote a "Muslim" agenda. The message was clearly aimed at Megawati. The appeal was echoed a day later by the KISDI head, Sumargono.[75] These attacks failed to hit their target, however. Indeed, my own research during these months indicated that the bullying pushed some fence-sitting Muslim moderates into the Megawati camp.

This auspicious beginning to a possible democratic transition remains clouded, however, by several uncertainties. The first concerns the role of the military. As the violence of 1997–98 demonstrated, the military's commitment to its "two functions" (*dwifungsi*) introduces a dangerous instability into elite politics. In particular, by failing to specify any limits on military involvement in domestic affairs, the doctrine invites abuse by unscrupulous individuals who invoke the formula to legitimate their own political adventurism. Although in the 1980s American political scientists portrayed the armed forces as ideologically cohesive,[76] the struggles of Soeharto's last years showed that this was no longer the case, if it was ever true. A handful of commanders engaged in violent adventurism, splitting the army leadership and attempting to create an anti-democratic constituency for Soeharto and, no less important, themselves. Inasmuch as the "red-and-white" moderates who opposed Prabowo are as Muslim and pious as their rivals, clearly the issue separating these two groups was never really Islam but rather whether Muslim politics should subordinate Islam's high ideals to violent and authoritarian ends.

Faced with stalemate among the elite, in early 1998 the Prabowo clique had reached out into society to mobilize ultraconservative civilians against its rivals. This desperate action showed that there was no neat opposition of state and society in Soeharto's final days; the state's loss of cohesion was not society's gain. If anything, in fact, the conflict resembled that of 1948 and 1965.[77] In those years, factionalism in the state led rival elites to exacerbate ethnoreligious antagonisms in society, creating segmentary alliances that exploited communal tensions for their own narrow ends. Indonesia paid an awful price for this elite adventurism. The price included not only a horrendous loss of life but a tragic run on the nation's reserves of civility and tolerance.

The fact remains, too, that the economic crisis of 1997–99 has worsened the ethnoreligious imbalance between Chinese and "indigenous" (pribumi) Indonesians. The economic crisis has also intensified the plight of the urban underclass, the overwhelming majority of whom are Muslim. In these circumstances, the divide between Christian-Chinese haves and Muslim have-nots will likely remain in the public eye for years to come. Inasmuch as this is so, we are likely to hear continuing appeals for affirmative action for Muslims, some of which will use the language of proportionalism in the state and economy.

This dispute over inequality and affirmative action is a legitimate issue for democratic discussion and should not be dismissed out of hand just because it was abused by Soeharto defenders. The issue can be made tractable, however, if the military and civilian leadership grasp two lessons from the anti-Soeharto struggle. The first is that all the country's leaders must work to socialize the awareness that the pluralism and compromise so visible in the prodemocracy struggle were not just momentary concessions on the road to victory but are democracy's most trying but essential requirements. The second is that the Muslim community's (and everyone else's) sense of participation in an open and fair political process must be decisively heightened so that it becomes easier to discredit unscrupulous actors who go outside the law into the netherworld of syndicate violence for their own narrow gain. Achieving this sense of fairness will require a just accounting of the abuses of the Soeharto years, including the violent repression of Muslims in the 1980s as well as the persecution of Chinese in 1998.

In any society, let alone one teetering on the edge of political-economic collapse, these would be difficult lessons to apply. But Indonesian democrats, both Muslim and non-Muslim, have shown themselves capable of greatness.

In June 1999, after a nightmare of state violence, the world saw this majority-Muslim nation repudiate the Soeharto regime's awful legacy of bloodshed and ethnoreligious hatred. Although many obstacles lie ahead, the struggle for a civil Islam and democratic Indonesia presses forward and continues to inspire hope.

A Postscript-Addendum

At the end of August 1999, as this book was moving toward publication, a referendum on independence was held in East Timor. After it became clear that some 80 percent of the population had voted for independence, anti-independence militias sprang into action, assisted by elements of the Indonesian military. The militias burned down most of East Timor's towns, killed an as yet unknown number of independence activists, and drove 200,000 people into exile in West Timor. The tactics of paramilitary terror, refined in the Soeharto era, thus continued, a blight on the body politic.

The violence in East Timor was distressing not only for its awful human cost for Timorese but for what it indicated about the scale of the challenge facing Indonesian democrats. The violence erupted just weeks before the People's Consultative Assembly was to meet to elect a president and vice president. However implausible in light of facts on the ground, ultraconservatives in the military and Habibie government portrayed the Timor violence as a "horizontal" dispute between supporters of independence and advocates of integration with Indonesia. Despite clear and compelling evidence otherwise, then, the message was the same as that used by regime defenders to explain away killings in Banyuwangi, West Java, Ambon, and elsewhere: Civilians are incapable of self-rule; only an iron fist can maintain Indonesia's security and integrity.

On October 20, 1999, Abdurrahman Wahid of Nahdlatul Ulama was elected president. The next day, Megawati Soekarnoputri was elected vice president. Amien Rais had been elected head of the People's Consultative Assembly a few days earlier. The triumph of these three long-suffering and courageous reformists was marred by outbreaks of mass violence in Jakarta, Medan, Solo, Denpasar, and several other cities. Although some of this violence may have been sparked by disappointed Megawati supporters (who had hoped she would win the presidency), most disturbances bore the telltale signs of agents provocateurs. Although its leaders have been removed from the heights of government, advocates of state terror remain ensconced in segments of the military and bureaucracy. The dismantlement of their shadowy network of vigilantes and gangsters will be one of the greatest challenges facing democratic Indonesia.

Chapter Eight

CONCLUSION:

MUSLIM POLITICS, GLOBAL MODERNITY

I N AN ARTICLE a few years ago the Turkish sociologist Serif Mardin offered a wryly inconclusive answer to the question of whether the ideals of
democracy and civil society are generalizable to the Muslim world. "Civil
society is a Western dream, a historical aspiration," he first avers. The dream
is premised on values that reach back to Greek times, entailing notions of moral
autonomy and individual self-creation. Given its cultural genealogy, Mardin
implies, the ideal of civil society will be of limited interest outside the West,
because the notions of personhood and agency on which it is based are incompatible with most cultures.[1]

Mardin's remarks capture well a relativist view of democracy and civil society
widespread in academic circles in the late 1990s. The argument was that democracy depends on a cultural history unique to the West more than it does
on liberties and powers widespread in our age (chapter 1). A gifted observer
of Islam and the West, however, Mardin himself begins to doubt this conclusion as he moves deeper into his discussion. He observes that civil society in
the West was not merely the product of ancient cultural precedents but of an
emergent modern organization. The power of the Church and its separation
from the state, urban autonomy, the rivalry between kings and feudal lords,
civic associations, and the eventual rise of an independent bourgeoisie—these
particularities were part of a general dynamic that helped to heighten civil
participation and create a countervailing balance of power.[2]

Mardin then observes that in recent years "bit and pieces" of this pluricentric
social organization have begun to appear even in non-Western contexts, including the Muslim world.[3] He cautions, however, that we should not assume
that either democracy or civil society is about to triumph in Muslim nations.
Although "many modern Muslim states are beginning to acquire a skeleton of
institutions similar to those" seen in the West, "the dream of Western societies
has not become the dream of Muslim societies." It has not yet done so, Mardin
suggests, because Muslim societies are heir to a "collective memory of a total
culture which once provided a 'civilized' life of a tone different from that of
the West." That culture's core values were not autonomy and self-determina-
tion but faithful adherence to an awesome revelation.[4]

In light of the Indonesian example, Mardin's portrayal of the Muslim imagination may be too textual and unitary for generalization to all Muslim societies.

The social imagination of Muslim Indonesians, we now realize, has been filled with disparate dreams. But Mardin's analysis correctly underscores a general truth concerning democratization. The process depends not just on formal elections and constitutions but on a delicate interaction between society and the state. On the one hand, democracy requires a civic *organization* character- ized by voluntarism, independent associations, and a balance of powers be- tween state and society as well as among civil organizations themselves. All these things help to create commitments and balances congenial to democratic habits of heart. But these activities are still not enough if they remain the stuff of isolated groupings. Democracy ultimately requires a public culture that draws on these separate experiences to promote universal habits of participa- tion and tolerance. This civic culture "scales up" (chapters 1, 2) the democratic habits learned in, among other places, civic associations, making their best features available to the whole of society.

Recent discussions of the conditions that make democracy work have all been consistent in emphasizing that democracy depends not just on the state but on cultures and organizations in society as a whole. Different authors have stressed one side of this latter duality as opposed to the other. Some insist, for example, that culture is the truly critical variable for democracy, as if civility and participation were only matters of getting discourse right. Others empha- size the mediating influence of civic organizations (chapter 2). In the end, however, democratization involves not one of these phenomena but both in mutual and ever emergent interaction.

The Indonesian example also makes clear, however, that these two develop- ments come to nothing if they are not reinforced by a third above and beyond society: the creation of a civilized and self-limiting state. As in Indonesia, the culture of civility remains vulnerable and incomplete if it is not accompanied by a transformation of state. This is to say, once again, that civil society is not opposed to the state but deeply dependent on its *civilization*. The state must open itself to public participation. At the same time, independent courts and watchdog agencies must be ready to intervene when, as inevitably happens, some citizen or official tries to replace democratic proceduralism with nether- world violence. As vigilantes and hate groups regularly remind us, not all orga- nizations in society are *civil*, and the state must act as a guardian of public civility as well as a vehicle of the popular will.

Observations like these remind us that democratization dances not just to the beat of one drum, least of all an ancient one, but to a contemporary rhythm of organizations and values. Inasmuch as this is so, then, the key to democra- cy's possibility is not singular but multiple. It builds on strategic interventions at many points in the democratic circle: civil associations, a free press and judiciary, the egalitarian diffusion of wealth and opportunity, and, always, public support for citizens and leaders committed to these goals. Even in the smoothest-running political systems, democracy is not all-or-nothing, but enduringly incremental.

A second conclusion follows from this first, namely, that there is no one-size-fits-all democracy but a variety of forms linked by family resemblances. Democracy's values of freedom, equality, and tolerance-in-pluralism do not come with unbending instructions for all places and times. The general values take their practical cues from the particularities of the place in which they would work. Even in modern Western Europe, we know, the balance struck among democratic values has varied across countries and epochs. In an earlier era when each nation was organized around a dominant religion and ethnicity, for example, the problem of tolerance loomed less large than it does today, as European nations become immigrant societies. Similarly, as societies change, people perceive old arrangements in a new light and shift the balance among democracy's values accordingly. The system of religious "pillars" that underlay Dutch democracy in the nineteenth century (chapter 2) is no longer popular among Dutch youth because it is seen as repressive rather than protective of their religious rights, in which many have lost interest. Or, similarly, gender and family roles once seen as central to Western civility are today questioned by those who would elevate individual freedom above family unity.

These examples remind us that even in the West the balance struck between community and individuality, public and private, and rights and duties change over time. Freedom, equality, and pluralism are highly generalized values, to say the least. As first principles of democracy they come with few instructions as to precisely where they should apply or how they should be balanced. This would not be a problem, of course, if the principles always worked in synergistic harmony, the promotion of one necessarily enhancing the others. However, modern history shows that these first principles come with no guarantee of easy compatibility. Private property may strengthen liberty while corroding equality. Affirmative actions to improve the lives of long marginalized groups may be seen as assaults on the rights of others. Demands for sexual freedom may offend believers who insist that promoting such values in their houses of worship denies them their freedom.

Democratic values are not realized, then, through their magic-wand absolutization in all social spheres. The practice of democracy requires a balance among its core values, and that balance inevitably varies over time and place. If the latter were not true, democracies would show none of the variation in freedoms and responsibilities that they do. Liberal philosophers might see this variation as a fatal flaw, wondering how democracy can flourish if the social achievement of freedom, equality, and tolerance is not everywhere the same. But because it depends on a culture larger than itself, democracy is not one structure but many related and flexible forms. Not everything can be relative, of course; certain value concerns remain the same. But the sameness is one of family resemblance rather than mechanical replication.

Inasmuch as variation of this sort exists in the West, we should not be surprised to see that democratization in the Muslim world will strike its own balance among values. Like Western civic democrats not long ago, Muslim democrats may prefer a stronger commitment to public moral education than contemporary Western liberals do. But this variation is not a deviation from the democratic plan but proof of its contextual realization.

Its daunting specificity aside, the Indonesian example illustrates clearly the fragility and variability of the democratic process. In this Southeast Asian country, there have been precedents for power-diffusing associations since the arrival of Islam more than five centuries ago. In a few city-states early in that history, local organizations converged with a remarkable economic dynamism to limit royal authority, disperse social power, support spiritual individualism, and inspire dreams of contractual government (chapter 2). The possibility that such contractual precedents might be drawn up into a broader reformation of Muslim politics was diminished, however, by an unholy alliance of absolutist monarchs and European power. Later, the secularizing policies of the Dutch unwittingly eroded the moral authority of imperial Islam. In so doing, European colonialism encouraged the emergence of a society-based popular Islam. It was this tradition, not the aristocratic Islam of the courts, that underlay new visions of Muslim politics in the twentieth century.

In that same century, however, Muslim scholars discovered that theirs was no longer the only voice claiming to represent society but one in a chorus with secularists, socialists, and multireligious nationalists. Muslim politics had met the pluralism of our age, and there was no going back. Although conservative scholars were unhappy with the new cacophony, the result was not a narrowing of the Muslim political voice but its enrichment. In the first decades of the twentieth century Muslims listened to the words of the nationalist anthem and made much of it their own. In the independence era they learned the language of democracy and constitutionality, and took enthusiastically to its forms. In matters of civic association Muslims showed themselves second to no one. None of their rivals could match the breadth and vitality of their associations. Even under the New Order, Muslims were better able than others to resist state controls and nurture alternative ideas of the public good.

This new politics of Muslim pluralism had difficulty, however, when it attempted to stand back and learn from its own history. Indonesian Muslims boast a proud legacy of tolerance, autonomy, and skepticism toward the all-pretending state. They deepened those civic habits in modern times. When it came to "scaling up" from this experience to devise principles of government, however, some scholars balked. The world in which they lived seemed less glorious than the golden age of Islam. Rather than generalizing from their own remarkable achievement, many looked away, toward a shimmering ideal of an "Islamic" state whose seamless union of governance and society risks subordinating Islam's high ideals to low politics. As had occurred with nationalism and socialism in the modern West, the very radiance of the high ideal caused a blindness toward context and interpretation.

But the problem of modern Muslim politics was not merely a matter of seeing things right. It was political, too. Fiercely uncivil rivalries with socialist, communist, and, later, conservative nationalists forced Muslim politicians onto the defensive. Pushed to the corner, they fought back, using simplistic rallying cries for solidarity against the enemy. They and their rivals spent themselves on uncivil wars rather than democratic consolidation. These zero-sum battles drained society's coffers of the social capital required for democratic reformation.

Despite thirty years of authoritarian rule, Indonesia today is witness to a remarkable effort to recover and amplify a Muslim and Indonesian culture of tolerance, equality, and civility. The proponents of civil Islam are a key part of this renaissance. Civil Muslims renounce the mythology of an Islamic state. Rather than relegating Islam to the realm of the private, however, they insist that there is a middle path between liberalism's privatization and conservative Islam's bully state. The path passes by way of a public religion that makes itself heard through independent associations, spirited public dialogue, and the demonstrated decency of believers.

This civil democratic Islam makes sense, of course, only if one believes that Islam is compatible with, or even founded on, democratic values. No one can deny that this conviction is a matter of interpretation, and conservative Muslims have the right to insist it is not theirs. Like many in the West in the early twentieth century, some among the latter still see all the opportunity but none of the dangers of the modern state. They would use the awesome power of state technologies to dissolve the wall between public and private, and force citizens to virtue. Inasmuch as they do this, however, these conservatives betray principles other Muslims hold dear: that their great faith insists there can be no compulsion in religion, and that it does indeed count freedom, equality, and justice among its core values.

In Indonesia, however, statist Islam has become the minority view. There is no denying that serious differences remain over the terms of Muslim representation in government and the economy. And there is also no denying that some politicians will use low appeals to Muslim exclusivity to blunt the drive for an inclusive Muslim politics. But the majority have learned that they make their understanding of God's commands more relevant when they relate them to an ecumenical interpretation of Indonesian history and culture. The majority have also learned from Soeharto's excesses that the critical skepticism of their forebears toward the all-subsuming state is an attitude still relevant for politics in our age.

In the end, then, Muslims are part of our shared world, and Muslim politics is part of our shared but plural modernity. Contrary to earlier forecasts, religion in our age has not everywhere declined, nor been domiciled within a sphere of interiority. Modernity has witnessed powerful religious revivals. Not a reaction *against* but a creative response *to* the modern world, the most successful of these religious reformations have thrived by drawing themselves down into mass society and away from exclusive elites. Having moved into the public realm in this manner, some among the refigured religions tap popular energies only to direct them toward authoritarian ends. Some replace plural economies of meaning with a homogeneous religious currency. But these repressive standardizations inevitably unleash contestive heterogenizations. Just as nineteenth-century America saw a struggle for Protestant hearts and minds, the Muslim world today witnesses fierce contests over the meaning and social relevance of religion.

Inasmuch as this great religious transformation has occurred, Muslims face choices similar to all us moderns. The refiguration of their tradition is taking place in a world of migrations, urbanizations, and communications that render borders permeable to transcultural flows.[5] In this setting, traditions laying claim to ultimate meanings face a common dilemma: how to maintain a steadied worldview and social engagement while acknowledging the pluralism of the age.

One response to this predicament, a repressively organic one, is to strap on the body armor, ready one's weapons, and launch a holy war for society as a whole. In today's world of bureaucratic leviathans, this option typically involves the seizure of state and, from there, the forced imposition of organic unity on an inorganic social body. This option has its enthusiasts not just among conservative Muslims but among antipluralist radicals in all modern societies. However, the history of the twentieth-century West, in particular, has shown that this option exacts an awful price. It oppresses minorities, antagonizes nonconformists among the majority, and robs society of the freedoms necessary for pacificity and dynamism. Nonetheless, as a strategy for holding power, this option may have an easy appeal, and self-serving elites may be willing to pay its price. In his final years Soeharto of Indonesia was willing to pay that price, and the violence of 1998 showed its awful consequence.

A second strategy for religion's reformation renounces organic totalism for separatist sectarianism. Like the Essenes of ancient Israel under Roman rule,[6] proponents of this option take refuge in the uncompromised purity of small circles of believers. In a complex society rather than a desolate desert retreat, however, this path brings with it regular reminders of one's marginality. Because most view their religion as public ethics as well as private devotion, however, this choice is unlikely to win as many followers among Muslims as it has in some other modern traditions.[7]

There is a third option for a refigured religion, a civil one. Rather than state conquest or separatist isolation, this approach accepts the diversity of public voices, acknowledging that this is, in some sense, the nature of modern things. What follows after this varies widely, but the underlying pluralist premise remains. The civil option may promote *public* religion, but distanced from the coercive machinery of state. It strides proudly into the public arena but insists that its message is clearest when its bearers guard their independence. Religious voices must be ready to balance and critique the state and the market, rather than give both a greater measure of social power.[8] Here is a religious reformation that works with, rather than against, the pluralizing realities of our age.

The option elected by any religious community will be determined, of course, not by the timeless truths of scripture but by the struggle for influence among rival bearers of the Word. In the Muslim case, we know that some will claim that the Word demands the dissolution of the fragile barriers separating state from society. They will insist that the state leviathan is needed to make people good. But the markets, media, and migrations of our age make any enduring institutionalization of such a statist Islam difficult. It may be attempted, but again and again it will fail. Virtue will give way to hypocrisy and abuse, and religion itself will be threatened. The arrangement fails because it is so out of step with the pluralism and movement of our age, and because, unchecked by any balance of power, rulers inevitably abuse the truths over which they claim rights of control. For Muslim believers, then, the real danger in the union of Islam and state is that it ends by subordinating Islam to state. Faced with this peril, other Muslims will look to democratic ideas, and some variant of civil Islam, to guard their great faith and maintain an ethical compass amid the roaring flux.

Plural in its origins, there is no single modernity; nor is there one final formula for civility and democracy. Certainly, as Serif Mardin noted above, Muslim societies should and will have their own dreams. However, the restructuring of life worlds that characterizes our age has become so massive that it guarantees that, more than any prior epoch, large numbers of people will continue to be drawn to ideas of a civil and democratic sort. The implementation of these ideals will, of course, vary; it always has. So, too, will the balance societies strike between public morality and private freedom or between individual liberty and communitarian good. But this variation only reminds us that the real key to democracy's cross-cultural appeal is not imitation or "Westernization" but dialogue and contextualization.

The lessons from Indonesia lead me to a closing observation, a normative one, and one that I, an American anthropologist who came of age in the 1960s and 1970s, was able to relearn only with the help of Muslim friends. The conclusion is that we believers in civility and democracy must show greater confidence in the relevance of these ideals for our age. This confidence has nothing to do with the alleged Occidental origins of democratic ideals, a mythic charter that, I have suggested, only clouds the issue by telling Muslims and others that their own experience is not what is most directly relevant to democracy's possibility. Rather than on grounds of genealogy, then, our democratic confidence should be based on the conviction that the message of freedom, equality, and plurality is not narrowly circumscribed, as some prophets of the new civilizational relativism argue. Democratic ideals are broadly appealing because they respond to circumstances and needs common across modern cultures.

This is not to suggest that the outcomes of today's democratic struggles, whether Indonesian or others, are guaranteed. There is no end of history, no definitive triumph of democratic ideals. Ours will remain an age of democratic trial, and, for better or for worse, history's verdict will vary. But of this the Indonesian experience should make us certain: that the desire for democracy and civil decency is not civilizationally circumscribed. This simple hope will remain a powerful force in public politics and religion for years to come.

NOTES

PREFACE

1. Bhikku Parekh, "The Cultural Particularity of Liberal Democracy," in David Held, ed., *Prospects for Democracy: North, South, East, West* (Stanford: Stanford University Press, 1993), p. 156.

2. Robert W. Hefner, *The Political Economy of Mountain Java: An Interpretive History* (Berkeley: University of California Press, 1990).

3. See, for example, Arjun Appadurai, *Modernity at Large: Cultural Dimensions of Globalization* (Minneapolis: University of Minnesota Press, 1996); Ulf Hannerz, *Transnational Connections: Culture, People, Places* (London: Routledge, 1996); Adam Kuper, *Conceptualizing Society* (London: Routledge, 1992); and Henrietta L. Moore, ed., *The Future of Anthropological Knowledge* (London: Routledge, 1996).

4. Denys Lombard, *Le carrefour Javanais: essai d'histoire globale*, 3 vols. (Paris: École des Hautes Études en Sciences Sociales, 1990); and Anthony Reid, *Southeast Asia in the Age of Commerce, 1450–1680*, 2 vols. (New Haven: Yale University Press, 1988; 1993).

5. Clifford Geertz, *The Religion of Java* (New York: Free Press).

6. M. Hodgson, *The Venture of Islam: Conscience and History in a World Civilization,* 3 vols. (Chicago: University of Chicago Press, 1974), p. 551.

CHAPTER ONE
DEMOCRATIZATION IN AN AGE OF RELIGIOUS REVITALIZATION

1. Not that this nonmodernist view is entirely new. Decades earlier, critics of Marxism and modernization theory made a similar point, denying that ethnicity and religion had been forever extinguished by capitalism and the nation state. See, for example, Frank Parkin, *Marxism and Class Theory: A Bourgeois Critique* (New York: Columbia University Press, 1979).

2. Charles Taylor's much-cited essay on multiculturalism demonstrates that the demand for recognition and cultural "authenticity" is not peculiar to developing countries but is a central feature of the late modern West. See his *Multiculturalism and "The Politics of Recognition"* (Princeton, N.J.: Princeton University Press, 1992).

3. Francis Fukuyama, "The End of History?" In *The National Interest* 16 (Summer 1989): 4. See also his more nuanced *The End of History and the Last Man* (New York: Free Press, 1992).

4. The scale of the conflict convinced many that it was an eruption of long suppressed "primordial" tensions. But the conflict owed more to contemporary intrigues than ancient urges. On a related point, see John R. Bowen, "The Myth of Global Ethnic Conflict," in *Journal of Democracy* 7:4 (October 1996): 3–14.

5. For an anthropological view, see Edwin N. Wilmsen and Patrick McAllister, eds., *The Politics of Difference: Ethnic Premises in a World of Power* (Chicago: University of Chicago Press, 1996).

6. John Gray, "From Post-Communism to Civil Society: The Reemergence of History and the Decline of the Western Model," in Ellen Frankel Paul, Fred D. Miller Jr., and

Jeffrey Paul, eds., *Liberalism and the Economic Order* (Cambridge: Cambridge University Press, 1993), p. 50.

7. See Samuel P. Huntington, *The Third Wave: Democratization in the Late Twentieth Century* (Norman: University of Oklahoma Press, 1991).

8. Samuel P. Huntington "The Clash of Civilizations?" *Foreign Affairs* 72:3 (Summer 1993): 29.

9. The Huntington debate was covered extensively in Southeast Asia. Displaying the generosity of spirit for which it was famous, the civil Islamic Indonesian journal, *Ulumul Qur'an*, translated and published the full text of Huntington's article, in conjunction with a judiciously balanced group of critical essays. See *Ulumul Qur'an* 4:5 (1993); 5:2 (1994).

10. On the stereotypes that inform this judgment, see Bruce B. Lawrence, *Shattering the Myth: Islam Beyond Violence* (Princeton, N.J.: Princeton University Press, 1998).

11. For a criticism of the "spurious prior reality . . . termed 'culture' " in analyses of Muslim politics, see Aziz Al-Azmeh, "Modern 'Culture' and the European Tribe," in Al-Azmeh, *Islams and Modernities* (London: Verso, 1993), pp. 1–17.

12. Robert D. Putnam, *Making Democracy Work: Civic Traditions in Modern Italy* (Princeton, N.J.: Princeton University Press, 1993).

13. John Gray, "Autonomy is not the only good," *Times Literary Supplement*, no. 4915 (June 13, 1997), p. 30.

14. Students of social theory will recognize that this concern for the conditions of democracy's possibility also underlay modernization theory in the 1960s. There is an important difference, however, between the two literatures. Although the best modernization theorists were aware of the world's cultural diversity, they had a greater confidence in the generalizability of Western modernity and a simpler and less plural understanding of the non-Western world. When the issue of democracy reemerged in the 1990s, it assumed a less polar understanding of modernity and tradition. The effort to acknowledge the unboundedness and internal complexity of small-scale societies has been part of this. See, for example, Adam Kuper, ed., *Conceptualizing Society* (London: Routledge, 1992); Richard Fardon, ed., *Counterworks: Managing the Diversity of Knowledge* (London: Routledge, 1995); Igor Kopytoff, "The Internal African Frontier: The Making of African Political Culture," in Kopytoff, ed., *The African Frontier: The Reproduction of Traditional African Societies* (Bloomington: Indiana University Press, 1987), pp. 3–84; and Terence Ranger, "The Local and the Global in Southern African Religious History," in Robert W. Hefner, ed., *Conversion to Christianity: Historical and Anthropological Perspectives on a Great Transformation* (Berkeley: University of California Press, 1993), pp. 65–98.

15. This last question is explored in José Casanova's *Public Religions in the Modern World* (Chicago: University of Chicago Press, 1994).

16. For an overview of the precrisis performance, see Hal Hill, *The Indonesian Economy Since 1966: Southeast Asia's Emerging Giant* (Cambridge: Cambridge University Press, 1996).

17. For contemporary comparisons, see Dale F. Eickelman and James Piscatori, *Muslim Politics* (Princeton, N.J.: Princeton University Press, 1996); and John L. Esposito and John O. Voll, *Islam and Democracy* (New York: Oxford University Press, 1996). On political ideas in medieval Islam, see Ann K. S. Lambton, *State and Government in Medi-*

eval Islam: An Introduction to the Study of Islamic Political Theory (Oxford: Oxford University Press, 1981).

18. See Ellis Goldberg, "Private Goods, Public Wrongs, and Civil Society in Some Medieval Arab Theory and Practice," in Ellis Goldberg, Resat Kasaba, and Joel S. Migdal, eds., *Rule and Rights in the Middle East: Democracy, Law, and Society* (Seattle: University of Washington Press, 1993), pp. 248–71; and Esposito and Voll, *Islam and Democracy*, pp. 4–10.

19. See Roy P. Mottahedeh, "Toward an Islamic Theology of Toleration," in Tore Lindholm and Kari Vogt, *Islamic Law Reform and Human Rights: Challenges and Rejoinders* (Copenhagen: Nordic Human Rights Publications, 1993), pp. 25–36.

20. On the separation of religious and state authority in classical Islam, see Ira M. Lapidus, "The Separation of State and Religion in the Development of Early Islamic Society," *International Journal of Middle East Studies* 6:4 (October 1975): 363–85.

21. For an examination of the relationship of these brotherhoods to the state and Islamic conversion, see Richard M. Eaton's *The Rise of Islam and the Bengal Frontier, 1204–1760* (Berkeley: University of California Press, 1993). For a contemporary example, see Leanardo A. Villalón, *Islamic Society and State Power in Senegal: Disciples and Citizens in Fatick* (Cambridge: Cambridge University Press, 1995), esp. pp. 200–265.

22. On the tension between contractual and "hierocratic" notions of kingship in Morocco, see Henry Munson Jr., *Religion and Power in Morocco* (New Haven: Yale University Press, 1993), esp. pp. 35–55; for a comparative anthropological treatment, see Charles Lindholm, *The Islamic Middle East: An Historical Anthropology* (Oxford: Blackwell, 1996).

23. See, for example, Nikki R. Keddie, *An Islamic Response to Imperialism: Political and Religious Writings of Sayyid Jamal ad-Din "Al-Afghani"* (Berkeley: University of California Press, 1968); and Ali Rahnema, ed., *Pioneers of Islamic Revival* (London: Zed, 1994).

24. Two examples of such movements were Hasan al-Banna's Muslim Brotherhood in Egypt (founded 1928) and, in south Asia, Abu al-Ala Mawdudi's Jamaat-i Islami (founded 1941). See Richard P. Mitchell, *The Society of the Muslim Brothers* (New York: Oxford University Press, 1969); and Seyyed Vali Reza Zasr, *The Vanguard of the Islamic Revolution: The Jama'at-i Islami of Pakistan* (Berkeley: University of California Press, 1994).

25. On the reception of nationalism among twentieth-century Muslims, see James P. Piscatori, *Islam in a World of Nation-States* (Cambridge: Cambridge University Press, 1986).

26. For anthropological studies of this transition, see Richard T. Antoun's *Muslim Preacher in the Modern World: A Jordanian Case Study in Comparative Perspective* (Princeton, N.J.: Princeton University Press, 1989); and Dale F. Eickelman, *Knowledge and Power in Morocco: The Education of a Twentieth-Century Notable* (Princeton, N.J.: Princeton University Press, 1985). For an Indonesian counterpart, see John R. Bowen's *Muslims Through Discourse: Religion and Ritual in Gayo Society* (Princeton, N.J.: Princeton University Press, 1993).

27. Ulf Hannerz, "The Global Ecumene as a Network of Networks," in Adam Kuper, ed., *Conceptualizing Society* (London: Routledge, 1992), pp. 34–56.

28. On democracy's globalization via vernacularization, see Chris Hann, "Introduction: Political Society and Civil Anthropology," in Chris Hann and Elizabeth Dunn, eds., *Civil Society: Challenging Western Models* (London: Routledge, 1996), pp. 1–26;

and Robert W. Hefner, "On the History and Cross-Cultural Possibility of a Democratic Ideal," in Hefner, ed., *Democratic Civility: The History and Cross-Cultural Possibility of a Modern Political Ideal* (New Brunswick, N.J.: Transaction, 1998), pp. 3–49.

29. Anthropology would seem to have been well positioned to appreciate this interaction, but, as Richard A. Wilson has observed, the discipline's "methodological emphasis on localism" and its elevation of "culture" as a supreme value slowed its response. Things are changing, however. See Richard A. Wilson, "Human Rights, Culture, and Context: An Introduction," in Wilson, ed., *Human Rights, Culture, and Context: Anthropological Perspectives* (London: Pluto, 1997), pp. 1–27. See also note 28, above.

30. This view challenges earlier models of solidarity and meaning in traditional societies. It also implies a less totalizing hold of culture on cognition, in which there is always more to an agent's mental processing than just "internalizing" culturally available symbols. On this point, see Maurice Bloch, *Ritual, History, and Power: Selected Papers in Anthropology* (London: Athlone, 1989 [LSE Monographs on Social Anthropology, no. 58]); and Dan Sperber, *La Contagion des Idées* (Paris: Editions Odil Jacob, 1996). On the same problem from the perspective of conversion, see Robert W. Hefner, "Introduction: World Building and the Rationality of Conversion," in Hefner, ed., *Conversion to Christianity: Historical and Anthropological Perspectives on a Great Transformation* (Berkeley: University of California Press, 1993), pp. 3–44.

31. Robert P. Weller, "Horizontal Ties and Civil Institutions in Chinese Societies," in Hefner, *Democratic Civility*, pp. 229–47.

32. This process of amplification and dampening is both sociological and psychocultural. My understanding draws on two otherwise unrelated bodies of research. The first is the model of mind and culture elaborated in cross-cultural studies of practical cognition, like those of Maurice Bloch and Arthur Kleinman. See Bloch, "From Cognition to Ideology," in Bloch, *Ritual, History, and Power*, pp. 106–36; and Kleinman, *Rethinking Psychiatry: From Cultural Category to Personal Experience* (New York: Free Press, 1988). My political-sociological reflections on amplification draw on Peter Evans's discussion of the "scaling up" of social capital in his "Government Action, Social Capital, and Development: Reviewing the Evidence on Synergy," in *World Development* 24:6 (1996): 1119–32.

33. Islam's egalitarianism, of course, lies more visible on the surface of the tradition than it does in Weller's Confucianism. On the tension in early Islam between hierarchy and egalitarianism, see Lindholm, *The Islamic Middle East*; and Louise Marlow, *Hierarchy and Egalitarianism in Islamic Thought* (Cambridge: Cambridge University Press, 1997).

34. For a classical statement of this view, see Bryan R. Wilson, *Religion in Secular Society* (London: Watts, 1966). A more nuanced view, emphasizing the shifting nature of "public" and "private" in the West, is presented in David Martin's *A General Theory of Secularization* (New York: Harper and Row, 1978). José Casanova's *Public Religions in the Modern World* takes Martin's reservations even further, questioning the privatization thesis outright and showing that some in the modern West have rediscovered a middle ground between religious establishment and privatization.

35. On post-Enlightenment religious revival, see D. Outram, *The Enlightenment* (Cambridge: Cambridge University Press, 1995), p. 34; and E. P. Thompson, *The Making of the English Working Class* (New York: Vintage, 1963), pp. 350–400.

36. Alexis de Tocqueville, *Democracy in America*, trans. George Lawrence, ed. J. P. Mayer (Garden City, N.Y.: Doubleday, 1969), 2 vols.

37. In this sense, the view that nineteenth-century America had a smoothly consensual "civic religion" is too simple. Public religion in the United States was not a matter of settled agreement but, like religion in today's Muslim world, was an ongoing and agonistic debate over identity and morality. For the classic view of American civic religion, see Robert N. Bellah, Richard Madsen, William M. Sullivan, Ann Swidler, and S.M. Tipton, *Habits of the Heart: Individualism and Commitment in American Life* (New York: Harper and Row, 1985). For a more pluralized view, see Robert Wuthnow, *The Restructuring of American Religion: Society and Faith Since the Second World War* (Princeton, N.J.: Princeton University Press, 1988); and (for the 1990s) his *Loose Connections: Joining Together in America's Fragmented Communities* (Cambridge: Harvard University Press, 1998).

38. As the activism of American bishops, conservative evangelicals, and civil rights preachers has shown, we should *not* assume that all Westerners accept this privatized view of religion. Recent years have seen a resurgence of *public* religion even in the West. Some might suggest that in America religion never gave up its public role. See Casanova, *Public Religions*, esp. pp. 211–34.

39. G. M. Marsden, *Fundamentalism and American Culture: The Shaping of Twentieth-Century Evangelicalism, 1870–1925* (Oxford: Oxford University Press, 1980); and Wuthnow, *The Restructuring of American Religion*.

40. Eickelman and Piscatori, *Muslim Politics*, p. 5.

41. On Islamic publishing, see George N. Atiyeh, "The Book in the Modern Arab World: The Cases of Lebanon and Egypt," in Atiyeh, ed., *The Book in the Islamic World: The Written Word and Communication in the Middle East* (Albany: State University of New York Press, 1995), pp. 232–53; Dale F. Eickelman, "Mass Higher Education and the Religious Imagination in Contemporary Arab Societies," *American Ethnologist* 19:4 (1992): 643–55; and Yves Gonzalez-Quijono, *Les gens du livre: Champ intellectuel et édition dans l'Égypte republicaine (1952–1993)*, Ph.D. dissertation, L'Institut d'Études Politiques, Paris, 1994. On the new popular Islamic arts, see Walter Armbrust, *Mass Culture and Modernism in Egypt* (Cambridge: Cambridge Studies in Social and Cultural Anthropology 102, 1996); and, for Indonesia, Kenneth M. George's delightful "Designs on Indonesia's Muslim Communities," *The Journal of Asian Studies* 57:3 (August 1998): 693–713.

42. On the politics of populist preaching, see Richard T. Antoun, *Muslim Preacher in the Modern World*; and Patrick D. Gaffney, *The Prophet's Pulpit: Islamic Preaching in Contemporary Egypt* (Berkeley: University of California Press, 1994). On neotraditionalist Sufis and mass politics, see Serif Mardin, *Religion and Social Change in Modern Turkey: The Case of Bediuzzaman Said Nursi* (Albany: State University of New York Press, 1989); and Leonardo A. Villalón, *Islamic Society and State Power in Senegal*. On secularly educated new Islamic intellectuals, see Michael E. Meeker, "The New Muslim Intellectuals in the Republic of Turkey," in Richard Tapper, ed., *Islam in Modern Turkey: Religion, Politics, and Literature in a Secular State* (London: Tauris, 1991), pp. 189–219; and Olivier Roy, *The Failure of Political Islam*, trans. Carol Volk (Cambridge, Mass.: Harvard University Press, 1994).

43. Roy, *The Failure of Political Islam*, p. 3.

44. On the populist tensions in Latin American evangelicalism, see David Martin, *Tongues of Fire: The Explosion of Protestantism in Latin America* (Oxford: Blackwell, 1991); and C. Smith, "The Spirit and Democracy: Base Communities, Protestantism, and

Democratization in Latin America," in W. H. Swatos Jr., ed., *Religion and Democracy in Latin America* (New Brunswick: Transaction, 1995), pp. 27–44.

45. Jurgen Habermas, *The Structural Transformation of the Public Sphere: An Inquiry into a Category of Bourgeois Society*, trans. Thomas Burger, with Frederick Lawrence (Cambridge, Mass.: MIT Press, 1989 [orig. 1962]).

46. The best collection on this theme is Craig Calhoun, ed., *Habermas and the Public Sphere* (Cambridge, Mass.: MIT Press, 1992). On Habermas and gender, see Joan B. Landes, *Women and the Public Sphere in the Age of the French Revolution* (Ithaca: Cornell University Press, 1988).

47. A claim also made by the Syrian sociologist Bassam Tibi when he argues that if Islam is to be modern, it must be "domiciled within the sphere of interiority." See *Islam and the Cultural Accommodation of Social Change* (Boulder, Colo.: Westview, 1990), p. 139. For a better cross-cultural perspective on public and private religion, see John R. Bowen, *Religions in Practice: An Approach to the Anthropology of Religion* (Boston: Allen and Bacon, 1998), pp. 234–56; and my own, "Multiple Modernities: Christianity, Islam, and Hinduism in a Globalizing Age," in *Annual Review of Anthropology* 27 (1998): 83–104.

48. Even a sophisticated writer like Charles Taylor can be drawn toward such simple conclusions. In *Multiculturalism and "The Politics of Recognition,"* p. 62, he writes,

> For mainstream Islam, there is no question of separating politics and religion the way we have come to expect in Western liberal society. Liberalism is not a possible meeting ground for all cultures, but is the political expression of one range of culture, and quite incompatible with other ranges. Moreover, as many Muslims are well aware, Western liberalism is not so much an expression of the secular, postreligious outlook that happens to be popular among liberal *intellectuals* as a more organic outgrowth of Christianity. . . . The division of church and state goes back to the earliest days of Christian civilization.

49. Bernard Lewis, *The Political Language of Islam* (Chicago: University of Chicago Press, 1988), p. 2.

50. This same point has been made by analysts from segments of the political spectrum different than Lewis. See, for example, Talal Asad, "The Limits of Religious Criticism in the Middle East: Notes on Islamic Public Argument," in Asad, *Genealogies of Religion: Discipline and Reasons of Power in Christianity and Islam* (Baltimore: The Johns Hopkins University Press, 1993), pp. 200–236. For a Hindu example of the varied constructions of the private and public, see Peter van der Veer, *Religious Nationalism: Hindus and Muslims in India* (Berkeley: University of California Press, 1994).

51. See G. E. Fuller, *Algeria: The Next Fundamentalist State?* (Santa Monica, Calif.: RAND Corp., 1996); Roy, *The Failure of Political Islam*.

52. On the aptness of this phrase, see Dale F. Eickelman, "Inside the Islamic Reformation," *Wilson Quarterly* 22:1 (Winter 1998): 80–89.

53. Mohammad Shahrour, "The Divine Text and Pluralism in Muslim Societies," *Muslim Politics Report* (Council of Foreign Relations, New York) 14 (July–August 1997), p. 8. On Shahrour, see Dale F. Eickelman, "Islamic Liberalism Strikes Back," *Middle East Studies Association Bulletin* 27 (1993): 163–68.

54. For an Iranian example, see Valla Vakili, "Debating Religion and Politics in Iran: The Political Thought of Abdolkarim Soroush" Council on Foreign Relations, 1996 (New York: [Studies Department Occasional Paper, no. 2]).

55. Invoking the maxim "power tends to corrupt," for example, Nurcholish Madjid calls for a separation of powers among the executive, legislature, and judiciary. He also observes, however, that such formal checks and balances are incomplete unless complemented by an equitable balance of power and resources in society as a whole. See his "Menata Kembali Kehidupan Bermasyarakat dan Bernegara Menuju Peradaban Baru Indonesia' [To rearrange our lives as a society and nation toward a new Indonesian civilization], in Madjid, *Cita-Cita Politik Islam Era Reformasi* [Islamic political ideals in an era of reformation] (Jakarta: Penerbit Paramadina, 1999), pp. 183–99. For other Indonesian examples of this genre, see Moeslim Abdurrahman, *Semarak Islam Semarak Demokrasi?* [The strengthening of Islam is the strengthening of democracy?] (Jakarta: Pustaka Firdaus, 1996); Nurcholish Madjid, *Islam: Agama Kemanusiaan* [Islam: Humanitarian religion] (Jakarta: Paramadina, 1995); Abdul Mu'im, ed., *Kebebasan Cendekiawan: Refleksi Kaum Muda* [Intellectuals' freedom: Reflections by youth] (Jakarta: Bentang Budaya, 1996); and Abdurrahman Wahid, *Tabayun Gus Dur: Pribumisasi Islam, Hak Minoritas, Reformasi Kultural* [Gus Dur's moves: Indigenizing Islam, minority rights, and cultural reformation] (Yogyakarta: LKiS, 1998). On the civil society debate in the Middle East, see Augustus Richard Norton, *Civil Society in the Middle East*, vol. 1 (Leiden: Brill, 1995).

56. Bhikhu Parekh, "The Cultural Particularity of Liberal Democracy," p. 158. This same issue lies at the center of the much heralded debate between "liberals" and "communitarians." See Charles Taylor, "Cross Purposes: The Liberal-Communitarian Debate," in Nancy L. Rosenblum, ed., *Liberalism and the Moral Life* (Cambridge, Mass.: Harvard University Press, 1989), pp. 159–82.

57. This tension between liberalism's philosophy and its actual practice is explored in Bernard Yack, "Liberalism and Its Communitarian Critics: Does Liberal Practice 'Live Down' to Liberal Theory?" in Charles H. Reynolds and Ralph V. Norman, eds., *Community in America: The Challenge of Habits of the Heart* (Berkeley: University of California Press, 1988), pp. 147–69. On the way that Dutch democracy balanced individual and communal interests, see Anton C. Zijderveld, "Civil Society, Pillarization, and the Welfare State," in Hefner, *Democratic Civility*, pp. 153–71.

58. Adam Seligman, *The Idea of Civil Society* (New York: Free Press, 1992); Michael J. Sandel, *Democracy's Discontent: America in Search of a Public Philosophy* (Cambridge, Mass.: Harvard University Press, 1996).

59. For a similar view of public religion's democratic function in Western society, see Casanova, *Public Religions in the Modern World*, and Wuthnow, *Loose Connections*.

60. This vision of a fused state and society was not unique to certain Indonesian Muslims but was also widespread among conservative nationalists. The most influential exponent was the great corporatist thinker S. Soepomo. A harsh critic of political Islam, Soepomo was equally opposed to liberal democracy. For him, if political leaders are close to the people then civil rights and a balance of powers are unnecessary. Although late in life he qualified these ideas, Soepomo influenced Indonesia's first president, Soekarno, as well as Soeharto and conservative members of the New Order military. See Adnan Buyung Nasution, *The Aspiration for Constitutional Government in Indonesia: A Socio-Legal Study of the Indonesian Konstituante, 1956–1959* (Jakarta: Sinar Harapan 1992); and Marsillam Simanjuntak, *Pandangan Negara Integralistik: Sumber, Unsur, dan Riwayatnya dalam Persiapan UUD 1945* [The perspective of the integralist state: Sources, elements, and history in the preparation of the 1945 Constitution] (Jakarta: Grafiti,

1994); and Douglas E. Ramage, *Politics in Indonesia: Democracy, Islam, and the Ideology of Tolerance* (New York: Routledge, 1995), pp. 125–130.

61. See John R. Bowen, *Muslims through Discourse*; Robert W. Hefner, "Islamizing Java? Religion and Politics in Rural East Java," *Journal of Asian Studies* 46:3 (August 1987): 533–54; and Martin Rossler, "Islamization and the Reshaping of Identities in Rural South Sulawesi," in Robert W. Hefner and Patricia Horvatich, eds., *Islam in an Era of Nation States: Politics and Religious Renewal in Muslim Southeast Asia* (Honolulu: University of Hawaii Press, 1997), pp. 275–306.

62. In Javanese, *abangan* literally means "red," but the term is a symbol for folk traditions generally. Javanese Muslims of this sort are also called *kejawen*, or "Javanist."

63. The classical study of the tension between Javanism and Islam is Clifford Geertz, *The Religion of Java*. Recent research has made clear that the tension did not always assume the polarized form evident in Geertz's time. On the variable nature of the relationship, see Denys Lombard, *Le Carrefour Javanais*, Vol. 2: *Les Réseaux Asiatiques*, pp. 77–208; and M. C. Ricklefs, *The Seen and Unseen Worlds in Java, 1726–1749: History, Literature, and Islam in the Court of Pakubuwana II* (St. Leonard's, Australia: Allen & Unwin, 1998). For a reflection from the perspective of Java arts, see Laurie J. Sears, *Shadows of Empire: Colonial Discourse and Javanese Tales* (Durham, N.C.: Duke University Press, 1996), pp. 34–74.

64. On modernist Javanism, see Kenji Tsuchiya's *Democracy and Leadership: The Rise of the Taman Siswa Movement in Indonesia*, trans. by Peter Hawkes (Honolulu: University of Hawaii Press, 1987).

65. Rita Smith Kipp's study of the Karo Batak shows that a similar differentiation of religion from ethnicity occurred among non-Muslim Indonesians. See her *Dissociated Identities: Ethnicity, Religion, and Class in an Indonesian Society* (Ann Arbor: University of Michigan Press, 1993).

66. Gavin W. Jones and Chris Manning, "Labour Force and Employment during the 1980s," in Anne Booth, ed., *The Oil Boom and After: Indonesian Economic Policy and Performance in the Soeharto Era* (Kuala Lumpur: Oxford University Press, 1992), pp. 363–410.

67. Terence H. Hull and Gavin W. Jones, "Demographic Perspectives," in Hal Hill, ed., *Indonesia's New Order: The Dynamics of Socio-Economic Transformation* (Honolulu: University of Hawaii Press, 1994), pp. 123–78.

68. For Sumatran examples, see Bowen, *Muslims through Discourse*; and Kipp, *Dissociated Identities*; for rural East Java, see Hefner, *The Political Economy of Mountain Java*.

69. Adam Schwarz, *A Nation in Waiting: Indonesia in the 1990s* (Boulder, Colo.: Westview, 1994), p. 164.

70. On government restrictions on business associations, see Andrew MacIntyre, *Business and Politics in Indonesia* (Sydney: Allen & Unwin, 1990).

71. It also meddled in the affairs of other religions. For a Hindu example, see Carol Warren, *Adat and Dinas: Balinese Communities in the Indonesian State* (Kuala Lumpur: Oxford University Press, 1993); for an example from a localized religion, see Joel C. Kuipers, *Power in Performance: The Creation of Textual Authority in Weyewa Ritual Speech* (Philadelphia: University of Pennsylvania Press, 1990).

72. Andrée Feillard, *Islam et armée dans l'Indonésie contemporaine* (Paris: L'Harmattan, 1995), pp. 146–50.

73. Among many fine anthropological studies, see Lorraine V. Aragon, "Revised Rituals in Central Sulawesi: The Maintenance of Traditional Cosmological Concepts in the Face of Allegiance to World Religion," *Anthropological Forum* 6:3 (1992): 371–84; Jane Atkinson, "Religions in Dialogue: The Construction of an Indonesian Minority Religion," *American Ethnologist* 10:4 (1983): 684–96; Kenneth M. George, *Showing Signs of Violence: The Cultural Politics of a Twentieth-Century Headhunting Ritual* (Berkeley: University of California Press, 1996); Janet Hoskins, "Entering the Bitter House: Spirit Worship and Conversion in West Sumba," in Rita Smith Kipp and Susan Rodgers, eds., *Indonesian Religions in Transition* (Tucson: University of Arizona Press, 1987), pp. 136–160; Kipp, *Dissociated Identities*; Patricia Spyer, "Serial Conversion/Conversion to Seriality: Religion, State, and Number in Aru, Eastern Indonesia," in P. van der Veer, ed., *Conversion to Modernities: The Globalization of Christianity* (London: Routledge, 1996), pp. 171–98; Mary Margaret Steedly, *Hanging Without a Rope: Narrative Experience in Colonial and Postcolonial Karoland* (Princeton, N.J.: Princeton University Press, 1993); and Toby Alice Volkman, *Feasts of Honor: Ritual and Change in the Toraja Highlands* (Urbana: University of Illinois Press, 1985).

74. Examples of the privatization of once public village traditions include Sven Cederroth's *Survival and Profit in Rural Java: The Case of an East Javanese Village* (London: Curzon, 1995); Kipp, *Dissociated Identities*; and M. Bambang Pranowo, "Creating Islamic Tradition in Rural Java," Ph.D. dissertation, Department of Anthropology and Sociology, Monash University, Melbourne, Australia, 1991.

75. On the killings, see Robert Cribb, ed., *The Indonesian Killings: Studies from Java and Bali* (Clayton, Victoria: Center for Southeast Asian Studies, Monash University, 1990); and Hefner, *The Political Economy*, pp. 193–227.

76. On diversion from Islam, see Hyung-Jun Kim, "Reformist Muslims in a Yogyakarta Village," Ph.D. dissertation, Department of Anthropology, Australian National University, Canberra, 1996; and Margaret L. Lyon, "Politics and Religious Identity: Genesis of a Javanese-Hindu Movement in Rural Central Java," Ph.D. dissertation, Department of Anthropology, University of California, Berkeley: 1977.

77. See Julia Day Howell, Subandi, and Peter L. Nelson, "Indonesian Sufism: Signs of Resurgence," in Peter B. Clarke, ed., *New Trends and Developments in the World of Islam* (Somerset, England: Luzac Oriental Press, 1998), pp. 277–97.

78. On the reception of democratic ideals by Muslim intellectuals, see Masykuri Abdillah, *Responses of Indonesian Muslim Intellectuals to the Concept of Democracy (1966–1993)* (Hamburg: Abera Verlag Meyer, 1997).

79. On government concessions to Islam, see Bahtiar Effendy, "Islam and the State: The Transformation of Islamic Political Ideas and Practices in Indonesia," Ph.D. dissertation, Department of Political Science, Ohio State University, Columbus, Ohio, 1994.

80. This impression of Soeharto as a pluralist and tolerant if authoritarian ruler informs Douglas Ramage's otherwise insightful *Politics in Indonesia*.

81. For an example of how rivalries among state elites exacerbated conflicts in society during the late Soekarno era, see the moving account in Geoffrey Robinson's *Dark Side of Paradise: Political Violence in Bali* (Ithaca: Cornell University Press, 1995).

CHAPTER TWO
CIVIL PRECEDENCE

1. See Max Weber, *The Protestant Ethic and the Spirit of Capitalism* (New York: Scribner's, 1958).

2. Max Weber, *Economy and Society: An Outline of Interpretive Sociology*, ed. Guenther Roth and Claus Wittich (Berkeley: University of California Press, 1968).

3. This was the methodological premise of Clifford Geertz's *Peddlers and Princes: Social Development and Economic Change in Two Indonesian Towns* (Chicago: University of Chicago Press, 1963). Geertz set out to identify actors in Java and Bali who could play an entrepreneurial role akin to that of the Weber's mythical Calvinist. Geertz's study succeeded in highlighting dimensions of Indonesian economic life overlooked in macroeconomic accounts. As an explanation of what is required to achieve market growth, however, Geertz's analysis was still sorely wanting, failing as it did to address the question of the state's role in capitalist growth.

4. These concepts of social capital resemble Pierre Bourdieu's notion of *symbolic capital* but also differ in that they apply only to markets and democracy. The two approaches agree in asserting that there are nonmaterial resources in society, such as status, trust, or good will, that can be accumulated by social agents and used as down payments for other social "goods." In Bourdieu's Algerian study, a Kabylian lineage head uses gifts to his subordinates to accumulate good will and allegiance deployable in later battles with rivals. Bourdieu's symbolic capital is a more general currency, then, deployed toward any number of ends, not just market efficiency or democratic politics. See Pierre Bourdieu, *Outline of a Theory of Practice* (Cambridge: Cambridge University Press, 1977).

5. Putnam, *Making Democracy Work*, p. 167.

6. On the role of networks in overseas Chinese capitalism, see Gary Hamilton, "Culture and Organization in Taiwan's Market Economy," in Robert W. Hefner, *Market Cultures: Society and Morality in the New Asian Capitalisms* (Boulder, Colo.: Westview, 1998), pp. 41–77.

7. On markets and "embeddedness," see Mark Granovetter, "Economic Action and Social Structure: The Problem of Embeddedness," *American Journal of Sociology* 91 (1985): 481–510. For a view from East Asia, see my "Introduction: Society and Morality in the New Asian Capitalisms," in Hefner, *Market Cultures*, pp. 1–38.

8. Alexis de Tocqueville, *Democracy in America*, trans. George Lawrence, ed. J. P. Mayer, vol. 1 (Garden City, N.Y.: Doubleday, 1969), p. 192.

9. Putnam, *Making Democracy Work*, p. 144.

10. Ibid., pp. 121.

11. Ibid., pp. 124–125.

12. Ibid., pp. 173–174.

13. Ibid., p. 176.

14. Anton C. Zijderveld, "Civil Society, Pillarization, and the Welfare State," in Hefner, *Democratic Civility*, pp. 153–171.

15. The quote here is from Peter Evans, "Government Action, Social Capital and Development," p. 1124.

16. For ethnographic examinations of Muslims and religious diversity, see John R. Bowen, *Muslims through Discourse,* esp. pp. 18–47; Mark R. Woodward, *Islam in Java: Normative Piety and Mysticism in the Sultanate of Yogyakarta* (Tucson: University of Arizona Press, 1989), esp. pp. 60–124; and my *Hindu Javanese: Tengger Tradition and Islam* (Princeton, N.J.: Princeton University Press, 1985), esp. pp. 126–41.

17. For anthropological critiques of the bounded-society model, see Fredrik Barth, "Towards Greater Naturalism in Conceptualizing Societies," in Kuper, *Conceptualizing Society,* pp. 17–33; and Ulf Hannerz, "The Global Ecumene as a Network of Networks," in *idem,* 34–56.

18. Anthony Reid, *Southeast Asia in the Age of Commerce, 1450–1680,* Vol. 2: *Expansion and Crisis* (New Haven: Yale University Press, 1993).

19. The classic essay on the political culture of these Indic states is R. von Heine-Geldern, "Concepts of State and Kingship in Southeast Asia, *Far Eastern Quarterly* 2 (1942): 15–30. Among the better recent treatments are O. W. Wolter, *The Fall of Srivijaya in Malay History* (Ithaca: Cornell University Press, 1970), esp. chap. 8; Theodore G. Th. Pigeaud, *Java in the Fourteenth Century: A Study in Cultural History,* 5 vols. (The Hague: Martinus Nijhoff, 1960–62); and Clifford Geertz, *Negara: The Theatre State in Nineteenth-Century Bali* (Princeton, N.J.: Princeton University Press, 1980).

20. John A. Hall, *Powers and Liberties: The Causes and Consequences of the Rise of the West* (Berkeley: University of California Press, 1985); Ernest Gellner, *Conditions of Liberty: Civil Society and Its Rivals* (New York: Penguin, 1994); and Max Weber, *The City* (New York: Free Press, 1958).

21. On the cultural interaction among Islam, Malay, and mercantilism in the early modern archipelago, see James T. Collins, *Malay, World Language: A Short History* (Kuala Lumpur: Dewan Bahasa dan Pustaka, 1998).

22. This is not to deny that there were numerous local instances of religious warfare.

23. For a West African example of "quarantined" Islam see Robin Horton, "African Conversion," in *Africa* 41 (1971): 85–108; and I. M. Lewis, "Introduction," in I. M. Lewis, ed., *Islam in Tropical Africa,* 2nd ed. (Bloomington: University of Indiana Press, 1980), pp. 1–98.

24. See Stuart Robson, "Java at the Crossroads," *Bijdragen tot de Taal-, Land-, en Volkenkunde,* 137 (1981): 259–92.

25. See, for example, Pierre-Yves Manguin, "L'introduction de l'Islam au Campa," in *Bulletin de l'Ecole Francaise d'Extreme-Orient* 66 (1979): 255–69; and Reid, *Southeast Asia in the Age of Commerce,* pp. 186–92.

26. See Thomas M. McKenna, "Appreciating Islam in the Muslim Philippines: Authority, Experience, and Identity in Cotabato," in Hefner and Horvatich, *Islam in an Era of Nation-States,* pp. 43–73.

27. Anthony Milner, "Islam and the Muslim State," in M. B. Hooker, ed., *Islam in South-East Asia* (Leiden: Brill, 1983), pp. 23–49.

28. See Theodore G. Th. Pigeaud and H. J. de Graaf, *Islamic States in Java, 1500–1700* (The Hague: Martinus Nijhoff, 1976); and H. J. de Graaf, *De Regering van Sultan Agung, vorst van Mataram, 1613–1646, en die van zign voorganger panembahan Seda-ing-Krapjak, 1601–1613,* no. 23 (The Hague: Verhandelingean van het Koninklijk Instituut voor Taal-, Land-, en Volkenkunde, 1958); and Stuart O. Robson, "Java at the Crossroads," in *Bijdragen tot de Taal-, Land-, en Volkenkunde* 137 (1981): 259–92.

29. Clifford Geertz, *Islam Observed: Religious Development in Morocco and Indonesia* (Chicago: University of Chicago Press, 1968).

30. On Islam in colonial Java's arts, see Laurie J. Sears, *Shadows of Empire*; and Nancy K. Florida, *Writing the Past, Inscribing the Future: History as Prophecy in Colonial Java* (Durham, N.C.: Duke University Press, 1995).

31. See Tomé Pires, *The Suma Oriental of Tomé Pires*, trans. Armando Cortesao (London: Hakluyt Society, 1944 [orig. 1515]), p. 177. See also Reid, *Southeast Asia*, pp. 178–79. In eastern Java, a small Hindu kingdom survived into the eighteenth century in the Blambangan region (across the straits from Bali). Just to the west in the Tengger mountains a population of mountain-dwelling Hindus has survived to this day. On Blambangan, see Andrew Beatty, *Varieties of Javanese Religion: An Anthropological Account* (Cambridge: Cambridge University Press, Studies in Social and Cultural Anthropology No. 111, 1999); on Tengger, see my own *Hindu Javanese: Tengger Tradition and Islam* (Princeton, N.J.: Princeton University Press, 1985), pp. 44–64, 126–41.

32. Milner, "Islam and the Muslim State"; Mark R. Woodward, *Islam in Java*.

33. Geertz, *The Religion of Java*; Woodward, *Islam in Java*.

34. Reid, *Southeast Asia*, pp. 182–83; see also B. Schrieke, "Ruler and Realm in Early Java," in *Indonesian Sociological Studies: Selected Writings of B. Schrieke*, vol. 2 (The Hague: Van Hoeve, 1955–57), pp. 102–3.

35. Sixteenth- and nineteenth-century Aceh provides some of the best examples of state-enforced orthodoxy. See Bowen, *Muslims through Discourse*, p. 20.

36. See, for instance, Milner, "Islam and the Muslim State," p. 29; Reid, *Southeast Asia*, p. 183.

37. See Thomas Stamford Raffles, *The History of Java*, vol. 2 (Kuala Lumpur: Oxford University Press, 1965 [orig. 1817]), p. 280; and M. B. Hooker, *A Concise Legal History of South-East Asia* (Oxford: Clarendon, 1978), p. 72. The subordination of *shariah* courts to royal authority is, of course, not peculiar to Southeast Asian Islam.

38. Reid, *Southeast Asia*, p. 253.

39. Ibid., p. 264.

40. See R. Michael Feener, "In the Realm of the Fifth Caliph: Sufism and the State in the Sultanate of Buton," unpublished paper, Department of Religious Studies, Boston University; and Andi' Zainal Abidin, "The Emergence of Early Kingdoms in South Sulawesi: A Preliminary Remark on Governmental Contracts from the Thirteenth to the Fifteenth Century," *Southeast Asian Studies* 20:4 (March 1983): 1–39.

41. Reid, *Southeast Asia*, p. 14.

42. See Lombard, *Le Carrefour Javanais*, Vol. 2: *Les réseaux asiatiques*, pp. 169–76.

43. See Martin van Gelderen, "The Machiavellian Moment and the Dutch Revolt: The Rise of Neostoicism and Dutch Republicanism," in G. Bock, Quentin Skinner, and Maurizio Viroli, eds., *Machiavelli and Republicanism* (Cambridge: Cambridge University Press, 1990), pp. 205–23.

44. See Anthony J. Reid, *The Contest for North Sumatra: Acheh, the Netherlands, and Britain, 1858–1898* (Kuala Lumpur: Oxford University Press, 1969); and M. C. Ricklefs, *A History of Modern Indonesia since c. 1300*, 2nd ed. (Bloomington: Indiana University Press, 1993), pp. 143–45.

45. On Dutch controls on the *ulama* and the pilgrimage, see Jacob Vredenbregt, "The Haddj: Some of Its Features and Functions in Indonesia," *Bijdragen tot de Taal-, Land- en Volkenkunde* 118 (1962): 92–153. On Snouck Hurgronje, see Harry J. Benda, *The*

Crescent and the Rising Sun: Indonesian Islam under the Japanese Occupation, 1942–1945 (Dordrecht: Foris, 1983 [orig. 1958]), pp. 20–22.

46. Roy F. Ellen, "Social Theory, Ethnography, and the Understanding of Practical Islam in South-East Asia," in M. B. Hooker, ed., *Islam in South-East Asia* (Leiden: Brill, 1983), p. 65; William R. Roff, "Islam Obscured? Some Reflections on Studies of Islam and Society in Southeast Asia," in *L'Islam en Indonésie, Archipel* 1 (special issue) (1985): 7–34.

47. This fine phrase is from Florida, *Writing the Past*, p. 29.

48. Ibid., pp. 26–30; cf. M. C. Ricklefs, *Jogjakarta under Sultan Mangkubumi, 1749–1792: A History of the Division of Java* (London: Oxford University Press, 1974), pp. 176–226.

49. See Sears, *Shadows of Empire*, esp. pp. 34–100.

50. Eric Hobsbawm and Terence Ranger, eds., *The Invention of Tradition* (Cambridge: Cambridge University Press, 1983).

51. M. B. Hooker, "Muhammadan Law and Islamic Law," in Hooker, *Islam in Southeast Asia*, pp. 160–82.

52. James T. Siegel, *The Rope of God* (Berkeley: University of California Press, 1969); Taufik Abdullah, "Adat and Islam: An Examination of Conflict in Minangkabau," *Indonesia* 2 (October 1966) 1–26.

53. Abdullah, "Adat and Islam," p. 10. See also Daniel S. Lev, *Islamic Courts in Indonesia: A Study in the Political Bases of Legal Institutions* (Berkeley: University of California Press,1972) p. 250.

54. On these points Dutch policies resembled those of the French in Berber regions of Morocco. There, too, in contrast with their policies among Arabs, colonial authorities highlighted ethnic tradition in an effort to undermine the influence of Islam. See Munson, *Religion and Power in Morocco*, p. 103.

55. Sartono Kartodirjo, "Agrarian Radicalism in Java: Its Setting and Development," in Claire Holt, ed., *Culture and Politics in Indonesia* (Ithaca: Cornell University Press, 1972), p. 89.

56. Kartodirdjo, "Agrarian Radicalism," p. 113. For a Sumatran comparison from a few decades earlier, see Christine Dobbin, *Islamic Revivalism in a Changing Peasant Economy: Central Sumatra, 1784–1847* (Copenhagen: Curzon, 1983), pp. 128–41. For an analysis of this same process in the early twentieth century, see Kenneth Young, *Islamic Peasants and the State: The 1908 Anti-Tax Rebellion in West Sumatra*, Monograph 40, (New Haven: Monograph 40, Yale Southeast Asia Studies, Yale Center for International and Area Studies, 1994).

57. See William R. Roff, *The Origins of Malay Nationalism*, 2nd ed. (Kuala Lumpur: Oxford University Press, 1994); and Clive S. Kessler, "Archaicism and Modernity: Contemporary Malay Political Culture," in Joel S. Kahn and Francis Loh Kok Wah, eds., *Fragmented Vision: Culture and Politics in Contemporary Malaysia* (Honolulu: University of Hawaii Press, 1992), pp. 133–57.

58. See Sidney Jones, "The Contraction and Expansion of the 'Umat' and the Role of Nahdatul Ulama in Indonesia," in *Indonesia* 38 (1984): 1–20; and my "Reimagined Community: A Social History of Muslim Education in Pasuruan, East Java," in Charles F. Keyes, Laurel Kendall, and Helen Hardacre, eds., *Asian Visions of Authority: Religion and the Modern States of East and Southeast Asia* (Honolulu: University of Hawaii Press, 1994), pp. 75–95.

59. See Feillard, *Islam et Armée*; and chaps. 5 and 7, below.

60. See, for example, Lance Castles, *Religion, Politics, and Economic Behavior in Java* (New Haven: Southeast Asian Studies, Yale University, 1967); and Clifford Geertz, *The Social History of an Indonesian Town* (Cambridge, Mass.: MIT Press, 1965).

61. This precedent for extra-state initiative was also evident in the growth of modern Islamic schools at the beginning of the twentieth century. See Taufik Abdullah, *Schools and Politics: The Kaum Muda Movement in West Sumatra (1927–1933)* (Ithaca: Monograph series, Modern Indonesia Project, Southeast Asia Program, Cornell University, 1971); and Pradjarta Dirdjosanjoto, *Memelihara Umat*, pp. 69–72. Pradjarta's study also demonstrates that, contrary to Clifford Geertz's observation, the founders of modern Islamic schools were not all theological modernists; some were traditionalists affiliated with Nahdlatul Ulama.

62. The sociologist Resat Kasaba examines a similar tension between traditionalist hierarchy and modern democracy among Sufis in contemporary Turkey. See his "Cohabitation? Islamist and Secular Groups in Modern Turkey," in Hefner, *Democratic Civility*, pp. 265–84.

63. See Abdurrahman Wahid, "Watak Mandiri Pesantren" [The independent face of pesantren], in *Cakrawala* 10: 3 (1977): 17–34; and Pradjarta Dirdjosanjoto, *Memelihara Umat: Kiai Pesantren -Kiai Langgar di Jawa* [To nurture the Muslim community: Pesantren leaders and local religious leaders in Java] (Yogyakarta: LKIS Press, 1999), pp. 140–51.

64. See Benda, *The Crescent and the Rising Sun*, pp. 20–31.

65. Feillard, *Islam et Armée*, pp. 29–30.

CHAPTER THREE
CONTESTS OF NATION

1. The Ottoman Empire had preserved the memory if not the form of a pan-Islamic caliphate until Turkey's national assembly abolished the institution in March 1924. Before this time, most Indonesian Muslims were only vaguely familiar with the institution, although in the 1870s the sultan of Aceh had appealed to the Ottoman sultan for support against Dutch invaders. As Martin van Bruinessen has shown, in the 1920s the growth of the anticolonial movement in the Dutch Indies led some modernist Muslims to become interested in proposals in Egypt and Arabia to revive the defunct institution. But nationalist fervor among Indonesians and the failure of these initiatives ensured that the caliphate and pan-Islamic politics attracted little attention after 1929. See Martin van Bruinessen, "Muslims of the Dutch East Indies and the Caliphate Question," in *Studia Islamika* 2:3 (1995): 115–40.

2. On Qur'anic sanctions and classical Muslim writings on statehood, see James P. Piscatori, *Islam in a World of Nation-States* (Cambridge: Cambridge University Press, 1986), pp. 45–48.

3. See, for example, Albert Hourani, *A History of the Arab Peoples* (Cambridge, Mass.: Belknap Press of Harvard University Press, 1991), pp. 343–49, 401–7.

4. See John L. Esposito, "Muhammad Iqbal and the Islamic State," in *Voices of Resurgent Islam*, ed. John L. Esposito (New York: Oxford University Press, 1983), pp. 175–90

5. On this consensus and nonconformist critiques, see Piscatori, *Islam in a World of Nation-States*. One of the most famous holdouts on nationhood was the journalist-

turned-militant Sayyid Qutb, executed by Egyptian authorities in 1966. See his "Muslim's Nationality and Belief," in *Milestones* (Indianapolis: American Trust Publications, 1993), pp. 101–10. For an overview of Qutb, see Ahmad S. Moussalli, *Radical Islamic Fundamentalism: The Ideological and Political Discourse of Sayyid Qutb* (Beiruit: American University of Beiruit, 1992).

6. The idea that religion may figure in nationalist appeals runs contrary to the modernist narratives that dominated Western social theory for most of the twentieth century and some postmodern critical scholarship still today. Although modernization theory has long since faded, its influence is sometimes still seen in unexpected places. In an important postmodernist essay on nationalism, for example, Benedict Anderson has implied that, by its very nature, the nation is secular:

> It [the nation] is imagined as *sovereign* because the concept was born in an age in which Enlightenment and Revolution were destroying the legitimacy of the divinely ordained, hierarchical dynastic realm. Coming to maturity at a stage of human history when even the most devout adherents of any universal religion were inescapably confronted with the living *pluralism* of such religions, and the allomorphism between each faith's ontological claims and territorial stretch, nations dream of being free, and, if under God, directly so.

See Benedict R. O'G. Anderson, *Imagined Communities: Reflections on the Origin and Spread of Nationalism*, rev. ed. (London: Verso, 1991), p. 7. If the nation and nationalism in Asia and the Middle East, not to mention the United States, have demonstrated anything, however, it is that believers' confrontation with the plurality of religions by no means pushes them to this "inescapable" conclusion. Religious nationalism often emerges in reaction *against* this pluralism. For Indian examples, see Peter van der Veer, *Religious Nationalism: Hindus and Muslims in India* (Berkeley: University of California Press, 1993); and T. N. Madan, "Secularism in Its Place," in *Journal of Asian Studies* 46:4 (1987): 747–59.

7. In the case of Indonesia, the term *nonconfessional*, or *multiconfessional*, *nationalism* captures the majority view among non-Islamist nationalists better than the term *secular nationalism*. *Secular nationalism* implies a high wall between religion and state, so that religion is personal not public. Indonesia's non-Muslim nationalists, like their counterparts in much of the Muslim world, have been less insistent than Western liberals on the need to privatize religion. Like Soekarno, many have been willing to grant religious organizations a prominent role in public life, although without giving any single religion a privileged role. Rather than being fully *secular*, then, Indonesian nationalism has tended to be *non-* or *multiconfessional*. The state ideology, or *Pancasila*, illustrates this tendency well.

8. For general analyses of the tension between secular and Islamic nationalism, see Roy, *The Failure of Political Islam*. For global comparisons, see Mark Juergensmeyer, *The New Cold War? Religious Nationalism Confronts the Secular State* (Berkeley: University of California Press, 1993).

9. See George Mc. T. Kahin, *Nationalism and Revolution in Indonesia* (Ithaca: Cornell University Press, 1952), pp. 65–77; and Harry J. Benda, *The Crescent and the Rising Sun: Indonesian Islam under the Japanese Occupation, 1942–1945* (Dordrecht: Foris, 1983), pp. 42–47.

10. For an analysis of this tension in the Solo region of Java, see Takashi Shiraishi, *An Age in Motion: Popular Radicalism in Java, 1912–1926* (Ithaca: Cornell University Press, 1990).

11. Anderson, *Imagined Communities*, p. 105.

12. Soekarno presented this view in his, "Apa Sebab Turki Memisah Agama dari Negara" [Why has Turkey separated religion from state?], in his collected essays, *Diba-wah Bendera Revolusi* [Under the flag of revolution] (Jakarta: Panitia Penerbitan, 1964), pp. 404–7.

13. This Islamic network preceded by more than a century the colonization of the late nineteenth century. On the cultural ties between the Middle East and the East Indies, see Azyumardi Azra, "The Transmission of Islamic Reformism to Indonesia: Networks of Middle Eastern and Malay-Indonesian 'Ulama' in the Seventeenth and Eighteenth Centuries," Ph.D. dissertation, Department of History, Columbia University, New York, 1992.

14. The speed with which reformist ideas spread in the Indies also shows why it is misleading to say that "in complete contrast" to government schools Muslim religious schools "were always local and personal enterprises" (see Anderson, *Imagined Communities*, p. 111). On the role of Islamic reformism as a carrier of a distinctively Islamic nationalism, see Taufik Abdullah, *Schools and Politics: The Kaum Muda Movement in West Sumatra (1927–1933)* (Ithaca: Cornell University, Southeast Asia Program, Modern Indonesia Project, Monograph series, 1971); and John R. Bowen, *Muslims through Discourse*, pp. 39–73.

15. On the connotations of ʿasabiyah in Islamic political discourse, see Fuad Baali, " ʿAsabiyah," in John L. Esposito, ed., *The Oxford Encyclopedia of the Modern Islamic World*, vol.1 (New York: Oxford University Press, 1996), p. 140.

16. For Muslim arguments against secular nationalism in the late-colonial era, see Deliar Noer, *The Modernist Muslim Movement in Indonesia, 1900–1942*; (Kuala Lumpur: Oxford University Press, 1973), pp. 259–66.

17. On contemporary Indonesian exponents of Islam as a "total" (*kaffah*) social and value system, see M. Syafi'i Anwar, *Pemikiran dan Aksi Islam Indonesia* (Jakarta: Penerbit Paramadina, 1995), pp. 175–78. On the appeal of Islam as a *nizam* (order, system), see Moussalli, *Radical Islamic Fundamentalism*, pp. 69–70, 87; and Richard P. Mitchell, *The Society of the Muslim Brothers* (New York: Oxford University Press, 1969), pp. 234–45.

18. On al-Afghani, see Nikki R. Keddie, *An Islamic Response to Imperialism: Political and Religious Writings of Sayyid Jamal ad-Din "al-Afghani"* (Berkeley: University of California Press, 1968). On Abduh, see Yvonne Haddad, "Muhammad Abduh: Pioneer of Islamic Reform," in Ali Rahnema, *Pioneers of Islamic Revival* (London: Zed, 1994), pp. 30–63.

19. See James L. Peacock, *Muslim Puritans: Reformist Psychology in Southeast Asian Islam* (Berkeley: University of California Press, 1978); Alfian, *Muhammadiyah: The Political Behavior of a Muslim Modernist Organization under Dutch Colonialism* (Yogyakarta: Gadjah Mada University Press, 1989); and Mitsuo Nakamura, *The Crescent Arises over the Banyan Tree: A Study of the Muhammadiyah Movement in a Central Javanese Town* (Yogyakarta: Gadjah Mada University Press, 1983).

20. After the founding of Nahdlatul Ulama in 1926, however, the so-called traditionalists introduced extensive educational and organizational reforms. These had a limited impact, however, on the authority of traditionalist scholars. On Islamic reform-

ism in NU, see Martin van Bruinessen, *NU: Tradisi, Relasi-Relasi Kuasa, Pencarian Wacana Baru*, pp. 24–45.

21. This was the general tendency, but it was by no means universal. Founded in Bandung, West Java, in 1923, the Persatuan Islam (Muslim Unity) was less vague on political and ideological matters than were its mainstream counterparts. Its ideology resembled the Muslim Brotherhoods in the Middle East and Mawdudi's Jama'at-i-Islami in Pakistan. It rejected the nation-state as secular, called for an Islamic state, and promoted the full application of Islamic criminal penalties (*hudud*). I discuss the relationship of the Pelajar Islam (PI; Muslim Pupils) to contemporary Indonesian organizations in chapter 5. See also Howard M. Federspiel, *Persatuan Islam: Islamic Reform in Twentieth Century Indonesia* (Ithaca: Cornell University, Southeast Asia Program, Modern Indonesia Project, Monograph series, 1970).

22. Perhaps the best example of such a figure was Indonesia's first vice president, Mohammad Hatta. A devout Muslim from Minangkabau, Sumatra, Hatta was an early supporter of the Nationalist Party, and an unusually articulate advocate of constitutional democracy and the rule of law. See Mavis Rose, *Indonesia Free: A Political Biography of Mohammad Hatta* (Ithaca: Cornell University, Southeast Asia Program, Modern Indonesia Project, Monograph series no. 67, 1987).

23. Japanese sensitivity to Islam is apparent in the report on a West Java village written by a Japanese researcher during the occupation. See Fukuo Ueno, *Desa Cimahi: Analysis of a Village on Java during the Japanese Occupation (1943)*, ed. W. J. Hendrix and S.C.N. de Jong (Rotterdam: Erasmus University, Comparative Asian Studies Program, 1988), esp. pp. 121–28.

24. See, for example, Benda, *The Crescent and the Rising Sun*, pp. 183–94.

25. On Soekarno and the *Pancasila*, see Kahin, *Nationalism and Revolution in Indonesia*, pp. 122–26. Although many people have dismissed the *Pancasila* as ideological mish-mash, Kahin's 1952 characterization captures well the doctrine's appeal. He writes:

> Soekarno formulated with clarity the ideas which were dominant but inchoate in the minds of many educated Indonesians and . . . he did so in a language and a symbolism much of which was and remains meaningful to the uneducated rank and file. Probably in no other exposition of principle can one find a better example of the synthesis of Western democratic, Modernist Islamic, Marxist, and indigenous-village democratic and communalistic ideas which forms the general basis of the social thought of so large a part of the post-war Indonesian political elite. (p. 123).

Recently Andrée Feillard has shown that Soekarno consulted with three prominent Muslim leaders before presenting the Pancasila to the public; all three leaders saw the principles as consistent with Islamic teachings. See Feillard, *Islam et Armée*, pp. 38–40.

26. On the circumstances surrounding formulation of the charter, see B. J. Boland, *The Struggle of Islam in Modern Indonesia* (The Hague: Martinus Nijhoff, 1982), pp. 25–33.

27. Although a small concession for some Muslims, this rephrasing had serious implications for non-Muslims. After the state began, after 1965, to enforce its requirement that citizens profess a religion, practitioners of ethnic religions came under great pressure to convert. At the same time, Buddhists and Hindus—whose religions were not recognized as official options for Indonesians until the early 1960s—were obliged to

reform their beliefs along monotheistic lines. On this challenge for Balinese Hindus, see F. L. Bakker, *The Struggle of the Hindu Balinese Intellectuals* (Amsterdam: VU University Press, 1993). For Chinese Indonesians, see, Leo Suryadinata, *The Culture of the Chinese Minority in Indonesia* (Singapore: Times Books International, 1997), pp. 125–94.

28. The sense of betrayal was vividly remembered in the 1980s and 1990s, when the Jakarta Charter was again debated. For a pro-charter view, see H. Endang Saifuddin Anshari, *Piagam Jakarta 22 Juni 1945 dan sejarah konsensus nasional antara nasionalis Islamis dan nasionalis sekular* [The Jakarta Charter of June 1945 and the history of the national consensus between Muslim and secular nationalists] (Bandung: Perpustakaan Salman ITB, Monograph no. 26, 1981).

29. See chapter 4 below, and Herbert Feith, *The Decline of Constitutional Democracy in Indonesia* (Ithaca: Cornell University Press, 1962), pp. 92–97.

30. See Herbert Feith, *The Indonesian Elections of 1955* (Ithaca: Cornell University, Interim Report series, Modern Indonesia Project, 1957), pp. 58–59.

31. A handful of delegates in the assembly advocated a third way between the Islamists and the *Pancasilaists*, a "socialist economic" road, but this option never attracted much support.

32. See Nasution, *The Aspiration for Constitutional Government in Indonesia*. For a discussion of the disputes relating to the Jakarta Charter, see Boland, *The Struggle of Islam*, pp. 85–99.

33. On Sjahrir's career and imprisonment, see Rudolf Mrazek, *Sjahrir: Politics and Exile in Indonesia* (Ithaca: Cornell University, Southeast Asia Program, 1994). There is still no full-length, English-language treatment of Natsir's role in Indonesian politics and Islam. Natsir's role in Muslim politics through 1965 is chronicled in Deliar Noer, *Partai Islam di Pentas Nasional* [Islamic parties on the national stage] (Jakarta: Grafiti Pers, 1987).

34. See Harold Crouch, *The Army and Politics in Indonesia* (Ithaca: Cornell University Press, 1978); Ulf Sundhaussen, "The Military: Structure, Procedures, and Effects on Indonesian Society," in Karl Jackson and Lucian Pye, eds., *Political Power and Communications in Indonesia* (Berkeley: University of California Press, 1978), pp. 45–81; and Robert Lowry, *The Armed Forces of Indonesia* (St. Leonards, Australia: Allen & Unwin, 1996).

35. On military support for Guided Democracy, see Daniel S. Lev, *The Transition to Guided Democracy: Indonesian Politics, 1957–1959* (Ithaca: Cornell University, Southeast Asia Program, Modern Indonesia Project, Monograph series, 1966) , pp. 182–200; and Crouch, *The Army and Politics*, pp. 43–68.

36. On Soekarno's ideological alchemy, see Ruth T. McVey, "Nationalism, Islam, and Marxism: The Management of Ideological Conflict in Indonesia," introduction to Soekarno's "Nationalism, Islam and Marxism" (Ithaca: Cornell University, Modern Indonesia Project, 1970), pp. 1–33.

37. On the army's role in the decline of the parliamentary system, see Lev, *The Transition to Guided Democracy*, pp. 44–74, 176–201.

38. R. William Liddle, "Modernizing Indonesian Politics," in Liddle, ed., *Political Participation in Modern Indonesia* (New Haven: Yale University, Southeast Asian Studies, Monograph series no. 19, 1973), p. 179.

39. Feith, *The Decline of Constitutional Democracy in Indonesia*, p. 134.

40. Allan A. Samson, "Religious Belief and Political Action in Indonesian Islamic Modernism," in Liddle, *Political Participation in Modern Indonesia*, p. 123. Compare his "Islam and Politics in Indonesia," Ph.D. dissertation, Department of Political Science, University of California, Berkeley, 1972, esp. pp. 213–53.

41. On the life and ideals of Anwar Harjono, see Lukman Hakiem, *Perjalanan Mencari Keadilan dan Persatuan: Biografi Dr. Anwar Harjono, S.H.* [A journey in search of justice and unity: A biography of Dr. Anwar Harjono] (Jakarta: Media Dakwah, 1993). Later in the New Order period Harjono would be active in the "Petition of 50" group that protested against the New Order government. In 1993 he would succeed Mohammad Natsir as head of the Dewan Dakwah Islamiyah Indonesia (DDII) and lead it in an unexpectedly accommodating direction. See chapters 5–7, below.

42. For an HMI member's view of this period, see Agussalim Sitompul, *HMI Dalam Pandangan Seorang Pendeta* [The Indonesian Muslim Students Association in the eyes of a Christian minister] (Jakarta: Gunung Agung, 1982), esp. pp. 56–73.

43. This information is based on interviews with local HMI activists in Malang and Jakarta in 1985, 1991, and 1992.

44. For an example of the impact of this proselytization, see my "The Political Economy of Islamic Conversion in Modern East Java," in William Roff, ed., *Islam and the Political Economy of Meaning: Comparative Studies of Muslim Discourse* (London: Croom Helm, 1987), pp. 53–78.

45. Lance Castles, *Religion, Politics, and Economic Behavior in Java: The Kudus Cigarette Industry* (New Haven: Yale University, Southeast Asia Studies, Cultural Report series no. 15, pp. 67–68.

46. See J.A.C. Mackie, *Konfrontasi: The Indonesia-Malaysia Dispute, 1963–1966* (New York: Oxford University Press [for the Australian Institute of International Affairs], 1974).

47. Rex Mortimer, *Indonesian Communism under Sukarno: Ideology and Politics, 1959–1965* (Ithaca: Cornell University Press, 1974), p. 300.

48. Mortimer, *Indonesian Communism under Sukarno*, p. 303.

49. On the Madiun rebellion, see M. C. Ricklefs, *A History of Modern Indonesia since c. 1300*, 2nd ed. (Stanford: Stanford University Press, 1993), pp. 227–30; and Ann Swift, *The Road to Madiun: The Indonesian Communist Uprising of 1948* (Ithaca: Cornell University, Monograph series no. 69, Modern Indonesia Project, 1989).

50. George Mc. Kahin, *Nationalism and Revolution*, p. 300.

51. Geertz, *The Religion of Java*; and Robert Jay, *Religion and Politics in Rural Central Java* (New Haven: Yale University, Southeast Asian Studies, Cultural Report series no. 12, 1963). For a moving account of the Madiun carnage, see Jay, "History and Personal Experience: Religious and Political Conflict in Java," in Robert F. Spencer, ed., *Religion and Change in Contemporary Asia* (Minneapolis: University of Minnesota Press, 1971), pp. 143–64.

52. See Mortimer, *Indonesian Communism under Sukarno*, p. 281; and Peter Edman, *"Communism a la Aidit": The Indonesian Communist Party under D. N. Aidit, 1950–1965* (Townsville, Australia: Centre for Southeast Asian Studies, Monograph no. 23, James Cook University, 1995), pp. 38–66.

53. Mortimer, *Indonesian Communism*, p. 403. The term *aliran* refers to the vertical "streams" in Indonesia organized around religious ideology. Solidarity within *aliran* is overdetermined by politics and social class, not just religion.

54. Ibid., p. 276.

55. See ibid., pp. 278–84.

56. See ibid., p. 279. Ethnographic materials confirm this tendency for some rural PKI cadre to come from middle or even privileged backgrounds. For the Kediri region, for example, see Robert Jay, *Javanese Villagers: Social Relations in Rural Modjokuto* (Cambridge, Mass.: MIT Press, 1969), p. 434; for upland Pasuruan, see my *Political Economy*, pp. 202–6. This tendency is not surprising, of course, particularly in strongly Javanist areas where affiliation with Muslim parties was unthinkable. In these communities the PKI was often not the party of class struggle but a populist alternative to the PNI establishment.

57. On the law's genesis and provisions, see E. Utrecht, "Land Reform in Indonesia," *Bulletin of Indonesian Economic Studies* 5:3 (November 1969): 71–88.

58. For examples of local conflicts, see Kenneth R. Young, "Local and National Influences in the Violence of 1965," in Robert Cribb, ed., *The Indonesian Killings, 1965–1966: Studies from Java and Bali* (Clayton, Victoria, Australia: Monash University, Centre of Southeast Asian Studies, Monash Papers no. 21, 1990), pp. 63–99. On the PKI campaign in general, see Mortimer, *Indonesian Communism*, pp. 295–303; and Gerrit Huizer, "Peasant Mobilisation and Land Reform in Indonesia," *Review of Indonesian and Malayan Affairs* 8 (1975): 81–138.

59. The NU's social organization differed profoundly from the PKI. The relationship between national leaders and local religious scholars was, in particular, notoriously ill coordinated. Although the NU's national administration had been reorganized in the 1950s, its rural base was not. Despite these flaws, NU proved effective at harnessing its supporters against the PKI, not least of all in the violence of 1965–66. On the organizational divide between the rural scholars and NU's national organization, see Andree Feillard, *Islam et Armée*, pp. 157–59.

60. See John Bresnan, *Managing Indonesia: The Modern Political Economy* (New York: Columbia University Press, 1993), pp. 16–17.

61. Ernest Utrecht, a Dutch Indonesian who had helped draft the legislation (later involved in a bitter conflict with the Muslim Students Organization), noted that one study indicated that in the whole of Java, Madura, South Sulawesi, Bali, and Lombok, only fifty-four hundred people owned more than the legal limit, though a greater number controlled holdings above these limits through rental and pawning. See Utrecht, "Land Reform in Indonesia," p.73.

62. One of the finest studies of this difference remains Castles's, *Religion, Politics, and Economic Behavior in Java*. For a recent view, see Pradjarta Dirdjosanjoto, *Memelihara Umat*.

63. Even in non-Muslim areas, there were parallel "communalizations" of politics. In Bali the PKI became embroiled in rivalries between caste groups. See Young, "Local and National Influences in the Violence of 1965," pp. 91–92; Robert Cribb, Soe Hok Gie et al., "The Mass Killings in Bali," in Cribb, *The Indonesian Killings*, pp. 241–60; and the haunting account in Geoffry Robinson, *The Dark Side of Paradise: Political Violence in Bali* (Ithaca: Cornell University Press, 1995).

64. See Young, "Local and National Influences in the Violence of 1965," p. 77.

65. In discussions with HMI and PII activists in East Java in the 1970s and 1980s, I was surprised to see that this incident is still vividly remembered.

66. See Jacob Walkin, "The Moslem-Communist Confrontation in East Java, 1964–1965," in *Orbis* 13:3 (Fall 1969): 829–30. Walkin was an American Foreign Service Officer stationed at the American Consulate in Surabaya.

67. Walkin, "The Moslem-Communist Confrontation," p. 829.

68. See Feillard, *Islam et Armée*, pp. 54–77.

69. Mortimer, *Indonesian Communism*, pp. 322–23.

70. Benedict R. O'G. Anderson, "Old State, New Society: Indonesia's New Order in Comparative Historical Perspective," in Anderson, *Language and Power: Exploring Political Cultures in Indonesia* (Ithaca: Cornell University Press, 1990 [orig. 1983]), p. 95.

71. Anderson, "Old State, New Society," pp. 102, 109.

72. See Benedict R. O'G. Anderson, "The Idea of Power in Javanese Culture," in Claire Holt, ed., *Culture and Politics in Indonesia* (Ithaca: Cornell University Press, 1972), pp. 1–69.

73. See Michael Mann, "The Autonomous Power of the State: Its Origins, Mechanisms, and Results," in John A. Hall, ed., *States in History* (Oxford: Blackwell, 1986), pp. 109–36.

74. See John A. Hall, "In Search of Civil Society," in Hall, ed., *Civil Society: Theory, History, Comparison* (Cambridge, Polity, 1995), pp. 1–31; and my "On the History and Cross-Cultural Possibility of a Democratic Ideal," in Hefner, *Democratic Civility*, pp. 3–49. In a paper presented a year before the 1997–98 crisis, Nurcholish Madjid made a similar point, emphasizing that state and civil society are not mutually antagonistic but necessarily interdependent. See Madjid, "Potensi Dukungan Budaya Nasional Bagi Reformasi Sosial Politik" [National cultural supports for sociopolitical reform], in Madjid, *Cita-Cita Politik Islam Era Reformasi*, pp. 131–59.

75. Anderson, "Old State, New Society," p. 107.

CHAPTER FOUR
AMBIVALENT ALLIANCES: RELIGION AND POLITICS IN THE EARLY NEW ORDER

1. The best sources on the coup and its aftermath are Cribb, *The Indonesia Killings*; Crouch, *The Army and Politics in Indonesia*, chapter 5; and Robinson, *The Dark Side of Paradise*, pp. 235–302. Benedict R. O'G. Anderson and Ruth McVey, in their *Preliminary Analysis of the October 1, 1965, Coup in Indonesia* (Ithaca: Cornell University, Southeast Asia Program, Modern Indonesia Project, Interim Report series, 1971), raise the controversial but still unresolved possibility that Soeharto himself may have known about the coup leaders' plans.

2. According to a retired officer I interviewed in 1995, the generals' confidence was also based on their belief that they had thoroughly penetrated the Central Committee of the PKI. According to this commander, General Yani boasted of receiving direct reports of each PKI Central Committee meeting just five hours after it occurred.

3. Although the military depends on extra-official revenues to supplement salaries, Nasution was famous for his spartan self-discipline and integrity. In 1993 one visitor to his home remarked to me that the furniture in Nasution's home seemed unchanged since the 1950s.

4. For the text of the announcement of the Thirtieth of September Movement, see "Selected Documents Relating to the 'September 30th Movement' and Its Epilogue," *Indonesia* 1 (April 1966): 134–35.

5. The most comprehensive account of the sequence of events in the coup remains Crouch's, "Coup Attempt," in his *Army and Politics in Indonesia*, pp. 97–134.

6. Again, this is not to say that the coup leaders had necessarily intended to carry out a blood purge. Crouch concluded that the Thirtieth of September Movement may have merely intended to arrest the seven generals, expose their alleged plot, and then hand them over to President Soekarno. For whatever reasons, however, the president refused to support this effort. Without his backing the rebels were doomed. See Crouch, *The Army and Politics*, pp. 125–26.

7. Crouch suggests that the coup leaders probably regarded Soeharto as a taciturn and generally apolitical officer, known for having been on less than cordial terms with Generals Nasution and Yani (two of the generals targeted by the rebels), and unlikely, therefore, to intervene if presented with the facts of the generals' arrest (*The Army and Politics*, pp. 124–25.)

8. Some theorists speculate that this PKI support for the coup was, in fact, a dirty trick carried out by agents provocateurs operating within the party. Certainly this is possible and consistent with much off-stage politics in the late New Order, but there is as yet no proof to confirm this allegation.

9. One retired military official whom I interviewed claimed that before the coup General Yani himself had known that Pranoto was a Communist sympathizer who was relaying information to the PKI (interview, June 25, 1995).

10. Crouch, *The Army and Politics*, pp. 128–34.

11. There were also incidents of sexual torture in killings by civilian vigilantes. See the anonymous "Additional Data on Counter-Revolutionary Cruelty in Indonesia, Especially East Java," in Cribb, *The Indonesian Killings*, pp. 169–76; and "Survival: Bu Yeti's Story," trans. Anto Lucas, in idem, pp. 227–39.

12. Many members of the urban middle class still insist today that they had no idea of the scale of the killing. Some of this denial seems genuine. In contrast, villagers in East Java where I lived can recount the names of victims and their manner of execution.

13. This was a perspective conveyed to me in 1985 and 1991 by an HMI activist who had worked with the East Javanese Brawijaya division during 1965 and again around Blitar in 1968. By his account, he and the action groups concluded in early October that because the PKI might not be banned, the best strategy was to strike quickly and massively, crippling the party forever. See Hefner, *The Political Economy of Mountain Java*, pp. 193–227; and Anonymous, "Report from East Java." Kenneth R. Young provides an excellent analysis of the killings in the Kediri region. There, civilian auxiliaries waited for a sign from the military before acting. But when they moved, they did so with such ferocity that the military had to intervene to limit the bloodshed. See Young, "Local and National Influences in the Violence of 1965," in Cribb, *The Indonesian Killings*, pp. 63–99.

14. On these later killings, see Robert Cribb's translation of Maskun Iskandar and Jopie Lasut, "The Purwodadi Killings: Two Accounts," in Cribb, *The Indonesia Killings*, pp. 195–226. In light of what we shall see shortly about the role of student activists in the anti-PKI campaign, it is interesting to note that these articles, with their allegations of torture and official misconduct, first appeared in *Harian KAMI*, mouthpiece of the anticommunist student action group KAMI. See below.

15. The precise number of people killed is a subject of dispute. A government fact-finding mission in December 1965 estimated that 78,500 people had been killed, but

this figure was dismissed even by commission members. A military study suggested that as many as 1,000,000 people died; another in 1976 put the toll at 500,000. Recently a former American chief of covert actions in Indonesia, B. Hugh Tovar, has suggested that the actual numbers were smaller. Although his analysis provides fascinating insight into American intelligence in 1965, his analysis of the limited scale of the killings lacks proof. See B. Hugh Tovar, "The Indonesian Crisis of 1965–1966: A Retrospective," *International Journal of Intelligence and Counterintelligence* 7:3 (1994) 313–38.

16. Michael van Langenberg, "Gestapu and State Power in Indonesia," in Cribb, *The Indonesian Killings*, p. 52.

17. This point was emphasized in Geoffrey Robinson's study of the violence in Bali, *The Dark Side of Paradise*, pp. 9–18. The problems segmentary violence like this poses for long-term democratic transitions are discussed in Guillermo O'Donnell and Philippe C. Schmitter, *Transitions from Authoritarian Rule: Tentative Conclusions about Uncertain Democracies* (Baltimore: The Johns Hopkins University Press, 1986).

18. Langenberg, "Gestapu and State Power," p. 53.

19. In a highly original study, Loren Ryter has shown that, in Medan and Jakarta during 1965, urban hoodlums affiliated with what was to become one of Indonesia's most powerful gangs, the Pemuda Pancasila, were recruited by the military to assist in attacks on Communists. In years to come they would be mobilized against other opponents of the regime. See Ryter's "Pemuda Pancasila: The Last Loyalist Free Men of Suharto's New Order," in *Indonesia* 66 (October 1998): 45–73.

20. See Crouch, *The Army and Politics*, pp. 167–71.

21. Ibid., p. 174.

22. Soekarno had good reason to be concerned about these officers' activities. In 1952 Brigadier General A. Kemal Idris had been involved in an army protest that included ringing the presidential palace with tanks and armored vehicles; in 1956 he was implicated in a plot against the foreign minister. See John Bresnan, "The Army Activists," in Bresnan, *Managing Indonesia*, pp. 38–40. For a biographical profile of these men, see Francois Raillon, *Les étudiants indonésiens et l'Ordre Nouveau: Politique et idéologie du Mahasiswa Indonésia (1966–1974)* (Paris: Éditions de la Maison des Sciences de l'Homme, 1984), pp. 335–36.

23. See ibid., p. 15.

24. Sulastomo, *Hari-Hari Yang Panjang, 1963–1966* [Long days: 1963–1966] (Jakarta: CV Haji Masagung, 1989), pp. 39–40. Sulastomo was chairman of the Central Bureau of the HMI from 1963 to 1966, though he was not living in Jakarta during the fall of 1965.

25. Raillon, *Les Étudiants Indonésiens*, p. 20.

26. A well-respected Chinese activist in anticommunist circles, Harry Chan was secretary general of the Catholic Party. Like other student activists, he developed a close working relationship with one of Soeharto's closest personal advisers, Ali Moertopo. In the early 1970s Tjan was among a group of Catholic Chinese who joined with Moertopo to form the Center for Strategic and International Studies (CSIS). The CSIS had close ties to the government through the early 1980s and was regarded by many Muslims as a key proponent of its "anti-Islamic" policies.

27. Reflecting the complexity of these alliances, KAPPI was dominated by modernist Muslim youth more than KAMI was. Its chairman was Husni Thamrin, the general secretary of the Indonesian Muslim Pupils a modernist organization with ties to the HMI and

Masyumi. Many of its early activities were, in addition, directed against the minister of education Prijono, a national-Marxist identified with the banned Murba Party (a labor party opposed to the PKI). See Crouch, *The Army and Politics*, pp. 184–85.

28. Bresnan, *Managing Indonesia*, p. 38. Loren Ryter's research shows that several local branches of KAMI and KAPPI developed ties not just with the military but with hoodlums linked to the Pemuda Pancasila. The latter took advantage of the political crisis to extort "struggle funds" (*dana perjuangan*) from hapless Chinese merchants. See Ryter, "Pemuda Pancasila," p. 59.

29. See Raillon, *Les Étudiants*, p. 21.

30. Ibid., p. 23, and Crouch, *The Army and Politics,* p. 174.

31. Semar is a comic but wise and beloved deity in Javanese shadow theater. The reference was indicative of the way Soeharto, in his early years, used Javanist imagery to popularize his policies.

32. See, for example, the story in the Catholic-owned national newspaper *Kompas* (April 3, 1987), on the remarks of T. B. Simatupang and Arief Budiman suggesting that the students were not an independent force during 1965–66. Simatupang and Budiman were well-known generation '66 activists but went on to become ardent critics of the government. Clearly offended by these remarks, Sulastomo, chairman of the HMI from 1963 to 1966, responded to these views in a chapter in his *Hari-hari yang panjang,* pp. 88–94.

33. R. William Liddle, "Modernizing Indonesian Politics," in Liddle, *Political Participation in Modern Indonesia*, p. 178.

34. As asserted, for example, in Douglas Ramage's otherwise insightful, *Politics in Indonesia*.

35. Herbert Feith and Lance Castles, *Indonesian Political Thinking, 1945–1965* (Ithaca: Cornell University Press, 1970), p. 227.

36. More recently, of course, the semantics of "liberal" have shifted again. The New Order government pushed the term's connotation from oligopolistic capitalism toward "Western" human rights and liberalism. Soeharto has sought to present the New Order as sailing a course between collectivistic communism, on the one hand and hyper-individualistic liberalism, on the other. "Liberalism," in this usage, refers to a legal and political order that defends the liberties of a few to the detriment of the many.

37. Feith and Castles, *Indonesian Political Thinking*, p. 227.

38. See Raillon, *Les Étudiants*, p. 148; and Monique Zaini-Lajoubert, "Vers un Societé et une Culture Nouvelles, L'Indonésie et la PréIndonesie," *Archipel* 11 (1978): 72–78.

39. For insight into this complex leader, see Benedict R. O'G. Anderson's "Introduction" to Sjahrir's *Our Struggle* (Ithaca: Cornell University, Southeast Asia Program, Modern Indonesia Project Translation series, 1968), pp. 1–16; and Rudolf Mrazek's political biography, *Sjahrir: Politics and Exile in Indonesia* (Ithaca: Cornell University, Southeast Asia Program, 1994). On Sjahrir's influence on post-1966 intellectuals, see R. William Liddle, "Modernizing Indonesian Politics," in Liddle, *Political Participation in Modern Indonesia*, esp. pp. 178–80.

40. See John Legge's comparison of Hatta and Sjahrir in his, *Intellectuals and Nationalism in Indonesia: A Study of the Following Recruited by Sutan Sjahrir in Occupation Jakarta* (Ithaca: Cornell University, Cornell Modern Indonesia Project, Monograph series, 1988), pp. 32–34.

41. Kahin, *Nationalism and Revolution*, p. 169.

42. Ibid., p. 319.
43. See Liddle, "Modernizing Indonesian Politics," p. 181; and Raillon, *Les Étudiants,* pp. 153–55.
44. Raillon, *Les Étudiants,* p. 72.
45. Liddle, "Modernizing Indonesian Politics," p. 178.
46. Raillon, *Les Étudiants,* pp. 36–37.
47. Ibid., p. 72.
48. On the New Order's economists, see John James MacDougall, "Technocrats as Modernizers: The Economists of Indonesia's New Order," Ph.D. dissertation, Department of Political Science, University of Michigan, 1975; and Bresnan, *Managing Indonesia,* pp. 72–79
49. In keeping with the New Order's interest in recognizing local culture while subjecting it to official categorizations, each of the pavilions is identified in provincial, not ethnic, terms. For example, a Minangkabau house is identified as "West Sumatran," not Minangkabau.
50. A close Soeharto ally, Amir Machmud was also one of the three generals who, on March 11, 1966, had managed to secure the "Supersemar" transfer of power from President Soekarno to General Soeharto.
51. See Raillon, *Les Étudiants,* p. 90.
52. See ibid., pp. 95–101.
53. Ibid., pp. 103–4.
54. See Richard Robison, *Indonesia: The Rise of Capital* (North Sydney, Australia: Allen & Unwin, 1986), pp. 131–249; and Bresnan, *Managing Indonesia,* pp. 164–93.
55. Raillon, in *Les Étudiants,* p. 61, briefly discusses this split between the Tolleng group and liberal-minded Muslims. The two most significant figures in the latter group were Adi Sasono and Dawam Rahardjo. Sasono became editor in chief of *Mimbar Demokrasi* and, with Dawam Rahardjo, helped to ensure that the journal became an important forum for the "renewalist" Islam discussed in the next chapter. See Fachry Ali and Bahtiar Effendy's portrait of Sasono and Rahardjo's early career in their *Merambah Jalan Baru Islam: Rekonstruksi Pemikiran Islam Indonesia Masa Orde Baru* [To clear a new Islamic path: The reconstruction of Indonesian Muslim thought in the New Order] (Bandung: Mizan, 1986), pp. 209–86. See also below, chapter 6.
56. Raillon, *Les Étudiants,* p. 208.
57. See Donald K. Emmerson, "The Bureaucracy in Political Context," in Karl D. Jackson and Lucian W. Pye, eds., *Political Power and Communications in Indonesia* (Berkeley: University of California Press, 1978), p. 95.
58. Raillon, *Les Étudiants,* p. 207. Even in East Java, after 1965–66 there were instances where zealous government officials sought to pressure non-Muslims and nominal-Muslims to conform to Islamic norms. See R. Hefner, "The Political Economy of Islamic Conversion in Modern East Java," in Roff, *Islam and the Political Economy of Meaning,* pp. 53–78.
59. Emmerson, "The Bureaucracy in Political Context," p. 97.
60. For the most complete treatment of the marriage law controversy, see Feillard, *Islam et Armée,* pp. 145–50.
61. See Leo Suryadinata, *Military Ascendancy and Political Culture: A Study of Indonesia's Golkar* (Athens: Ohio University, Southeast Asia series, Monographs in International Studies, no. 85, 1989), pp. 66–69. Cf. Feillard, *Islam et Armée,* p. 145.

62. Liddle, "Modernizing Indonesian Politics," p. 198.

63. An activist member of the Generation of '66, Goenawan Mohamad was the co-founder and editor of Indonesia's distinguished newsweekly, *Tempo. Tempo* was banned in June 1994 after criticizing the business dealings of Minister of Technology B. J. Habibie. On Goenawan, see R. William Liddle, "Improvising Political Cultural Change: Three Indonesian Cases," in Liddle, *Leadership and Culture in Indonesian Politics* (Sydney: Asian Studies Association of Australia, in association with Allen & Unwin, 1996), pp. 143–78.

64. Raillon, *Les Étudiants*, pp. 263, 267.

65. Emmerson, "The Bureaucracy in Political Context," p. 96. In subsequent years Emmerson revised his views and presented some of the best early analyses of the state's changing policy on Islam.

66. One hears an echo of this anachronistic model, for example, in the following: "Dominant New Order authorities are themselves committed to, obsessively devoted to, the ideal of a traditional culture, 'particularly' . . . a traditional Javanese culture" (J. Pemberton, *On the Subject of "Java"* [Ithaca: Cornell University Press 1994], p. 10). The folk Javanists with whom I worked in East Java in the late 1970s and mid-1980s, and who watched as their traditions were ravaged by New Order programs, had no such illusions as to the elite's "devotion."

67. See Crouch, *The Army and Politics,* p. 37; David Reeve, *Golkar of Indonesia: An Alternative to the Party System* (Singapore: Oxford University Press, 1985), p. 313; and David Jenkins, *Soeharto and His Generals: Indonesian Military Politics 1975–1983* (Ithaca: Cornell University, Southeast Asia Program, Modern Indonesia Project, Monograph no. 64, 1984), p. 21 n.17.

68. On the fate of several such left-wing mystical groups, see my "Islamizing Java?"

69. See Hung-Jun Kim, "Reformist Muslims in a Yogyakarta Village"; and Bambang Pranowo, "Creating Islamic Tradition." In an intriguing study from rural East Java, the Swedish anthropologist Sven Cederroth has observed that in his village (once "a stronghold for traditional syncretist Islam") "orthodox Islam has gained considerable ground . . . during the last few decades" (p. 232). While conceding Islam's advance, however, Cederroth adds that it is the public or communal ceremonialism of folk Javanism that has declined. Syncretist and mystical ideas have fared better by becoming less public, less communal, and more individuo-mystical. These "mysticist movements," he observes have become "the major alternative to Islamic orthodoxy" (p. 277). Cederoth is right to insist that we should distinguish decommunalization and individualization, which were occurring already, from the outright decline of Javanism. And he is right to assert that mysticism remains an alternative to orthodox Islam for some. Nonetheless it is important not to forget that, at one time, Javanist spirituality aspired to project itself as a public alternative to Islam. The policies of the New Order state made such a full-blown public Javanism untenable.

70. See Geertz, *Religion of Java*, pp. 77–85.

71. This generalization does *not* apply, however, to Javanese artistic traditions. These enjoyed considerable regime support, not least of all because they were seen as an attractive item for tourist promotion.

72. None of this is to say, of course, that pious Muslims are in full agreement on this matter. As is well known, many variants of Sufi mysticism elevate individual experience of divinity to a position of central religious importance. Some nominally Islamic

Javanese mystics take this sacralized individuality one step further. They identify *rasa* (feeling, intuition, conscience) with in-dwelling divinity, asserting that inner conscious-ness is itself an aspect of the divine. For subtle analyses of this monistic tradition, see Beatty, *Varieties of Javanese Religion*, pp. 193–98; and Paul Stange, *Politik Perhatian: Rasa dalam Kebudayaan Jawa* [The politics of attentiveness: Rasa in Javanese culture] (Yogyakarta: LKiS Press, 1998).

73. Although committed to classical jurisprudence (*fiqh*) and established schools of law (*madhab*), NU transformed that tradition in the twentieth century. Since its found-ing in 1926, NU has responded to modernist critiques on the importance of general education by introducing reforms of its own. For an overview of this tension between tradition and renewal in NU, see Martin van Bruinessen, *NU: Tradisi, Relasi-relasi Kuasa, Pencarian Wacana Baru* [NU: Traditions, power relations, and the search for a new discourse] (Yogyakarta: LKiS, 1994); and his *Kitab Kuning: Pesantren dan Tarekat* [Tradi-tionalist scriptures: Pesantren and tarikat] (Bandung: Mizan, 1995).

74. Feillard, *Islam et Armée*, p. 32; also see chapter 3, above.

75. Samson, "Islam and Politics in Indonesia," p. 171.

76. In a rare comment on Islam, Benedict Anderson echoed Samson's views, in his "Religion and Politics in Indonesia since Independence," in Anderson, ed., *Religion and Social Ethos in Indonesia* (Clayton, Victoria: Monash University, Centre of Southeast Asian Studies, 1977), pp. 21–32. Noting that secularists tend to see NU as "thoroughly corrupt" and a "failure" by ordinary political standards, he adds that such a judgment overlooks that NU's primary concern is not power as such but the desire to "preserve and extend a religious way of life" (p. 24).

77. See Feillard, *Islam et Armée*, p. 27; and van Bruinessen, *NU: Tradisi, Relasi-Relasi Kuasa*, p. 39.

78. See Feillard, *Islam et Armée*, pp. 45–47; and Choirul Anam, *Pertumbuhan dan Perkembangan Nahdlatul Ulama* [The growth and development of Nahdlatul Ulama] (Surabaya: Jatayu Sala, 1985), pp. 196–97.

79. On all these points, NU differs from its modernist rival, the Muhammadiyah (chapter 3). Whereas schools and welfare programs linked to NU are owned by individ-ual scholars (the *ulama*), Muhammadiyah schools, hospitals, orphanages, and universi-ties are operated by the national organization. Muhammadiyah also lacks the charis-matic lineages so central to NU leadership. As was illustrated in the 1980s with the ascent of Abdurrahman Wahid (grandson of NU's founder), most NU leaders come from well-pedigreed families. For the NU rank-and-file, genealogical ties of this sort carry real weight, linked as they are to the folk Islamic belief that some of a living saint's spiritual power (A., *barakah*; J., *berkat*) can be transmitted to his descendants.

80. See H. Kamen, *The Rise of Toleration* (London: Weidenfeld and Nicolson, 1967).

81. See Sidney Jones, "The Contraction and Expansion of the 'Umat' and the Role of *Nahdlatul Ulama* in Indonesia," *Indonesia* 38 (October 1984): 1–20.

82. Reeve, *Golkar of Indonesia*, p. 211.

83. See Crouch, *The Army and Politics*, pp. 65, 153.

84. Cited in Feillard, *Islam et Armée*, p. 79.

85. Ibid., p. 70.

86. Personal interviews with HMI and NU activists, June 1995. Cf. Crouch, *The Army and Politics*, p. 141.

87. Feillard, *Islam et Armée*, p. 70 n. 5.

88. See Bresnan, *Managing Indonesia*, p. 46.

89. Feillard, *Islam et Armée*, p. 106

90. Ken Ward, *The 1971 Election in Indonesia: An East Java Case Study* (Clayton, Victoria: Monash University, Centre of Southeast Asian Studies, Monash Papers on Southeast Asia, no. 2, 1974), p. 7; and Feillard, *Islam et Armée*, p. 86.

91. Ward, *The 1971 Election*, p. 8.

92. On the decline of the textile industry, see Bresnan, *Managing Indonesia*, pp. 149–52; for the Muslim reaction, see Feillard, *Islam et Armée*, p. 92.

93. Feillard, *Islam et Armée*, p. 90.

94. Pierre Labrousse and Farida Soemargono, "De L'Islam comme morale du développement. L'action des bureaux de propagation de la foi (*Lembaga Dakwah*) vue de Surabaya." In *Archipel*, no. 30, Special Issue on "L'Islam en Indonésie" (2 vols.), 2. (1985): p. 222.

CHAPTER FIVE
THE MODERNIST TRAVAIL

1. See Adnan Buyung Nasution, *The Aspiration for Constitutional Government in Indonesia*; and Ahmad Syafii Maarif, *Islam dan Masalah Kenegaraan: Studi Tentang Percaturan dalam Konstituante* [Islam and the problem of state: A study of the Constitutional Assembly] (Jakarta: LP3ES, 1985).

2. See Lev, *The Transition to Guided Democracy*, p. 72.

3. See ibid., p. 79; and Crouch, *The Army and Politics in Indonesia*, pp. 273–303.

4. The label Islamic "renewal" (*pembaruan*) is most often applied to Indonesia's leading neo-modernist intellectual, Nurcholish Madjid. Although Madjid looms large in the present account, my concern here is with all those who distanced themselves from the senior Masyumi leadership and sought to develop new perspectives on pluralism and civility.

5. On the logic of the collaboration linking modernist Muslims and PSI-style secular nationalists in New Order planning agencies, see John James MacDougall, "Technocrats as Modernizers: The Economists of Indonesia's New Order"; and M. Syafi'i Anwar, *Pemikiran dan Aksi Islam Indonesia, Sebuah Kajian Politik Tentang Cendekiawan Muslim Orde Baru* [Indonesian Muslim thought and action: A political analysis of New Order Muslim intellectuals] (Jakarta: Paramadina, 1995), p. 26.

6. Allan A. Samson provides the best English-language description of these events in his "Islam in Indonesian Politics," *Asian Survey* 7:12 (December 1968): 1001–16.

7. Allan A. Samson, "Army and Islam in Indonesia," *Pacific Affairs* 44:4 (Winter 1971–72), p. 548.

8. Technically Golkar was established by the military in 1964, as an alliance of civilians and the military against the Communist Party. It was the New Order, however, that transformed this corporatist skeleton into a powerful political body. See Reeve, *Golkar of Indonesia*.

9. In 1992–93 the single-loyalty policy was challenged by the prodemocracy Muslim activist Sri Bintang Pamungkas. Elected to the national assembly as a representative of the Muslim PPP, Sri Bintang maintained his professorship at the state-run University of Indonesia. As a legislative representative for the PPP, however, his party affiliation contradicted the monoloyalty regulation. During his first two years in the assembly Sri

Bintang was a fearless critic of corruption and presidential abuse. Sri Bintang's independence was at first seen as evidence that the government's talk of a new spirit of "openness" (*keterbukaan*) in the early 1990s was for real. But the impression proved short-lived. In 1996, in the aftermath of the president's visit to Germany, Sri Bintang was accused of organizing demonstrations against the president and defaming him with his criticism. Sri Bintang was convicted and imprisoned. He was among the first political prisoners freed by the Habibie government in May 1998 after Soeharto's downfall. See chapter 7.

10. See Marshall Hodgson, *The Venture of Islam*, 3 vols. (Chicago: University of Chicago Press, 1974).

11. See Mohammad Natsir, "Agama dan Negara" [Religion and state], in M. Isa Anshary, ed., *Falsafah Perjuangan Islam* (Medan: Saiful, 1951), pp. 27–99. One of the finest Indonesian-language texts to situate Natsir's thought in its historical context is Maarif's *Islam dan Masalah Kenegaraan*. The best English-language survey is Peter Burns's *Revelation and Revolution: Natsir and the Panca Sila* (Townsville, Australia: James Cook University, Committee of South-East Asian Studies, Southeast Asian Monograph no. 9, 1981).

12. See Federspiel, *Persatuan Islam*, p. 16. For an Indonesian-language discussion of Ahmad Hassan, see Syafiq A. Mughni's, *Hassan Bandung: Pemikir Islam Radikal* [Hassan Bandung: A radical Muslim thinker] (Surabaya: Bina Ilmu, 1980).

13. To call Maududi a conservative is to oversimplify this complex man. In discussions of democracy and human rights in the Muslim community today, however, his ideas are invoked to support conservative claims that "Western" democracy is incompatible with Islam. On Maududi's career and vision, see Seyyed Vali Reza Nasr, *The Vanguard of the Islamic Revolution*; see also Esposito and Voll, *Islam and Democracy*, pp. 23–24.

14. Samson, "Islam and Politics in Indonesia."

15. On New Order cinema, see Karl G. Heider, *Indonesian Cinema: National Culture on Screen* (Honolulu: University of Hawaii Press, 1991); and Krisha Sen, *Indonesian Cinema: Framing the New Order* (London: Zed, 1994).

16. On the politics and economics of the Muslim middle class, see Aswab Mahasin, "The Santri Middle Class: An Insider's View," in Richard Tanter and Kenneth Young, eds., *The Politics of Middle Class Indonesia* (Clayton, Australia: Monash University, Centre of Southeast Asian Studies, 1990), pp. 138–44; and Robert W. Hefner, "Markets and Justice for Muslim Indonesians," in Hefner, *Market Cultures*, pp. 237–72. On the changing nature of the Indonesian middle class generally, see Howard W. Dick, "The Rise of a Middle Class and the Changing Concept of Equity in Indonesia—An Interpretation," in *Indonesia* 39 (1985): 71–92.

17. On Persis, see Federspiel, *Persatuan Islam*; and Noer, *The Modernist Muslim Movement*, pp. 259–95.

18. Federspiel, *Persatuan Islam*, p. 146.

19. Adam Schwarz provides a wry comment on a similar attitude among conservative modernists:

> The modernists tend to skip over the ideological and doctrinal differences which divide the Muslim community; instead, they claim to speak for all Indonesian Muslims. When talking about politics, the modernists downplay the idea of a *santri-*

abangan split. The *abangan* world view, they believe, is not a sustainable condition but is, rather, a sort of way station for the uninformed. (*A Nation in Waiting*, p. 183)

For more sustained Muslim Indonesian reflections on pluralism, however, see Alwi Shihab, *Islam Inklusif: Menuju Sikap Terbuka Dalam Beragama* [Inclusive Islam: Toward an open attitude in religion] (Bandung: Mizan, 1997); and Abdul Munir Mulkhan, *Teologi Kebudayaan dan Demokrasi Modernitas* [A cultural theology and democracy of modernity] (Yogyakarta: Pustaka Pelajar, 1995).

20. A view Natisir voiced even in print. See his *Politik Melalui Jalur Dakwah* [Politics by way of Dakwah], 2nd ed. (Jakarta: PT Abadi, 1998).

21. On Muhammadiyah, see Mitsuo Nakamura, *The Crescent Arises over the Banyan Tree: A Study of the Muhammadiyah Movement in a Central Javanese Town* (Yogyakarta: Gadjah Mada University Press, 1983); and James L. Peacock, *Purifying the Faith: The Muhammadiyah Movement in Indonesian Islam* (Menlo Park, Calif.: Benjamin/Cummings, 1978).

22. See, for example, Avery T. Willis, *The Indonesian Revival: Why Two Million Came to Christ* (Pasadena: William Carey Library, 1977).

23. Willis, *Indonesian Revival*, p. 192. Cf. Hyung-Jun Kim, "Reformist Muslims in a Yogyakarta Village," p. 236.

24. This is based on my research among Christians in East Java in 1979 and 1985.

25. On the NU editorial, see Feillard, *Islam et Armée*, p. 64. The Muhammadiyah statement first appeared in the organization's weekly, *Suara Muhammadiyah*, on November 9, 1965. The text is reproduced in an English version in B. J. Boland, *The Struggle of Islam in Modern Indonesia* (The Hague: Verhandelingen van Het Koninklijk Instituut voor Taal-, Land-, en Volkenkunde No. 59, rev. 2nd ed., 1982), p. 146.

26. Two ethnographic studies provide compelling accounts of just such outreach and Islamization of once *abangan* populations. See Pranowo, "Creating Islamic Tradition in Rural Java"; and Hyung-Jun Kim, "Reformist Muslims in a Yogyakarta Village."

27. See Feillard, *Islam et Armée*, pp. 93, 111.

28. Willis, *Indonesian Revival*, p. 110.

29. Samson, "Islam and Politics in Indonesia," p. 231.

30. See Agussalim Sitompul, *HMI Dalam Pandangan Seorang Pendeta*, p. 25.

31. See ibid., p. 28.

32. In 1990 the DDII sent preachers into the Tengger highlands in East Java and sponsored the construction of a mosque in a predominantly Hindu region where I had done research in the late 1970s and in 1985. According to DDII preachers whom I interviewed in 1991(one was a friend of mine from the 1970s), military officials in the provincial capital were angered by this move and sought unsuccessfully to have the missionaries expelled. The DDII has sponsored similar initiatives in Christian areas of Eastern Indonesia and in the northern portions of the Yogyakarta district where Christian conversion occurred after 1965–66.

33. I base this claim that Soeharto himself approved the predication efforts on interviews I conducted with two members of his cabinet in 1994.

34. On Dr. Sjadzali's role in promoting contextual methodologies in the study of Islamic law, see Muhamad Wahyuni Nafis, ed., *Kontekstualisasi Ajaran Islam: 70 Tahun Prof. Dr. H. Munawir Sjadzali, M.A.* [Contextualizing the teachings of Islam: 70 years of Prof. Dr. H. Munawir Sjadzali] (Jakarta: Paramadina, 1995).

35. The former rector of the Jakarta State Islamic Institute Colleges (IAIN), Harun Nasution, has been an advocate of Islamic tolerance, making the case by way of muʿtazilist rationalism. Although his theological grounds differ from Madjid, Nasution's critique reaches a similar conclusion that the Muslim community has often confused what is local and relative for what is absolute. He has also spoken out against the idea that jurisprudential commentary (*fiqh*) should be the main instrument of religious reflection. See Saiful Muzani, "Muʿtazilah and the Modernization of the Indonesian Muslim Community: Intellectual Portrait of Harun Nasution," in *Studia Islamika* 1:1 (April 1994): 91–131; and Richard C. Martin and Mark R. Woodward, *Defenders of Reason in Islam: Muʿtazilism from Medieval School to Modern Symbol* (Oxford: One World, 1997).

36. What follows is based on interviews with Anwar Harjono (DDII head), June 14, 1995; Lukman Hakiem and Aru Syeif Asad (*MD* reporters), January 7, 1997; Natsir Zubaidi (a former writer for *MD*), January 10, 1997; and sources in *Media Dakwah*.

37. It was no coincidence that in February 1998, at the height of the Soeharto regime's last political crisis, *Media Dakwah* obtained a general publication license. It was widely believed that Soeharto's son-in-law, Prabowo Subianto, intervened to secure the license. On Prabowo's ties to Muslim ultraconservatives, see chapters 6, 7.

38. For an English-language selection of Goenawan's writings, see his *Sidelines: Writings from Tempo, Indonesia's Banned Magazine*, trans. Jennifer Lindsay (South Melbourne, Australia: Hyland House, in assoc. with the Monash Asia Institute, 1994). On Goenawan as a public intellectual, see R. William Liddle, "Improvising Political Cultural Change: Three Indonesian Cases," in *Leadership and Culture*, pp. 143–78.

39. A detailed presentation of *MD*'s views on the Catholic-owned Kompas-Gramedia group is presented in the magazine's analysis of the *Monitor* affair (chapter 7, below). See "Membedah Jantung Monitor" [To expose the heart of *Monitor*], *Media Dakwah* (December 1990): 25–30.

40. Interview with *Kompas* associate editor S. T. Soelarto, January 11, 1997, and former *Tempo* reporters, January 1997 and June 1995.

41. Interviews with Djohan Effendi, Dawam Rahardjo, Usep Fathudin, and Utomo Danadjaya, July 1993. Danadjaja and Fathudin were leaders of the moderate wing of the Pelajar Islam, forced from the organization in 1971. A. Wahib, Dawam Rahardjo, and Djohan Effendi were members of the "Lingkaran Limited Discussion Group," a discussion group in Yogyakarta organized by Mutki Ali, who would become minister of religion in 1971. The role of this Yogya-based group has sometimes been neglected in outsiders' accounts of the *pembaruan* (renewal) movement. An exception is Greg Barton's thoughtful overview of Indonesian neo-modernism, "Neo-Modernism: A Vital Synthesis of Traditionalist and Modernist Islamic Thought in Indonesia," in *Studia Islamika* 2:3 (1995): 1–75.

42. See Madjid's "Modernisasi Ialah Rasionalisasi Bukan Westernisasi" [Modernization is rationalization not Westernization], "Keharusan Pemikiran Islam dan Masalah Integrasi Umat" [The necessity of Islamic thought and the problem of the integration of the community of believers], "Sekali Lagi Tentang Sekularisasi" [Once more on secularization], and "Perspectif Pembaruan Pemikiran Dalam Islam" [The perspective of intellectual renewal in Islam], in Madjid, *Islam, Kemodernan, dan KeIndonesiaan* [Islam, modernity, and Indonesianness] (Bandung: Mizan, 1984), pp. 171–203, 204–14, 221–33, and 234–39. English-language versions of the essays are available in Muhammad

Kamal Hassan, *Muslim Intellectual Responses to "New Order" Modernization in Indonesia* (Kuala Lumpur: Dewan Bahasa dan Pustaka, 1982), pp. 187–233.

43. In recent writings Madjid delves more extensively into classical Muslim commentary. Some observers see in this evidence of a greater "conservatism" in Madjid's mature writing. However, this reading has more to do with his efforts to demonstrate that conservative modernists have overlooked the pluralistic richness of classical scholarship.

44. See Nurcholish Madjid, *Ibn Taymiyya on Kalam and Falsafa (A Problem of Reason and Revelation in Islam)*, Ph.D. dissertation, Department of Near Eastern Languages and Civilizations, University of Chicago, 1984.

45. The posthumously published diaries of Ahmad Wahib provide additional insight into the fervor surrounding the rethinking of Islam and politics at this time. Killed in a motorcycle accident in 1973, Wahib was active in HMI circles. Through an Islamic study group known as the "Limited Discussion Group," he and his friends in Yogyakarta discussed the question of how to revitalize Islamic culture and politics. Along with friends Djohan Effendi and Dawam Rahardjo, and under the protective sponsorship of Mukti Ali, a professor at an Islamic university who would later become minister of religion, Wahib criticized what he called the stagnation of Islamic modernism. Having originated as a bold and dynamic response to modernity, Wahib felt, modernism had degenerated into an orthodoxy that hinders freedom of thought. He blamed the subordination of Islam to party politics for much of this stagnation. As early as mid-1967 Wahib and his Yogyakarta colleagues argued that the HMI should repudiate the idea of an Islamic state and embrace the *Pancasila*. In 1968 their public airing of this view provoked stern condemnation by the Jakarta branch of the HMI, which accused the Jogja chapter of secular and "socialist" thought. In fact, however, no less a figure than the national chairman of the HMI, Nurcholish Madjid, was privately moving toward a similar conclusion. Published eight years after his untimely death, Wahib's diaries remain a bestseller to this day in Indonesia—and a regular object of condemnation by conservative Muslim writers. See Ahmad Wahib, *Pergolakan Pemikiran Islam: Catatan Harian Ahmad Wahib* [Upheaval in Islamic thought: The diaries of Ahmad Wahib], ed. Djohan Effendi and Ismed Natsir (Jakarta: LP3ES Press, 1981). For an English-language commentary on Wahib's influence, see Anthony H. Johns, "An Islamic System or Islamic Values? Nucleus of a Debate in Contemporary Indonesia," in William R. Roff, ed., *Islam and the Political Economy of Meaning* (London: Croom Helm, 1987), pp. 254–80. On DDII portrayals of Wahib as a heretic, see Hefner, "Print Islam: Mass Media and Ideological Rivalries in Indonesian Islam," in *Indonesia* 64 (October 1997): 77–103.

46. On the view that this argument distorts the variegated relationship between religion and state in Islamic civilization, see Eickelman and Piscatori, *Muslim Politics*, p. 46; and Lapidus, "The Separation of State and Religion in Early Islamic Society."

47. See Mohammad Natsir's commentary on the writings of Mohammad Iqbal, *Dapatkah Dipisahkan Politik dari Agama?* [Can politics be separated from religion?] (Jakarta: Mutiara, 1953).

48. See Madjid, "Sekali Lagi Tentang Sekularisasi," p. 222.

49. Madjid, "Modernisasi Ialah Rasionalisasi Bukan Westernisasi," p. 174.

50. See, for example, ibid., pp. 175–81; and Madjid, "Keharusan Pembaruan," pp. 204–14.

51. This, for example, is the substance of the Malaysian scholar Kamal Hassan's mordant criticism of Madjid in Hassan's *Muslim Intellectual Responses to "New Order" Modernization in Indonesia,* esp. pp. 121–23. Compare Ali and Effendy's measured assessment in their *Merambah Jalan Baru,* pp. 134–43.

52. For book-length versions of these critiques, see Muhammad Rasjidi, *Koreksi Terhadap Drs. Nurcholish Madjid Tentang Sekularisasi* [A correction to Nurcholish Madjid on secularization] (Jakarta: Bulan Bintang, 1972); and Endang Saefuddin Anshary, *Kritik atas Faham dan Gerakan "Pembaruan" Drs. Nurcholish Madjid* [A criticism of the concept and movement for "renewal" of Nurcholish Madjid] (Bandung: Bulan Sabit, 1973).

53. Hassan, *Muslim Intellectual Responses,* pp. 114, 123.

54. See Madjid, "Sekali Lagi," pp. 221–33; and his "Sekularisasi Ditinjau Kembali" [Secularization revisited], in Madjid, *Islam, Kemodernan, dan Keindonesiaan,"* pp. 257–60.

55. See Nurcholish Madjid, *Islam: Doktrin dan Peradaban* [Islam: Doctrine and civilization] (Jakarta: Paramadina, 1992). Accused of writing only for intellectuals, in the 1990s Madjid made an effort to present his views to the broader Muslim public. See his *Pintu-Pintu Menuju Tuhan* [Doorways to God] (Jakarta: Paramadina, 1995); and his *Islam: Agama Kemanusiaan: Membangun Tradisi dan Visi Baru Islam Indonesia* [Islam: Humanitarian religion: To create a new tradition and vision of Indonesian Islam] (Jakarta: Paramadina, 1995). The latter work was written in the aftermath of interreligious violence, and is notable for its uncompromising defense of pluralism.

56. In our discussion on June 19, 1993, Madjid again affirmed that he is "still quite comfortable" with his views on secularism and secularization, "though it is not economical to use these terms, inviting as they do such emotional reactions from people."

57. Ali and Effendi, *Merambah Jalan Baru,* p. 133.

58. For a related description of this change, see Howard M. Federspiel, *Muslim Intellectuals and National Development in Indonesia* (New York: Nova Science, 1992) pp. 7–12.

59. See Abdulaziz, Imam Tholkhah, and Soetarman, *Gerakan Islam Kontemporer di Indonesia* [Islamic movements in contemporary Indonesia] (Jakarta: Pustaka Firdaus, 1991); and M. Nasir Tamara, "Islam as a Political Force in Indonesia: 1965–1985," (Cambridge, Mass.: Harvard University, Center for International Affairs, Occasional Paper, 1985), pp. 23–25.

60. Gavin W. Jones and Chris Manning, "Labour Force and Employment during the 1980s," in Anne Booth, ed., *The Oil Boom and After: Indonesian Economic Policy and Performance in the Soeharto Era* (Kuala Lumpur: Oxford University Press, 1992), pp. 363–410. For a Middle Eastern comparison, see Dale F. Eickelman, "Mass Higher Education and the Religious Imagination in Contemporary Arab Societies," in *American Ethnologist* 19:4 (1992): 1–13.

61. Terence H. Hull and Gavin W. Jones, "Demographic Perspectives," in Hal Hill, ed., *Indonesia's New Order: The Dynamics of Socio-Economic Transformation,* (Honolulu: University of Hawaii Press, 1994), pp. 123–78.

62. See Jeroen Peeters, "Prophets and Profits: The Internal Structure of the Islamic Book Industry in Indonesia," paper presented at the conference "Mass Media and the Transformation of Islamic Discourse," International Institute for Asian Studies, Leiden, March 24, 1997.

63. See Feillard, *Islam et Armée,* pp. 145–50.

64. See M. Bambang Pranowo, "Which Islam and Which Pancasila? Islam and the State in Indonesia: A Comment," in Arief Budiman, ed., *State and Civil Society in Indonesia* (Clayton, Australia: Monash University, Centre of Southeast Asian Studies, Monash Papers on Southeast Asia, no. 22, 1990), p. 493.

65. These statistics are from Mitsuo Nakamura, "The Emergence of an Islamizing Middle Class and the Dialectics of Political Islam in the New Order of Indonesia: Prelude to the Formation of the ICMI," paper presented at the conference "Islam and the Social Construction of Identities: Comparative Perspectives on Southeast Asian Muslims," Center for Southeast Asian Studies, University of Hawaii-Manoa, Honolulu, Hawaii, August 4–6, 1993. See also Lombard, *Le Carrefour Javanais*, vol. 2, pp. 123, 126.

66. These figures are from assorted statistical sources in the Office of Statistics in Central and East Java. See also "Setelah boom Sarjana Islam" [After the Boom in Islamic scholars], *Tempo* (December 8, 1990): 34–37.

67. Syamsuddin Haris, "PPP and Politics under the New Order," in *Prisma* 49 (1985): 31–51; and Cees van Dijk, "Survey of Political Developments in Indonesia in the Second Half of 1984: The National Congress of the PPP and the Pancasila Principle," *Review of Indonesian and Malaysian Affairs* 19:1 (1985): 177–202.

68. NU's action was not based on a repudiation of politics but on the conviction that the price of opposition to the government was so high, and the PPP so ineffectual, that it was best to leave the formal political sphere, at least temporarily. See van Bruinessen, *NU: Tradisi, Relasi-Relasi Kuasa*, pp. 115–49; and Andrée Feillard, *Islam et Armée*, pp. 157–92.

69. Ramage, *Politics in Indonesia*, p. 83.

70. Interview, June 19, 1993.

71. Compare Pranowo's *Making Islamic Traditions* on the Islamic resurgence in the Magelang regency of Central Java to the process in Pasuruan, East Java, as described in my *Political Economy of Mountain Java*, pp. 193–227. Evidence of Islamization can be found, however, in unexpected places. In a study of Javanist mysticism in the mid-1980s the historian Paul Stange wrote that "even though Islam may be politically on the defensive, in the religious sphere it has been gaining ground. . . . Islamic discourse, I would argue, increasingly defines the context of Javanese mysticism." See Paul Stange, " 'Legitimate' Mysticism in Indonesia," *Review of Indonesian and Malaysian Affairs* 22:2 (1986): 79–80.

72. This discussion of "reversion" from Hinduism to Islam is based on my field observations in South Malang, East Java, and Gunung Kidul, Yogyakarta. In an interview on July 3, 1993, Dr. Th. Sumartana, director of the Institute for Inter-Faith Dialogue in Indonesia at the Universitas Kristen Satya Wacana, noted that studies conducted by his institute indicate that Christian converts in some areas of Central Java are also backsliding, although not on the scale reported among Hindus.

73. Howard W. Dick, "The Rise of a Middle Class and the Changing Concept of Equity in Indonesia: An Interpretation," *Indonesia* 39 (1990): 71–92.

74. Interviews with University of Indonesia students, July 1992, and with Imaduddin Abdulrahim, August 1992 and June 1993. Ali and Effendy place the Salman revival in the context of other developments among urban Muslims (Meramblah Jalan Baru, p. 308).

75. See Richard Robison, "The Middle Class and the Bourgeoisie in Indonesia," in Richard Robison and David S. G. Goodman, eds., *The New Rich in Asia* (New York: Routledge, 1996), pp. 79–101.

76. Benedict R. O'G. Anderson, "Cartoons and Monuments: The Evolution of Political Communication under the New Order," in Karl D. Jackson and Lucian W. Pye, eds., *Political Power and Communications in Indonesia* (Berkeley: University of California Press, 1978), p. 315.

77. Kuntowijoyo *Paradigma Islam: Interpretasi Untuk Aksi* (Bandung: Mizan, 1991), pp. 370–71.

78. Ibid., p. 373.

79. Zifirdaus Adnan, "Islamic Religion: Yes, Islamic Ideology: No! Islam and State in Indonesia," in Budiman, *State and Civil Society in Indonesia*, p. 459.

80. For Middle Eastern comparisons, see Eickelman and Piscatori, *Muslim Politics*. In its mixture of media savvy, personalism, and rhetorical accessibility, this segment of the Islamic resurgence resembles the evangelical boom in the Americas. Compare, for example, "Dai-Dai Baru Bak Matahari Terbit" [New Muslim preachers rise], *Tempo* (April 11, 1992): 14–23, to David Martin's portrait of Latin American evangelicalism in his *Tongues of Fire*.

81. ICMI [no author], *Membangun Masyarakat Indonesia Abad XXI: Prosiding Simposium Nasional Cendekiawan Muslim, 1991* [To build a twenty-first-century Indonesian people: Proceedings of the 1991 National Symposium of Muslim Intellectuals] (Jakarta: ICMI National Office), pp. 203–10.

82. Interview in Boston, December 9, 1992.

CHAPTER SIX
ISLAM DEFERRED: REGIMIST ISLAM AND THE STRUGGLE FOR THE MIDDLE CLASS

1. See, for example, "ICMI Jaring Cendekiawan Konsep Minimal" [ICMI: A minimal concept for an intellectual network], *Kompas*, December 5, 1990; and "Hari Ini Presiden Soeharto Buka Simposium Cendekiawan" [Today President Soeharto opens an intellectual symposium], *Pelita*, December 6, 1990.

2. In what was widely regarded as one of his best cabinet choices, President B. J. Habibie appointed Malik Fadjar minister of religion in the *Reformasi* cabinet that took shape in June 1998, after Soeharto's resignation. One of Fadjar's first acts as minister was to visit Abudurrahman Wahid, who was recovering from a stroke at the time.

3. Interviews, 1993 and 1995. See also Dawam Rahardjo's brief account of these events in his "Visi Dan Misi Kehadiran ICMI: Sebuah Pengantar" [The vision and mission of ICMI: An introduction], in Rahardjo, ed., *ICMI: Antara status quo dan demokratisasi* [ICMI: Between the status quo and democratization] (Bandung: Mizan, 1996), pp. 25–43. There was an even earlier precedent for this effort to unite Muslim intellectuals under a single organizational banner. In 1964 the Union of Muslim Scholars (Persatuan Sarjana Muslim Indonesia, or Persami) was established to combat the growing influence of the Communist Party. Persami was backed by the armed forces, and the organization was active in supporting General Soeharto from 1965 to 1967. Like so many of Soeharto's allies, however, Persami declined after 1968, as a result of leadership disputes and the regime's interest in curtailing organizations inclined to question its policies.

4. What follows draws on interviews with Imaduddin Abdulrahim, Syafi Anwar, Dawam Rahardjo, Nurcholish Madjid, Wardiman Djojonegoro, and Aswab Mahasin in August 1992 and June–July 1993.

5. Interview, June 5, 1993.

6. See MacDougall, "Technocrats as Modernizers: The Economists of Indonesia's New Order."

7. On Suntowo and the Pertamina crisis, see Bresnan, *Managing Indonesia*, pp. 164–93. During his first years back in Indonesia in the 1970s, Habibie was usually identified as part of the "economic nationalist" camp by Indonesian observers. But this disparate group was united more by their reservations toward export-oriented industrialization and foreign investment than any consensus on economic policy. Some of the group's key members later emerged as rivals to Habibie—especially junior minister of production (and in the late Soeharto and Habibie administrations, minister of industry), Ginanjar Kartasasmita, and state secretary (and vice president, 1988–93) Soedharmono.

8. Anonymous interview with a former cabinet minister, June 12, 1995.

9. Despite his nationalist background, Wardiman learned to play by the rules of the new political game. In 1991–92 he spoke out against what he regarded as Chinese Christian dominance in education and the media. As minister of education after 1993, Wardiman was widely expected to shift lucrative orders for schoolbooks away from the Chinese-owned firms that dominated the market. However, by 1996–97, almost no such new deals had occurred, and reform activists expressed bitter disappointment with the minister's sweetheart deals.

10. Habibie's speech to the Malang symposium illustrated this vigorously "non-Islamic" emphasis. He devoted most of his presentation to general discussion of the technological challenges of the twenty-first century. When he referred to Islam, he did so in a general fashion, stressing the importance of religion in development and avoiding any mention of Muslim politics.

11. See Ruth McVey, "The Materialization of the Southeast Asian Entrepreneur," in McVey, ed., *Southeast Asian Capitalists* (Ithaca: Cornell University Southeast Asia Program, 1992), p. 11.

12. On the social organization of overseas Chinese business, see Gary Hamilton, "Overseas Chinese Capitalism," in Tu Wei-Ming, ed., *Confucian Traditions in East Asian Modernity: Moral Education and Economic Culture in Japan and the Four Mini-Dragons* (Cambridge: Harvard University Press, 1996), pp. 328–44; on the question of a Chinese "comparative cultural advantage," see Hefner, "Society and Morality in the New Asian Capitalisms," in Hefner, *Market Cultures*, pp. 1–38; and Tania Li, "Constituting Capitalist Culture: The Singapore Malay Problem and Entrepreneurship Reconsidered," in *Market Cultures*, pp. 147–72.

13. On the relationship of Chinese business to the New Order elite, see Richard Robison, *Indonesia: The Rise of Capital* (Sydney: Allen & Unwin, 1986); and also his "Industrialization and the Economic and Political Development of Capital: The Case of Indonesia," in McVey, *Southeast Asian Capitalists*, pp. 65–88.

14. This point is nicely analyzed in Ramage's *Politics in Indonesia*, p. 101.

15. A high-ranking ICMI officer with whom I spoke in 1994 estimated that 337 people in the MPR could be counted as "ICMI." Journalists with whom I spoke typically cited a slightly lower figure.

16. I base this remark in part on interviews conducted in May 1993 and March 1994 with Indonesian students in Cambridge, Massachusetts; Ithaca, New York; and Washington, D.C.

17. Ramage, *Politics in Indonesia*, p. 76.

18. Madjid based his argument in part on his reading of the great fourteenth-century Muslim reformer (*mujaddid*) Ibn Taymiyya. Taymiyya was a fierce critic of Sufi mysticism and Islamic Hellenism, and has often been adopted as a model by conservative Islamic modernists. In his graduate studies at the University of Chicago in the 1970s and early 1980s, however, Madjid attempted to strengthen the grounds for his tolerant interpretation of Muslim politics by contesting conservatives on their own grounds. His choice of Taymiyya was a particularly strategic one, showing that Muslim conservatives overlook pluralistic themes in Taymiyya's work. See Madjid, "Ibn Taymiyya on Kalam and Falsafa (A Problem of Reason and Revelation in Islam)," Ph.D. dissertation, Department of Near Eastern Languages and Civilizations, University of Chicago, 1994. For the written version of Madjid's 1992 presentation, see his "Kehidupan Keagamaan untuk Generasi Mendatang" [Religious life for future generations], in *Ulumul Qur'an* 1:4 (1993): 4–25. See also his bold comments on the "borderlessness" of Islam in his interview in "Islam yang Hanif Itu borderless" [Spiritual Islam is Borderless], in *Detik* 2:563 (November 1992): 23.

19. Madjid's views bear a striking resemblance to those of the great Syrian Muslim scholar and civil democrat Mohammad Sharour (chapter 1). See his "Divine Text and Pluralism in Muslim Societies," in *Muslim Politics Report* 14 (July–August 1997): 1–9 (New York: Council on Foreign Relations Study Program).

20. See Mohammad Natsir, *Islam Sebagai Dasar Negara* [Islam as the basis of the state] (Jakarta: Masyumi, 1957). On the problem of popular sovereignty, see Masykuri Abdillah, *Responses of Indonesian Muslim Intellectuals to the Concept of Democracy (1966–1993)* (Hamburg: Abera Verlay Meyer, 1997), pp. 70–72.

21. See Abdillah, *Responses of Indonesian Muslim Intellectuals*, pp. 102–6.

22. Grounded as the inheritance rule is on a passage in the Qur'an (Qur. 4:11), this attempt was greeted with skepticism in *ulama* circles. Abdurrahman Wahid agreed with the minister, but many other democratic-minded scholars thought it wisest not to expend their moral capital on so difficult an issue.

23. On the importance of public spheres for dialogue and debate in modern democracy, see Jean L. Cohen and Andrew Arato, *Civil Society and Political Theory* (Cambridge, Mass.: MIT Press, 1992); and, from a mainstream liberal perspective, Amy Gutmann and Dennis Thompson, *Democracy and Disagreement: Why Moral conflict Cannot Be Avoided in Politics, and What Should Be Done about It* (Cambridge, Mass.: Harvard University Press, 1996). On the significance of such civil-democratic insights for religion in modern times, see Casanova, *Public Religions in the Modern World*.

24. LP3ES (Institute for Economic and Social Research, Education, and Information) was established by democratic Muslims and PSI-style social democrats with the assistance of the German Neumann Institute and (later) the Ford Foundation. LP3ES also publishes what was, during the 1980s, Indonesia's most distinguished journal of policy and political debate, *Prisma*. During its heyday, LP3ES's board of advisers included Dawam Rahardjo, Arselan Harahap, Ismid Hadad, Adi Sasono, Aswab Mahasin, Abdurrahman Wahid, and other luminaries from the democratic wing of Jakarta's Muslim community. By the late 1980s most of these men had gone their separate ways. Several,

like Aswab Mahasin and Ismid Hadad, remained on good terms with their former colleagues. But others, like Adi Sasono and Abdurrahman Wahid, developed a deep mutual antipathy (see chapter 7).

25. In 1993 Probosutedjo sought to enhance his stature as a spokesperson for indigenous enterprise with the publication of a 106-page book entitled *Upaya Menghapus Kecemburuan Sosial Pada Era Kebangkitan Nasional Kedua* [The effort to eliminate social jealousy in the second era of national revival] (nd., n.p.). The book was said to have been ghostwritten by regimist Muslims in ICMI and was never sanctioned for general distribution. The book repeatedly denounces conglomerates and "rich people," without mentioning Chinese by name until its last pages. But it makes clear (not least of all from its cover, which shows a greedy Chinese developer eyeing an innocent-looking indigenous citizen) that the "conglomerates" it has in mind are Chinese, not the first family's.

26. On the travails of organized labor under the New Order, see Vedi R. Hadiz, *Workers and the State in New Order Indonesia* (London: Routledge, 1997).

27. My information here is based on interviews with two of Adi's supporters in the labor initiative, interviewed (on promise of anonymity) in June 1995.

28. This was not the end of Adi Sasono's labor intrigues. In March 1998, at the height of the Soeharto regime's crisis, Eggy Sudjana, an Adi lieutenant, announced the formation of a new Muslim labor federation. The timing of the establishment raised eyebrows among political observers, including anti-Soeharto Muslims. Muslim intellectuals familiar with Eggi Sudjana complained bitterly that the organization was clearly intended to split the labor opposition along religious lines, so as to undermine opposition to Soeharto.

29. Some of the clearest-headed writing on ICMI has been done by ICMI authors from the independent intellectual camp. See Anwar, *Pemikiran dan Aksi Islam*; Eep Saefulloh Fatah, *Politik Orde Baru: Catatan atas Gagalnya* [New Order politics: Notes on its failure] (Yogyakarta: Pustaka Pelajar, 1998); and Masika Editorial Board, eds., *Kebebasan Cendekiawan: Refleksi Kaum Muda* [Intellectuals' freedom: Reflections from youth] (Jakarta: Pustaka Republika, 1996).

30. In Muhammadiyah, Din Syamsuddin was allied to Lukman Harun (of the ultra-conservative KISDI) in opposition to Amien Rais, the head of Muhammdiyah and a democratic reformist.

31. Eggy Sudjana was outspoken in his insistence on the incompatibility of "Western" democracy with Muslim politics. See his *HAM, Demokrasi, dan Lingkungan Hidup: Perspektif Islam* [Human rights, democracy, and the environment: Islamic perspectives] (Bogor: As-Syahidah, 1998).

32. Din Syamsuddin of the CPDS was also a political adviser and speech writer for the hardline "green" general, Feisal Tanjung during these years. He wrote an introduction to a collection of the general's essays celebrating the new, collaborative relationship between (regimist) Islam and ABRI. See Feisal Tanjung, *ABRI-Islam: Mitra Sejati* [ABRI-Islam: True partners] (Jakarta: Sinar Harapan, 1997).

33. One more indication of how little the generals' actions were based on a higher commitment to Islam is that two "green" generals had played leading roles in the government's repression of rebels in Aceh, rebels often seen as "Islamist" in outlook. Syarwan Hamid was active in the campaign when stationed in the province in 1991. Prabowo reportedly masterminded the whole Aceh campaign, which made systematic use of torture, rape, civilian vigilantes, and grisly public executions. Prabowo had earlier re-

fined these same techniques in East Timor. On Prabowo and Aceh, see Geoffrey Robinson, "Rawan Is as Rawan Does: The Origins of Disorder in New Order Aceh," *Indonesia* 66 (October 1998): 127–56.

34. In commenting on Soeharto's reshuffling of the ABRI leadership in 1994, Douglas Ramage notes that Feisal Tanjung and Hartono were sympathetic to Islam but "warned against politicking on the basis of religious affiliation" (*Politics in Indonesia*, p. 113). When Feisal and Hartono issued warnings like these, however, the people they had in mind were Abdurrahman Wahid and the reform activists in ICMI. As their involvement in the CPDS showed, the generals had no problem with those who promoted regimist Islam to defend Soeharto (below and chapter 7).

35. Din's dissertation provides an intelligent, balanced overview of Islam and politics under the New Order. It ends, however, by advocating a new Muslim *realpolitik* centered on collaboration with the Soeharto regime. See M. Sirajuddin Syamsuddin, "Religion and Politics in Islam: The Case of Muhammadiyah in Indonesia's New Order," Ph.D. dissertation, Program in Islamic Studies, University of California–Los Angeles, 1991.

36. See Benedict R. O'G. Anderson, "Old State, New Society: Indonesia's New Order in Comparative Historical Perspective," *Journal of Asian Studies* 42 (1983): 477–96; and David Reeve, *Golkar of Indonesia: An Alternative to the Party System* (Singapore: Oxford University Press, 1985), pp. 322–64.

37. On integralism in Indonesian political discourse, see Adam Schwarz *A Nation in Waiting: Indonesia in the 1990s* (Boulder, Colo.: Westview, 1994), pp. 230–63; and Ramage, *Politics in Indonesia*, chap. 4.

38. See Andrew MacIntyre, *Business and Politics in Indonesia* (Sydney: Allen & Unwin, 1990).

39. Interview, August 6, 1992.

40. Interview, June 16, 1993.

41. ICMI's national newspaper, *Republika*, was launched on January 3, 1993; *Ummat* was launched in 1994. *Republika*'s circulation grew from 45,000 in January 1993 to about 175,000 in 1997. See "Islam Kosmopolitan dalam Berita" [Cosmopolitan Islam in the news], *Tempo* (January 9, 1993): 33. On the founding of the government-supported Islamic bank, Bank Muamalat Indonesia (BMI), see "Mengapa Baru Sekarang BMI Berdiri" [Why the Islamic bank has only now been established], *Prospek*, November 2, 1991. See also Robert W. Hefner, "Islamizing Capitalism: On the Founding of Indonesia's First Islamic Bank," in Mark R. Woodward, ed., *Toward a New Paradigm: Recent Developments in Indonesian Islamic Thought* (Tempe, Ariz.: Arizona State University Press, Program for Southeast Asian Studies, 1996), pp. 291–322.

42. See Rahardjo's sharp comments in *Berita Buana*, January 14, 1991. Other Muslim independents voiced similar concerns about the subordination of ICMI to bureaucratic power during the weeks preceding Habibie's announcement on February 14. See, for example, *Suara Karya*, January 31, 1991, p. 1; and *Pelita*, January 31, 1991, p. 1.

43. Based on interviews with junior ICMI staff involved in the conference preparations, July 1992. Although reporters from several news organizations were present at the human rights conference, the police closure was mentioned in only one press report, "ICMI pun Kena Sempit," *Tempo*, May 9, 1992.

44. With Adnan Buyung Nasution (a Muslim), Todung Mulya Lubis (a Catholic) has been one of Indonesia's most courageous human rights lawyers. See his *In Search of*

Human Rights: Legal-Political Dilemmas of Indonesia's New Order, 1966–1990 (Jakarta: PT Gramedia Pustaka Utama, 1993).

45. There were, of course, other Muslim critics of ICMI, such as the distinguished historians Deliar Noer and Taufik Abdullah, and the politician Ridwan Saidi. All three men argued that ICMI was no more than a vehicle to mobilize Muslim support for the president.

46. Earlier examples of military infighting are analyzed in David Jenkins, *Soeharto and His Generals: Indonesian Military Politics, 1975–1983* (Ithaca: Cornell University, Modern Indonesia Project, Monograph Series No. 64, 1984).

47. For a discussion of the breech, see Editors, "Current Data on the Indonesian Military Elite: July 1–January 1, 1992," *Indonesia* 53 (1993): 93–136.

48. Jamie Mackie and Andrew MacIntyre, "Politics," in Hall Hill, ed., *Indonesia's New Order: The Dynamics of Socio-Economic Transformation* (Honolulu: University of Hawaii Press, 1994), p. 8.

49. Adam Schwarz provides an overview of the first family's assets in his *A Nation in Waiting*, pp. 133–61. Ruth McVey examines the logic of the shift from rent seeking to business control among the first family, and among Southeast Asian elites as a whole, in her "The Materialization of the Southeast Asian Entrepreneur."

50. See Schwarz, *A Nation in Waiting*, p. 146.

51. My information on this exchange comes from an anonymous interview with an American military attaché close to Moerdani.

52. Schwarz, *A Nation in Waiting*, p. 285.

53. Whatever the president's motives, armed forces leaders believed that the president intended to punish them. This was a theme in my interviews with military commanders, and comes across, too, in Ramage, *Politics in Indonesia*, esp. p. 154.

54. A trademark perhaps most vividly illustrated in two studies: Jenkins, *Soeharto and His Generals*; and Liddle, *Leadership and Culture in Indonesian Politics*.

55. Publicly, however, the military press remained suspicious, urging the organization to stick to its goals of national unity and development. See, for example, the editorial in the military newspaper, *Angkatan Bersenjata*, "ICMI, Selamat Datang" [ICMI welcome], December 10, 1990. Behind-the-scenes, military criticism continued, prompting Dr. Habibie to make a much-publicized visit to the offices of the chief of staff Try Sutrisno, on February 22, 1992, in an effort to dispel rumors that the military opposed ICMI. The armed forces commander subsequently released the text of his statement to Habibie. The document's twenty-five short paragraphs make no fewer than twenty references to the *Pancasila*, religious pluralism, and the need for vigilance against those who threaten national unity.

56. See *Kompas*, June 18, 1993, p. 1.

57. Schwarz, *A Nation in Waiting*, p. 288.

58. Ibid., p. 275.

59. Feillard's *Islam et Armée*, especially, explores NU's early commitment to Indonesian nationalism.

60. See Abdillah, *Responses of Indonesian Muslim Intellectuals to the Concept of Democracy*, p. 56.

61. The best English-language summaries of the incident are in Ramage, *Politics in Indonesia*, pp. 87–89; and Schwarz, *A Nation in Waiting*, p. 191. See also chapter 7 below.

62. Interviews, June 17, 1991. See also Schwarz, *A Nation in Waiting*, p. 191; and Ramage, *Politics in Indonesia*, p. 88.

63. During the first five minutes of my first interview with Wahid in June 1991, he volunteered a thumbnail sketch of the tensions in ABRI, especially over the matter of the president and Islam. Although conservative Muslims denounced Wahid as a friend of Moerdani, Wahid had a coolly objective analysis of both Moerdani and Sutrisno. He blamed both for actions that led to the killings of Muslims in Lampung (1989) and Tanjung Priok (1984).

64. See the statements of military officials in, "ABRI Officer Says Openness Cause of Indonesia's Dilemma," in *Jakarta Post*, July 8, 1994.

65. Ramage, *Politics in Indonesia*, p. 57.

66. Ibid., pp. 59–61.

67. Interview with Wahid in Boston, Massachusetts, March 15, 1992.

68. Wahid subsequently sent a letter protesting the president's actions against the Grand Assembly and his courtship of conservative Islam in general. I never saw a copy of the letter, although its content, as summarized by Ramage (*Politics in Indonesia*, p. 66) and Schwartz (*A Nation in Waiting*, pp. 192–93) appears consistent with Wahid's comments to me in Boston in March 1992.

69. See "Belum Saatnya Proyek Untung" [No profit yet], *Tempo* (October 31, 1992): 27–29. See also "Engineering the Future," *The Economist* (April 17, 1993): 12–13 (special supplement).

70. See the critical evaluations of Habibie's economic programs in Schwarz, *A Nation in Waiting*, pp. 89–97.

71. In June 1995 reporters with whom I spoke at the ICMI newspaper, *Republika*, insisted that the president had demanded that the three papers be banned. But some of their colleagues at the ICMI magazine, *Ummat* (which had a reputation for greater independence than *Republika*), insisted that Habibie was involved as well. In my discussion with him in June 1995, *Tempo*'s editor, Goenawan Mohamad, blamed Habibie squarely for the ban.

72. Interview, June 12, 1995.

73. Showing how much an insider he had become, Adi Sasono joined with regime conservatives to urge Muslims not to join the protests against the press banning. Unlike the ultraconservatives who were happy to see the magazines go, however, Adi did not try to defend the government's actions. He simply insisted that it was important not to let the incident jeopardize the improving relationship between the president and Muslims. See the interview, "Sebagai Umat Jangan Na'if" [As Muslims, let's not be naive], *Media Dakwah* (August 1994): 18.

CHAPTER SEVEN
UNCIVIL STATE: MUSLIMS AND VIOLENCE IN SOEHARTO'S FALL

1. After government meddling allowed John Naro to become chairman of the PPP in 1978, the modernist wing of the PPP was given the lion's shares of the party's seats in the National Assembly, despite the fact that the NU faction in the PPP was larger than the modernists'. This marginalization convinced many mainstream NU party members of the wisdom of Wahid's and Siddiq's rejection of the PPP.

2. Soeharto's peaceful coexistence with Wahid was short-lived. Wahid was not reappointed to the MPR in 1993.

3. Van Bruinessen, *NU: Tradisi, Relasi-Relasi Kuasa, Pencarian Wacana Baru*, p. 116; Feillard, *Islam et Armée*, pp. 193–96.

4. Interview, June 9, 1992. Feillard's *Islam et Armée* makes a similar point, describing the new policy not as a retreat from politics but a "provisional displacement" (p. 196). Feillard also provides a compelling overview of the organizational and financial problems NU faced in the early 1980s. See Feillard, *Islam et Armée*, pp. 213–28.

5. By this time Wahid was controversial not merely because of his views on the PPP and Golkar but because of statements he had made on religious matters. He expressed appreciation for Shi'ism and Mutazilah rationalism (both long vilified among NU's conservative scholars), appealed for an "indigenization" (*pribumisasi*) of Indonesian Islam, and supported efforts by young scholars like Masdar Mas'udi to promote a critical rereading of Muslim jurisprudence. See Imron Hamzah and Choirul Anam, eds., *Gus Dur Diadili Kiai-Kiai* [Gus Dur (Abdurrahman Wahid) judged by the scholars] (Surabaya: Jawa Pos, 1989). See also van Bruinessen, *NU*, pp. 185–87; and Greg Barton, "The Liberal, Progressive Roots of Abdurrahman Wahid's Thought," in Greg Barton and Greg Fealy, eds., *Nahdlatul Ulama: Traditional Islam and Modernity in Indonesia* (Clayton, Victoria [Australia]: Monash University, Monash Asia Institute, 1996), pp. 190–226.

6. See van Bruinessen, *NU*, p. 191. At the same meeting Benny Moerdani was greeted coldly, a clear sign that at this time most of the NU delegates favored Soeharto.

7. Interview with Wahid, March 9, 1993.

8. Interviews with *Republika* reporters, June 1995.

9. Some hostile observers had long since concluded that the *Republika* reporters were willing instruments of Soeharto-Habibie propaganda. But this was far from true. Although the majority of *Republika* reporters were critical of Wahid, most resented government interference in their affairs. They feared that if they gave in to government pressures they would discredit the Muslim community as a whole. Unfortunately, in the repeated confrontations that pitted *Republika* reporters against the government, these reporters almost always lost, and by 1997 most of the courageous junior reporters had left. See my "Print Islam: Mass Media and Ideological Rivalries among Indonesian Muslims," in *Indonesia* 64 (October 1997): 77–103.

10. See Greg Fealy, "The 1994 NU Congress and Aftermath: Abdurrahman Wahid, *Suksesi*, and the Battle for Control of NU," in Barton and Fealy, *Nahdlatul Ulama*, p. 268.

11. I was shown these documents in July 1995 by an ICMI activist who objected to the effort against Wahid.

12. As most famously developed in Geertz's *Religion of Java*; see also chapter 1 above.

13. What follows here is based on interviews with Wahid and NU activist youth in June 1995, as well as press sources. See also Fealy's, "The 1994 NU Congress and Aftermath," pp. 257–77.

14. My account is based on discussions with Muslim journalists and two junior members of the CPDS.

15. See, for example, "Permadi, Kaset, dan Soeyono" [Permadi, cassettes, and Soeyono], *Media Indonesia* (March 12, 1985): 8–9.

16. See "Yang Saya Lakukan itu Jelas Tindakan Politik" [What I am doing is of course a political action], *Forum Keadilan* 4:1 (April 27, 1995): 86–90.

17. See the interview with K. H. Hasan Basri in *Tiras* (1:9 [March 30, 1995]: 24), "Dia Melecehkan Akidah Islamiah" [He insulted the Muslim faith].

18. See the *Forum Keadilan* interview, 4:1 (April 27, 1995): 87.

19. See, "Peramal Politik Yang Terganjal" [A political predictor is cornered], *Tiras* 1:9 (March 30, 1995): 16–29.

20. See, "Permadi, Ramalan, dan Protes Kemudian" [Permadi, predictions, and the subsequent protest], *Forum Keadilan* 3:26 (April 13, 1995): 19–26.

21. See, for example, the wry observations of Moeslim Abdurrahman, "Dosa 'Eyang' Permadi" [Permadi's sins], *Tiras* 1:9 (March 30, 1995): 28–29.

22. Amien Rais protested that he had left the room during the question-and-answer period of the seminar.

23. See "Menghujat Golkar, Presiden, dan Nabi Muhammad" [Slandering Golkar, the president, and the Prophet Muhammad], *Media Dakwah* (April 1995): 9–16.

24. The former Masyumi leader and DDII founder, Mohammad Natsir, died in 1993—two years before the DDII bolted from the opposition into the ranks of regime supporters.

25. The appreciation was mutual. In late 1996 Wahid made public statements praising Moerdiono as the leader best qualified to lead the nation after Soeharto.

26. Anonymous interview with Muhammadiyah officer, June 1995.

27. On the government-contrived challenges to Megawati's leadership, see "Mega Digoyang, Mega Bertahan" [Mega destabilized, Mega endures], *Forum Keadilan* 3:16 (November 24, 1996): 101–8. On the East Java governor's attitude, see his interview, "Basofi Soedirman: 'Nggak Ada Tugas Menjatuhkan Mega' " [Basofi Soedirman: There's no assignment to topple Mega], *Forum Keadilan* 3:26 (April 13, 1995): 14.

28. See "Jusuf Merukh Bentuk DPP PDI Tandingan" [Jusuf Merukh forms a rival PDI executive board], *Merdeka* (December 31, 1994): 1.

29. See "Bersih Diri" [Self-cleansing], *Tiras* 1:1 (January 12, 1995): 17–30.

30. See "Nasib Perjalanan Sebuah Partai" [The fate of a party], *Tiras* 1:2 (February 9, 1995): 16–29.

31. My information came from a political scientist who had at one time worked with the CPDS.

32. PDI activists I interviewed after the violence insisted that the single largest constituency among the attackers were recruits from the Pancasila Youth (*Pemuda Pancasila*). Based on his study of the gang, however, Loren Ryter concludes that Pancasila Youth may have well been involved in the attack, but they probably were not the "prime movers"; poor residents from North Jakarta were also hired. See Ryter, "Pemuda Pancasila," p. 68.

33. The commission's finding that some people were still missing embarrassed the government, which had previously cited a lower figure. See "Kemanakah Mereka Pergi?" [Where did they all go?], *D&R* (September 14, 1996): 10–15.

34. In the aftermath of the riots, PDI activists claimed that some of the people involved in the rioting were actually undercover personnel linked to Prabowo.

35. Jakartan observers in 1997 pointed the finger of accusation at Adi Sasono of CIDES. But Sasono himself denied these charges. It is worth noting, however, that even as he criticized the PRD for being naively leftist he refused to join in the formal

condemnation of the organization. To do so, he believed, was to neglect the larger problems that had given rise to the PRD. See "Adi Sasono: Sekarang Masanya Maling Teriak Maling" [Adi Sasono: Now is the time when thieves cry 'thief'], *Forum Keadilan* 5:12 (September 23, 1996): 94–98.

36. Interview, January 12, 1997. See also the interview, "Perubahan Harus Konstitusional" [Change has to be constitutional], *Ummat* 2:4 (August 19, 1996): 35–36.

37. See "Megawati Harus Belajar Dari Kasus Ini" [Megawati has to learn from this case], *Ummat* 2:4 (August 19, 1996): 31–32.

38. Even in late August 1996, as moderate Muslims were beginning to doubt the government's claims, Amien Rais kept close to the government line, saying the Peoples Democratic Party may be only "naively" communist, but it was dangerous nonetheless.

39. See "Perbuhan, Yes, Revolusi, No" [Change yes, revolution no], *Ummat* 2:4 (August 19, 1996): 30.

40. It is important to keep these dissidents in mind so as not to paint the DDII with too broad a stroke. Even in the 1990s, many people continued to affiliate with the DDII out of a sense of loyalty to Masyumi, which had been so unfairly repressed in the 1960s. Hints of the unease felt by some DDII members over the new pro-regime policy were apparent even on the pages of *Media Dakwah*. One example was a surprisingly blunt article by Zulkifli Halim. He warned that collaboration with those in power might backfire and reminded Muslims that a politics based on presidential favor was "unhealthy." See "Perlunya Umat Mempelajari Seni Berpolitik" [Muslims need to study political art], *Media Dakwah* 265 (August 1996): 50.

41. See the thoughtful article by the sociologist Laode Ida on the effort to isolate Abdurrahman Wahid, "Gus Dur dan 'Pernyataan Kutukan' " [Gus Dur and the statement of condemnation], *Forum Keadilan* 5:11 (September 9, 1996): 94. On the pro-government rally, see "Mawas Diri Setelah Sabtu Kelabu" [Self-correction after gray saturday], *Ummat* 2:5 (September 2, 1996): 31–40.

42. See Sasono's unusually blunt attack on Wahid in his "Sekarang Masanya Maling Teriak Maling," pp. 94–98.

43. Interview, January 4, 1997. Nasution also observed that he felt that the prodemocracy movement had erred in placing all its hope in the PDI as the locomotive of democratic reform. He argued that democratization had to be pursued on several fronts, including legal and electoral. See the interview "Yang Berbeda Pendapat Dianggap Musuh" [Those who disagree are considered enemies], *D&R* (October 26, 1996): 76–81.

44. *Masyarakat* means "people" or "society." *Madani* is the adjectival form of the root related to the Indonesian *medan* (square, public space) and the Arabic phrase for "urban" or "public".

45. See "Ketua Umum PBNU Mohon Maaf" [The executive chairman of the NU apologizes], *Kompas* (October 14, 1996), p. 1.

46. Local security officials denied, of course, that the death had anything to do with torture. See "Matinya Ahmad Siddiq" [The death of Ahmad Siddiq], *Forum Keadilan* 5:19 (December 30, 1996): p. 25.

47. For descriptions of the extraordinary meeting, see "Harapan Pasca-Salaman" [Hope after the handshake], *Ummat* 2:11 (November 25, 1996): 29–39.

48. See "NU Akan Mendukung Pak Harto" [NU will support Soeharto], *Surabaya Post*, November 4, 1996.

49. See, "Makna Politis Pertemuan Genggong" [The political meaning of the cottage meeting], *Jawa Pos*, November 8, 1996.

50. See, for example, the November 17, 1996 appeal of the ICMI intellectual, Fachry Ali, "Gus Dur Harus Ketemu Habibie" [Gus Dur has to meet Habibie], *Jawa Pos*, November 18, 1996.

51. Although some people suggested that in making these visits Wahid had deserted Megawati, she insisted this was not so. See "Megawati: Gus Dur Tak Tinggalkan Saya" [Megawati: Gus Dur didn't desert me], *Kompas Online*, April 11, 1997.

52. See "Letjen TNI Syarwan Hamid Tentang PDI: ABRI Turut Prihatin" [Lieutenant General Syarwan Hamid on the PDI: The armed forces is concerned], *Kompas Online*, June 4, 1997.

53. See "Hartono Berpeluang Ketua Umum ICMI" [Hartono ready to become head of ICMI], *Kompas Online*, August 7, 1997.

54. See Andrew MacIntyre, "The Indonesian Debacle: What Americans Need to Know and Do," in *The National Interest* 53 (Fall 1998): 41–52.

55. "Amien Rais: Saya Siap Jadi Capres" [I am ready to run for president], *Jawa Pos*, September 26, 1997.

56. On Rais's critique and the furor caused by his removal, see Hamid Basyaib and Ibrahim Ali-Fauzi, eds., *Ada Udang di Balik Busang: Dokumentasi Pers Kasus Amien Rais* [Behind the Busang scandal: Press documentation on the Amien Rais case] (Bandung: Mizan, 1997).

57. The lessons from Amien's expulsion were not lost on the mass media. See, for example, "Amien Rais dan Kemandirian ICMI" [Amien Rais and the independence of ICMI], *Suara Merdeka Online*, March 2, 1997.

58. Rais's last appearance at a KISDI event took place in early October 1997, in support of a KISDI effort to censure the Catholic-owned newspaper *Kompas* over alleged bias in its reporting on violence in Algeria. See "Amien Rais: Ada Yang tak Wajar dalam Kehidupan Nasional" [There is something not right in national life], *Kompas*, October 6, 1997.

59. On KISDI attacks on *Republika*, see my "Print Islam."

60. I was given a copy of these documents by a Muslim activist present at the meeting and shocked by its discussion. Portions of the booklet were subsequently circulated in conservative Islamist circles and also made available through KISDI's web page on the Internet.

61. *Konspirasi Mengguling Soeharto*, p. 4.

62. Ibid., pp. 3–4.

63. Ibid., p. 20.

64. Ibid., p. 56.

65. See "Panglima ABRI telepon 13 Konglomerat" [ABRI general telephones 13 conglomerates], *Kompas*, January 15, 1998. For an early but insightful analysis of these tensions, see John T. Sidel, "*Macet Total*: Logics of Circulation and Accumulation in the Demise of Indonesia's New Order," in *Indonesia* 66 (October 1998); 159–94.

66. "Berbohongan Liem Bian Koen" [The lies of Liem Bian Koen (Sofyan Wanandi)], KISDI Website, February 8, 1998.

67. Human rights workers who investigated the rapes were themselves threatened with violence. In November 1998 an eighteen-year-old Chinese-Indonesian counselor

to some of the rape victims was herself raped and murdered. A one-day police investigation claimed that she had been killed by a deranged neighbor.

68. For an early journalistic analysis of the violence, see Julius Pour, *Jakarta Semasa Lengser Keprabon* [Jakarta at the time of the fall from power] (Jakarta: Media Komputindo, 1998). For a first-wave academic analysis, see Geoff Forrester and R. J. May, eds., *The Fall of Soeharto* (Singapore: Select Books, 1999).

69. This information was provided to me by an aide to Rais.

70. See the special issue of *Abadi*, the weekly newspaper of the Partai Bulan Bintang, "Benny Moerdani Kembali" (Benny Moerdani returns), 1:20 (March 25, 1999): 14–19. In the same issue, the Prabowo ally and executive director of the IPS, Fadli Zon, attacked Habibie for failing to protect "Muslim generals" against "non-Muslim circles." See his "Skenario Pemilu 1999" [The election scenario 1999] (19).

71. See "KISDI Tuntut Pelaksanaan Penegakan Hukum" [KISDI demands the strengthening of law], *Kompas*, October 15, 1998. For an anthropological analysis of the gendered nature of the reporting, see Ariel Heryanto, "Rape, Race, and Reporting," a paper presented at the International Conference, "Democracy in Indonesia? The Crisis and Beyond," Monash University and the University of Melbourne, Melbourne, Australia, December 11–12, 1998.

72. See "Habibie Comments under Fire," *Tempo Interaktif*, July 21, 1998.

73. See "KISDI tuding RMS dibalik kerusuhan Ambon" [KISDI charges RMS is behind the Ambon conflict], SIAR online, January 30, 1999.

74. See "Wawancara Khusus Dengan Pak Harto" [Exclusive interview with Soeharto]. *Siar Edisi*, April 13, 19–25, 1999.

75. See "MUI sets 'guidelines' for Muslims to vote." *Tempo Interactif*, March 6, 1999.

76. This is, for example, the impression of the military leadership conveyed in Liddle's *Leadership and Culture in Indonesian Politics*.

77. On this point, see Geoffrey Robinson's analysis, in his *Dark Side of Paradise*, of how rivalries among state elites contributed to the ferocity of the anticommunist massacres in Bali during 1965–66. Robinson's theoretical conclusion also resonates here: "Divisions within a state may create opportunities for the emergence of political protest, resistance, or conflict. In states that are incohesive or divided, it is argued, there is a greater tendency for open political conflict. The reason lies not simply in the absence or weakness of state authority but in the active participation of elements of the state apparatus in the process of political protest or conflict" (*Dark Side of Paradise*, p. 11).

CHAPTER EIGHT
CONCLUSION: MUSLIM POLITICS, GLOBAL MODERNITY

1. Serif Mardin, "Civil Society and Islam," in John A. Hall, ed., *Civil Society: Theory, History, Comparison* (Cambridge: Polity, 1995), p. 278. In an important anthropological overview of civil society literature, Chris Hann at first reaches a similar conclusion, arguing that the idea of civil society "developed in historical conditions that cannot be replicated in any other part of the world today," especially in as much as it assumes "the universality of modern Western notions of the person." By the end of his essay, however, Hann sees a silver lining in this democratic cloud, arguing, as I have attempted to do in this book, that civil society "is not the unique product of the West after all; others have developed important elements of it." See Chris Hann, "Introduction: Politi-

cal Society and Civil Anthropology," in Chris Hann and Elizabeth Dunn, eds., *Civil Society: Challenging Western Models* (London: Routledge, 1996), pp. 1–26.

2. On Western pluricentrism, see John A. Hall, *Powers and Liberties: The Causes and Consequences of the Rise of the West* (Berkeley: University of California Press, 1985).

3. Mardin, "Civil Society and Islam," p. 295.

4. Ibid., p. 290.

5. For recent explorations of this change, see Arjun Appadurai, *Modernity at Large: Cultural Dimensions of Globalization* (Minneapolis: University of Minnesota Press, 1996); and Ulf Hannerz, *Cultural Complexity: Studies in the Social Organization of Meaning* (New York: Columbia University Press, 1996).

6. Howard Clark Kee, "From the Jesus Movement toward Institutional Church," in Hefner, *Conversion to Christianity*, pp. 47–63

7. David Martin has shown that the separatist option was popular among poor converts to evangelical Protestantism in Latin America in the 1960s and 1970s. The converts chose to live apart on "islands of piety" so as to minimize the threat of political repression and social stigmatization. Martin also shows, however, that second-generation converts often chafe at their isolation, as well as the conservatism of their elders, and choose to integrate themselves on new and more egalitarian terms back into the society their poor parents fled. See Martin, *Tongues of Fire*.

8. For a similar conclusion from a Christian context, see José Casanova, *Public Religions*.